Global Forest Resources

Global Forest Resources

Alexander S. Mather

Timber Press
Portland, Oregon

First published in Great Britain in 1990 by
Belhaven Press (a division of Pinter Publishers),
25 Floral Street, London WC2E 9DS

First published in North America in 1990 by
Timber Press, Inc.
9999 S.W. Wilshire
Portland, Oregon 97225, U.S.A.

ISBN 0-88192-178-5

Printed and bound in Great Britain

CONTENTS

ACKNOWLEDGEMENTS

I am grateful for the following for permission to use material in tables and figures: Organisation for Economic Co-operation and Development (Table 1.1); Cambridge University Press (Table 2.1); Naturgeografiska Institutionen, Göteborgs Universitet (Figure 2.3); University of Chicago Press (Figure 3.2); American Association for the Advancement of Science and Dr Marion Clawson (Figures 3.3, 3.4, 3.5 and 3.6); Royal Swedish Academy of Sciences (Table 4.4 and Figure 8.3); American Meteorological Society (Table 4.5); Elsevier Applied Science Publishers (Figure 4.6); Zed Books (Table 6.11); Food and Agriculture Organisation of the United Nations (Table 6.12 and Figure 6.16); International Union for the Conservation of Nature (Table 6.17); Macmillan Magazines and Dr L.W. Blank and other authors (Figure 7.3); National Center for Atmospheric Research (Table 7.1 and Figure 7.1 a and b); Springer-Verlag Heidelberg (Figure 7.5); British Ecological Society (Figure 7.6 and Table 7.6).

The figures were drafted in the Drawing Office of the Department of Geography, University of Aberdeen, the assistance of which is gratefully acknowledged.

FIGURES

TABLES

1 INTRODUCTION

Global forest resources now attract unprecedented attention. They give rise to more widespread concern than at any time in history, even though they are no longer a vital part of the power base of major countries as they were before the days of coal and steel. This concern extends both to their value and usefulness as a resource, and to the environmental effects of their use. The destruction of tropical forests attracts much more attention today than similar episodes of forest destruction, for example in Europe or North America, did in the past. This interest extends far beyond those peoples and areas immediately affected: indeed tropical deforestation is a global issue. The health of forests in Europe and North America, and their fate in the face of air pollution and possible climate change, is a topic of similar concern. The forest is not only a source of many useful products and services: it is also a symbol of environmental purity. Symptoms of malaise are therefore unwelcome and worrying, and contribute to the emergence of world forests as a major issue of the day.

The depletion of world forests and other natural resources is an issue about which one-third or more of the population of many developed countries are 'very concerned', as Table 1.1 indicates.

The table suggests that the depletion of forests and other natural resources gives rise to similar extents of concern as related environmental issues such as the extinction of plant and animal species and possible climatic change resulting from the increasing content of carbon dioxide in the atmosphere. Other surveys confirm the centrality of forest resources as a major environmental issue of the day. One report, quoted by Whitby and Ollerenshaw (1988), suggests that up to 72 per cent of the population in the European Community indicate an interest in it. Only relatively small numbers of people directly depend on forests for their livelihood, but vast numbers are concerned about their use and condition. Paradoxically, the more separated people become from the forest in their daily lives, the more interested and concerned they seem to become about its condition and extent.

Mankind and the forest

The relationship between mankind and the forest has a complex and ambivalent history. While it has at times been a refuge, a home and a source

1

Table 1.1   Perception of environmental issues

	Extinction of some plant or animal species	Depletion of world forest and natural resources	Possible climatic change brought about by CO_2
	(percentage of population 'very concerned')		
Belgium	28	27	28
Denmark	47	44	44
Germany	38	26	32
Greece	35	33	38
Ireland	21	22	30
Italy	45	40	46
Luxembourg	58	36	48
Netherlands	47	33	28
Portugal	40	37	32
Spain	51	46	43
United Kingdom	43	40	37
EEC	42	35	38
Japan	11	33	16
Finland	38	41	29

Note: Data for EEC countries relate to 1986; those for Finland and Japan to 1983 and 1984, respectively.
Source: OECD (1987)

of raw materials, it has also been feared and attacked as an obstacle to development and welfare. It has variously been a source of strategic raw materials on which military power was based, a fund of natural resources on which economic development could proceed, and an obstacle which had to be removed before agriculture could begin. Great significance has been ascribed to it: for example according to Braudel (1979, p. 363), 'One of the reasons for Europe's power lay in its being so plentifully endowed with forests. Against it, Islam was in the long run undermined by the poverty of its wood resources and their gradual exhaustion'. However accurate this assessment may be, man's attitudes to the forest have rarely been neutral. Nor have they been explicable solely in material terms. The forest may be a useful source of raw materials or it can be an obstacle that must be cleared before food production or some other activity can proceed, but it also affects the mind of man. Whether it depresses, humbles or inspires awe perhaps depends at least in part on technology and lifestyle, but it cannot be doubted that there is a psychological dimension to these attitudes as well as a physical or material one.

Perceptions have altered radically through history: the forest that was once dreaded and attacked with a vigour that could be understood only partly in terms of the need for agricultural advancement is now cherished as a valued environment in much of Europe and North America. This transformation has not occurred simultaneously throughout a people or country and still less has it taken place throughout the world. In Thailand, for example, the perception of the forest as a source of danger and its association with backwardness still survives: the most common Thai word for forest, *paa*, also means wild or backward (Hirsch, 1988a). The negative association with development survives there and in many other parts of the developing world as it once did in nineteenth-century North America or medieval Europe. And indeed the continuing and often pejorative use of the terms 'backwoods' and 'backwoodsmen' would suggest that the negative associations are still not dead even in the developed world.

Different individuals and groups, and on a different level different peoples and nations, are characterised by different relationships to the forest. In much of the developed world, the forest is now widely valued as a resource for recreation and wildlife conservation: equally, it is seen by others primarily as a source of raw material for forest-products industries. Clashes and conflicts arise between these values, and although they can be curbed and contained by compromise, they cannot fundamentally be resolved as long as contrasting perceptions remain. The same forest can be perceived very differently as a natural resource, and indeed it can be perceived as a non-resource or anti-resource that must be removed before the underlying land resource can be brought into use. In much of the developing world, the removal of forests is rapidly proceeding as more land is required (or is thought to be required) for food production. Here the resource value for recreation or wildlife conservation is unlikely to be a serious concern of the small cultivator struggling to feed his family. Just as these contrasts in perception are readily appreciated, so also are those at the level of nations and world divisions easily understandable. Having devastated its own forests in the past and having come to a realisation of their value, the developed world can view the current trends in the developing countries with concern. On the other hand the developing world can legitimately point to the inconsistencies and self-righteousness of voices from developed countries which preach rather than practise sustainable forms of development.

Varying perceptions of the forest reflect the varying relationship between humans and their environment and pose questions about the basic nature of the relationship between forests, human culture and civilisation. Mankind has had an uneasy relationship with the forest throughout history. Its darkness and mysterious or eerie sounds have endowed it with supernatural attributes, and it features in the religious beliefs of many primitive peoples around the world. More arid regions with grasslands or scanty forests probably formed the cradles of civilisation and of agriculture: technology had to be developed before denser forest lands could be used for farming. A leading American forester of his day, Raphael Zon (1920), concluded that three stages existed in the relationship between man and forest. Initially, man was dominated by the forest, and at his time of writing Zon suggested that areas such as Central Africa and South America were characterised by that stage of development. He considered that contemporary man was overcoming the forest in areas such as North America and Asia, while in Europe and part of the United States civilisation was dominating the forests. Perhaps terms such as 'dominating' and 'overcoming' are unhelpful, suggesting as they do a necessarily aggressive rather than harmonious relationship. There is little doubt, however, as to the fact that forests are more fully under the control of man in some parts of the world than in others, and that the extent of management is generally greater in what is now called the developed world than in the developing world. As will be discussed in subsequent chapters, trends in forest area, use and management are strongly differentiated between developed and developing worlds, although this is not to suggest or imply that uniformity exists within either of these divisions.

Forests as natural resources

In addition to covering around one-third of the face of the earth, forests represent a major category of natural resources. Conventionally, natural resources are subdivided into those that are renewable and those that are non-renewable. These sub-divisions correspond to flow and stock or fund resources, respectively. Like land and soil, forests are a particular type of natural resource, which can behave either as a flow resource or as a stock resource. Some forms of use can be carried on indefinitely, and under such regimes forests function as flow or renewable resources. Other types of use, however, inevitably lead to the depletion and eventually to exhaustion of the resource. In this case the forest is 'mined' just like coal or a mineral ore, and the capacity for self-renewal disappears. The forest becomes a stock resource, which is used *up* as it is used.

Forests therefore occupy an intermediate position in the spectrum of natural resources. At one end lie flow resources such as solar energy and water or wind power, which are in practical terms independent of human action and which are permanently renewable. At the other end are the stock resources such as coal, oil and minerals, where use means depletion and which are, at least on the human time-scale, not renewable. Forests are an example of what Rees (1985) describes as *critical zone* resources: if depletion proceeds beyond a *critical zone*, full recovery to the original condition of the resource may not take place even if no further use occurs. The *critical zone* relates to a level or intensity of harvesting beyond which the reproduction of the resource is endangered. In crude terms, if the rate of harvesting is greater than that of growth over a long period, then the resource ceases to reproduce itself.

An alternative classification is that of a *potentially renewable* resource. This alternative may be preferable for a number of reasons. First, the history of forest use shows that it has been treated (wittingly or otherwise) as a stock resource more often than not. Its potential renewability has all too frequently not been realised. Second, its survival and 'flow' capacity depend not just on the use made of it, but also on external factors such as changing climate or air pollution. The resource may shrink or deteriorate not only because the level of use has passed a 'critical zone' but also because of factors unconnected with direct use of the resource.

'Resource' is a term that is used as loosely as it is widely. In this volume, it is used to refer to a useful or valued part of the natural environment. Human perceptions are obviously implicit in such a definition. Many years ago, Erich Zimmerman (1951) encapsulated this idea in his memorable aphorism that 'resources are not, they become'. Such a statement accords closely with the changing perception (through both time and space) of the usefulness and value of forests. Zimmerman illustrates his concept of resources in terms of a wedge of 'culture' that penetrates the 'neutral stuff' of the natural environment (Figure 1.1).

Figure 1.1   The perception of natural (forest) resources

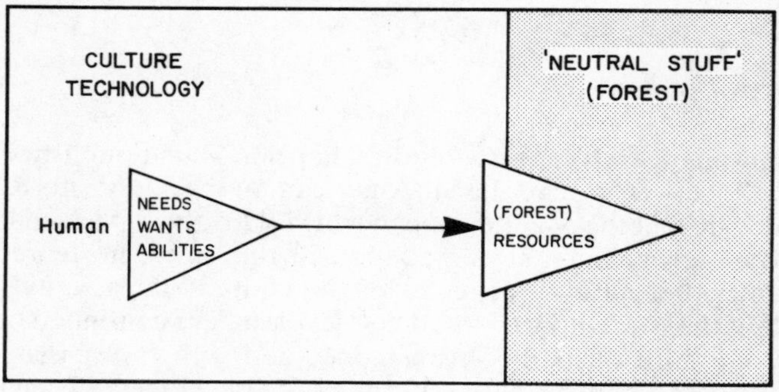

Source: Modified after Zimmerman, 1951

Such a depiction has its limitations, and in particular fails to convey the negative perception of a forest as an 'anti-resource' or 'resistance' that has to be overcome or removed before the land it occupies can be used for farming. Nevertheless, it conveys something of the dynamism of resource perceptions. It accurately portrays, for example, the widening perception and definition of timber resources in recent centuries. During this period, an ever-increasing forest area has been called into service for timber production, and at the same time, within individual forest types, an increasing range of tree species has been perceived as useful and valuable for this purpose.

Perhaps Zimmerman's 'wedge' should be shown as hollow, because all too often its passage or penetration has left a trail of destruction or degradation. Perhaps also the diagram should include a plurality or multiplicity of 'wedges', each representing a sense in which the forest is perceived as useful or valuable. It is a resource not only for timber supply, but also for recreation and for several other goods and services. Several 'wedges', with varying degrees of penetration and representing different resources, should perhaps thus be incorporated.

Use and abuse of the forest resource

The use and abuse of the forest resource have occupied centre stage in the unfolding drama of human use of the earth and of human impact on the environment. Forest issues have been foci of interest and concern amongst eminent conservationists and in popular conservation movements. These issues vary in form, ranging from long-standing fears of a shortage of timber, which as yet have been more valid at the national than at the global level, to concerns about the environmental effects of the use of the forest. The prominent role of forest issues in contributing to the growing environmental awareness of the late twentieth century merely continues a long history, although the scale of awareness, interest and concern is now global. In previous centuries it was largely confined to the local, regional or national level.

Forest destruction

In the mid-nineteenth century, George Perkins Marsh published *Man and Nature*. Marsh, who had been American ambassador in Rome, had travelled widely in the Mediterranean world. Deeply impressed by what he regarded as environmental degradation in that area, he feared that the forests and other natural resources of the United States would suffer the same fate if the contemporary mode of development continued unchecked. Around one-third of his book was concerned with forest issues. On the basis of observation in his native Vermont, he developed a keen awareness of the environmental impact of forest removal, especially in respect of soil erosion and hydrological change. While others had earlier lamented the extent of forest removal because of fears of a scarcity of timber, Marsh was one of the first to draw attention effectively to its environmental conse- quences. He was also one of the first to advocate that some areas of forest should be retained or preserved in their pristine condition. As such, he is one of the originators of the concept of the nature reserve or protected area. Perhaps it is significant that this manifestation of conservation originated with concern about the forest.

According to Marsh, 'the vast forests of the United States and Canada cannot long resist the improvident habits of the backwoodsman and the increased demand for lumber', and he concluded that 'we have now felled forest enough everywhere, in many districts far too much' (Lowenthal, 1965, pp. 257, 280). Human treatment of the forest – and the conse- quences of this treatment – epitomised to Marsh the wider (and dis- harmonious) relationship between mankind and the environment.

Initially, Marsh may have been a lone voice in a wilderness, but within thirty years steps were being taken at federal level to preserve at least some areas of forest. In little more than half a century the rate of forest destruction in the United States had greatly slowed, to a point where the forest area stabilised. In parts of Europe, writers such as Reclus (1871) were also expressing concern about the fate of the forest resource, and about the consequences of forest removal in terms of flooding and removal. This concern arose in particular from conditions in the French Alps, where growing population pressure had led to deforestation and increased erosion and flooding – conditions remarkably similar to those in parts of the developing world at the present day.

In addition to identifying the damaging effects of forest removal, commentators of the nineteenth and early twentieth centuries postulated various theories, models or generalisations about the nature of its relationship to progress and development. For example Ernst Friedrich, a German geographer, suggested at the turn of the century that *Raubwirtschaft* (robber economy) or destructive exploitation was a stage in the development in culture and civilisation (Whitaker, 1940; Speth, 1977). He saw it as an attribute of civilised cultures, especially in the recently colonised, newer lands. While primitive peoples were associated only with milder forms of exploitation (*Sammelwirtschaft*), *Raubwirtschaft* was seen by Friedrich as an indicator of progress. Heedless exploitation was a temporary phase: temporary want would heighten awareness of the need for conservation, which in turn would lead to improvement and foresight in the use of resources. In short, destructive exploitation was an evolutionary stage in progress towards conservation of natural resources and efficient resource management.

Such a belief leads, of course, to a relaxed attitude to destructive use: it is seen merely as a passing phase in the development of an area. The question of the necessity or inevitability of such a phase is overlooked. Furthermore, the possibility or indeed the reality of irreversible environmental change, such as the complete elimination of a forest, the extinction of plant or animal species or the complete stripping of soil, is not easily accommodated in this concept. It is not surprising, therefore, that many subsequent commentators, such as Carl Sauer, were vigorously opposed to destructive exploitation as practised in the United States. In particular they doubted whether the passing of the frontier would be accompanied by the passing of 'frontier' attitudes towards the environment in general or the forest in particular. According to Sauer (1938), the ' "frontier" attitude has the recklessness of an optimism that has become habitual, but which is residual from the brave days when north-European freebooters overran the world and put it under tribute' (p. 154).

The view that destructive exploitation was a direct consequence of the rapid colonisation of the United States has been very persistent (e.g. van Hise, 1910; Moncrief, 1970). The question of its validity is obviously of primary importance, both in relation to the United States historically and more generally to other, more recently developing areas. The question is a complex one. Some commentators have seen a difference between the hostility of early settlers to the forest and a pervasive enmity that seemed to continue after the forest had been 'conquered'. For example the American conservationist Nathaniel Shaler, writing in the 1880s and 1890s, found the former understandable and indeed almost inevitable, but the latter objectionable (Livingstone, 1980). Perhaps what he identified was the almost ubiquitous ingredient of human-environmental (and indeed also social) relations, namely disharmony and alienation. Whether the eventual 'turn-round' of forest area in the United States would have lightened Shaler's gloom is debatable. In subsequent chapters the reality of this 'turn-round' in the extent of forest area around the developed world will be considered further. Statistical evidence can be produced to support the idea that a *Raubwirtschaft* phase has eventually been succeeded by one in which forest conservation plays a larger part, and in which forest destruction is succeeded by forest re-creation, at least in terms of area. To conclude that phases or episodes have existed, of course, does not necessarily correlate with a positive or developmental view of destructive exploitation, of the type propounded by Friedrich.

Regardless of how valid concepts of phases or cycles of forest resource use (and their relationship with stages of cultural development) may be, there is ample evidence that the bitter lessons learned in some parts of the world are not heeded in others. More than half a century ago, Dietrich (1928, p. 141) wrote: 'Nearly every [European] country . . . has learned by bitter experience that complete denudation without reforestation is detrimental to the best interest of the state, and the sound economic development of its industries.' He went on to observe that 'America profited only in slight measure by the experience of Europe.' We could now add that the same is true of many other countries. The same destructive exploitation continues in country after country, and some countries with unhappy histories of forest resource use in their own lands have been instrumental in the destructive exploitation of overseas forests.

Control of the forest resource

Destructive exploitation is only one of a number of issues that have been associated with the forest resource over many centuries. Another is the struggle for control of the resource. In Europe there is a long history of conflict between the peasant and the proprietor about rights over forest products and services. In many instances this tussle focused on the conflict between the preservation of hunting and sporting rights on the one hand, and forest encroachment and the taking of forest produce on the other. In one part of medieval Scotland, for example, the penalty prescribed for the unfortunate peasant found encroaching on the reserved forest was to be pinned by the ear to a tree, by 'ane ten penny nail' (Anderson, 1967). Similar if less drastic attempts to reserve forest rights, in the face of growing population pressure, were common across much of Europe, and have their modern counterparts in the struggles between indigenous forest groups and capitalistic exploiters of the tropical forest. Another parallel is found in the conflict between the forest guards and park keepers of protected forests and would-be colonists or exploiters.

The question of control of the resource is related to, rather than distinct from, that of destructive exploitation. In much of Europe in the medieval and early modern periods, there was a long and bitter struggle between landowners and peasants for the control of the forest resource. This struggle was simply the precursor of more recent tussles in areas such as parts of Amazonia. Realising the commercial value, and especially the timber value, of the forest has usually meant extinguishing pre-existing rights. The struggle for the control and use of the forest resource in Germany was an influence on the thinking of Karl Marx (Westoby, 1989). He attacked control of the forest by large owners, and argued that the state should defend customary law against what he regarded as the rapacity of the rich landowner. In practice, the state has more often played a positive role in the transition from communal to individual control, and has often enabled or facilitated the exploiting of timber values at the expense of other forest resource values.

Marx viewed deforestation as essentially a correlate of capitalism:

> The long period production time (which comprises a relatively small period of working time) and the great length of the periods of turnover entailed make forestry an industry of little attraction to private and therefore capitalist enterprise . . . The development of culture and of industry in general has ever evinced itself in . . . energetic destruction of forests. (Parsons, 1977)

Other nineteenth-century writers such as George Perkins Marsh also associated the political and economic character of industrial capitalism with the destruction of natural resources such as forests (e.g. Robbins, 1985). Even if such views were simplistic (to say the least), there is little doubt that the nature of the control of the resource is directly related to its condition and trends. The synthesis of cyclical models of resource control and of concepts of phases of destruction and re-creation of the forest resource is an elusive goal. It is, however, clear that questions of control and condition of the resource cannot be divorced from each other, any more than those of the interrelationships between the use, control and condition of the resource. Successive phases of control certainly appear to exist, and seem to be correlated with successive phases of perception of the resource and of its use. Perhaps the major problems of forest resource use occur at times of transition from one phase to another: much of the tropical forest is in the throes of such a transition at present.

Aim and structure

The purpose of this volume is not to lament the sorry history of the world forest resource, but to review the use of the resource within a framework of organising concepts that is sufficiently robust to offer a context and possible means of making sense of the myriad of factual details, without being so rigid as to stifle or distort. It is concerned with the extent, control, status and use of the world forest resource. It begins with a brief review of the nature of the resource base, in which particular attention is paid to those ecological characteristics that are of central significance for the use of the forest. It then proceeds to present some historical perspectives on the use of the forest resource, and to outline the dimensions of world forests, in Chapters 3 and 4 respectively. Chapter 5 addresses the subject of the ownership, control and management of the forest resource, while its use is discussed in Chapter 6. The relationships between the forest resource and the wider environment are summarised in Chapter 7. The tropical forest, a major component of the world forest resource and one which is undergoing rapid change at present, is singled out for closer attention in Chapter 8. Chapter 9 considers 'people and policies', and leads to the concluding chapter, which is a brief review.

The aim of the volume is severalfold. First, it is to present a concise review of the state of the world forest resource in the late twentieth century. It does not seek to give a comprehensive country-by-country review of forest resources and is in no sense intended to emulate the monumental accounts of Zon and Sparhawk (1923) or Haden-Guest et al. (1956). Instead it is the intention to outline major trends and issues in the use of the forest resource, on a systematic basis.

Second, the aim is to present this review within the framework of the perception of the forest as a natural resource, and of a number of concepts of forest-resource use. Amongst the latter are included models of trends in forest area, and sequential models of ownership and control. It is further suggested that three major generalisations or models, namely that of the 'pre-industrial', 'industrial' and 'post-industrial' forests, are helpful in providing an organising framework within which the use of the forest resource can be considered. Such a framework, it is hoped, will provide a means by which the use of a particular area of forest at a particular time can be viewed within a wider background or context.

Third, it is hoped that the volume can serve, in a limited way, as a source book and starting-point not only for further development of concepts and models of forest resource use but also for empirical work on other related issues. One of the major difficulties confronting work on forest resources is the diverse and widely scattered literature. A subsidiary aim is to provide a listing of at least a few references. Textual references are therefore included, on the basis that detriment to readability is at least partly counterbalanced by benefit to the student (in the widest sense) of the subject.

A comprehensive review of the world forest resource is impossible. The resource is bewildering in its extent and its complexity. The histories and patterns of resource use are equally bewildering in their diversity. And above all there is a confusing combination of a plethora of statistical information and a paucity of data – especially of uniform quality, coverage and form. Information is scattered and diverse, and attempts at compilation and synthesis are all too rare. To state the predictable and obvious, it is difficult to see the wood for the trees, and indeed not even all the trees are in focus. The aim is to attempt to provide at least some general context for considering individual and specific forest issues of the day.

2 THE FOREST RESOURCE BASE

The world's forest resource base is mind-boggling in its extent, complexity and diversity. Much of the earth surface is or has been capable of supporting woods or forests, and despite centuries or even millenia of clearance perhaps as much as one-third retains a tree cover. Perhaps as much as 80 per cent of the pre-agricultural forest area survives, although the pattern of clearance has been very variable (see Chapter 4). Forests and woodlands still occupy around 4,000 million hectares, and in some areas such as parts of Canada and Siberia they still give the impression of being almost limitless. On the other hand, the impression created when the forest area is related to the human population is rather different. The average forest area per person has now shrunk to around three-quarters of a hectare, or an area similar to that of a soccer pitch. The average forest area per person is of course an abstraction: the distribution of dense population and densely forested areas are almost mutually exclusive at all scales from the global to the local. And the distributions of forest areas and forest types are remarkably uneven. This is one of the key characteristics of the forest resource base, and it is a factor of fundamental significance for the use of the resource. Another fundamental factor is the ecological character and type of the forest. Forest ecosystems vary greatly in their structure and dynamics. The usefulness of a forest, in terms of the products and services it provides, depends in part on ecological characteristics. In addition, these characteristics may determine the way in which the forest responds to use and is modified by it. In short, forest ecosystems provide the base on which resource use, and its consequences, take place.

The purpose of this chapter is to present a brief review of the forest resource base and its distribution pattern, in order to provide context and background for the ensuing discussion of resource use. The focus is on the forest *resource base*, rather than on forests *per se*. For more detailed reviews of forest vegetation and its various types, the reader is referred to texts such as those of Eyre (1963), Richards (1952) and Walter (1985), and the volumes in the series 'Ecosystems of the world' (e.g. Ovington, 1983). The nature and characteristics of the forest resource base are outlined in this chapter, whilst its extent and trends therein are reviewed in Chapter 4.

Distribution

At the global scale, the ultimate limiting factor in forest growth and distribution is climate, while climate and geographical location (in relation

11

to the origin and dispersal of tree species) are the main natural determinants of the distribution of forest types. Two climatic elements are of fundamental importance: temperature and rainfall. Temperature, in conjunction with wind exposure, determines the northern latitudinal limits of the forest as well as its altitudinal limits. Rainfall is the main control on the mid-latitude distribution of lowland forests, and its relative absence accounts for the desert and steppe zones which separate tropical and temperate forests.

Much effort has been devoted to identifying the climatic values which coincide with and therefore appear to determine natural forest distributions. The search for perfect fits between forest margins and specific lines of temperature or rainfall values is somewhat futile: local variations in soil type, drainage and slope will always be complicating factors. Nevertheless, the isotherm of 10°C for the warmest month has long been regarded as coinciding approximately with the poleward limit of forest growth. The fit is far from perfect, with the forest margin lying polewards of the isotherm in maritime regions and equatorwards in more continental areas, and attempted refinements have sought to make use of data on other variables such as length of growing season.

If temperature is the determining influence on the poleward extent of forest, rainfall is the limiting factor in mid-latitudes. The effectiveness of rainfall for plant or tree growth depends on its seasonal distribution and on the amount of evaporation, which in turn is related to temperature. Again, perfect coincidence between lines of equal rainfall (isohyets) and forest limits cannot be expected, but in practice little woodland is found in areas of less than 400 to 500 millimetres annual rainfall.

Forest types and distribution

Figure 2.1 illustrates the broad distribution of the natural forest within its basic climatic controls of temperature and rainfall, and also indicates something of the diversity of forest types. It is important to emphasise that this is merely a highly generalised version of the pattern that would exist under purely natural conditions, in the absence of human interference. It also omits local variations arising from different soil types and mountain ranges, for example. The pattern portrayed, therefore, is not that of existing forests: indeed that pattern is very different, as will be discussed later. Much of the mid-latitude forest has long since been cleared, and the boreal (northern) coniferous forest and tropical moist forest together account for most of the remaining area of the global forest. Tropical forests, including evergreen and deciduous moist forest and dry, open woodlands, make up about half of the world area of forest and woodland, and the high-latitude (mainly) coniferous forest around one-third (Brünig, 1987a). Subtropical and mid-latitude forests are now therefore relatively insignificant in areal extent at the global scale.

Figure 2.1 Forest distribution

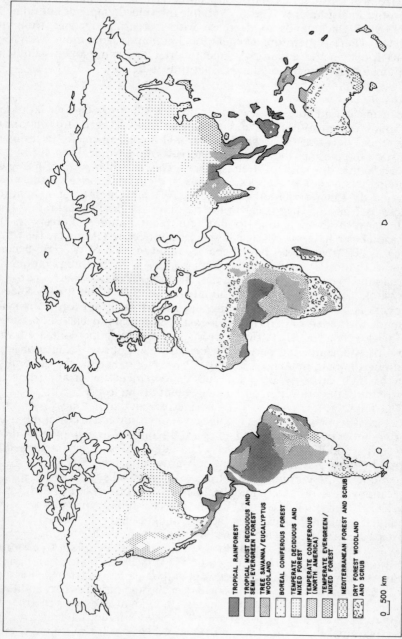

TROPICAL RAINFOREST

TROPICAL MOIST DECIDUOUS AND
SEMI-EVERGREEN FOREST

TREE SAVANNA/EUCALYPTUS
WOODLAND

BOREAL CONIFEROUS FOREST

TEMPERATE DECIDUOUS AND
MIXED FOREST

TEMPERATE CONIFEROUS
(NORTH AMERICA)

TEMPERATE EVERGREEN/
MIXED FOREST

MEDITERRANEAN FOREST AND SCRUB

DRY FOREST WOODLAND
AND SCRUB

0 500 km

Source: Compiled from various sources, including Eyre (1962), Sommer (1976) and Walter (1985)

The tropical forest

The tropical forest varies in its character and composition along latitudinal and altitudinal gradients. The key variable on which it depends latitudinally is rainfall, which tends to decrease with increasing distance from the equator. There is therefore a vegetational gradation from moist evergreen (rain) forest in the equatorial zone to drier and more open woodland merging into savannah grasslands as latitude increases.

Tropical rain forest

The tropical rain forest is found in three main areas of low latitudes, in South America, Africa and south-east Asia. There are important differences between these widely separated areas, especially in terms of floristics, but perhaps the main characteristic of the tropical rain forest as a whole is the diversity of tree species. The Brazilian Amazon region contains around 6,000 tree species, many of them endemic to specific areas (Correa de Lima and Mercado, 1985). As many as fifty or a hundred species per hectare may occur in the tree layer of the tropical rain forest, and many of them belong to different plant families. Forests in the Amazon basin have on average 87 species per hectare (Ramade, 1984). As many as 300 tree species have been recorded in each of two one-hectare plots in Iquitos, Peru, while ten similar plots in Kalimantan, Indonesia, were found to contain 700 tree species: the number of tree species native to the whole of North America is about the same (Wilson, 1989). Species diversity is not equally high throughout the tropical rain forest area: for example the forests of parts of south-east Asia contain species of only a few families. Furthermore, African forests are species-poor compared with those of Amazonia and parts of south-east Asia, partly because of long-continued human influence (Jacobs, 1988). Nevertheless, the generalisation of high diversity is valid, and is extremely important from the viewpoint of the utilisation and management of the forest.

The tallest trees reach to over 50 metres, and sometimes a stratified structure is recognisable. The highest level or storey consists of a relatively small number of giants forming an open, discontinuous canopy well above the denser middle and lower levels. The tallest trees are characterised by enormous buttress roots radiating outwards from the base of the trunk. When one of these upper-storey trees eventually falls, a gap is opened in the canopy and ultimately may be filled by a replacement of a different species, the original tree probably having no saplings of its own species immediately below it because of the lack of light under the dense canopies. Perhaps several tree generations may pass before the original species returns to the site. Since the light intensities below the main tree storeys are usually poor, forest-floor vegetation is very limited, although most of the trees themselves are festooned with climbing plants such as lianas.

Climatic conditions are warm and moist throughout the year, and there is no climatically-limited growing season. Individual trees shed their leaves at different times, and the forest as a whole is evergreen. Fallen leaves and other plant debris accumulate on the relatively bare forest floor, where a

Table 2.1 Lowland–mountain tropical rain forest contrasts

a) Mount Maquiling, Philippine Islands

Forest Altitude Number of tree storeys	Dipterocarp (450m) 3	Mid-mountain (700m) 2	Mossy (1020m) 1
Average height of storeys (m)	27,16,10	17,4	6
No. of species of woody plants	92	70	21

b) Eastern Zaïre/Belgian *Congo*	*Tropical* *rain forest*	*Transition* *forest*	*Montane* *rain forest*
No. of trunks (>20 cm diam.)/ha	115	180	200
Mean height of boles (m)	13	12	10
Mean diameter of trunks (cm)	60	40	35
Timber volume per ha (m^3)	400–600	300	200

Source: Based on data in Richards (1952).

litter layer forms. Decomposition of the plant litter proceeds very rapidly under the continuously hot and damp conditions, and the plant nutrients are rapidly released for subsequent uptake. Despite the apparent luxuriance of the vegetation, the soils in many equatorial areas are usually very old, weathered and leached. They are often very poor in nutrients and acid in reaction. Most of the plant nutrients are contained in plant material, rather than in the soil, and these nutrients are rapidly cycled from plant to forest floor. If the tree layers are removed, for example by burning, the plant-nutrient cycle is disrupted, and the nutrient reserves are suddenly and abruptly leached. A major loss of nutrients from the local ecosystem results, and the impoverished soils may be capable of supporting only grasses or other non-tree species. The pattern of nutrient cycling in the tropical rain forest is therefore of crucial significance and has profound implications both for the utilisation and management of the forest itself, and also for the conversion of the forest into agricultural land.

As in other latitudinal zones, the nature of the forest changes in mountainous areas, where characteristics of both temperature and rainfall differ from those in the lowlands. Rainfall is higher at normal cloud level, which often lies between 1,000 and 2,500 metres, and the cloud forests which occur in this zone are characterised by ferns and mosses which drape the branches of the trees. Above the cloud level, rainfall decreases rapidly, and tree species suited to the drier environment (for example *Podocarpus* conifers) may be found. With increasing exposure to wind, the trees become shorter and more gnarled and stunted, and eventually the forest

Figure 2.2   Tropical rain forest: species richness and altitude (metres) (Brunei)

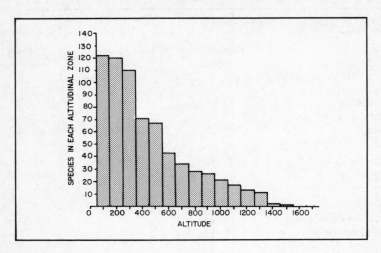

Source: Modified after Ashton (1964)

gives way to a shrub zone. Well before that stage is reached, however, and at altitudes of only a few hundred metres, clear contrasts between the lowland and mountain forest can become apparent. The number of tree storeys may drop from three to two and their average height rapidly decreases. Average trunk diameter also decreases, as does the timber volume per unit area. At the same time, the number of tree species per unit area decreases. Table 2.1 summarises these characteristics, while Figure 2.2 illustrates the relationship between species richness and altitude for the example of Brunei.

In short, the mountain forests are less rich both in timber and in diversity of species than their lowland counterparts. The more inaccessible mountain forests are amongst those least likely to be cleared or converted: it is unfortunate that they are also the least diverse in terms of species.

Tropical seasonal forests

Outwards from the equator, the seasonality of rainfall becomes more pronounced than in the uniformly wet equatorial zone, and the character of the forest changes as dry seasons become longer and clearer. Semi-evergreen forests are widespread in the northern part of South America and in the form of monsoon forests in parts of the area stretching from north-east India to northern Australia (Indo-Malaysia). They are less well developed in Africa. Compared with the tropical rain forest, their structure is generally simpler and lower. There are usually only two tree storeys, with the upper one reaching to between 20 and 30 metres. Most of the tree species in the lower layer are evergreen, but a proportion of those making up the upper storey are deciduous. This forest type is represented by the so-called moist teak forests of Burma and neighbouring areas: teak, however, is only one of a number of tree species found in these areas of seasonal rainfall, and rarely occupies more than 10 per cent of a stand.

Where the pattern of rainfall becomes more seasonal, the nutrient cycle differs from that of the tropical rain forest. The leaf fall at the beginning of the dry season forms a deep layer of litter which does not begin to decay rapidly until the following wet season. Similarly, with higher light intensities during the 'winter', more profuse and diverse undergrowth and forest-floor vegetation may develop.

With longer dry seasons and lower rainfall, the semi-evergreen forest gives way to one more correctly designated 'tropical deciduous'. In Central and South America and in Indo-Malaysia, this forest typically has a two-storey structure, with an upper storey at around 20 metres composed mainly of deciduous species, below which may lie a lower, mainly evergreen layer. In Indo-Malaysia, this type is represented by the so-called dry teak forest, where the associated species differ from those of the moist variant.

Tropical deciduous forest is less well represented in Africa. It is typically discontinuous rather than continuous, and usually takes the form of stands of tall deciduous trees separated by open grassland or parkland. The relative proportion of the former is greatest in the belt of *miombo* forest which stretches across Africa from Angola to Tanzania. Here, and in a number of similar but smaller areas to the north of the equator, the dominant trees are usually flat-topped and under 20 metres in height. Tall grasses, and shrubs in some areas, dominate the undergrowth. *Miombo* forest grades into more open parkland or savannah where the trees may have similar form but become more scattered and the woodland is more open. *Acacia* spp. are usually the most common species in this zone. With decreasing rainfall the tree savannah becomes increasingly open and merges into thorn scrub and grassland (mapped as dry forest in Figure 2.1). In terms of industrial timber production, the native woodlands of the more open savannahs and dry forests are unimportant, but in relation to the supply of fuelwood their significance is much greater.

Climate, especially in the form of low rainfall, and soil conditions may both be limiting factors to forest growth over large areas of the savannah zone, but fire is a major ecological factor. During the dry season of several months, the plant litter is highly combustible, and frequent fires over a long period of time are probably responsible for the present character of much of the dry forest zone. The chances of survival of tree seedlings or saplings are low, and most of the trees making up the open woodland are of fire-resistant species such as the baobab (*Adansonia digitata*). Where fire has been excluded in experimental areas, increases in woody growth have taken place, and commercial plantations have been established in many parts of the savannah zone.

Boreal coniferous forest

Outside the tropics, the boreal coniferous forest is by far the most extensive surviving forest type. It occupies two great zones, one stretching across North America from Alaska to Newfoundland and the other from the Atlantic coast of Scandinavia to the Pacific coast of Siberia. In these zones, the climate is characterised by short growing seasons and long, cold winters. The forests are dominated by conifers, most of which are evergreen. Their dominance is ensured by an ability to survive the harsh winter conditions by minimising water-loss through their needle-like leaves and to begin photosynthesis and growth rapidly during the short growing season.

Although there are similarities of form and structure between the North American and Eurasian parts of the boreal coniferous forest, there are important differences in species composition both between and within these areas. The European section is much poorer in species than its counterparts in North America and eastern Asia. Scots pine and Norway spruce dominate in the European section, on the drier and wetter soils respectively. Siberian species gradually increase eastwards. Spruce gradually decreases towards the most continental areas of eastern Siberia, and its place is taken by larch, a deciduous conifer. The shallow-rooted Dahurian larch is the dominant species over huge areas of permafrost. Larch forests occupy some 2.5 million square kilometres in Siberia (Walter, 1985). Further east again, towards the Pacific coast, firs and spruce again become dominant although larch remains common in northern Japan and Manchuria.

In terms of species diversity, the North American section more closely resembles the east Asian part of the boreal forest than the European area. As in Eurasia, however, there is a west–east gradation. In eastern Canada the white and black spruces are commonly found on areas of better and poorer drainage respectively and give way to species such as jack pine on poorer soils. The species pattern in the west is complicated by mountain chains, but the eastern dominants give way to lodgepole pine and western species of spruce and fir.

A distinctive feature of the boreal forest is the frequent occurrence of almost pure, single-species stands. This facilitates exploitation on a large scale, but when extensive areas of pure stands are removed by felling or fire they may not regenerate directly. Deciduous species such as birch and aspen may be the first trees to invade, and may in turn themselves form even-aged stands. Conifers such as jack pine may eventually displace the birch or aspen, and in turn may themselves be followed by the probable climatic-climax dominants such as white spruce and balsam fir.

Both the structural and functional characteristics of the boreal forest ecosystem mean that utilisation and management face problems quite different from those of the tropical rainforest, for example. In contrast to the rainforest, the plant litter on the forest floor decomposes only slowly in the cool conditions. The mean residence time for organic matter on the forest floor is quoted by Cole (1986) as 350 years, compared with four years and 0.7 years respectively for temperate deciduous and tropical forests. In the boreal forests most of the nutrients are found in the litter and in the tropical rain forest in the vegetation. Indeed the forest-floor litter contains as much as 84 per cent of the above-ground nitrogen and 71 per cent of the potassium, whereas for the tropical rainforest the corresponding figures are only 6 per cent and 1 per cent respectively. Nutrient reserves in the leached podzolic soils of the boreal forest are poor, but the tree roots generally possess mycorrhizal fungi which may help to make the nutrients contained in the raw litter more easily available. In addition, the boreal forest appears to be able to make more efficient use of available nitrogen (as indicated by the amount of biomass produced per unit of nitrogen uptake) than most other forest types.

Other forests

Although the greater part of the remaining forest area is contained within the boreal and tropical forest belts, forests in intermediate latitudes have been of primary importance as the hearths of modern silviculture and forest management.

Temperate deciduous forest
To the south of the boreal forest zone lies temperate mixed and deciduous forest. The boundary between the coniferous and deciduous forest is rarely as sharp as Figure 2.1 suggests. Wide belts of transition occur in both Eurasia and North America, with the detailed pattern of distribution of conifers depending on local conditions of relief, soil and drainage. The deciduous forests of Europe stretched from the Atlantic to the Urals and were dominated by the pedunculate oak over vast areas. Depending on soils, climate and drainage, the oak was usually associated with a number of species including elm, ash and beech. Beech, for example, was prominent or dominant on some calcareous areas and on areas of well-drained and rich soils as far north as the south of Sweden. It also occured widely at intermediate altitudes in the Alps and the Mediterranean peninsulas, where it frequently occupied a zone below the coniferous mountain forest. In the southern part of the temperate belt of Europe, oak often remained dominant (for example in areas such as northern Spain and Italy), but was represented by species different from those of north-west Europe.

In North America prior to the arrival of European settlers, the deciduous forest occupied a block of country between the Atlantic and the Mississippi. Much of this forest has now been removed or modified, as in Europe, but it seems that many structural similarities existed between the two continents. The upper storey of trees usually formed a canopy sufficiently open to allow sunlight to penetrate and support a rich shrub layer. On the other hand the American formation is characterised by a wider range of species. In New England and much of the Appalachians beech and maple are usually dominant, and are found in association with a range of other broadleaf species as well as conifers such as hemlock in some areas. Further south, the beech–maple forest gives way to one of oak and chestnut, while in the drier areas to the west oak–hickory forest predominated. Similar deciduous forest, usually dominated by oak species, occupied large areas in northern China, Korea and the south-eastern part of the Soviet Union. The oaks of Shantung at one time provided food for the silkworms which produced local 'wild silk'.

In contrast to the extensive blocks of deciduous forests in the eastern parts of North America and Asia, narrow belts are found to the south of the boreal forest in the interiors of both continents. In Canada this belt is only 75–150 kilometres wide and is dominated by balsam, poplar and aspen. Aspen is also often dominant in the Siberian belt, where it is usually associated with birch. In both continents these deciduous belts have proved to be more attractive for settlement than either the boreal forest to the north or the grasslands to the south. The Trans-Siberian railway, for example, closely follows the narrow belt of deciduous forest. In both continental and maritime deciduous forests, soils are usually better than those in the boreal forest zone, and the more rapid decomposition of the plant litter in the warmer climate allows faster recycling of nutrients. Throughout the zone, therefore, the deciduous forest has been extensively cleared for agriculture, and most areas of forest that have not been cleared have been heavily modified.

Temperate coniferous forest
Extensive areas of coniferous forest are also found outside the boreal forest, notably in North America. The so-called 'lake forest' occupied a huge area stretching from Minnesota to New England, but like the deciduous forest has been severely modified by clearance and logging. White and red pine and eastern hemlock were the predominant species. To the south and east, forests dominated by loblolly and other species of pine occupied much of the coastal plain from New Jersey to northern Florida and westwards to Texas. This forest is characterised by pure stands of mainly pine species on low-lying sandy or marshy soil along the coastlands. The uncompromising nature of the typical soils meant that there was little incentive to clear the land for agricultural purposes, and this forest has survived better than much of the deciduous and lake forests to the north. The western forests of North America form a third type of non-boreal coniferous forest. The 'coast forest' is dominated by Sitka spruce from the coastal lowlands of Alaska south to British Columbia, and from there southwards is gradually replaced by western hemlock and western cedar, which attain heights of 60–80 metres. From Oregon southwards these species in turn are challenged by the even larger coastal redwood. Douglas fir occurs extensively both in the coast forest of British Columbia and Washington, and in the drier mountain forests inland from the coast. In the former areas, its presence may be related to successions following extensive fires rather than directly to the nature of the climate.

Mediterranean forest
Each of these types of coniferous forests in North America, as well as the other forest types previously outlined, have posed their own problems for forest management and have provided the settings for successive phases of forest utilisation and development of the lumber industry. At a much earlier stage of human history, the forests around the Mediterranean did likewise. Most of these Mediterranean forests were typically mixed and evergreen. Evergreen oak species such as the holm oak were common and widespread, while pines such as the stone, maritime and Aleppo pines also occurred widely around the Mediterranean basin. As long ago as classical times it was known that a continual supply of small timbers could be obtained from stump growths (coppicing) of oak, but this knowledge did not safeguard the forest resource base. Extensive deforestation and forest destruction or modification are long established, and with them came the hydrological changes and soil erosion that are still associated with modern forest removal in other parts of the world. Much of the original forest has now been totally destroyed or reduced to scrub by centuries of grazing and burning, especially in the drier areas. Today's forests in Mediterranean Europe and Turkey occupy only 5 per cent of their original area (Ramade, 1984). On the other hand in the cooler and moister mountains, the mixed forest of the lowlands typically gave way to coniferous forests, including the well-known cedar forests of parts of North Africa and Lebanon.

Areas of Mediterranean-type climate outside the European area – for example in parts of California, South Africa and Australia – have been less severely modified by humans and are characterised by genera and species different from those of the Old World Mediterranean area. In these areas of dry woodland and scrub, summer drought is a major limiting factor, and the tree and plant species making up the natural vegetation of open 'sclerophylous' woodland or scrub are characterised by small leaves with thick cuticles, adapted to minimise transpiration.

Other temperate evergreen and mixed forest
Mixed evergreen forests are also found in the Southern Hemisphere, in South America, South Africa, and Tasmania and New Zealand. The tree species comprising these forests are usually quite different from those in the Northern Hemisphere. In Chile, for example, the dominant species is Araucaria pine, which is often associated with beech (*Nothofagus* spp.). Forests of similar structure are found in New Zealand, but with different species: for example the kauri pine (*Agathis australis*) is associated with the northern part of the country, while various pines of *Podocarpus* spp. are found along with broad-leaved evergreens elsewhere in the islands.

Evergreen forests dominated mainly by broad-leaved species occur in restricted areas in both hemispheres. In the Northern Hemisphere the main occurrence was in central China and southern Japan, where a range of evergreen oaks was predominant, often occurring in association with laurel, magnolias and some conifers. Forests of this type also covered much of south-east and south-west Australia prior to European settlement. These forests were dominated by drought-resistant species of *Eucalyptus*.

Trees of this species are typically very tall, but cast only a light shade. They are therefore associated with a well-developed undergrowth of grass and scrub. Because of these characteristics of drought-resistance and light shade, *Eucalyptus* species have been widely used in agro-forestry projects and in other forms of planting in many parts of the world far removed from their native Australia. Evergreen broad-leaved forests also occupy parts of New Zealand with much wetter climates than those found in most of Australia: for example many of the slopes of the Southern Alps are clothed in a rain forest composed mainly of southern beech (*Nothofagus* spp.).

The forest resource base is therefore highly varied in its structure, composition and ecological characteristics. Although climate is a determining factor in forest type and distribution, it is not the only one. Variations in soil type, for example, may complicate the simple relationship between type of forest and type of climate, as for example in the case of the pine forests of the eastern coastlands of the United States. Furthermore, the history of changing climate over the last few thousand years is a major complicating factor. Forest type and distribution may not yet have adjusted to an equilibrium state in some areas. Locational or plant-geographical factors are obvious: although life forms may be similar in forests of both hemispheres the tree species are often quite different. Human interference has been a major factor, selectively removing some species or causing indirect modification by practices such as grazing. The pre-human character of some forest types remains uncertain or unknown, simply because few completely untouched areas have survived. Forests in mountains and in areas of poor soils are more likely to have escaped clearance for agricultural purposes than forests in lowlands and more fertile areas.

With a selective pattern of forest survival, the basis for our understanding of forest ecology may be somewhat biased, especially in relation to the former forests of the now densely populated and severely modified parts of the world. Furthermore, the concepts and systems of management that evolved in response to the ecology of one type of forest may be less appropriate in other settings. For example the tenets of silviculture that evolved in the temperate deciduous forest of west-central Europe were not necessarily appropriate for the coniferous forests of North America. At the same time humans have themselves become a major factor in the distribution of tree species as well as of forests. Tree species for use in forest plantations have been transported from continent to continent and even from hemisphere to hemisphere. The most usual direction of movement in temperate latitudes has been from the west coast of North America to Europe and Asia: movement from Europe to North America has been less successful (Zobel et al., 1987). The extensive use of Monterey pine (*Pinus radiata*), a native of California, in plantations in Chile, Australia and New Zealand is a major example, as is the use of Sitka spruce (*Picea sitchensis*) from the Pacific coast of North America in the man-made forests of Britain and Ireland. The expansion of eucalyptus outwards from Australia to many low-latitude lands is another major example. But while species can be taken from area to area and while a certain amount can be done to modify drainage and soil factors locally, the ultimate control of climate remains as an unyielding limiting factor. It is this factor above all others that determines forest growth and productivity.

Forest ecosystems: growth and volume

The forest resource-base is perhaps even more variable in its timber volume and growth rates than it is in its structure and composition. Tremendous contrasts in volume per hectare and rates of growth exist between different types of forests. Rainfall and length of growing season are major determinants of these variables. The volume of standing timber varies from around 350 cubic metres per hectare in the tropical rainforest to 50 cubic metres in savannah woodland and perhaps 150 cubic metres in the temperate forest (Persson, 1974). It is estimated that around 20 to 25 per cent of the photosynthetic matter produced on earth is in the form of wood, as is about half of the total biomass produced by the forest (Spurr and Vaux, 1976).

There is a voluminous literature on the amounts of living matter found in the various ecological zones, and on its rate of growth. Net primary productivity (NPP) is the rate of increment of plant material, and is usually expressed in terms of dry matter per square metre per year. One measure of the extent of human use of ecological resources is the proportion of terrestrial NPP used or directed by humans. This amounts to around 40 per cent. Whilst the use of the forest resource accounts for over one quarter of the 'human' proportion, much of this fraction arises from forest clearing for cultivation and other forms of forest destruction without beneficial use (for example during forest harvesting). The part represented by wood actually used as lumber or for paper or firewood is equivalent to little more than one-twentieth of the NPP used or directed by humans, and to around 2 per cent of all terrestrial NPP. (Diamond, 1987).

Table 2.2 shows illustrative figures for productivity, production and biomass in the main forest types. A wide range of NPP values is indicated for most of the divisions, and different sources quote different estimates for mean values. For example, Lieth (1976) quotes a figure of 2.8 kilograms per square metre per year for the tropical rain forest, while Eyre (1978) estimates the mean value at 2,500 grams per square metre per year. (See also Cannell (1982) for a compilation of numerous reports of net production and biomass relating to different tree species and conditions world wide.)

As Table 2.2 clearly indicates, the tropical rainforest is the most productive forest type, and has the highest biomass. Net primary productivity is up to four times greater than that in the boreal forest, and twice that in the warm temperate mixed forest. As Jordan (1983) observes, there is almost unanimous agreement amongst professional ecologists that productivity in tropical forests is higher than in any other forest type. Productivity tends to decline along gradients towards zones with seasonal humid and semi-arid climates, and also with altitude, on poorer soils and in

Table 2.2   Net primary productivity

	Area (10⁶ km²)	Net primary productivity Range (g/m²/year)	Net primary productivity Approx. (g/m²/year)	Total production (10⁹t)	Mean biomass (t/ha)
Forests	50.0		1290	64.5	
Tropical rain forest	17.0	1000–3500	2000	34.0	450
Raingreen forest	7.5	600–3500	1500	11.3	
Summergreen forest	7.0	400–2500	1000	7.0	
Mediterranean forest	1.5	250–1500	800	1.2	
Warm temp. mixed forest	5.0	1000–1500	1000	5.0	300
Boreal forest	12.0	200–1500	500	6.0	200
Woodland	7.0	200–1000	600	4.2	

Source: Compiled from data in Lieth (1975) and Jones (1979)

areas of very high rainfall (Brünig, 1987). In this latter respect the gradient of a primary productivity resembles those of forest structure and complexity, and of species richness.

The tropical rain forest is also dominant in terms of total production and biomass per unit area. It will be apparent from the earlier part of the chapter that the composition of the biomass varies greatly between different forest types, in terms of both the relative role of wood and the composition of tree species. A distinction needs to be drawn between total net primary productivity and wood production. Little more than half of the biomass may consist of the stems of trees in the temperate forest: for example these account for 52 per cent of the plant biomass in Russian oak forests (Walter, 1985). (Stems, of course, comprise a greater proportion of tree biomass. For example Pardé [1980] quotes a range of 65–70 per cent for mature spruce forest in Canada.) Although the tropical rain forest is characterised by high rates of NPP, these do not necessarily extend to wood production. In the words of Wadsworth (1983, p. 284), 'The relevance of the level of primary productivity to that of usable wood . . . is apparently no greater than that of primary forest luxuriance to soil fertility in the tropics'. In the same way that explorers and colonisers have often mistakenly assumed that luxuriance of tropical vegetation meant fertile soils, so also have politicians, planners and entrepreneurs often assumed that high NPPs meant rapid growth of useful timber. Furthermore, timber growth is spread across numerous tree species, whereas in the boreal forest, most of the tree biomass is composed of only one or two species. Commercial harvesting (for timber) of the former is more difficult and more costly for the former, especially since only a few of the species may be useful or valuable, than it is for the latter. In short, while total NPP is much higher in tropical forests than in those in the temperate zone, those for wood only may be much more comparable. Considerable variations exist for the latter in both zones, and especially in the temperate zone.

Table 2.3 Distribution of forest area by type and timber volume

Type	Area (million ha)	Mean volume (m³/ha)	Total volume (1000 million m³)
Tropical wet evergreen	560 (20.0)	350	196 (49.5)
Tropical moist deciduous	308 (11.0)	160	49 (12.3)
Tropical and sub-tropical dry	784 (28.0)	50	39 (9.8)
Other sub-tropical	28 (1.0)	80–200	4.6 (1.6)
Temperate	448 (16.0)	150	67 (16.9)
Boreal	672 (24.0)	60	40 (10.1)
Total	2800	157	396

Note: Figures in parentheses indicate column percentages
Source: Compiled from data in Persson (1974)

These variations are related especially to climate, and in particular to radiation balance and rainfall.

Estimates of timber volume per hectare in different forest types have been assembled by Persson (1974) and have been used, in conjunction with his estimates of forest areas, to obtain estimates of the total volume of standing timber. These estimates are illustrated in Table 2.3, which relates to closed forest only. In the table, the dominant role of tropical and boreal zones is clearly indicated: together they account for over three-quarters of the forest area and nearly 80 per cent of the volume of standing timber.

In natural forests and other stable, climatic-climax communities, both NPP and biomass are constant: new growth is matched by death and decay. When management is introduced, however, changes may occur. Tree growth rates vary with age, and after reaching a peak begin to slow down. If management aims at maximising timber yield, therefore, it may adjust the length of rotation to the pattern of growth. In this way the productive characteristics of the managed forest may differ from those of the natural forest. In the mainly managed forests of temperate regions such as Europe, North America and Japan, annual growth rates or net annual increments are usually equivalent to between 1 and 6 per cent of growing stock, and are usually of the order of a few cubic metres per hectare per annum, with gradients of variation paralleling those of temperature and rainfall. In the Soviet Union, Canada and the United States for example, annual increments per hectare are respectively 1.2, 1.5 and 3.1 cubic metres. King (1975) has suggested a global average increment of around 1.1 cubic metres per hectare, equivalent to over 3,000 million cubic metres per year or around 1 per cent of the growing stock.

Potential productivity

In order to estimate the *potential* productivity of the world's forests, Paterson (1956) attempted to relate *ideal site* class, or productive capacity of forested lands under conditions where rotation length and management are geared to maximising yield, to climate. He derived a CVP (climate vegetation productivity) index in which data on temperature, rainfall and growing season were incorporated. This index was closely and positively correlated ($r = +0.90$) with values for ideal site class. Difficulty was experienced in obtaining acceptable values for ideal site class, and although a few of his values came from Africa and North America, the majority were taken from Sweden. From the statistical relationship that he established between the CVP index and ideal site class, he proceeded to estimate the potential productivity of the world's forests on the basis of available climatic statistics. The resulting pattern of variation is shown in Figure 2.3.

Since the map is based on a climatic index, it will be apparent that influences from factors such as soils are not portrayed, and, furthermore, the climatic index itself does not incorporate certain elements such as wind exposure. Nevertheless, even though it is an oversimplification, the map shows an interesting pattern of variation in estimated potential productivity. A degree of correlation exists, as might be expected, with the map of forest distribution and type, with high values in much of the tropical zone and low values in the boreal forest zone. In most of the equatorial zone and the humid tropics, the calculated potential productivity is in excess of 12 cubic metres per hectare per year, compared with under 3 cubic metres in the boreal forest. Potential productivity is relatively high in the humid temperate climates of north-west Europe and eastern North America, and in parts of eastern Australia and New Zealand. On the other hand the limiting factor of moisture means that potential productivity in much of Africa and western Asia is zero or negligible.

Plantations

In practice much higher growth rates than those indicated in Figure 2.3 can be obtained in plantations, and these may have the additional advantage of higher proportions of potentially useful stemwood than in natural forests. Their real comparative advantage, in practical terms, may therefore be greater than the apparent one. Caution needs to be exercised in comparing plantations with each other and with natural forests. Plantation records usually refer only to yield, and indicate nothing of the inputs (Jordan, 1983). Furthermore, plantation figures are often quoted over-bark, which may be thick (up to 45 per cent by volume) in young pines in particular, whereas in the temperate zone the usual practice is to quote under-bark (Zobel et al., 1987). These points need to be borne in mind in considering Table 2.4, which illustrates some examples of annual growth rates achieved in tropical plantations. (Zobel et al. quote some exceptionally high rates of up to 60 or even 100 cubic metres per hectare per year.) Some figures for non-tropical plantations are included for comparison as well as some data for other managed forests.

The table suggests that growth rates in tropical plantations are much

Figure 2.3 Potential productivity

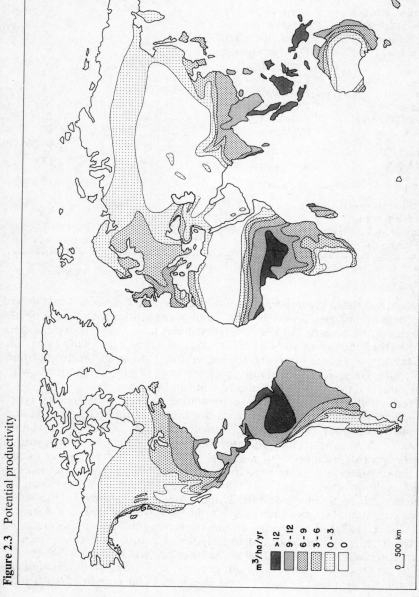

m³/ha/yr

> 12
9 – 12
6 – 9
3 – 6
0 – 3
0

0 ___ 500 km

Source: Based on Paterson (1956)

Table 2.4 Examples of average growth rates (mean annual increments (MAI)) achieved in plantations

Country	Species	Rotation length (yr)	MAI (m³/ha/yr)
Brazil Amazonia	*Gmelina arborea*	10	35
	Pinus caribaea	16	27
Central	*Eucalyptus* spp	—	25
Costa Rica	*Pinus caribaea*	8	40
Chile	*Pinus radiata*	25	22
New Zealand	*Pinus radiata*	18	25
Swaziland	*Pinus patula*	15	19
Malawi	*Pinus patula*	16	18
Gambia/Senegal	*Gmelina* spp	10	15
Philippines	*Albizzia falcataria*	10	28
South USA	*Pinus taeda*	30	12
NW USA	*Pseudotsuga menziesii*	40	13
Scandinavia	*Picea abies*	50	5
Canada (average)		—	1
Sweden (average)		60–100	3
Tropical high forest (managed)		—	0.5–7

Source: Compiled from data in Evans (1982) and Sedjo (1984)

greater than those in temperate zones, and it is usually assumed that this is so. Some authorities, however, have cautioned that this assumption needs to be viewed with care. Jordan (1983) concludes from a review of published figures that the *wood only* productivities of temperate plantations are similar to (and sometimes slightly higher than) those in the tropics and subtropics. Whether this is simply a reflection of length of experience with silviculture in the respective zones remains to be seen.

Productivity or growth rate in plantations varies with species type, management (including the nature and intensity of inputs), soil type and climate. In Europe, for example, growth rates vary with climate in two different dimensions. One gradient, determined mainly by temperature, slopes upwards from north to south. The other is from extreme oceanicity of climate in western Ireland to extreme continentality in the Soviet Union. This gradient operates differentially between different species. Oceanic species such as Sitka spruce attain their maximum growth in the west. More continental species such as Scots pine grow well in east (e.g. Christie and Lines, 1979). Knowledge of the characteristics and preferences of species (and provenances) and experience in use of exotics are rapidly increasing, and hence growth rates can be expected to increase.

The area under plantations in general and tropical plantations in particular is increasing rapidly, and this expansion combined with high productivities is likely to mean that an increasing proportion of industrial wood requirements will be supplied from this source. On the other hand some controversy exists over the sustainability of high productivities beyond the first rotation in tropical plantations, and pests and diseases may yet be problems (see Chapter 7). It should perhaps also be borne in mind that the expansion of plantations itself reflects the existence of some pressure on the forest resource base.

3 HISTORICAL PERSPECTIVES ON FOREST RESOURCE USE

The management and use of the forest resource are sometimes seen as problems peculiar to the late twentieth century. We read much about shrinking forests and shortages of wood, and about the floods and accelerated soil erosion that are alleged to follow the removal of the forest. Topical as these problems are, however, they are not new. Although the scale of some of them may be greater than in the past, they affected our forefathers as well as ourselves. In his arrogance, modern 'technical' man may assume that both his perception of modern problems and his responses to them are (and must be) unique, and that he has little to learn from the past. If he takes this view, he is limiting his vision as effectively as if he wore blinkers.

In many parts of the world a sequential pattern of use of the forest resource can be demonstrated (Table 3.1). Initially, the forest is seen as an almost unlimited resource, with little danger of exhaustion and little need of conservation. Trends in forest use and area are perceived in neutral or positive terms: a reduction in forest area may be welcomed in allowing an expansion of the agricultural area. As this phase of resource destruction proceeds, some voices begin to call for conservation. Initially they are largely ignored, but from the faint stirrings a clamour may arise and may eventually lead to legislation or other government action aimed at halting the trends. The effectiveness of these voices has been variable. In some countries forest destruction was halted while significant forest areas still survived. In others it continued to a point where the forest resource was all but exhausted. In some instances, near-exhaustion was followed by attempts at the re-creation of the resource, and in a few of these cases the expansion of the forest area has recently attracted adverse reaction. Perhaps there may also (at least in theory) be a phase of equilibrium, when the resource is neither expanding nor contracting. Such phases, however, have been in reality few and far between.

This three or four-phase cyclical model can be demonstrated at various scales. For many centuries, the forests of Britain suffered contraction before a dramatic turn-round in the early twentieth century led to expansion which has continued ever since. In detail the model is not quite so simple as the outline may suggest: the late eighteenth and early nineteenth centuries saw a 'false dawn' of forest expansion which was not

30

Table 3.1   Sequential model of forest resource trends

Stage	Trend in resource area	Perception of trend
1 'Unlimited' resource	contraction	positive or neutral
2 Depleting resource	contraction	negative
– – – – –	forest transition – – – – –	
3 Expanding resource	re-creation/expansion	neutral/negative
4 Equilibrium?	(stability)	na

sustained. Nevertheless in general terms it appears to be as valid as it is simple. Different parts of the world have reached different stages in the model, while at the global scale we are still firmly in the phase of resource destruction.

At the same time we can perhaps conceive of management of the forest resource in terms of the model or analogy of hunting/gathering and agriculture. Initially, utilisation of the forest resource resembles hunting or gathering rather than farming. It involves the direct use of an ecological resource with little or no management or manipulation. Only later is management applied, and later still trees are grown under conditions as 'artificial' as those under which crops such as wheat or rice are produced. Again the model is perhaps not simple or linear: there may be deviations and reversals. Nevertheless, the transition from hunting/gathering to farming the forest has been made in many parts of the world, although in many others it has still to begin.

An important contextual factor is the incorporation of an area for the first time into the wider world economy. This process brings new demands for forest products, as well as new forms of control. It often coincides in time with rapid population growth, and severe pressures may be exerted on the forest resource. These may eventually be followed by a shift from one exploitation phase to the next, and by a transition from hunting/gathering to farming. Incorporation may be an important trigger factor, but the time-lag between it and the response appears to be as variable in length as it is critical for the condition of the forest resource.

While the sequential and hunting/gathering models both provide a background against which current trends in the forest resource can be viewed, they are perhaps of more value in combination than they are separately. The driving-force in the shift from hunting/gathering to farming the forest also provides the dynamic for the progression from the phase of destruction to that of conservation or re-establishment. It may thus be both meaningful and helpful to think in terms of a forest transition, from a 'hunted', dwindling forest resource to one which is 'farmed' and stable or expanding in area. Two separate transitions may occur – the one from hunting/gathering to farming and the other from contraction to stability or expansion – but in practice they often coincide in time.

In this chapter, forest resource use is initially considered in two contrasting areas – the Mediterranean basin in the Old World, and the United States and neighbouring areas in the New World. These histories are then considered in relation to other parts of the world, and in particular to the expanding world economy.

The Mediterranean basin

The Mediterranean region has been described as the 'type situation' of an unhappy history of forest management and its consequences (Thirgood, 1981, p. 163). Its degraded scrub vegetation, denuded slopes and silted river mouths are widely perceived as symptoms of mismanagement of the environment in general and of the forest in particular. Some have gone so far as to implicate this environmental mismanagement in the decline of classical civilisations (Hughes and Thirgood, 1982). The long and troubled relationship between man and the Mediterranean forest gives ample scope for thought. Several classical writers refer to the rate at which forests were being replaced by fields, pastures or scrub. Perhaps there is a parallel between the Mediterranean forest of 2,000 years ago and the tropical forest of today.

Resource demands

In classical Greece and Rome, the forest was the source of fuel, building material and war *matériel*. Furthermore, the forest had to be cleared before agriculture could be practised, and in areas remaining uncleared its shrub and field layers offered grazing and browsing. It is not surprising, therefore, that the forest resource was subjected to severe pressure: perhaps it is more surprising that so much of it survived the classical civilisations.

With growing populations in the city-states, more and more forest land had to be cleared for agriculture, and this was perhaps the main cause of contraction of the forest area as indeed it is today. Forest clearance occurred not only around the cities themselves, but also further afield in Greek colonies and in Africa and in other Roman provinces. And even if direct clearance did not occur, the same result was produced by grazing, which also prevented the recovery or regeneration of forests previously cleared or degraded.

The biggest single demand for wood was for fuel. In the absence of significant use of coal and oil, the Greeks and Romans had to look to the forest for fuel for both domestic and industrial purposes. According to Hughes with Thirgood (1982), probably close to 90 per cent of wood consumption was as fuel, as it is in many developing countries today. Charcoal, rather than wood, probably accounted for much of this consumption, and its production employed thousands. As a more easily transportable material than timber, it could be economically produced at greater distances from the cities and allowed urban demand to be met from some of the remoter mountain forests. Timber for building material, on the other hand, was less easily transported though more valuable. Even when timber scarcities led to the more extensive use of stone as a building material, with the accompanying flowering of classical architecture, some timber was still required for purposes such as scaffolding as well as for fitting out the buildings. It was also required for shipbuilding, and became a strategic raw material of primary importance. In short, with the growth of city-states of substantial populations numbered in hundreds of thousands, demand for forest products escalated at an unprecedented rate.

It is not surprising that this demand resulted in the local destruction of the forest resource around the main cities. Many classical writers refer to deforestation, and indeed it seems that the area around Athens was already bare by the time of Plato. Many also refer to the difficulty of obtaining timber suitable for shipbuilding and construction, and Plato describes the permanent damage to the environment that could result from deforestation. The loss of soil from the deforested slopes was a particular problem in both Greek and Roman times. Post-deforestation erosion products now form deposits 10 metres thick in parts of the Roman provinces of Syria and Africa (Simmons, 1989). Indeed most of the environmental concerns of the present day, with the possible exception of fears about the loss of genetic diversity, were voiced two thousand or more years ago.

Yet although the areas around the main cities may have been extensively deforested, the regional forest resource was not completely destroyed. Although some writers have assumed that Plato's description of deforestation in Attica applied also to other parts of classical Greece, it is unlikely that this was so. In the words of Thirgood (1981, p.46). 'The overall conclusion is that, despite considerable inroads, and with the exception of the more arid, thin-soiled conditions, extensive timber forests, though often depleted, still remained at the end of the classical period, and that natural regeneration was able to maintain the forests in being'. That some of the forest resource was able to survive these unprecedented pressures was probably at least partly due to a combination of technical and organisational ability. Knowledge of coppicing could ensure a continuing supply of timber without the elimination of the forest. Methods of sowing and planting were understood, as was the practice of thinning. Without an appropriate institutional framework, however, such technical knowledge would have been of little practical use. In the past, as at present, the major problem was organisational rather than technical.

Resource management
Government controls on forest use were imposed in both Greece and Rome. Since ship timber in particular was an important strategic material, Athens banned the export and re-export of all such material, and indeed strict export control characterised states with significant forest resources. Those lacking these resources often sought to enter into treaty arrangements with peoples still in possession of forests. Athens and the other powers that controlled the Macedonian forests at various times tried to manage them for national purposes and applied controls to this end,

although both then and in more recent times short-term national security overshadowed long-term conservation as a policy objective.

The association of state control with forest management was even more clearly demonstrated in the case of Rome. Forests were in effect under state ownership and administration. In both unoccupied and conquered areas, government ownership was assumed, but elsewhere some areas were leased to syndicates of businessmen for commercial development and in some of the settled areas forests were included in the larger *latifundia*. The potentially damaging effects of grazing animals on forest regeneration were understood and reflected in at least some colony charters by clauses prohibiting grazing on land where young trees were growing (Meiggs, 1982). In theory, then, an effective framework existed for the management and conservation of the forest resource. A forest guard service gradually evolved and became responsible for various aspects of forest management, including what would now be termed watershed protection.

Both in classical times and more recently, however, this framework was perhaps necessary but not sufficient for sound management. Then, as now, governments from time to time sought to raise revenue by selling or leasing forest land to private owners, who would proceed to clear it or exploit it by producing timber or other forest products for the market, or even by turning it into residential subdivisions. Furthermore, a Roman law of 111 BC confirmed that anyone who had occupied public land of up to 30 acres (12 hectares) for purposes of bringing it under cultivation had a full legal right to ownership (Meiggs, 1982). Sizeable areas of woodland might be retained (or even planted) on the larger farms and products such as honey, nuts and resin produced, but on the smaller farms and residential subdivisions significant areas of woodland were less likely to be found. Then, as now, the nature of the rural population and settlement pattern helped to determine the nature of the forest.

Forest survival and forest destruction
The survival of the forest, therefore, depended on several factors. Consistent government control was one of the most important. Location was another. After the exhaustion of resources in the immediate vicinity of the city-states, those forests along rivers where logs could be floated and those around potential seaports were the next to be utilised. Conversely, the more inaccessible mountain forests were more likely to remain intact. The third major variable was the nature of the physical environment, and especially of climate. In the drier areas of the eastern Mediterranean, the forest was initially sparser and subsequently less resilient than in the better-watered areas. The drier limestone areas were especially vulnerable, and parts of eastern Greece and the neighbouring Aegean islands and coasts were amongst the first to experience complete loss of forest and the associated loss of soil. The end stage of the process was the reduction of the forest to little more than bare rock (Figure 3.1).

The fate of the forest, therefore, depended on a combination of climate, location and control, as well as on demands for agricultural land and forest products. These were, of course, related to population trends. If one of

Figure 3.1　Forest degeneration resulting from clearance and grazing in the Mediterranean world

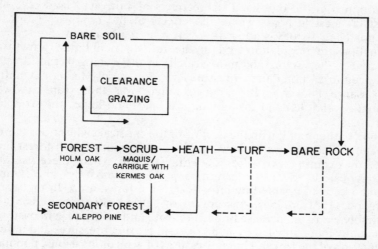

Source: Generalised from various sources

these factors were favourable, it could to a large degree mitigate the adverse effects of the others. Even in the unlikely desert climate of Egypt, forests of considerable extent survived as late as the eleventh or twelfth centuries along the Nile Valley and in the desert fringes and in some of the wadis (Thirgood, 1981). As early as the Ptolemaic period (332–30 BC), there was government control of felling and programmes of tree-planting on wasteland and along the banks of rivers and canals. Later all forests became state property, and an efficient central government strove to conserve the limited forest estate. Only with the breakdown of this control, and with the extension of the cultivated area in the Nile valley in the face of population growth, did forest depletion occur. Indeed remnants of the ancient Egyptian forest survived as late as 1880, when according to Thirgood, contemporary writers were predicting its exhaustion within twenty years.

The forest and political instability
Perhaps the significance of control and management is best illustrated by what happened during periods of strife, instability and power vacuums. From the Persian invasion of Greece in the sixth century BC through the Roman siege of Jerusalem in AD 70 to the depletion of the surviving forest of the Levant coast by the Turks during the First World War, there are numerous reports to the effect that the forest was, if not the first, then a significant casualty of war. It is claimed, for example, that Lebanon lost 60 per cent of its remaining trees as railway fuel during the first three years of the First World War. But instability did not have to develop to such

extreme forms as warfare and conquest for the forest to be threatened. With the decline in the classical civilisations, two opposing trends were set in motion. On the one hand, large tracts of cultivated land reverted to forest, at least in areas where the effects of the removal of the forest had not been so devastating as to prevent regeneration. Subsequently, fluctuations in population and in the rate of population growth were reflected in the waxing and more usually in the waning of the forest. For many centuries population pressures were generally light: not until the Renaissance Period in Italy, for example, was there rapid growth in population and demand for agricultural land, and hence the stripping of the forests.

On the other hand, with the decline of the classical civilisations there was a decline in administration and in the enforcement of such forest laws as were still extant. Laws were now enforced only where there was strong rule: repeatedly over the centuries political weakness, uncertainty or change was accompanied by inroads into the forest area. In the words of Thirgood (1981, p. 59), 'disruption of settled government has almost inevitably led to an increase of pastoralism', and an increase in pastoralism has equally inevitably led to an increase in grazing pressures and in further attenuation of the forest. Under pressures of wars or invasions, populations might seek refuge in previously unoccupied mountains and the forests rapidly converted to crops or pastureland. Major upheavals such as the Arab Conquest of the Maghreb and subsequent mass immigration set in motion what Thirgood (1986a) describes as a process of inexorable decay of the forest.

The adverse effects of political instability continued until the nineteenth and twentieth centuries. In the upheaval that followed the Greek War of Independence in 1821, for example, many forest areas that had previously been protected by their inaccessibility were now destroyed or degraded. In North Africa, the coming of French colonists led to the partial displacement of the native population to the hills, bringing new demands for fuelwood and new intensities of grazing in the forests. Loss of traditional grazing grounds in the plains gave rise to bitterness expressed in the deliberate burning of lowland forests (Meiggs, 1982). More recently still, the political unrest that accompanied the Independence movement in Cyprus in the late 1950s and 1960s was itself accompanied by an increase in fire damage to the remaining forests, and indeed the island suffered the worst fires in its known history at the time of the Turkish invasion in 1974 (Thirgood 1981, 1986b, 1987).

A hundred years earlier, the forests of Cyprus were in a sorry state: in the third quarter of the nineteenth century it was estimated that in the previous twenty years they had decreased in area by one-third and in volume by one-half. This spectacular degradation of the Cyprus forests during the latter phase of Ottoman rule was caused mainly by the depredations of the goat, that well-known enemy of the Mediterranean forest. Both in Cyprus and in many other parts of the Mediterranean, the traditional woodland grazing economy had begun to break down in the face of rapidly growing population and growing (and uncontrolled) grazing pressures from increasing numbers of nomadic shepherds and their herds and flocks. Pastoralism was of course not a new activity nor were its damaging effects on the forest previously unknown. In Spain, for example, the large-scale annual migrations of sheep flocks had done much to reduce the forest area over the centuries (Darby, 1956). By the nineteenth century, however, the scale, extent and intensity had greatly increased.

To these pressures were added in many parts of the Mediterranean those arising from changing accessibility. In the age of the railway, previously inaccessible forests could now be exploited. The railway age witnessed the destruction of the forest resource in some of the more mountainous and previously inaccessible areas. During the same period changing political structures probably contributed to the destruction. Since 1870 the modern Italian state had the unenviable task of unifying the forest organisations (such as they were) of the many small states and principalities which it succeeded. The finances of the new state were desperately weak. Many estates on former papal lands were sold, and the purchasers proceeded to clear-fell the timber they carried (Meiggs, 1982). Earlier in the century, huge areas of forest in the public domain in Spain were sold to private owners and obligations for woodland protection and management in privately owned forests were removed (Thirgood, 1981). At the other end of the Mediterranean, nineteenth-century travellers in the Levant repeatedly referred to contemporary and extensive forest destruction.

There is, therefore, considerable evidence to suggest that the nineteenth century was a decisive period for much of the Mediterranean forest. Previous periods had witnessed resource destruction (and partial recovery) in relatively localised areas, but the new pressures meant destruction on a wider scale, and extended to better-watered, more resilient areas that had previously escaped destruction or that had regenerated. These pressures included spectacular growth in population, greatly increased demand for timber for fuelwood and building, and increased numbers of nomadic shepherds and heavier grazing pressures in the woods. They also resulted from the arrival of the railway, and the transformation of transport and accessibility. Forests previously protected by virtue of remoteness and inaccessibility were now vulnerable. Finally, the century saw great changes in political organisation, and at a time of political change forest laws and efficient management practices could not easily be enforced. With the pressures and the resulting deforestation (especially on vulnerable mountain slopes) there came the inevitable consequences of soil erosion and environmental degradation, epitomised in the bare slopes of areas such as Calabria.

A model for modern forest resource use?
This Mediterranean combination of pressures is perhaps unique in detail, but in more general terms is matched in much of the developing world in the second half of the twentieth century. If the phase of resource destruction reached a climax in the Mediterranean in the nineteenth century (and locally in small areas much earlier), then perhaps much of the developing world is experiencing similar changes today. The Mediterranean

experience in the present century would suggest that the turn-round from the phase of destruction to the phase of re-creation (or at least stabilisation) is difficult but not impossible. Forestry histories such as that of Cyprus (Thirgood, 1987: Dunbar, 1983) relate the setbacks and disappointments as well as the successes, but in most of the region the forest area has once more expanded or at least stabilised, despite continuing problems of fire and other hazards. At the very least, the rate of forest destruction has slowed down. Tree 'farming' in the shape of the establishment of forest plantations has expanded far beyond its very limited extent of classical and medieval times. Nineteenth-century projections of the Mediterranean forest would in all probability have indicated the complete exhaustion of the forest resource long before the late twentieth century. The fact that this has happened neither here nor in North America, where projections were similar, is significant, and offers grounds for some optimism about trends in the tropical forest today. On the other hand, the Mediterranean experience is also acutely depressing. Technical knowledge about forest management and conservation was available from classical times. There were some technical triumphs, such as the silver fir plantations in the Tuscan hills, managed initially to ensure a supply of ship masts for the Florentine state and still maintained today. But consistent application of that technology was sadly lacking, at least until very recent times. The result was that all but a tiny fraction of the forest was destroyed or degraded. This history of the Mediterranean forest is characterised by destructive exploitation, spread over several eras in some areas. This exploitation has at best been followed by only partial transition to forest conservation and more efficient use. It has been accompanied by changing perceptions of what constituted potentially useful resources, especially as transport and accessibility underwent fundamental change. It has also been accompanied by severe resource shortages and by serious environmental damage. In short, the Mediterranean forest resource model does not bode well for the future of the world forest.

North America

If the forest history of the Mediterranean area is a rather depressing one of deforestation and environmental degradation, that of North America perhaps gives more grounds for optimism. There the turn-round from deforestation to forest stability or expansion occurred more abruptly and at a less advanced stage in the process of forest removal. Despite forecasts of timber famines dating from more than a hundred years ago, there have in fact been increases in forest volume during the present century. Many of the worst environmental effects arising from the use of the forest resource have been curbed, and while it would be wrong to suggest that the problems of use of the forest resource have been solved, the present situation is less gloomy than might have been predicted at the end of the last century. It is debatable whether the American model of forest-resource use can be applied to the developing world or its constituent parts today, but the model certainly offers a thought-provoking perspective for modern problems of global forest resources.

The pre-industrial forest

The history of use of the American forest is more concentrated and more dramatic than that of the Mediterranean. Indigenous peoples for centuries had used the forest for hunting, and as a source of numerous domestic and medicinal products, as well as for limited agriculture. Human impact on the forest was not absent: some timber was exported as early as Viking times (Cox et al., 1985), and crops such as beans, corn and pumpkins were produced in forest clearings in New England when English colonists arrived in the seventeenth century (Carroll, 1973). The use of the forest by the Indians resembled the shifting agriculture of the tropical forest of today. Further south, Mayan exploitation of the tropical fruit of south-east Mexico actually increased the number of useful tree species (Edwards, 1986). Human impact was therefore not absent. In addition to the effects of gathering and of agriculture, those of fire were also widespread. When the first Europeans arrived, portions of forest had already been changed to more open, parklike vegetation, and forest composition in some areas is also likely to have been altered (Williams, 1989a). Nor did the first European settlers in other parts of the world always encounter completely natural enviroments. In New Zealand, for example, the introduction of the potato at the end of the eighteenth century caused a great expansion of shifting cultivation over forest land, and an increased use of fire (Cameron, 1964). There is little doubt, however, that the arrival of Europeans in North America was soon followed by increased impact.

The quickening pace of destruction

From the seventeenth to the nineteenth centuries the North American forest shrank at an accelerating rate. Initially the forest was both a resource and an obstacle. It provided ample fuel and building materials, and it had to be cleared to provide agricultural land. It was also perceived as a threat, in both physical terms in harbouring dangerous wild animals and hostile Indians and in psychological or spiritual terms as an untamed wilderness or domain of Satan (Cox et al., 1985). The clearing of the forest had an almost sacred motive as well as a secular one: it was the wild, dark and horrible abode of the supernatural and the fantastic (Williams, 1989a). The attitude of early settlers in Ontario, for example, was one of outright antagonism: 'They attacked the forest with a savagery greater than that justified by the need to clear land for cultivation, for the forest smothered, threatened and oppressed them' (Kelly, 1974).

The apparently endless forest seemed inexhaustible, and its removal was as much a key to agricultural expansion as it was a symbol of control or dominion in the erstwhile wilderness: removal of the forest was the first step towards civilisation. Under such conditions, therefore, it is not surprising that the conservation ethic was not at the forefront of forest management. At the close of the eighteenth century, British North America was largely a wilderness covered by forest. In the words of Lower (1973,

p. 31), 'no one could possibly think of forest conservation, the inscrutable forest . . . was itself the enemy. Against it settlers would wage a century long war.'

Even in this unpromising climate, however, the relationship between the settlers and the forest was not wholly destructive. Although 200,000 hectares of woodland had been cleared by the end of the seventeenth century, the cutting of timber was restricted (at least in certain areas) by various laws. Perhaps these were motivated in part by memories of the timber shortage in England: in addition at least some of the settlers considered that wanton destruction of timberland was 'displeasing to Almightie God, who abhorreth all willfull waste and spoil of his good Creatures' (Carroll, 1973).

This early chapter of the history of the use of the American forest is not without its paradoxes. On the one hand there is the contradiction between expressed attitudes towards this part of God's creation and the exhibited behaviour of forest removal. On the other hand, it has been suggested that migrants from the better-wooded areas of Europe (such as German settlers in Pennsylvania) were more appreciative of the forest and more careful of its use than those from England, where the near-exhaustion of the forest had already resulted in a timber shortage (Cox et al., 1985).

Although most of the early forest clearance was related to agricultural expansion and to procurement of firewood and building materials, commercial exploitation for export markets began very early. As early as the seventeenth century, some timber was shipped to the colonies in the West Indies, to southern Europe, and to England (Carroll, 1973). This trade, however, was on a very small scale, and consisted largely of valuable products such as ships' masts, by now in short supply in much of maritime Europe. (See, for example, Albion [1926] and Bamford [1956].) Indeed the British Crown attempted to reserve the best of the pines along the New England rivers, by means of the 'broad arrow' marked by the surveyors of the 'Kings Woods'. Even with an acute timber shortage in England, the export trade was largely restricted to the most valuable timber such as masts, and the stormy Atlantic remained a formidable obstacle for bulky, low-value cargoes of timber for other purposes.

In what is now Canada, the timber export trade took off at the beginning of the nineteenth century. Up until that time, the British Navy relied strongly on timber from the Baltic lands, and with supplies threatened during the Napoleonic Wars it began to look more intently across the Atlantic. In 1800 British imports of timber from the colonies were negligible. In 1803 they amounted to 10,000 loads and in 1811 to 175,000 (Lower, 1973). By 1810 timber had replaced fur as Canada's leading export (Mackay, 1979). The Atlantic trade in timber continued after Napoleon's blockade of the Baltic was lifted in 1812. By then, Canadian timber merchants had become established in British markets. Furthermore, in order to encourage secure imports from North America, the British government in 1810 doubled duty on timber imports from northern Europe, while imports from the colonies were duty free and those from America attracted only a low duty. This preference lasted until 1866, and stimulated a rapid expansion of timber extraction in coastal areas such as New Brunswick, where exports multiplied nearly twentyfold between 1805 and 1812 (Wynn, 1981). In that province, the next few decades saw the unfolding of a story which has been often repeated in more recent times. At first, only the finest and soundest pines were taken for masts, but a more general demand for timber meant that progressively smaller timber was taken. Initially, squared timber was produced, and this form of exploitation utilised relatively few trees in a stand. Around mid-century, demand for lumber grew rapidly from the rapidly growing American cities, and far more trees were utilised. Furthermore, large amounts of slash were produced in the course of logging, and became a major fire hazard (Head, 1975).

This progressive use of increasing proportions of trees per stand and of small trees has been accompanied in many areas by a progressive widening of the range of utilised species. In Quebec, for example, pine and oak were selectively lumbered at the beginning of the nineteenth century. Subsequently other species, including hemlock, spruce, maple, yellow birch and beech were lumbered in a second generation of forest exploitation (Bouchard et al., 1989). A similar sequence was witnessed in the Lake States half a century later: the exploitation of pine was followed by that of hemlock and hardwoods, which were initially perceived not to be of value (Whitney, 1987; Williams, 1989a). With passing time and changing technology, the Zimmerman 'wedge' of resources (Chapter 1) occupied an increasing proportion of the forest.

In the early years of exploitation in areas such as New Brunswick, most of the timber was cut by small operators, combining the seasonal activity with farming. Gradually, however, operations increased in scale, and a Glasgow-based timber company dominated much of the north-east of the province. The growth of capitalist organisation accompanied the incorporation of the area into the expanding world economy. With this development came the emergence of a powerful entrepreneurial class and a growing proletariat (Wynn, 1981). The forms of control and use of the forest were being transformed. Whereas in earlier times control and use were local, both were now geared to the much larger scale of the North Atlantic. In practice, control was now external, as was the destination of both products and profits. In the words of an early historian of New Brunswick,

> The wealth that has come into it, has passed as through a thoroughfare. . . . The persons principally engaged in shipping the timber have been strangers who have taken no interest in the welfare of the country, but have merely occupied a spot to make what they could in the shortest possible time. . . . the capital of the country has been wasted . . . the forests are stripped and nothing is left in prospect, but the gloomy apprehension when the timber is gone, of sinking into insignificance and poverty. (Lower, 1973, p. 32)

While the colonial exploitation of the forests of New Brunswick and other areas was proceeding apace during the first half of the nineteenth century, the forests of the United States were being cleared primarily for agriculture. It is estimated that at the very least 40 million hectares of forest had been cleared, and a further 15 million by 1860 (Williams, 1982, 1989a). Perhaps 60 million hectares had been cleared by 1860, compared with about one-twelfth of that amount cleared as a result of industrial lumber, mining and urban development (Cox et al., 1985). The consumption of timber was enormous: for example farm fencing in the state of Kentucky alone during the 1870s was estimated to consume 10 million trees annually (Clark, 1984). In some Midwest states such as Ohio, clearing reached a peak during the 1870s, when 1.46 million hectares were removed. Extrapolation of such rates of forest removal caused local concern and alarm, pointing as it did to timber shortages or famines by the early decades of the twentieth century. These fears prompted a questionnaire survey of 'all township officials and intelligent farmers': agricultural clearance was perceived as the primary cause in 90 per cent of the state's eighty-eight counties, compared with use as fuel and construction in 9 per cent, and grazing by cattle and sheep in one county (Williams, 1983). By the end of the century, the formerly continuous forest of many states had been reduced to a few isolated patches (Figure 3.2).

Figure 3.2 Changing forest area (stippled), Cadiz Township, Green County, Wisconsin, 1831, 1882, 1902, and 1950

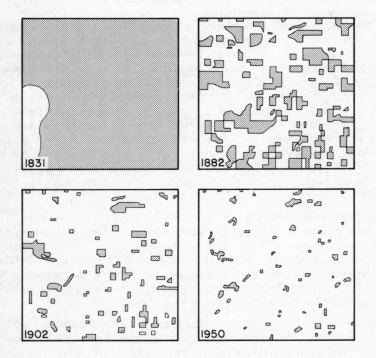

Source: Curtis, 1965

Table 3.2   Lumber production in parts of the United States, 1900–20

	Lake States	Gulf South	Pacific States
		(billion board feet)	
1900	9	5	5
1910	5	9.5	7.5
1920	2.4	8	10

Source: Compiled from data in Cox et al. (1985)

After 1860, however, the rate of clearing for agriculture declined sharply, while the rate of cutting for industrial purposes rose. The next few decades witnessed the quasi-colonial exploitation of successive forest areas in New England, the Lake States, the South and the Pacific Northwest. With the exhaustion of the forest resources of one area, the lumber industry simply moved on to a new one. Successive areas waxed and waned (Table 3.2). Between 1870 and 1910, the industry went through its period of greatest growth, production and destructiveness: the cutover land, great fires, and big mills 'assured to the Lake States an indelible image as the epitome of destructive lumber exploitation' (Williams, 1989a, p. 237). The legacy was not only of devastated forest lands but also of unfettered capitalist exploitation, and of reactions, attitudes and ideals that have continued to influence American forest policy to this day.

Reaction
From the beginning of this period of almost unbridled exploitation, calls for more careful husbanding of resources and fears of timber famines were voiced. These came first from New England, the earliest area to suffer, but while new timberland could be obtained in the west or south for as little as $1.25 per acre, it was more profitable for operators in Maine or Pennsylvania to relocate than to stay where they were and reforest their cutover lands (Cox et al., 1985). By the turn of the century, however, the last frontier had been reached in the Pacific Northwest. No new areas of virgin forest remained, and in any case the increasing capital investments in mills and equipment could no longer be lightly abandoned. The relationship between the 'cut and get out' approach and that of 'stay put and reforest' was now changing.

With many men and much equipment in the forests in the late nineteenth century, and huge quantities of slash, it is not surprising that devastating forest fires broke out. Some of these destroyed the organic layers of the soil over which they passed as well as neighbouring stands of timber. The lumberman's promise that 'the plow follows the ax' did not always hold good: at least half of the cutover land was not converted into farms, and a quarter of that was left barren, without trees or people. The devastated area amounted to over 30 million hectares (Cox et al., 1983). The lumber industry was characterised by the features typical of the expanding industrial capitalism of the period, with price fluctuations, severe competition and periodic overproduction. Associated with the volatility of the market were waste, devastation and disrupted communities – features common to a number of resource-based industries at the time. Agricultural clearing, as well as industrial lumbering, was now recognised as a source of environmental damage. Over 90 per cent of the respondents to an Ohio survey in the 1880s perceived it as having damaging effects (Williams, 1989a). The perceptions of George Perkins Marsh (Chapter 1) were now rapidly spreading.

By the turn of the century, the use of the American forest resource epitomised all that was inharmonious in the relationship between man and environment, and reaction was beginning to set in. Devastation of the forest became a powerful symbol for the first American conservation movement during Theodore Roosevelt's presidency in the early years of the century. The leading figure in that movement, Gifford Pinchot, was head of the new forest service, whose creation was in itself a reflection of growing unease about the use of the forest resource.

During the nineteenth century, people to whom the American forest had seemed inexhaustible began to realise that it was, after all, finite. This dawning realisation gave rise to the Forest Reserve Act of 1891, under which forest reserves, later to become national forests, were first established. Although initially there was uncertainty about the role and management of these forests, in practice they were safeguarded, under federal control, from private exploitation. Even before the peak of lumber production in 1909, it was becoming clear that attitudes towards the forest resource were undergoing a fundamental change. From the 1870s onwards, various government officials were referring to prospects of timber scarcity or famine. Thirty years later, the president himself publicly espoused such fears. Addressing the American Forest Congress in 1905, President Roosevelt declared that 'if the present rate of forest destruction is allowed to continue, with nothing to offset it, a timber famine in the future is inevitable' (quoted in Olson, 1971, p. 1).

The forest turn-round
By the end of the nineteenth century, professional foresters, recreationists and wilderness preservationists, government agencies and even the lumber industry itself were advocating change (Rakestraw, 1955; Williams, 1989a). The first step towards a fundamental change in forest resource use was an awareness of malaise in the existing pattern of use. From this growing awareness, which was itself reinforced by the apparently unsatiable demand for lumber during the First World War and by the devastation wrought by the forest industry in the South at this time (Clark, 1984), there emerged a radical change in the fortunes of American forests. Whereas forest area and timber volume had progressively decreased for many decades, a turn-round towards stability and expansion now began to occur. This happened over a period of decades rather than overnight, and the transition was not effected without difficulties and setbacks. Nevertheless, a fundamental transition did occur, and the predicted timber famines failed to materialise.

Figure 3.3 Total utilization of US-grown wood (in roundwood equivalent), by major form of use

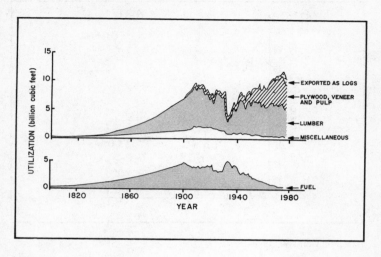

Source: Clawson, 1979

If the historical model of American forest-resource use is applicable to the forests of the developing world today, the factors underlying the transition are of crucial significance. Several are important, one of which is changing demand. In the nineteenth century, timber consumption rose steadily and apparently exponentially (Figure 3.3).

Timber was plentiful and cheap: it was a major source of fuel as well as constructional material. The extrapolation of these nineteenth-century trends must have indeed been worrying, and if that extrapolation had been valid there is little doubt that the consequences would have been serious. But the pattern of demand changed radically after the early years of the century. Electricity and gas supplied growing proportions of domestic fuel, while demand for constructional and industrial timber declined. The railways, for example, consumed about one-fifth of the timber harvest at the beginning of the century but only 3–4 per cent by the 1960s (Olson, 1971). Substitutes such as steel and concrete were increasingly employed: predictions of timber famine themselves encouraged the search for substitute materials. Consumption for the basic domestic and industrial uses steadily decreased during the first few decades of the century (Figures 3.3 and 3.4), and were only very partially offset by rising consumption of pulp and plywood. In short, the nature and magnitude of demand underwent a fundamental change, which completely undermined the validity of contemporary projections.

Major changes were also taking place in the management of the resource, and hence in potential supply. Predictions of timber famine were based on the fact that consumption was outstripping growth: indeed as late

Figure 3.4   Per capita consumption of timber products, United States

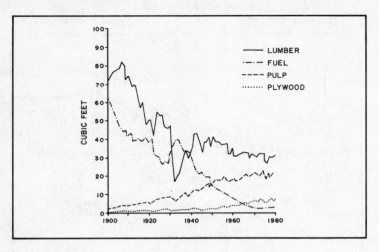

Source: Based on Clawson, 1979

as 1920 consumption was estimated at 26 billion cubic feet compared with growth of only 6 billion (Cox et al., 1985). Such a ratio was anathema to proponents of sustained-yield policy: simple logic seemed to indicate that this state of affairs could not continue indefinitely.

Professional and technical forestry in the United States had its roots in the managed forests of central Europe, where the concept of sustained yield was well established. The concept, however, could not be easily transplanted to the essentially natural forests of North America. In natural forests, timber volume is relatively constant, and no *net* growth takes place as long as a state of equilibrium is maintained. Growth is balanced by loss through age, disease and fire. In this state, timber *volume* is at a maximum, but net *growth* is much higher in younger stands of trees (Figure 3.5).

In other words, exploitation of the 'old growth' of mature natural forests resulted in a reduction in timber volume, as it must inevitably do whenever such forests are harvested, but not in annual growth. The application of the sustained-yield principle, in its strict sense of matching growth and removals, presents special problems when management is first introduced into natural or virgin forests (Eckmüllner and Madas, 1984). Initially, removals must exceed growth and cause a reduction in volume, and yield appears not to be sustained. If the old, mature stands are replaced, however, then growth will occur, and eventually growth and removals can be matched. There would be a time lag between the cutting of the old growth and the time when the new forest would be producing at its optimal rate. This time lag was inevitable in the transition from the unmanaged to the managed forest.

Since the implications of this basic principle were not widely appreciated at the time, it is not surprising that commentators of the day were

Figure 3.5 Timber age–volume relationships (A maximum stand volume, B maximum mean annual growth)

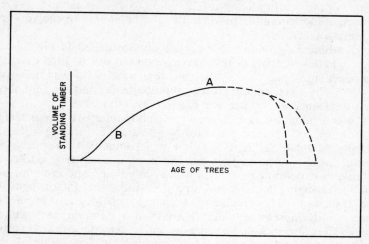

Source: Based on Clawson, 1979

Figure 3.6 Annual net growth of timber in the United States, and US Forest Service projections of future growth made in 1933 (33), 1946 (46), 1952 (52), 1962 (62) and 1970 (70)

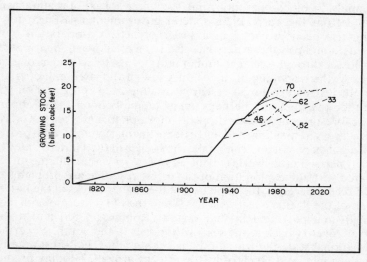

Source: Based on Clawson, 1979

concerned at the disparity between consumption and growth. In practice, annual growth has steadily increased from around 6 billion cubic feet at the beginning of the century to almost 22 billion by 1977 (Clawson, 1979). The downward trend to famine predicted at the beginning of the century has not materialised (Figure 3.6).

The trendlines of growth and cut gradually converged during the present century: whereas the US Forest Service pointed out in 1920 that logging was proceeding at nine times the rate that new wood was being grown (Cox, 1983), by 1963, annual growth of timber exceeded the annual cut for the first time since record keeping began (Cox et al., 1985).

This spectacular reversal of resource trends reflects a major transition from 'hunting and gathering' the forest resource to 'farming' it (eg Sedjo and Clawson, 1984; Sedjo, 1987). It was accompanied by another major transition, from a resource that was shrinking in areal terms, to one that was stable or expanding in area as well as in volume and growth rates. In addition to changing demand and supply, various other factors contributed to the transition. They included a changing perception of the forest resource, with increasing value placed on recreation and wilderness qualities. They also included a reaction against the concentrated pattern of capitalist control and use of the forest resource, and a climate of opinion that favoured increased government intervention and involvement in forestry matters.

This transition from a shrinking forest resource, apparently heading for exhaustion, to one which is now expanding, has taken place against a background of forest ownership divided between government, industry and private individuals. From the early years of the century, government has sought to influence the private sector in its forest management. Initially there was much debate about whether government policy should be based on compulsion or co-operation, but the theme of co-operation won the day, and from the early 1920s federal government assistance for tree-planting has been provided in a series of acts. Co-operation between government and private owners has also been effective in greatly reducing timber losses through fire. The timber industry itself has undergone radical change. At the beginning of the century few of the large mill operators in the South invested in forest research or supported reforestation (Clark, 1984); then the tradition, perhaps understandably in an age of apparently limitless forest resources, was simply to move on to a new area. Today with no such areas remaining and huge investments in mills and processing plants, a policy of 'cut and run' makes less sense in the United States (if not in other parts of the world). This is not to say that all the problems associated with the exploitation of the forest resource are problems of the past. In recent decades, the depletion of the timber stocks in the last 'forest frontier' of the Pacific Northwest has led to the old pattern of mill closures and high unemployment in that region (Robbins, 1985) and a shift in industrial forestry back to the regrowth forests of the South. Nevertheless, at the national scale the transition has been made. The forest area is now relatively stable, and much of it is in effect 'farmed'. Gloomy predictions of timber famine have not materialised, although the fact that these predictions were made may well in itself have helped to ensure that they did not come to pass. What was at risk were the virgin forests of the Pacific Northwest (and of other areas previously) and their aesthetic, amenity and conservation values, rather than their timber-producing potential. Indeed these values were extensively and permanently destroyed, while the timber-producing potential was not harmed.

There are several implications for other parts of the world at the present. The fact that a clear transition took place after a phase of destructive exploitation is one. The fact that a growth in recreational and preservational values contributed to the transition is another. The fact that the last frontier had been reached is perhaps a third. Perhaps more serious and ominous is the fact that a century elapsed between the voicing of the first concerns and the eventual turn-round, and almost half a century intervened between the first popular warnings of environmental consequences (such as those of Marsh) and the peak of the forest conservation movement around the turn of the century. A speedier transition will be required if the tropical forest is to survive.

Models of forest resource use and the expanding world economy

The contrasting histories of the Mediterranean and American forests offer different models of forest resource use, the one leading to the virtual exhaustion of the resource and the other suggesting that a fundamental transition (in area as well as in management) can be made while substantial areas of forest remain. In the former case, the transition was long-delayed and was slow, hesitant, and incomplete. In the latter, a transition was effected not only relatively earlier in the history of forest depletion, but also more quickly and completely.

If the models are to have validity or utility as perspective on modern trends in forest resource use and depletion world-wide, they need to be evaluated against the experience of other parts of the world. The remaining part of this chapter attempts such an evaluation and also considers the dynamic of expansion of the world economy (and incorporation of new areas into it) as a driving-force or trigger for destructive exploitation.

Many European countries conform to a greater or lesser degree to one or other of these models. For example, in the case of the United Kingdom and the Republic of Ireland, the resemblance is to the Mediterranean model, even though the original forest and the details of its removal are very different. In these countries, the native forest all but disappeared before a transition (in area) occurred in the twentieth century. On the other hand most central European countries conform more closely to the American model, even if once more there are many differences in detail and timing.

A basic outline of forest trends can be roughly sketched for many parts of the world, but detailed time-series data are rarely available. This deficiency is understandable: as Chapter 4 indicates, there are conflicting estimates of the forest area even today. It seriously limits the extent to which the models or generalisations constructed for one area can be evaluated for more general applicability. In the words of Richards (1986, p. 61), 'More precise, better documented data on the extent and rate of depletion for each individual forest would do much to correct our perspectives of the global process [of deforestation].'

Despite the deficiency of data, there is clear evidence of a transition in area (as well as in management) in many countries during the nineteenth century. For example, forests covered 18.6 per cent of Swiss territory in 1863 and 31.8 per cent in 1983 (de Saussay, 1987), while in Denmark the forest cover is now 11 per cent, compared with 4 per cent in 1800 (Knudsen, 1987). Forest trends are illustrated for the examples of France and Hungary in Table 3.3 (a and b).

In countries such as Austria and Finland, for example, legislation to safeguard the remaining forest area was enacted in response to the growing demand for timber (in both the local and wider economies) during the second half of the nineteenth century (Raumolin, 1984; Johann, 1984), and in effect marks the beginning of a relatively abrupt and complete transition.

Perhaps the earliest forest transition was in Japan. Japan suffered a timber shortage in the early modern period, as a result of a combination of factors including warfare, urbanisation, intensified agriculture and growth in population. Prior to the Tokuwaga era (1600–1868), deforestation was not a significant problem. According to Osaka (1983), villagers had free access to the forest but exercised restraint in their use of forest products because of their respect for fellow villagers and for nature. From the seventeenth century, however, pressures on the forest increased, not least because of the huge quantities of timber used in the construction of castles and cities. In addition, demand was created by the growing urban population, and increasing areas of land were cleared for agricultural purposes (Totman, 1984). Indeed during the seventeenth century the new pressures on the forest gave rise to a set of problems similar to those in many parts of the world today. Amongst these problems were flooding, soil erosion, shortages of timber and fuelwood, and endless wrangles over rights of forest use (Totman, 1986). In response the *daimyos* or lords took over the village forests. Conservation measures based on complete or partial prohibitions on the use of forest products were introduced and rigorously enforced, along with regulation of use in other areas and with compulsory reforestation (Osaka, 1983). From the time of the Meiji Restoration in 1868, most of the forests owned by the *daimyos* became in effect government property, and regulation of production was maintained despite peasant resistance. Japan remained self-sufficient in fuel and other forest products until late in the nineteenth century, and still retains an unusually high degree of forest cover (see Chapter 4).

The case of Japan is instructive for at least two reasons. First, it reveals a forest transition at a much earlier date than that in America, and probably one at an earlier stage of forest depletion. Second, it shows that deforestation was experienced, and was perceived as a problem, during the early stages of population growth and even before industrialisation or incorporation

Table 3.3 The changing extent of forest

(a) France	*Date*	*Wooded area as percentage of total*
	3000 BC	80
	0	50
	1400	33
	1650	25
	1789	14
	1862	17
	1912	19
	1963	21
	1970	23
	1977	24

(b) Hungary (present boundaries)	*Date*	*Area (000 ha)*
	1800	2765.8
	1925	1090.8
	1938	1106.0
	1946	1124.2
	1950	1165.9
	1960	1306.2
	1970	1470.7
	1980	1610.2

(c) Central America	*Date*	*Percentage of land surface*
	1700	92.0
	1800	91.8
	1850	85.0
	1900	77.8
	1940	70.7
	1950	67.7
	1960	62.4
	1970	55.4
	1977	50.9

(d) Ivory Coast	*Date*	*Area (000 ha)*
	1900	14 500
	1955	11 800
	1965	8 983
	1973	6 200
	1980	3 945

continued

Table 3.3   *continued*

(e) Thailand	Date	Percentage of land area
	1913	75
	1930	70
	1949	69
	1959	58
	1969/70	52
	1978	25

(f) Northern India	Date	Percentage of land area
	1870	24.6
	1890	21.5
	1910	19.2
	1930	18.2
	1950	16.2
	1970	13.7

(combined total for 'forest woods' and 'interrupted woods')

(g) Liberia	Date	Area (000 ha)
	1920	6475
	c.1950	5520
	1968	2500
	1980	2000

(h) Ghana	Date	Area (000 ha)
	1920	9871
	1937/8	4789
	1948/9	4236
	1953	2810
	1958	2493
	1960/1	2424
	1968	2207
	1980	1718

Sources: Compiled from data in Prieur (1988) (a), Keresztesi (1984) (b), Keogh (1986) (c), Bertrand (1983) (d), Feeny* (1988) (e), Richards et al. (1985) (f) and Gronitz (1985) (g and h).

* Feeny tabulates numerous estimates of the forest area made by different commentators using different bases. This is a selection from his data.

into the world economy, which are so often associated with environmental deterioration in general and forest depletion in particular.

Nevertheless, this is not to invalidate the association between these factors and forest depletion. Numerous examples could be cited of how the expansion of the world economy through the imposition of colonial control and development in the nineteenth and twentieth centuries has led to new pressures on forest resources, and indeed also to new regimes of management. In many parts of what is now called the developing world, forests were cleared for the production of cash crops such as tea in Assam (Tucker, 1988), rice in Burma (Adas, 1983) and cotton in the Bombay Deccan (Richards and McAlpin, 1983). The physical integration of such areas with the world economy through the construction of railway systems itself brought new pressures to bear on forest resources, with new demands for fuel and for timber for railway sleepers (Tucker, 1983). Similarly the processing of some of these new cash crops consumed large quantities of timber. The forest in the Philippines, for example, suffered not only direct clearance for sugar-growing, but also for wood to fuel refineries (Roth, 1983).

The displacement of indigenous peoples from areas cleared for cash crops meant new pressures on the forest in areas of resettlement, which frequently were in the more fragile mountain environments less coveted for cash crops. For example Thirgood (1986a) records such displacement following the French colonisation of Algeria. This is but one specific example of a widespread process identified by Westoby (1989) as a major cause of forest problems. Similarly, the clearing of land for the subsistence needs of peasants who had been plantation workers made inroads into the remaining areas of forest. Tucker and Richards (1983, p. xvii) conclude that 'We may well find that these secondary effects of the international economy were the most important, as well as the most difficult to measure, of all causes of forest degradation until the massively mechanised agriculture of very recent years.'

The incorporation of new areas into the world economy in the nineteenth and twentieth centuries was often accompanied by devastating effects on the forest, irrespective of whether the colonialism was external (as for example in the nineteenth-century case of New Brunswick) or internal. In Brazil, for example, perhaps as much as 30,000 square kilometres of forest were cleared for coffee-planting during the nineteenth century (Dean, 1983). McNeill (1988) has documented the disastrous effects of the incorporation of parts of southern Brazil in the present century. Of the original 20 to 25 million hectares of Araucaria forest, only 445,000 remained in 1980. Deforestation as a result of clearance for agriculture proceeded gradually during the first three decades of the century before accelerating to reach a peak during the period from 1945 to 1970. The waste of timber has been tremendous; perhaps as much as 1 billion cubic metres of Araucaria wood may have simply been burned. The forests have ceased to exist as an economic asset; logging and sawmilling, once the largest source of employment in Parana state, have greatly diminished, and the drainage basin of the Iguacu river has been so disturbed that navigation is no longer possible.

In neighbouring Chile, the twentieth-century history of the forest resource has been similar, if on a smaller scale. In the province of Aysen, the pastoral settlement of the interior was promoted by the government for strategic reasons in the 1920s. Massive clearance of *lenga* forest (dominated by *Nothofagus pumilio*) took place. Half of the original forest cover was burned to make way for cattle and sheep grazing with the familiar result of accelerated erosion and destabilised slopes. Ironically, the value of *lenga* was not perceived until the late 1970s, when exports of its decorative hardwood to Europe began (Veblen, 1984).

Perhaps the story of southern Brazil and similar areas in the twentieth century is no more than a repeat of that of many other areas of expanding frontiers in the nineteenth century. It reminds us that external colonial powers need not be directly involved for this type of development to occur, any more than they were in the case of nineteenth-century America. The effects in terms of displacement of indigenous population and forest clearance seems to be similar whether the colonial process is driven internally or externally. Characteristically, pioneers have tended to have exploitative or antagonistic attitudes towards the forest. Perhaps these attitudes are at least in part a reaction against the hardships and dangers of life on the frontier, and to the insecurity that they engendered. It is suggested by Wynn (1979) that the unusually early conservation response in New Zealand, in the form of the Forest Bill of 1874, may be related to the presence of a significant number of emigrants from the middle and upper ranks of British society. Their reserves of capital insulated them from some of the rigours and uncertainties of the pioneer life, and permitted a more benign and concerned attitude towards the forest than was common in similar territories. Perhaps New Zealand was also unusual in that much of the timber felled in the course of clearing land for agriculture was turned to profit (Arnold, 1976). In the case of southern Brazil, as in many other areas in the nineteenth and twentieth centuries, clearing was associated with tremendous waste of timber. Exploitation was often inefficient and wasteful, as well as destructive.

With the arrival of colonial power and the expansion of cash crops, there might come the first positive measures to protect the remaining forest area. Colonial powers might seek to reserve forest areas in order that forest conservation might be achieved for both environmental and commercial reasons; for the avoidance of soil erosion and other adverse processes as well as for safeguarding timber resources. In parts of India, for example, trends in forest resources began to worry the colonial authorities as early as the 1850s, and in 1864 Dr Dietrich Brandis, a German forester, was appointed Inspector-General of Forests. The enactment of forest laws in 1878 provided the legal basis for government ownership and management of parts of the remaining forest area, through the creation of forest reserves. In some areas, policies of forest preservation were accompanied by early attempts at planting exotic species. Such attempts began in 1902 in Kenya, for example (Ofcansky, 1984), and by 1914 over 4,000 hectares of forest land had been replanted in Punjab and Uttar Pradesh (Tucker, 1983). Similar attempts at forest regulation and replanting began half a

Table 3.4   Characteristics of colonial forestry departments in Africa

● Emphasis on commercial forestry, and on growing timber that could be sold either within the country (primarily for mines and industries) or for export.

● Corresponding emphasis on exotic species (especially pines and *Eucalyptus* spp.)

● Conversely, little interest in indigenous species, which for the most part were ignored.

● Little enthusiasm for ethno-botany of local people, who were usually regarded as ignorant about forestry and as spoilers of the environment.

● Most forest officials were dedicated to setting aside certain proportions (e.g. 6 per cent) of the total land area for forest reserves.

● Foresters were regarded by local people as a sort of auxiliary police, since one of their functions was to keep people out of reserves and to prosecute them for infringement of regulations.

Source: Based on Little and Brokensha, 1987.

century earlier in New Zealand (Roche, 1984), and within thirty-five years of having become a British colony the 1874 Forest Bill was enacted to 'make provision for preserving the soil and climate by tree planting, for providing timber for future industrial purposes, [and] for subjecting some portion of the native forests to skilled management and proper control' (Wynn, 1979, p. 172).

The imposition of external or colonial control gave rise to many and persistent problems. In Africa and India in particular, these problems have been very long-lasting (e.g. Anderson (1987); Shiva and Bandyopadhyay, 1988). In Africa, for example, many colonial forestry departments shared a number of commons aims, which are summarised in Table 3.4.

In detail the role of a department might be complex: in Kenya, for example, a three-sided political struggle developed between it, the company that had leased the forest for commercial exploitation, and the indigenous peoples (Anderson, 1987). In general terms, however, the new regime reflected Western notions of conservation and management, and alienation was often the inevitable result of the new orientation. The policing of forest reserves, with their symbolism in terms of alien control and regulation of traditional resources, posed many problems and not infrequently met with the response of incendiarism (see, for example, Castro [1988] and Tucker [1988] for discussions of forest reserves in Kenya and India respectively). Nevertheless, such reserves may have helped to reduce the attrition on the forest, even if they failed to reverse the downward trend of forest area. In many developing countries and regions, no real transition in the trend of forest area has yet occurred (Table 3.3 c–h), and indeed the rate of forest contraction in recent decades has been comparable to that in the United States in the nineteenth century.

In some instances the incorporation of new areas into the world economy led to the lessening, rather than intensification of pressures on the forest. For example, Goucher (1988) has shown that the decline of the local iron industry during the colonial period in Togo in West Africa reduced the local demand for charcoal and thus relieved one of the greatest pressures on the remaining forest. More usually, however, this incorporation, whether carried out by colonialism or imperialism, was accompanied by fundamental changes in the relationship between man and land, including a revised perception of the forest resource. The usual result was the diminution or degradation of the forest. Exploitation was often destructive, but the phase of destructive exploitation was by no means always followed by a clear shift towards conservation and more efficient use of the forest resource (Chapter 1). Perhaps the existence of external control (political or economic) meant that the transition from *Raubwirtschaft* to resource conservation, as indicated in Friedrich's theory, was far more difficult to achieve in peripheral than in core areas of the world economy. Perhaps the case of Cuba is instructive. At the beginning of the nineteenth century, forests covered 90 per cent of the land area, but by 1946 it had shrunk to 11 per cent. The expansion of sugar-growing and ranching, organised as 'peripheral' activities geared to the American market, was a major factor in that contraction. Following the overthrow of the Batista regime in 1959 and its replacement by Fidel Castro, a form of forest transition was achieved. By the early 1980s, the forest area occupied 26 per cent of the land surface.

The incorporation could apparently be set at various scales. In seventeenth-century Britain, for example, timber shortages in England gave rise to widening searches and to the exploitation of forests in the north of Scotland for naval timber. A century later, British companies expanded their activities to eastern Europe: one, for example, began to exploit Belorussian forests for timber in 1793 (French, 1983). This exploitation, as in many similar 'expanding frontier' episodes, was typically destructive. This was but one contribution to the widespread clearing of the Russian forest in modern and early modern times. From the end of the seventeenth century to 1914 about 70 million hectares of forest were cleared in European Russia alone, including 3 million hectares between 1888 and 1908 (Barr and Braden, 1988). Growth in population coincided with incorporation into the wider economy to unleash pressures on the forest comparable to those in the United States last century and in the tropical world today. One facet was the growing demand for timber in Sweden in the second half of the nineteenth century, which could not be satisfied from the traditional producing areas in the south of the country and which led to 'frontier' development in the north (Gaunitz, 1984) and as far east as the White Sea (Bjorklund, 1984). On a much larger scale, the nineteenth-century colonial period in Africa and Asia, and the same era in colonial and independent Latin America, witnessed the first impact of the global economy as it began to penetrate the tropical forest zone (e.g. Tucker, 1986).

This incorporation may be a sufficient condition for forest contraction, but it appears not to be a necessary one. In countries as disparate as Scotland and China, the forest resource has been largely exhausted even without (or before) radical changes in economic structures or organisation. Scotland was largely deforested even before its growing incorporation into the wider British economy was followed by the exploitation of some of its surviving forests. On a much larger scale China was effectively denuded of forest cover by the nineteenth century. This denudation took place over a very long period, beginning as long ago as 3000 BC and accelerating with the diffusion of bronze and then iron tools, but most of all with population pressures in the context of deteriorating economic, social and political orders from the seventeenth century onwards. Most of the deforestation was caused by peasant use of wood for fuel, building and coffins (Murphey, 1983), rather than by 'colonial' exploitation.

Perhaps the experience of countries such as Scotland and China (as well as parts of the Mediterranean world) suggests that when pressures on forest resources build up gradually over long periods, the forest transition is both late and uncertain. On the other hand, the examples of America and Japan may suggest that a relatively sudden build-up of pressures gives rise to perceptions that lead to effective responses and in turn to relatively early and complete forest transitions. A sudden build-up of pressures may lead, in other words, to a literal crisis. In theory the process of incorporation into the world economy may thus be the impulse that ultimately gives rise to the transition, but in practice a long time lag is usually involved. The fact that there is usually little local control or political power in the newly incorporated area means that the government action crucial in effecting the transition is weak, delayed or completely absent.

Natural forests all but disappeared in countries such as Scotland and China, but nevertheless there has been a form of forest transition even in these countries. In both cases the forest area is now increasing. In Scotland, the forest area has almost doubled since the Second World War, while some reports indicate that at least a partial transition may also have taken place in China. According to Li Jinchang et al., (1988), the forest area in China increased from under 9 to 12 per cent between 1950 and 1981, and there are numerous reports of ambitious and grandiose afforestation plans (see also Chapter 4). On the other hand it is suggested by come commentators (e.g. Forestier, 1989) that the forest area is still shrinking. It can safely be concluded, however, that strenuous attempts are being made to achieve a transition, even if the transition has not yet been successfully effected.

Perhaps the Mediterranean model can be applied to them, as to other long-settled countries, with some validity. In at least some of the newer lands, there are perhaps grounds for optimism that the American model can be applied despite the vicissitudes of colonial or imperial incorporation into the world economy, and that a turn-round in the trend of the forest area achieved well before forest exhaustion looms. A changing perception of the forest resource, and a growing appreciation of recreational and preservational values, underlay the American transition. Perhaps similar shifts will eventually lead to a comparable transition in the tropical forest.

4 THE EXTENT AND DISTRIBUTION OF THE RESOURCE

> We know quite a lot about the moon but do not know how much of the world's surface is covered by forests and woodlands (Persson, 1974, p.237).

This was the despairing conclusion reached by Persson at the end of a major assessment of world forest resources which he carried out whilst working in the Forestry Department of the Food and Agriculture Organisation (FAO) of the United Nations. Since the early 1970s, our knowledge may have improved to some extent, but many uncertainties remain. Since we do not know with accuracy and precision the present extent of the forest resource, we cannot reliably estimate the fraction of the original resource that still remains, nor can we evaluate the current trends of gains and losses in relation to the global extent of forest. Even during the last two decades, estimates of the forest area have varied from under 3000 to over 6000 million hectares, or from 20 to 45 per cent of the global land surface. One of the earliest estimates, made by Zon and Sparhawk as long ago as 1923, is not unlike some modern figures, and is considerably lower than some of those made more recently. It cannot be concluded from this, however, that the forest area has been static or increasing. Since such diverse estimates have been suggested, some of which are illustrated in Table 4.1, it is apparent that reliable time-series data cannot readily be assembled.

Differing definitions of forest and woodland are one of the main reasons for the apparently conflicting estimates illustrated in Table 4.1. As has been suggested in Chapter 2, forests are extremely varied in their structure and composition, and range from dense assemblages of trees to open woodland and scrub. Some definitions are required to provide context for these and other estimates. *Forest and woodland* is land under natural or planted stands of trees, and in FAO statistics includes land from which forests have been cleared but which will be reforested in the foreseeable future. *Closed forest* is land with a forest cover, with tree crowns covering more than 20 per cent of the land area. Land under shifting cultivation is included if it is expected to return to forest in the foreseeable future. *Open woodland*, on the other hand, consists of land with tree-crown cover of 5–20 per cent of the surface area, and includes the savannah belts of the

Table 4.1 Estimates of global area of forest and woodland

Source	Category	Area (10^6) ha
Zon and Sparhawk (1923)	Forest Area	3031
FAO (1946/1937)	Forest	3650
Haden-Guest et al. (1956)	Forest	3914
FAO (1963)	Forest land	4126
Persson (197)	Forest land	4030
	Closed forest	2800
Eyre (1978)	Total forest	6050
Global 2000 (1975)	Closed forest 2563	3763
(Barney, 1980)	Open woodlands 1200	
Matthews (1983)	Forest 3927	5237
	Woodland 1310	
World Resources Institute	Closed forest 2865	4147
(WRI 1986)	Open forest 1282	
	Other wooded land*	1081
	Total wooded area	5228
FAO (1987)	Forest and woodland	4087

* including forest fallow

tropics even if crown cover sometimes exceeds 20 per cent. The most convenient and comprehensive source of statistics of the extent of the forest and woodland resource is the *FAO Production Yearbook*. This publication lists areal statistics for forest and woodland on a country basis. The apparent degree of comprehensiveness may to some extent be misleading, since the same data are quoted for some countries over periods of several years, and on the other hand major changes may occur from year to year. FAO depends largely on the returns made by individual countries; and the degree of precision (and indeed also of accuracy) is variable. Nevertheless, the source remains the most convenient one in terms of availability, completeness and frequency of cover, despite the fact that it quotes figures only for 'forest and woodland' and not for 'closed forests'. (Some other FAO publications do distinguish between closed and other forests.)

Forest area and distribution

The total area of forest and woodland in the mid-1980s, as listed in *FAO Production Yearbook*, is just over 4,000 million hectares, or 31 per cent of the world land surface. Of that area, between 2,500 and 3,000 million hectares (c. 20 per cent) are closed forest. Perhaps the most detailed and authoritative estimate of the closed-forest area, at the global scale, is that made by Persson (1974) in the course of work intended to contribute to the never-completed fifth World Forest Inventory. His work is characterised by carefulness and comprehensiveness, but he clearly warns the reader of possible inaccuracies, and indeed indicates the estimated level of accuracy of his data. Few countries fall within his narrowest range of −5 to +5 per cent, and many lie in his lowest accuracy class of from −50 to +100 per cent. Such a range of possible error is a salutary reminder of the uncertainties that still surround our knowledge of the world forest area, and provides a context in which his and other estimates may be considered. Persson's estimate of the closed-forest area around 1970 is 2,800 million hectares; the World Resource Institute (WRI)(1986) estimated the closed forest area to be 2,865 million hectares in 1985, compared with 2,948 million hectares in 1980. Just under 40 per cent of that area consists of coniferous forest: WRI figures suggest that the coniferous forest is increasing in both absolute and relative terms (from 38.0 to 39.8 per cent between 1980 and in 1985), as the broad-leaved forests contract and coniferous ones expand through afforestation and reafforestation.

As Chapter 2 indicates, both the volume of growing stock per hectare and growth rate vary from area to area, depending on environmental factors and forest type. On the basis of information that he was able to assemble for 70 per cent of the closed-forest area, Persson (1974) concluded that the average volume of standing timber was around 110 cubic metres per hectare, and that the total volume was around 310,000 million cubic metres, of which perhaps 100,000 million cubic metres were coniferous. The former figure compares with one of around 400,000 million cubic metres derived from the application of average figures to estimated extents of forest types (Table 2.3). To these closed-forest figures must be added timber in open woodland areas, estimated at around 30,000 million cubic metres with perhaps a similar volume in trees outside forest land. His overall estimate for the total volume of growing stock was around 350,000 million cubic metres. This estimate should be viewed with caution, as Persson himself carefully emphasised: his ' "guestimate" may be far from the truth' (p.230).

The distribution of closed forest and open woodland by area and growing stock is indicated in Table 4.2. Among the main features emerging from the table are the dominant position occupied by the Soviet Union in terms of both area and volume, and the significance of open woodland in Africa in terms of area and, to a lesser extent, volume.

The distribution of closed forest is strongly concentrated: the Soviet Union, Canada and Brazil account for close on half of the total area, and the Soviet Union alone accounts for over a fifth of the area, nearly a quarter of its growing stock, and 50–60 per cent of its coniferous volume (Sutton, 1975; Barr, 1988). South America stands out as having the most extensive closed forest in the developing world, and Brazil comprises much of that area. Open woodland is even more concentrated in distribution, with Africa accounting for more than half of the area.

The extent of forest and woodland in relation to total land area is shown in Figure 4.1. Countries with an extent of forest and woodland greater than

Table 4.2 Distribution by area and growing stock

Region	Closed forest area (mill ha)	Closed forest volume (100 mill m³)	Open woodland area (mill ha)	Open woodland volume (100 mill m³)
North America	630 (459)	585 (503)	– (275)	–
Central America	60	55	2	1
South America	530	915	150	40
Africa	190	250	570	140
Europe	140 (145)	120 (160)	29 (35)	8
USSR	765 (791)	733 (841)	115 (138)	56
Asia	400	380	60	20
Pacific	80	60	105	25
World	2 800	3 100	(1000)	(300)

Figures in brackets are from UNECE/FAO (1985), and in columns 1 and 2 are for *exploitable* closed forest only. Differences compared with Persson's data reflect redefinition rather than physical changes.

Sources: Compiled from data in Persson (1974) and UNECE/FAO (1985).

the world average are to a large degree concentrated in the high and low latitudes, reflecting the areal dominance of the boreal and tropical forests. Japan and the Koreas stand out as well-forested areas in mid-latitudes. Outside these exceptions, the highest percentages for cover of forest and woodland are found on the one hand in Finland and Sweden, which fall largely within the boreal forest belt, and in parts of the equatorial zone such as Surinam, French Guiana and Guyana in Latin America, Congo, Gabon and Zaïre in Africa, and Papua New Guinea. It is noticeable from Figure 4.1 that the most poorly endowed countries are not only those of the arid and semi-arid intermediate latitudes: Britain, Ireland and some neighbouring countries in north-west Europe also fall into this group. The controls on the pattern are obviously human as well as climatic.

Forest area and population
In general terms, there is an inverse relationship between forest cover and population density. Densely peopled countries generally have low degrees of forest cover, while the reverse is true of sparsely populated areas with physical environments suitable for forest growth. For example Palo (1987) reports a correlation coefficient between forest cover and population density of –0.334 for 72 tropical countries, while Palo and Mery (1986) quote much higher coefficients for individual continents (–0.80 for Latin America, –0.96 for Asia) and areas (–0.80 for moist Africa). A highly significant relationship ($r^2 = 0.62$, $P = 0.0001$) was found for the Greater Caribbean area by Lugo et al., (1981).

The area of forest and woodland per head of population at the global scale is now around 0.8 hectares while that of closed forest is little more

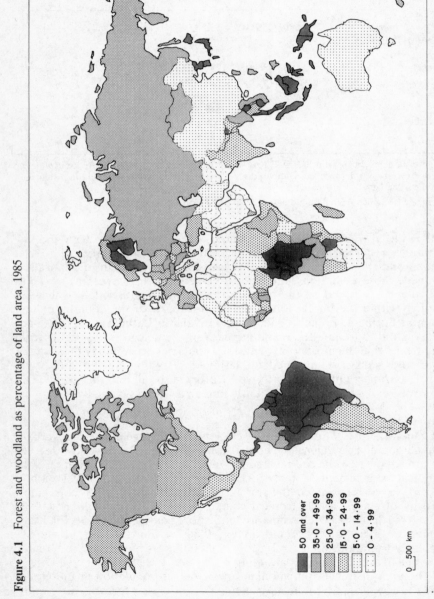

Figure 4.1   Forest and woodland as percentage of land area, 1985

50 and over

35·0 - 49·99

25·0 - 34·99

15·0 - 24·99

5·0 - 14·99

0 - 4·99

0   500 km

Source: Compiled from data in FAO *Production Yearbook*

Figure 4.2 Per capita area of closed forest (early 1970s) (ha)

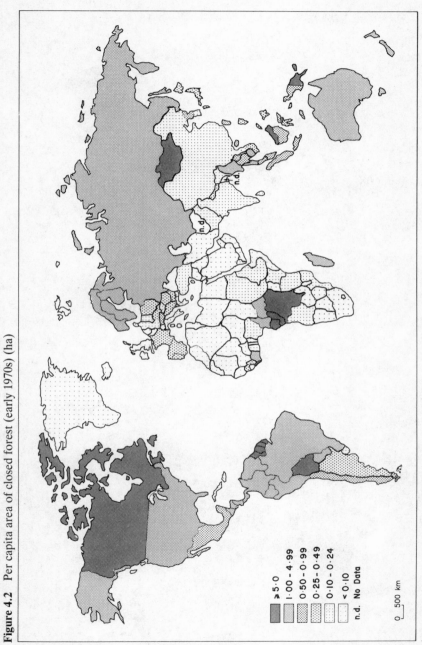

> 5·0
1·00 - 4·99
0·50 - 0·99
0·25 - 0·49
0·10 - 0·24
< 0·10
n.d. No Data

0 500 km

Source: Compiled from data in Persson (1974) and FAO *Production Yearbook*

Figure 4.3 Per capita area of forest and woodland 1985 (ha)

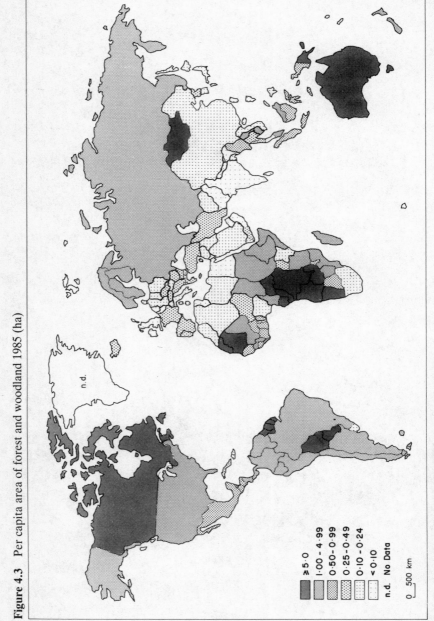

Source: Compiled from data in FAO Production Yearbook

than 0.5 hectares. (For comparison, the corresponding figures for arable land (with permanent crops) and permanent pasture are approximately 0.3 and 0.6 hectares respectively.) The unevenness of the per capita distribution of both closed forest and of forest and woodland is very pronounced, as Figure 4.2 and 4.3 illustrate.

Figure 4.2 clearly depicts a division into the 'haves' and 'have nots' in terms of the closed-forest resource at the level of individual countries. It is based on data assembled by Persson (1974): separate data for closed forest are not published in FAO *Yearbooks*. Ratios of more than one hectare of closed forest per head of population are largely confined to a few low-latitude countries, and to the Soviet Union and North America. On the other hand most of Africa and Asia (outside the Soviet Union) have less than one-quarter of a hectare per head, as indeed also has a group of densely populated countries in north-west Europe. Several significant features emerge from the pattern. One is that some tropical countries that are (or have been) associated with dense forests and active utilisation of the forest resource were near or below the world average even around 1970, since when the ratio has further declined with increasing population and decreasing forest area. Several countries in east and west Africa (for example Uganda and Nigeria) fall into this category, as do some in south-east Asia (including for instance the Philippines and Sri Lanka). Closed forest is a scarce resource in both absolute and relative terms throughout much of Africa and Asia, and not just in the areas traditionally associated with treelessness. Huge tracts in Africa, as well as in south-west Asia, have less than one-tenth of a hectare of closed forest per person.

Perhaps the picture portrayed in Figure 4.3 is slightly less gloomy, reflecting as it does an apparently more generous per capita endowment. Here other woodland is added to the category of closed forest. Caution is necessary in assessing the pattern, since the definition of 'forest and woodland' employed for some countries is a wide one, embracing scrub and brushland. Few would expect the north-west European countries, for example, to be less well endowed with forest and woodland, on a per capita basis, than countries such as Iceland, Mauritania, Libya or Saudi Arabia. Nevertheless, these north-west European countries (Ireland, United Kingdom, Belgium, Netherlands and Denmark) stand out as poorly endowed in terms of both closed forest and forest and woodland. On the other hand significant differences also occur between Figure 4.2 and 4.3. Much of Africa appears in a better light when other woodland is added to closed forest, and this applies especially in the savannah area in general and in the Sahel in particular. Again too much significance should not be attached to individual countries since statistics on the areas in question may be of doubtful accuracy, but the broad pattern reflects the basic fact that much of Africa is much better off in terms of open woodland than it is in terms of closed forest.

Both the volume of the growing stock in open woodland and its annual growth are, of course, low compared with the closed forest. Indeed volume per capita is probably a much more significant indicator of resource potential and stress than forest area, although it is less easily established.

On the basis of Persson's estimates for volume, combined with 1985 estimates of population, the world per capita volume in closed forest and forest land is respectively around 65 and 70 cubic metres. In Africa, the figures fall to about 45 and 70 cubic metres, whilst at the other extreme in the Soviet Union the ratios are around 280 cubic metres per person. Major disparities occur even at the scale of continents and large regions: at the intra-continental scale these disparities are of course much greater.

The dynamics of the forest area

Trends and patterns of deforestation

If uncertainty exists about the total area of forest and woodland, our knowledge about trends in that area is even more unsure. Huge differences exist amongst estimates of the annual rate of forest loss. Some of these differences may arise from different concepts of loss. For example two careful and prestigious studies estimated the annual rate of disturbance in tropical closed forests respectively to be 7.4 and 22.0 million hectares in the late 1970s (Lanly, 1982; Myers, 1980a). A subsequent comparison concluded that these apparently irreconcilable estimates could in fact be largely reconciled (Melillo et al., 1985)(see also Chapter 8). One study had estimated deforestation, whilst the other had measured conversion. In addition, there were differences in the initial assumptions, one study having considered all forests in the tropics and the other only broad-leaved forests. When adjustment was made for such differences, the remaining disagreement was minor, and hinged largely on the use of different figures for four countries.

Data sources

In addition to possible confusion between deforestation and conversion, there may also be problems of definition of categories. In the FAO *Yearbooks*, 'forest land' includes areas that have been felled but are intended for reforestation, and the distinction between such areas and those deforested is likely to be at best imprecise. Particular problems are encountered as woodland opens out to grassland. Shortening rotations of shifting cultivation may gradually reduce the forest, whilst on the other hand the gradual encroachment of the forest onto land abandoned by agriculture may similarly give rise to problems of definition and criteria. Neither increases nor reductions in the area of forest and woodland are easily capable of precise measurement, and therefore the net change is the balance between estimates of two quantities which are both likely to be subject to inaccuracies. The data on apparent changes in area of forest and woodland that are readily calculable from the *FAO Production Yearbooks* must therefore be viewed with caution. Myers (1980a) suggests that the FAO has been unable to apply vigorous appraisal to nationally reported statistics for fear of threats to funding, and refers to specific cases such as that of Indonesia, for which at his time of writing the published figure for forest cover was more than twenty years out of date and took no account of continuing logging and shifting cultivation. The quality of data has probably increased considerably in recent years, but in general terms, estimates of deforestation are usually five to seven years out of date, and while the use of remote-sensing techniques such as the analysis of LANDSAT imagery is a major step forward, their usefulness may be limited by the difficulty of differentiating between original forest and areas of regeneration (Salati and Vose, 1983), as well as by problems of cloudiness.

With these provisos in mind, we can conclude from *FAO Production Yearbooks* that the total area of forest and woodland appears to have decreased by approximately 2 per cent during the period from 1975 to 1985. During this period the net change has amounted to around 80 million hectares, or an area more than three times the size of Britain. The annual net change during the 1980s is around 5 million hectares, equivalent to around two-thirds the size of Scotland. The definition of forest land, as discussed earlier, is likely to mean that this figure is an underestimate of the area cleared, as 'forest land' includes those areas where there is an intention of eventual reforestation. Furthermore, data from the *Yearbook* relate to change in the aggregate forest area rather than to deforestation. Net changes in the forest area result from the balance between the area 'deforested' and the area 'reforested': the data therefore understate 'gross' deforestation. This important proviso should be borne in mind in considering the ensuing figures and discussion.

Data from the *Yearbooks* suggest that the annual rate of change increased from around 4 million hectares during the first half of the 1970s to over 10 million during the second half, before slowing to the more recent rate. Gross deforestation is of course very much more extensive, and net deforestation in the tropics is likely to be greater than that in the world as a whole.

Attempts to measure rates of change encounter great problems of source data as well as of definitions. Well-known examples of estimates of rates of tropical deforestation include those of Sommer (1976), Myers (1980a), and Lanly (1982). The latter concluded that the annual rate of clearance of tropical forests around 1980 was 11.3 million hectares of which 7.5 million were in closed forests and the remainder in open woodlands (see also Chapter 8). This corresponded to around 0.60 per cent of the tropical closed forest area. Whereas Lanly estimated that the rate was similar in the three major tropical areas, more recently Arnold (1987) has reported annual deforestation rates of 0.77 per cent in Africa, 0.67 per cent in Asia and 0.60 per cent in America.

Of Lanly's total area of 11.3 million hectares, 6.2 million hectares were transferred to other land uses while the remainder retained some tree cover. Myers (1983a) concluded that a minimum of 10 million hectares is eliminated each year, and that the overall conversion rate is around 24.5 million hectares. Some recent work based on remote sensing in the Amazon region suggests that up to 20 million hectares per year may be burned in that area alone (e.g. *The Times*, 6 August 1988), and indicates that the rate of deforestation increased exponentially between 1975 and 1985 (Malingreau and Tucker, 1988). The use of remote sensing in some other parts of the world has also suggested that other sources may have given rise to underestimates. For example, it has been alleged that while the forest cover of India was officially reported to extend to 74 million hectares in the early 1980s, its extent as determined by remote sensing was only 37.9 million hectares (Bowonder et al., 1987). It must be emphasised, therefore, that there are serious limitations to the accuracy of the data in the *FAO Production Yearbooks*: on the other hand the latter source is unrivalled in terms of its convenience and availability.

Patterns
The broad pattern of distribution of change is indicated in Table 4.3, from which it clearly emerges that reductions in area of forest land are primarily characteristic of the developing world, which accounts for some 70 million of the 80 million hectares apparently cleared between 1975 and 1985. The net change in Latin America alone is almost two-thirds of the net global figure, and Africa also registers a large decrease. In Brazil, forest land contracted by over 24 million hectares between 1975 and 1985 — an area larger than the whole of Britain. Colombia, Ecuador and Venezuela also appear to have suffered large reductions of the scale of millions of hectares, while in Africa the largest decreases were in Ivory Coast, Nigeria, Sudan and Zaïre. The apparent net increase in Asia results from the expansion of forest land in China (by a reported 22 million hectares, but it is alleged by Smil (1983) that much of the claimed afforestation indicates the target rather than the achievement) and to a lesser degree in India: countries such as the Philippines and Malaysia experienced substantial decreases. These trends between 1975 and 1985 merely continue those that have been operating for several decades. For example in Sri Lanka, natural forest cover shrank from 50 to 24.9 per cent between 1950 and 1981 (Erdelen, 1988). In Thailand, forest cover decreased from 70 per cent in 1945 to 53 per cent in 1961 and 18–19 per cent in 1988 (Lohmann, 1989).

Reforestation and afforestation.
If dwindling areas of forest land are a characteristic of much of the developing world, much of the developed world has undergone expansion. This is particularly true of Europe and the Soviet Union. As Table 4.3 indicates, expanding forest land appears to be a particular feature of the centrally planned economies. The reported increase in the Soviet forest area between 1961 and 1978 amounted to 52 million hectares (Barr, 1984), or more than twice the entire land area of Britain. The pattern of annual cut and replanting, however, indicated that the forest area should have been declining, and at least some of the reported change may be more apparent than real. Barr (1988) suggests that increases in the total forested area and volume of growing stock may reflect changes in survey techniques more than real changes in these parameters. Even if expansion in the Soviet Union and

Table 4.3 Net changes in area of forest and woodland 1975–85

	area *(million hectares)*	*per cent*
World	– 82.9	– 1.99
Developed world	– 12.9	– 0.70
Developing world	– 70.0	– 3.01
Centrally planned ecs.	+ 60.7	+ 5.55
Latin America	– 54.1	– 5.21
Africa	– 29.0	– 3.99
Asia	+ 13.8	+ 2.51
Europe	+ 2.0	+ 1.29
USSR	+ 38.0	+ 4.24

Source: Compiled from data in *FAO Production Yearbooks*

China is overstated, however, perhaps a three-world model can be applied effectively, with expansion and contraction characteristics respectively of the 'Second' and 'Third' worlds, and a mixture of expansion and contraction in the 'First'.

Patterns of change

A more detailed spatial pattern of change in forest land is depicted in Figure 4.4. Here the note of caution about the validity and reliability of statistics for individual countries needs to be sounded yet again: while the overall pattern is probably valid, overreliance should not be placed on the values shown for small areas. It should also be emphasised that the change is net, and is based on data in FAO *Yearbooks*. It is likely, therefore, to understate gross deforestation.

At the general level, forest contraction is shown to be almost ubiquitous in the tropics. The whole of central America from the US border to Ecuador, with the sole exception of Panama, experienced a loss of 10 per cent or more during the period from 1975 to 1985, together with large areas in the Sahel and west Africa, and part of south-east Asia. While high percentage rates of change are most likely to be found in small countries, the spatial propinquity of the areas in question is a notable feature of Figure 4.4. Furthermore, comparison with data for the decade of the 1970s suggests that the 'high loss' areas are expanding. Mexico, Guatemala and Ecuador have been added to the Latin America group and Malaysia has joined the 'high' group of Thailand and Indonesia in south-east Asia. Outside the tropics, reductions in forest land are most notable in the United States and Australia, where high agricultural prices in the 1970s and early 1980s contributed to forest clearance, and a few other small and isolated areas. In the case of the United States, at least part of the forest

Figure 4.4   Percentage change in area of forest and woodland, 1975–85

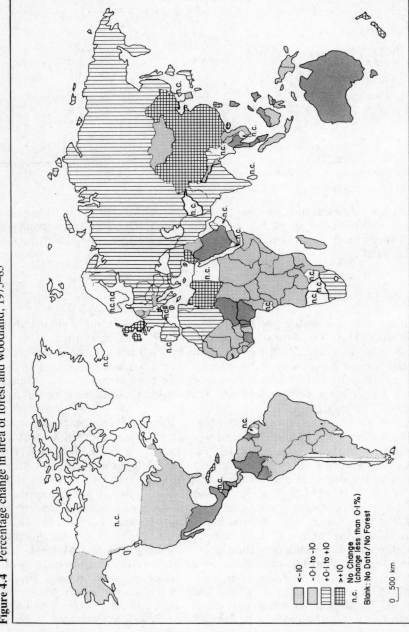

Source: FAO Production Yearbooks

Note: 'No change' relates to the areas as listed in the sources; it does not necessarily imply that the area remained constant. Please see text for

loss incurred during the 1970s may soon be replaced under a programme for the afforestation of erodible cropland.

The association between forest contraction in the tropics and expansion in the higher latitudes is reflected at the continental and national levels in South America and Africa, as well as at the global scale. High rates of increase are mainly confined to countries where the forest area is small. Almost all the centrally planned economies, including the Soviet Union and eastern Europe as well as China, stand out as areas of apparent forest expansion. Similarly, almost the whole of Europe, with the exception of Austria and the Benelux countries, has seen expansion even in the period before the agricultural surpluses of the mid-1980s began to encourage a faster transfer of land into forest. This trend applies even in countries such as Iceland, which is not traditionally associated with extensive forests. Its case, incidentally, illustrates the general point about the deficiency of data on which the map is based. The source indicates no change in forest area, but other reports suggest that by 1987, some 41,000 hectares were enclosed for afforestation, of which some 5,000 hectares had already been planted (Blondal, 1987). Previously, the extent of Icelandic birch woods had decreased by a factor of ten since the early eighteenth century, with the clearing of woodlands for fields, fuel and lumber (Arnalds, 1987).

Trends in forest area clearly do not exist in isolation, but are closely interrelated with trends in agricultural area. In particular, a relationship appears to exist between arable and forest areas. This relationship is depicted in Figure 4.5, where arable and forest trends are plotted for a large group of countries. Most of these countries are located in the parts of the graph indicating arable expansion combined with forest shrinkage, and vice versa (despite the fact that these two categories of land cover comprise just over 40 per cent of the total land area). Most European countries occupy the top left quadrant of the graph. In France, for example, the forest area has increased from 20 per cent of the land area in 1959 to 27 per cent in the mid-1980s (Devaud, 1987). In the Netherlands, the forest area has grown from 250,000 hectares during the Second World War to 330,000 hectares by the mid-1980s (Grandjean, 1987). Most developing countries, on the other hand, are in the lower-right part, indicating a combination of agricultural expansion and forest contraction.

Population trends and deforestation

The patterns indicated in Figures 4.4 and 4.5 suggest a relationship between forest trends and population trends at the global scale, and an example of a similar relationship at the national scale is contained in Figure 4.6. In countries with rapidly expanding populations the forest land area is rapidly contracting. Conversely, where the population is stagnating or growing only slowly, forest land is expanding. Probable errors in the published data values for both population and forest land area complicate the measurement of the statistical correlation between these two trends, but significant relationships between population growth, expansion of the

Figure 4.5 Distribution of countries by percentage change in arable and forest area, 1975–85. The section of the upper diagram indicated by the dashed lines is enlarged in the lower section.

Country code
2 China
9 Malaysia
10 Pakistan
11 Philippines
12 Saudi Arabia
13 Thailand
15 Yemen D.R.
16 Costa Rica
17 Cuba
18 Dominican
    Republic
19 El Salvador
20 Guatemala
21 Haiti
22 Honduras
24 Mexico
25 Nicaragua
29 Brazil
31 Colombia
32 Ecuador
33 Guyana
34 Peru
35 Surinam
48 Gambia
51 Madagascar
52 Malawi
53 Mali
55 Nigeria
57 Sierra Leone
62 Togo
63 Uganda
80 Ireland
90 Australia
91 New Zealand
111 Libya
112 Tunisia

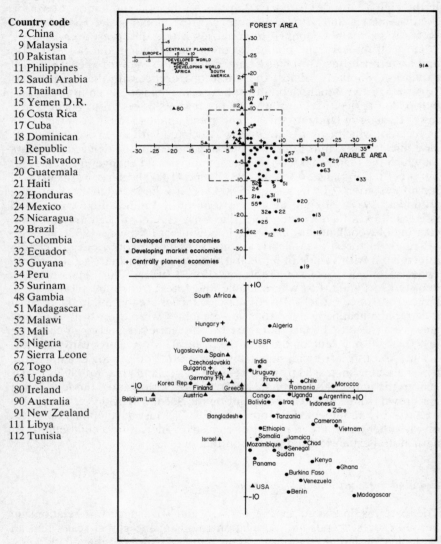

Source: Compiled from data in FAO *Production Yearbooks*

arable area and contraction of the forest land area have been confirmed for developing countries by Allen and Barnes (1985) on the basis of data from *FAO Production Yearbooks*. They conclude that recent population growth and change in arable area are associated with deforestation, and also show that the relationship is stronger in Asia and Africa than it is in Latin America, where presumably other factors play relatively stronger roles. Over the longer term, a similar relationship has been reported for Parana State, Brazil, between 1900 and 1973, although few details are presented (Palo and Mery, 1986).

The implication is that agricultural expansion in response to population growth is a major factor influencing or determining forest clearance, and probably the predominant one. In addition, forest clearance means that supplies of fuelwood may decrease in some areas, leading to the increasing use of crop residues and dung as fuel and hence declining agricultural yields and thus further pressure for forest clearance (e.g. Pimentel et al., 1986). This may be an oversimplification, since some dung could be used for fuel during the non-growing season without undue effect on crop yields (Bajracharya, 1983a). On the other hand fuelwood collection may itself be an agent of deforestation if the population pressure is high and the forest growth rate low. Open tree formations such as those in savannah areas are usually the most likely to be affected by this process. The likelihood of deforestation from this cause is perhaps greatest around cities, especially in the Sahel and in India. In the case of the latter, forest cover within 100 kilometres of India's major cities decreased by 15 per cent or more in less than a decade (Bowonder et al., 1987b). The effects of this pressure, however, are not confined to the vicinity of cities: the production of charcoal can affect forests far from the centres of consumption.

If there is a causal relationship between population growth and deforestation then there are two important implications. First, if population growth is the driving-force behind deforestation, then an increasing area of forest is likely to be cleared each year in response to it. Even if the absolute area cleared were constant, this would represent an increasing proportion of the dwindling forest area. At first a given area of deforestation might represent a very small percentage of the total area, but subsequently that percentage would rapidly increase. An accelerating decrease in the forest area may therefore occur. Since the later stages of deforestation may be so rapid, it is thus perhaps not surprising that some countries can effectively be almost completely denuded of forest before remedial action begins. Even so, deforestation appears unlikely ever to be complete: small residual areas are likely to be perceived to have high conservation value and in any case are likely to be located in inaccessible areas where there is a measure of insulation against both agricultural and commercial forces.

Second, the patterns depicted on Figures 4.4 and 4.5 combined with the concept of interrelationship between population and forest trends and the historical background of the use of the forest resource as sketched in Chapter 3, points to a sequential model of forest trends. During periods of rapid population growth, the forest area is likely to contract, while during periods of relatively stable population it is likely to stabilise or even to

Figure 4.6 Trends in population (POP) and forest cover (FC) in Sri Lanka. Population is in millions: forest cover is expressed as a percentage of land area

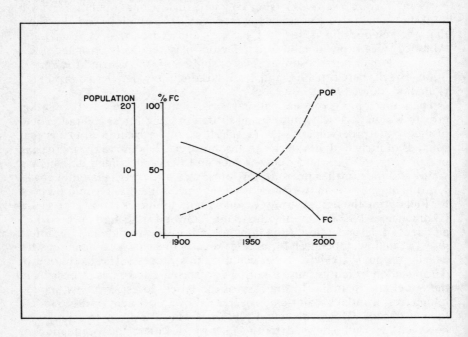

Source: Erdelen (1988)

expand. Forest clearance in nineteenth-century Europe has now given way to forest expansion, and the high rates of forest destruction in the second half of the nineteenth century in North America have not been matched in the second half of the twentieth century. While precise, quantitative evidence to refine and evaluate the model is scarcely available at the national level, far less at the global scale, it is tempting to speculate that the model may also be valid globally, and that at present we are in a phase corresponding to that of parts of Europe and North America a century or more ago. The problem lies in predicting when and how the downward curve of the forest area will 'bottom out', and whether it will do so while significant areas of forest still survive (Figure 4.6).

Third, it should perhaps be emphasised that the relationship between population trends and deforestation is neither especially close nor deterministic. An association between the variables can be demonstrated, but this association may itself vary through time, as in the case of the United States, and other factors such as the upheavals created by war, revolution and political reorganisation as well as more gradual changes in both popular and governmental attitudes may be followed by dramatic changes in forest trends. To attempt to portray the forest area 'transition' as a mirror image of the population transition is therefore an oversimplification, although this is not to say that it is devoid of validity.

Causes of deforestation

The dominant trend in forest area at present is that of deforestation, which is largly concentrated in the tropical zone. Trends in tropical forest areas are discussed further in Chapter 8: here the major causes of deforestation are outlined briefly. As Figures 4.4 and 4.5 imply, an inverse relationship appears to exist between trends in population and the forest area. This relationship, however, is far from perfect. Several factors account for the imperfect nature of the statistical relationship between population trends and deforestation. One is that the pressure of population growth on the forest may be expressed in the form of shifting cultivation or of sedentary agriculture, and that different effects may result. The former is believed to account for around 45 per cent of the annual rate of loss of tropical forest (Lanly, 1982). Shifting cultivation is identified as the principal cause of deforestation in all three tropical regions, accounting for 70, 50 and 35 per cent respectively in Africa, Asia and tropical America. About 500 million people and 240 million hectares of closed forest are involved in shifting cultivation, which is increasing at an average annual rate of 1.25 per cent. More than 5 million hectares of new forest fallow are being created annually (Lanly, 1985). As population increases, fallow periods grow shorter and forest recovery between periods of cultivation becomes impossible.

Another factor is that forest clearance occurs for reasons that are related to internal fiscal or development policies or to export markets in the developed world, rather than to population growth in the developing world. This may be one of the factors that accounts for the existence of a weaker relationship between population trends and deforestation in Latin America than exists in Africa and Asia. Large tracts of tropical forest in Latin America have been cleared for cattle-ranching to produce cheap beef for North America (Myers, 1981), although in recent years beef exports to the United States have decreased as a result of a combination of factors including decreasing beef consumption as well as political tensions in Central America.

Deforestation for conversion to pasture, however, is not only a result of international commodity markets — the so-called 'hamburger connection' — but also occurs for domestic reasons, especially in Brazil (e.g. Hecht, 1989). Forest clearance for cattle-grazing has been carried out by small peasants as well as by large ranchers, not least in order to strengthen land claims and secure fiscal incentives and tax holidays. In addition, the market value of cleared land increases, and forest removal may be a hedge against inflation: Browder (1988) suggests that the rate of forest conversion is positively correlated with Brazilian inflation. Even although cattle-ranching *per se* may not be economic in Amazonia, the related economic circumstances are a powerful driving-force for deforestation. Real-estate speculation in particular is a major factor (Fearnside, 1989).

Conversion to pasture has been identified as the foremost cause of deforestation in Brazil, accounting for 72 per cent of the forest clearance up to 1980 (Browder, 1988). This compares with a contribution of 10 per cent from small farmers and shifting cultivators. It is believed that at least 325,000 square kilometres of Latin American tropical forests were cleared for pasture between 1962 and 1985, and at least in the case of Brazil, almost none of the wood cleared was disposed of as commercial timber (Myers, 1983b). According to Myers, this represents a lost timber value of over $10 billion. Much of the Brazilian forest clearance for pasture development was encouraged indirectly by the development authority, the Superintendancy of Amazonia (SUDAM): merchantable timber was recovered on only 18 per cent of SUDAM-assisted ranches, and the loss of timber on these ranches alone is estimated at over 200 million cubic metres, perhaps representing a social opportunity cost of $1 billion to $2 billion (Browder, 1988).

Forest clearance for pastures and for export-oriented commercial agriculture is not confined to modern Latin America: as Chapter 3 indicated, it occurred in areas such as Burma and the Philippines during the nineteenth century, and has continued in recent times in countries such as Ivory Coast (Bertrand, 1983) and Nigeria (Osemeobo, 1988).

Large-scale commercial clearance may occur alongside peasant colonisation and government-sponsored settlement schemes for small farmers, as in the case of Brazil (e.g. Fearnside and Salati, 1985). Deforestation for subsistence production is not a major cause of deforestation in Brazil at present (Fearnside, 1989a), but land cleared by small-scale farmers may in turn be amalgamated into larger farms or ranches, and the process of small-scale clearing repeated. The government-sponsored 'transmigration' of millions of Javanese to outlying parts of Indonesia, including Sumatra, Kalimantan and Sulawesi, has resulted in extensive forest removal, perhaps amounting to 3 million hectares, in these areas (e.g. Ross, 1985; Repetto, 1988). Deforestation may also be carried out in some areas as evidence that a government has taken steps to establish an interest, and hence sovereignty, in a frontier area. Such action is reported, for example, from southern Venezuela (Buschbacher, 1987).

Timber production in general and commercial logging in particular may also be contributory factors. In some areas this has as yet been a minor factor. In Brazilian Amazonia, for example, loggers remove around 4 million cubic metres annually—around 0.01 per cent of the areas's 50,000 million cubic metres of timber (Westoby, 1989). Commercial logging is rapidly becoming a major disturbance even in Amazonia, however, as the forests in other parts of the tropics are depleted (Fearnside, 1989a). In parts of south-east Asia timber production has been a much more significant factor.

Allen and Barnes (1985) found that per capita wood production was not significantly related to change of forest area in their 'short-run' model, but when they allowed for a time lag effect by relating wood production in 1968 to change in the forest area over the following decade, their conclusion was that wood-harvesting does result in deforestation, albeit with a delayed effect. In their analysis, harvesting for both fuel and export was considered. Commercial logging, often geared to export markets, may be an important cause of deforestation at the local or national scale if reforestation is not enforced, even although it is not a major factor at the global scale (Lundgren, 1985). And even if logging is not significant as a direct cause of deforestation, it plays a vital part in a two-step process. Commercial loggers construct roads in order to extract timber, and thereby greatly improve accessibility. Settlers or forest farmers can then move in and proceed either to clear parts of the forest or to prevent its regeneration (Walker, 1987). In more general terms, the construction of roads and the resulting change in forest accessibility is a major factor in deforestation: for example Malingreau and Tucker (1988) link recent acceleration of deforestation in part of Amazonia to the paving of highway BR-364 and the consequent surge of migrants.

Various other factors may contribute to deforestation. Overgrazing has been damaging in some parts of the world, especially in mountainous areas such as north Pakistan (Allan, 1986; 1987) and in open or dry forests such as those of Saudi Arabia (Abo-Hassan, 1983). Fire is also a major hazard, especially in parts of southern Europe: in Greece, for example, 25,000–120,000 hectares are damaged or lost each year through fire, urban growth or agricultural expansion, while reforestation averages only 3,000–4,000 hectares (Modinos and Tsekouras, 1987). Political instability or strife may also be a contributory factor. In Pakistan, for example, the resettlement of Afghan refugees resulted in the destruction of forest, and Pakistani nationals took advantage of the confusion to participate in illegal logging (Allan, 1987). In southern Africa, incendiarism arising from disgruntlement amongst the rural population has damaged the Zambezi teak forests, as have accidental fires started by cultivators, honey gatherers and hunters (Piearce, 1986).

During the Vietnam conflict, an area of around 1.25 million hectares was sprayed with herbicides and defoliants, and more than 4 million hectares were damaged by shells (Lanly, 1982). In the south, 5.6 million hectares of upland forest were damaged, but more forest—around 200,000 hectares per year—has been lost in Vietnam since the war than during it (Kemf, 1988). There is a long history of destruction of forests during wars. This dates back to classical times (Chapter 3) and probably earlier. More recently, vast areas of forest in Pomerania were cut down by the Swedes during the Thirty Years War, with the result that many districts were invaded by sand dunes (Braudel, 1979). In the Soviet Union, forest depredation by the Japanese was suffered on Sakhalin between 1905 and 1945, and 20 million hectares of forest were felled or destroyed in areas occupied by the Nazis or subject to military activities (Barr, 1988).

Elsewhere, urban expansion may encroach on forest land. In the United States, the rate of conversion of forest land to urban uses increased dramatically during the 1970s, and amounted to almost 250,000 hectares in 1981 (Miller and Rose, 1985). At the global scale the area of forest affected in this way may be small, but the forest land affected may be of prime quality (as for example in the case of British Columbia (Redpath et al., 1986)) and the loss of timber production disproportionately high.

It is apparent, therefore, that several factors contribute to deforestation. Myers (1980a) has attempted to estimate their relative importance in terms of area. Of his estimated conversion (as opposed to deforestation) rate of

Table 4.4   Causes of deforestation in Jamaica, 1986

	Percentage of deforested land
Peasant agriculture	52.2
Pasture	11.0
Coffee	9.3
Residential etc.	8.8
Horticulture	6.5
Logging and fuelwood	4.5
Bananas	2.9
Cannabis (marijuana)	2.7
Other commercial agriculture	2.2
Conifer plantations	0.2

Source: Eyre (1987)

245,000 square kilometres per year, he estimates that commercial logging combined with follow-on cultivation accounts for 200,000 square kilometres, commercial logging alone between 19,000 and 29,000, fuelwood-cutting 25,000 and ranching 20,000 square kilometres.

The relative importance of these factors varies from place to place, and such estimates may have little validity at the national level. The nature of deforestation at all levels from the global to the local level is very complex. This is shown by the case of Jamaica, which is illustrated in Table 4.4. As the table indicates, a variety of causes including commercial and peasant cultivation, logging and the creation of coniferous plantations have all contributed. The compiler of data is careful to set them in context by referring to the possibility of cyclical trends related to climatic variability and to economic conditions (Eyre, 1987). An illustration of the possible significance of climate change or fluctuation in relation to woodland area comes from Mauritania, from where it is reported that drought during the 1970s seriously depleted the riverine woodlands, with the result that almost 7,000 out of a total of 16,000 hectares were lost (Pellek, 1983). Economic fluctuations were also associated with fluctuations in the forest area in the past: for example Eyre indicates that Jamaica had a smaller forest area in the plantation era than it has at present: during the second half of the nineteenth century regrowth occurred over substantial areas. Changes in the forest area may therefore be complex in terms of cause and amplitude: although the long-term trend may be downwards there may also be periods of regrowth, at least at the local or national scale.

Causes of afforestation

At the global scale, expanding forest area is correlated with low rates of population growth, in the same way as deforestation is associated with

Table 4.5 Pre-agricultural and recent forest cover

	Pre-agricultural area	Present area*	Percentage converted to cultivation
	(million km²)		
Forest: total	46.8	39.3	15.2
Tropical evergreen rain forest	12.8	12.3	3.8
Tropical/subtropical evergreen seasonal broad leaved forest	4.0	3.3	19.0
Tropical/subtropical drought deciduous forest	4.0	3.0	25.0
Temperate evergreen seasonal broad leaved forest, summer rain	1.2	0.8	32.0
Temperate/sub-polar evergreen needle-leaved forest	9.6	9.3	4.0
Cold deciduous forest, with evergreens	7.8	5.2	33.0
Cold deciduous forest, without evergreens	5.5	4.0	28.0
Xeromorphic forest/woodland	3.1	2.7	13.0
Woodland	15.2	13.1	13.8
Shrubland	13.0	12.1	6.7

* 'Present' relates to data extracted from sources mostly published in 1960s and 1970s

NB: Only forest types extending to over 1 million km² are indicated: the total figure therefore exceeds the sum of those indicated for specific types.

Source: Adapted from data in Matthews (1983)

rapid growth. In many parts of the developed world, areas that previously suffered rapid deforestation are now undergoing reforestation. In the French Alps, for example, extensive reforestation has occurred both by natural regeneration and by planting. It followed a decrease in population, the abandonment of agricultural land, and a reduction in numbers of grazing animals (Douguedroit, 1981). In the Alps and in many other parts of the developed world, population growth in the eighteenth and nineteenth centuries led to an expansion of the agricultural areas and increased agricultural pressures in previously wooded areas. More recent times have seen an abandonment of many of these agricultural areas and regrowth of the forest. Furthermore, afforestation has been carried out, or encouraged, by governments as a means of reducing the agricultural area at times of overproduction, of providing protection against erosion, or of building up reserves and supplies of timber. Until recently, most afforestation was carried on poor or marginal agricultural areas, but there are now indications that it is extending onto better qualities of land in countries such as New Zealand, Britain, and other parts of the European Community.

Long-term forest trends

If there is great uncertainty over the present dynamics of the forest area, our knowledge about historical rates of deforestation is even more deficient. Matthews (1983) has attempted to compare the present extent of forest and woodland with the 'pre-agricultural' extent, using numerous altases complemented by satellite imagery. Most of the atlases from which she worked were published during the 1960s and 1970s, and probably rely heavily on considerably earlier data. The results of such an exercise are, of course, no more robust than the original data, but they are nevertheless interesting and are summarised in Table 4.5.

The estimated reduction in the area of forest and woodland is approximately 900 million hectares, or approximately 15 per cent. Of this reduction, around 775 million hectares came from forests, and the remainder from woodland. A feature of her figures is the small reduction reported for the tropical rain forest. This amounted to only 50 million hectares or around 4 per cent of the 'pre-agricultural' extent: a similar reduction is indicated for the boreal coniferous forest. The clearing of mainly deciduous forests in Europe and the eastern United States, and of temperate evergreen forests in Asia, accounts for most of the reduction. Nevertheless, none of the conversion figures listed in the table exceeds one-third. These results seem low in comparison with current rates of change, and Sommer (1976) has suggested that the reduction in the tropical rainforest area alone may have amounted to 40 per cent. They nevertheless appear to be in broad agreement with the estimates of Wiliams (1989b), who concluded after assembling historical data on deforestation that a total of between approximately 750 and 800 million hectares had been cleared.

Such estimates can be interpreted in various ways. On the one hand, the apparent fact that around 85 per cent of the original forest area has survived to the second half of the twentieth century (at least in extent, if not necessarily in terms of composition) is a useful counterbalance to current fears about the fate of the world forest. On the other hand, an area of around 400 million hectares of forest and woodland may have been cleared between 1860 and 1978 (Williams, 1989b; Richards, 1986). The area of forest and woodland may thus have contracted as much during the last century as it did throughout earlier times. Furthermore, a net contraction of around 5 million hectares per year (as indicated by statistics in FAO *Yearbooks*) would indicate an accelerating rate of loss, even within the modern period. And it should be borne in mind that estimates of the annual gross loss of forest may be several times greater. The theme of accelerating loss is highlighted by comparing Matthews' estimated reduction of the area of the tropical rain forest (4 per cent) with recent estimates of annual loss of around 0.6 per cent, or even more strikingly by comparing her 'historical' figure of around 50 million hectares with estimates of recent annual losses of at least 7–11 million hectares.

Whilst it is impossible to construct a reliable set of global time-series data for the changing forest area (even with a time-scale of only a few decades), it is probable that rates of deforestation have closely paralleled rates of population growth at the medium and long terms as well as in the shorter term. If the historical relationship between population and forest area persists, it seems unlikely that the latter will stabilise before the former does so, perhaps well over a century from now. Any projection of historical trends to that time is completely speculative: such an exercise, however, would suggest that a further 15–20 per cent of the 'original' area might disappear. Optimists may prefer to think in terms that such a projection would still indicate the survival of around 70 per cent of the 'original' area. At a net rate of contraction of 5 million hectares per year, the estimated 2,800 million hectares of closed forest would disappear in 560 years (assuming rather unrealistically that all the contraction would be concentrated in the closed forest). More strikingly, the straight-line projections of Lanly's (1982) figures indicate the complete disappearance of the tropical rainforest by 2057 (Guppy, 1984). While there is, of course, no logical reason why such extrapolation should have any predictive value, it is rather disconcerting that the projected end of the forest should be so imminent, when human pressures throughout history have as yet caused the removal of perhaps only 15–20 per cent of the 'original' forest.

Plantations

Plantations constitute a significant but inadequately known part of the world forest area. Many countries have adopted forestry policies which have incorporated elements of plantation establishment, especially during the twentieth century. Such policies have frequently been motivated by concern about forest trends (nationally or globally) and their perceived implications for timber supplies. Fears of timber famine or shortage have underlain policies of this nature in settings as diverse as the United States during the 1920s (see Chapter 3), in New Zealand in the same decade (Roche, 1986) and in Britain around 1980. A related goal is to achieve complete or increased self-sufficiency. In Venezuela, for example, around 200,000 hectares of plantations had been established by 1986, with the goal of self-sufficiency of raw material for pulp and paper (Fahnestock et al., 1987). On the other hand the export potential for forest products may also be a motivating factor, as in the cases of New Zealand in the 1970s (Le Heron, 1986) and Chile (Postel and Heise, 1988). Environmental protection has also been a motive for planting in some instances, such as, for example, in the French Alps (e.g. Buttond, 1986). Whatever the driving-force may be, plantations may be created by government itself through state forestry services, or encouragement for afforestation may be offered in the form of planting grants and tax incentives. There may also be less direct incentives for landowners to afforest in some countries: in Ecuador, for example, forest land is likely to be safeguarded against land reform and some landowners may carry out afforestation for this reason (e.g. Gondard, 1988).

No convenient source of data such as the *FAO Production Yearbooks* exists for plantation areas, and most of the available compilations are based on diverse sources that relate to a variety of dates and are based on uncertain or differing definitions. Sometimes planting and regeneration are not clearly distinguished. Plantations may include both reforestation immediately after felling and the creation of new forests on land that at least in recent times (sometimes defined as within fifty years) has not supported forests, and it is not surprising that different definitions are adopted in different countries.

Despite these problems of data sources, there is some agreement that the total area of plantations world-wide in the early to mid-1980s was in excess of 100 million hectares, or approximately 3 per cent of the closed forest area. Evans (1986) estimates the area as between 120 and 140 million hectares, while in the early 1970s Persson (1974) assembled data, which he emphasised varied greatly in quality, indicating that the total area of man-made forest then was around 95 million hectares. That figure compares with an estimate of 81 million hectares in 1965 (Logan, 1967).

Postel and Heise (1988) have compiled estimates for the world-wide area of industrial forest plantations around 1985: these indicate that the total amounts to approximately 92 million hectares (Table 4.6). To the latter should be added areas of plantations established for fuelwood, environmental protection and other non-industrial purposes: for example 40,000 hectares/year or just under half of the total afforestation effort in Africa in recent years has been for these purposes (Evans, 1986): world-wide, 54 per cent of tropical plantations in the late 1970s were intended for industrial purposes and the remainder for fuelwood, environmental protection, and a variety of minor purposes (Evans, 1982). Lanly (1982) quotes broadly similar proportions of 60 per cent industrial and 40 per cent non-industrial.

The total annual rate of planting world-wide is uncertain, not least because of problems of definition and in particular of distinguishing between different forms of regeneration and between reforestation and afforestation. It was estimated by the World Resources Institute (WRI, 1986) that by 1980, 14.5 million hectares of forest land had been reforested or renewed annually. This is likely to represent an overestimate of the area actually planted. Table 4.6 sets out rates for a variety of countries, but it should be emphasised that no definitions are given in many of the individual sources from which the table is compiled.

As Table 4.6 indicates, plantations are very unevenly distributed. While some uncertainty may surround the extent to which the establishment of plantations in the Soviet Union and China has been successful, together they account for over 40 per cent of the plantation area. Europe, Japan and the United States are the other major areas, each having around 10 million hectares or more of industrial plantations. In Europe, Sweden alone has in excess of 5 million hectares of plantations (Savill and Evans, 1986).

It is notable that the four largest individual countries in terms of plantation area lie wholly or mainly in the temperate zone, as indeed do the majority of the countries listed in the table. Probably less than one-quarter of the plantation area lies within the tropics. Tropical regions account for around 17 million hectares if China is excluded (Lanly, 1982) but that figure may rise to nearer 25 million hectares if southern China and

Table 4.6 Estimated area of industrial forest plantations, c.1985

	(million ha)
USSR	21.9
China	17.5–28.0
USA	12.0
Japan	10.0
Brazil	5.0
South Korea	2.9
India	2.0
Indonesia	1.8
Canada*	1.5
Chile	1.3
South Africa	1.1
New Zealand	1.1
Australia	0.8
Argentina	0.8

* Plantations established since 1975

NB: Data for European countries are omitted. Most of the forest area in countries such as Britain and Hungary is in the form of plantations: in each of these two countries alone, the forest area is in excess of 2 million ha.

Source: Compiled from data in Postel and Heise (1987), and Savill and Evans (1986).

other countries just outside the true tropics are included (Evans, 1986). Much uncertainty surrounds plantation area and planting rates in China. One estimate of the open-land area planted between 1950 and 1983 is as high as 124 million hectares, with a further 8.8 million hectares having been planted following logging in natural forests (Zhu et al., 1987). The same source estimates recent planting rates averaging 4–5 million hectares per year. In addition, 'four sides' planting along rivers, roads, houses and streams amounted to 9.5 billion trees in 1981–2 (Hsiung, 1983). In 1981 it was resolved that all Chinese citizens above the age of eleven years should be obliged to plant three to five trees each year (Yuan, 1986). Although the reported planting rates are very impressive, survival rates have been low. They averaged only 31 per cent over the period from 1950 to 1983 (Zhu et al., 1987). It is officially claimed that 65 per cent of trees planted survive, but some estimates are as low as 10 per cent (Forestier, 1989).

In some north-west European countries and Japan, there is a long tradition of forest-planting, extending back for several centuries. Most of the plantation area, however, has been established during the twentieth century. In Sweden, for example, a rapid increase in the replanting rate has occurred over the last fifteen years (Hagner, 1986). Even in countries such as Japan with long traditions of forest expansion (Chapter 3), many of the plantations are comparatively young: a programme of reafforestation involving approximately 10 million hectares began after the Second World War (Guillard, 1983; Sedjo, 1987). Peak planting rates of over 400,000 hectares were achieved in the 1950s and early 1960s, as compared with post-war averages of around 200,000 hectares (Matsui, 1980; Tsay, 1987). Planting rates fell by half during the ten years prior to 1983. This decrease was related to an economic depression in Japanese forestry resulting from the effects of timber imports (Ohba, 1983).

Much of the 12 million hectares area of plantations in the United States was planted in the south-east of the country during the 1930s (see, for example, Clark, 1984). The annual area planted or direct-seeded in the United States increased from 200,000 hectares in 1950 to 800,000 hectares in 1978 (USDA, 1982). The agricultural Conservation Reserve Program introduced in the mid-1980s may lead to the planting of millions of hectares of farmland (e.g. Cubbage and Gunter, 1987), and is potentially one of the biggest afforestation exercises in American history. In countries such as the Soviet Union and Canada the replanting of forests is of recent origin. In the former, annual rates of forest establishment by seeding and planting increased from 582,000 hectares in 1955 to 1.33 million hectares in 1981 (Barr, 1984). In Canada, little attention was paid until recently to regeneration of cut-over areas, and the remaining forest stands became increasingly remote from mills (Fox, 1988). This has led to a rapidly expanding programme of replanting or regeneration. The total area planted per year increased from 128,000 hectares in 1975 to 192,000 in 1982, of which nearly half was in British Columbia (Canadian Forestry Service, 1988). In British Columbia, the annual planting rate doubled between 1973 and 1983. Even so, little more than half of the area logged in 1983–4 was replanted (Pearse et al., 1986). Despite recent increases in replanting rates, over 450,000 hectares of forest land in Canada go out of production annually as not being satisfactorily restocked with commercial species (Honer, 1986). Only about 20 per cent of the area cut each year in the late 1970s and early 1980s was replanted (Weetman, 1986).

Substantial expansion of plantations in the form of new or replacement forests has also occurred in Europe. In Sweden and Finland, for example, over 170,000 hectares and over 100,000 hectares per year respectively were being planted by the early 1980s (Savill and Evans, 1986; Tilastokestus, 1985–6). The forest area in Hungary increased by nearly 50 per cent between 1950 and 1980 (based on Keresztesi, 1984), and the planting rate in Bulgaria has exceeded 40,000 hectares per year (Grouev, 1984).

One of the most spectacular increases in the plantation area is in Brazil, where the plantation area increased from 500,000 to 3.7 million hectares between 1966 and 1979, and which has subsequently grown to over 5 million hectares (Postel and Heise, 1988). During the 1970s, Brazil established over 250,000 hectares of plantations per year (Sedjo, 1987). Most of this planting was carried out by private companies benefiting from the tax-saving incentives of forestry investment. An incidental effect of this type of incentive has been the dominance of large-scale investments and large plantations (Victor et al., 1986). Another South American country in which the plantation area has rapidly expanded is Chile. Over 300,000 hectares of pine plantations were established by 1974, largely through the government-owned National Forestry Corporation. Planting accelerated to 77,500 hectares per year during the second half of the 1970s (Husch, 1982), and by 1985 the area had expanded to 1.1 million hectares, largely because of the incentive of a 75 per cent reimbursement of costs incurred by the private sector in establishing and maintaining plantations (Postel and Heise, 1988). Over 100,000 hectares were reforested in 1976, but by the end of the decade the rate had fallen to about 50,000 hectares as the National Forestry Corporation was phased out (Solbrig, 1984). There has also been rapid expansion in South Korea and in countries such as New Zealand, where planting targets increased from 9–12,000 hectares per year in 1958–9 to 45,000 in 1981 (Abbiss, 1986). Annual planting rates averaged 44,000 hectares between the mid-1970s and mid-1980s (White, 1987). In New Zealand afforestation grants met 45 per cent of establish-ment costs, but were withdrawn in 1986. In Tasmania, planting rates increased from under 20 hectares per year prior to the early 1970s to over 1,500 hectares per year by 1982–4. This increase is attributable to the advent of a ready market for eucalyptus pulpwood with the growth of export woodchipping, and the introduction of planting assistance schemes (Tibbits, 1986).

Numerous other countries are also engaged in planting programmes which although modest in absolute terms are very significant in relation to the national forest area. For example, afforestation is proceeding in Israel at a rate of about 2,500 hectares per year (Cohen, 1985), and over 60 per cent of the national forest area now consists of plantations (Gottfried, 1982).

Although 1.0–1.2 million hectares of new plantations are now estab-lished annually in the tropics, subtropical and non-tropical areas account for most of the plantation area and also for much of the current planting (Tables 4.6 and 4.7). Nevertheless, the tropical plantation area has been rapidly expanding in recent years. The establishment of plantations in the tropics began in the Indian subcontinent in the mid-nineteenth century, but until recently the area of tropical plantations was very small. More than 90 per cent of the plantations existing in 1980 were created after 1951 and 40 per cent of the area after 1975 (Lanly, 1982). Between 1965 and 1980 the forest plantation area in the tropics trebled from under 7 to almost 18 million hectares (Evans, 1982) (Evans defined the tropics as lying between 27 degrees north and south of the equator). The tropics' share of the world plantation area increased from 8 per cent in 1965 to 13 per cent in 1979. This trend is likely to continue as more countries embark on planting programmes. For example, it was decided in 1981 that 188,000 hectares of forest plantations should be established in peninsular Malaysia, to offset a projected wood deficit and to reduce pressure on national forests. By 1988, 29,000 hectares had been planted (Mead, 1989). In Indonesia, it is projected that 4.4 million hectares of timber estates, consisting partly of fast-growing pines, will be established between 1985 and 2000 (Meulen-hoff, 1986). In East Kalimantan, a programme aimed at establishing fifteen estates each of 50,000 hectares of industrial plantations has been agreed, together with the rehabilitation of 60,000–70,000 hectares of logged areas by enrichment planting each year (Priasukmana, 1986).

Within the tropics, some forest areas have been cleared for industrial

Table 4.7 Annual rates of forest plantation establishment, selected countries, 1980s

	(ha)	
China	4.8 million	(Zhu et al., 1987)
USA	1.8 million	(WRI 1986)
USSR	1.3 million	(Barr, 1984)
India	370 000	(Evans, 1982) (Bowonder et al. 1987a) report that government envisages 3–5 million ha of afforestation per year 1987–90)
Brazil	250 000	(Sedjo, 1987)
Indonesia	200 000	(Evans, 1982)
Japan	200 000	(Tsay, 1987)
Vietnam	200 000	(Kemf, 1989)
Canada	192 000	(Canadian Forestry Service, 1988)
Turkey	150 000	(WRI, 1986)
Finland	114 000	(Tilastokeskus, 1985)
Chile	77 500	(Husch, 1982)
Sudan	60 000	(Evans, 1982)
Philippines	58 000	(Evans, 1982)
Nigeria	45 000	(Evans, 1982)
New Zealand	44 000	(White, 1987)
Bulgaria	40 000	(Grouev, 1984)
Australia	32 000	(Bureau of Agricultural Economics, 1985)
Britain	20 000	(Annual Reports, Forestry Commission)

Note: See also Grainger (1986) for areas of plantations established in Africa 1976–80

plantations but most of the plantations are on savannah, *cerrado* or other forms of grassland that has not been forested in recent times. A complex pattern of transfer may occur whereby forest is cleared for agriculture, and eventually, after the abandonment of cultivation and reversion to grassland, afforestation takes place. An illustration of this process comes from Ecuador, for instance: high-altitude natural forest is eventually replaced, after clearance, abandonment and reversion to grassland, by plantations (Gondard, 1988). Huge areas of tropical grassland are physically suitable for planting, some of which were at one time wooded and at another cultivated, and it is in this zone that much of the expansion of the forest area is likely to occur in the foreseeable future.

While the plantation area is growing at an accelerating rate, it is apparent that it matches the rate of deforestation in neither aggregate nor spatial terms. As has already been indicated, the net deforestation rate has in recent years been running at an annual rate of at least 5 million hectares, and the areas of deforestation and reforestation coincide at neither the global nor the national scales. Most of the deforestation is concentrated in low latitudes, while much of the reforestation is in the temperate or subtropical zones. Some tropical countries such as the Philippines claim that reforestation now exceeds deforestation (Durst, 1981), but the experience of Nigeria, where deforestation exceeds reforestation by a factor of ten, is more typical (Osemeobo, 1988). A similar ratio is reported for the tropical world as a whole, while in individual continents the ratio ranges from 1:29 in the case of Africa to 1:4.5 in Asia (Lanly, 1982). In countries such as Brazil, most of the deforestation is in Amazonia, while most of the new plantations are in the south of the country. (There are, of course, some exceptions to this generalisation, such as the huge plantations at Jari (e.g. Palmer, 1986).) Deforestation and reforestation are typically separated in both time and space, and it is apparent that the creation of plantations is not a substitute for the loss of natural forests.

This latter point applies in terms of species composition as well as area. Modern plantations are typically simple in composition, and indeed are frequently composed of a single species. Species of *Eucalyptus, Pinus and Tectona* account for 85 per cent of all plantations in the tropics (Evans, 1982), and in countries such as Brazil almost all the new forests are composed of either eucalyptus or pine, which, according to Sedjo (1980), comprised plantations amounting to 3.8 million hectares by 1979. It is estimated that a total of nearly 1.5 million hectares of southern pine species alone were planted world-wide in 1985 (McDonald and Krugman, 1986). A few species also dominate plantations in temperate and subtropical zones: for example plantations in Chile and New Zealand are composed mainly of *Pinus radiata*, while in the higher latitudes of Britain and Ireland *Picea sitchensis* and *Pinus contorta* play dominant roles. The latter species, of North American origin, is also widely used in Swedish plantations (Hagner, 1983; Gamlin, 1988).

While plantations cannot replace natural forests either in terms of area or of composition, they can play crucial roles in the overall pattern of forest resource use. As was indicated in Chapter 2, they are characterised by high productivities compared with natural forests in similar environments, and they are playing an increasingly important part in the supply of industrial wood in particular. In Latin America, for example, industrial plantations make up less than 1 per cent of the forest area but account for 30 per cent of industrial wood production: this proportion will rise to at least 50 per cent by the end of the century (Evans, 1987). In Australia, production from plantations will begin to exceed that from native forests sometime between 1990 and 2000 (Booth, 1984). In the United States, where at present around 14 per cent of the commercial forest area is in the form of plantations, it is expected that plantations will account for half of the wood-fibre production by 2000 (Sedjo, 1987).

Especially in relation to the production of industrial wood, therefore, the significance of plantations is disproportionate to their area. By offering the possibility of supplying large quantities of timber from relatively small areas of land, they may help to reduce at least one of the pressures on the natural forest and hence help to slow down its rate of contraction.

5 THE CONTROL AND MANAGEMENT OF THE RESOURCE

The use of the forest resource depends on the way in which it is controlled. The nature of this control, and in particular the form of ownership, provides the essential link between the forest resource and its use. Regimes of control or ownership also have a strong influence on the condition of the resource. Whilst the relationship between control, use and condition of the resource is not constant, broad correlations exist between systems of control and patterns of use. It is also clear that some forms of control are more likely than others to be associated with destructive exploitation. In particular sudden and abrupt changes in control systems may trigger phases of resource destruction or degradation.

Political history determines the character of landownership in general and the control of the forest resource in particular. In addition, political factors determine the degree to which regulation is imposed or influence exerted on private forest owners. The political background to forest resource use is therefore of profound and fundamental significance, and without an awareness of it little understanding of current forestry issues can be achieved. The nature of ownership and tenure influences the objectives of use of the forest resource and the nature of its management. In the United States, for example, national forests are managed for a variety of purposes, of which timber production is only one. Ownership by the forest-products industry, on the other hand, is characterised by the primacy of timber production and of economic criteria. Ownership by farmers and other individuals is usually intermediate in character (USDA, 1982). The person or organisation in immediate control of the resource may in turn be subject to various external constraints such as government regulation. The type of control exercised by government is of obvious significance in terms of regulating the extent of use and the nature of forestry practices.

The prevailing pattern of control of the forest resource has altered through time in most countries. The nature of this alteration varies in detail from area to area, but broad evolutionary patterns can be identified. These patterns consist of different phases, which frequently but not always follow each other in regular order. The chronological timing of these phases is highly variable, as is their respective durations. In general terms, however, a regular sequential pattern can be discerned in many parts of the world.

Ownership

Inadequacy of data

Since neither the forest area nor its rate of change is known precisely, it is not surprising that uncertainty surrounds the nature of ownership and tenure of the forest resource. Detailed statistical information on the structure of forest ownership is available for some countries, but for many others our knowledge is deficient in detail or quality. For many countries only a crude breakdown into the public and private sectors is available, and there is little information on the relative extent of different types of private ownership, for example. Furthermore, the actual status of ownership of forest land may not always be adequately defined (for example in some Latin American countries (Sedjo, 1987) and more generally in parts of the developing world (McNeil, 1981)), and hence it is not surprising that there are deficiencies in available data.

There are obvious reasons for the inadequacy of our knowledge of forest ownership. Ownership usually has no formal expression in the forest landscape, for example, and cannot be established by techniques such as remote sensing or field survey. The monitoring of changes in forest ownership is difficult to organise at the national level, and is well-nigh impossible to administer on a global scale. Furthermore, the structure of ownership may be extremely complex: the trees and the land on which they stand may in some instances have different owners, and indeed in some cases different tree species may even be under different ownership. In addition to the practical difficulties of measurement and monitoring, the nature of forest ownership may have political implications in some countries, and governments may not always be anxious to compile statistics showing how concentrated the structure of ownership, for example, may be. For various reasons, therefore, our knowledge about forest ownership is imperfect.

Forest ownership: a model

Despite these deficiences, sufficient data exist for the general nature of forest ownership to be established, and for a sequential model of the evolution of ownership through time to be tentatively suggested (Figure 5.1). Initially, the forest is common property, or the property of a particular tribe or clan, whose members enjoy rights of use of forest products but not the right to dispose of it. This form of communal ownership has been followed in many parts of the world by appropriation by the state, often in the form of a colonial power. In turn the state-owned

Figure 5.1 Sequential model of forest ownership, objectives of resource use and forest stage. Solid lines indicate main sequential trend of ownership; pecked lines shown subsidiary trends.

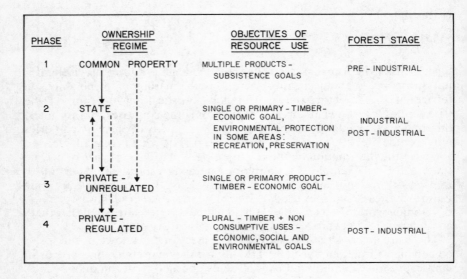

forest has been at least in part alienated into private ownership, and in some countries such ownership has become very fragmented.

This sequential model of communal, state and private ownership is, like most models, an oversimplification. In some countries, especially in Europe, the transition from communal to private ownership occurred without an intervening phase of direct state ownership. Also the phase of state ownership is characterised by a wide variety of forms of tenure: in some cases state ownership is combined with direct state management, while in others it is associated with the granting of forest utilisation contracts or concessions to private companies or individuals. Furthermore, the 'late' phase in which private ownership is prominent appears increasingly to be one in which indirect state influence through environmental and silvicultural controls becomes prominent. The private phase is therefore subdivided into 'unregulated' and 'regulated' sections. Also it should be emphasised that the phases of the model do not correlate directly with chronological time: different degrees of progress through the model have been achieved in different parts of the world, and indeed it is not unknown for reversions to 'earlier' evolutionary stages to have occurred. In many countries there have been short-term alternating phases of liberalism, characterised by privatisation, and government intervention, reflected in state afforestation. Nineteenth-century France is one example (de Montgolfier, 1989).

Despite its simplistic and imperfect nature, the model has some value in providing a framework and context in which the bewildering array of types of ownership and tenure can be considered. In addition, some correlation is apparent between ownership regime and the objectives of forest use. The combination of type of ownership and type of use is the basis for recognising three different stages of forest resource use (pre-industrial, industrial and post-industrial). These are indicated on Figure 5.1, and are further discussed in Chapter 6.

Phase 1: the common-property resource

Common-property ownership by indigenous peoples probably accounted for most of the world forest area until recently. It survived in parts of Europe until modern or early modern times. In much of Asia, Africa and America this form of ownership survived until the nineteenth century, and in some areas it is still extant in the late twentieth century. In Papua New Guinea, for example, forest land is held by the clan, but individual trees may be individually owned (Wigston, 1984). Similar systems applied in parts of Africa. A few trees, and especially large hardwoods and valuable building trees, were regarded as owned by individual clans or persons, but with these exceptions all were normally recognised as common property (Little and Brokensha, 1987).

In Africa and parts of the other developing continents, the arrival of European colonial powers marked a major turning-point. In general terms, they considered any land under common-property or group ownership to be unoccupied or ownerless, and in effect appropriated it (e.g. de Saussay (1987)). The replacement of traditional communal ownership by state ownership has continued to take place in very recent times. Forests in Nepal, for example, underwent such a change during the 1950s (Thompson and Warburton, 1988). With this change in the status of the forest there came a change in management. Under traditional common-property ownership the use of forest products was self-regulated by an informal form of policy consisting of rules or guidelines handed down from generation to generation.

The perception and use of the forest resource during this phase varied considerably. In North America, for example, the relationship between Indians and forests differed from place to place: in some cases the forest yielded building materials and food, while in others it was seen as an obstacle to cultivation (Bonnicksen, 1982). Typically, however, the range of forest products that were used was very wide, and some forms of management beyond simple gathering of products were utilised in at least some areas. For example the Kayapo Indians in Amazonia utilised a wide variety of plants, some of which were concentrated by transplanting in special forest areas (Posey, 1985).

With the advent of state ownership, the traditional pattern of self-regulation has tended to weaken or collapse. In the case of parts of Nepal, for example, management was taken out of local hands, and the indigenous management system, based on a rotating village office of forest guardian, that had worked successfully for centuries began to break down (Thompson and Warburton, 1988). People began to take too much wood from the forest closest to the village, instead of spreading the pressures over wider areas. Similar and long-lasting problems were encountered in India. Traditional forest resource management was disrupted as an alienated local population, now denied traditional rights, made destructive inroads into the forest (Shiva and Banyopadhyay, 1988). At the same time, local people began to perceive forestry officials as 'gendarmes' (Douglas, 1983; Westoby, 1989), policing the local use of the forest in favour of the faceless and remote new owner.

Another recent example of this widespread process is Ghana, where government took direct control of the forests in 1973, having previously held them in trust for local traditional communities. What followed has been described as a 'tragedy of the commons' (Gillis, 1988a). While this change in status may be intended to secure control and benefit for the whole country, all too often the state lacks sufficient administrative ability and control to manage the forests effectively. Furthermore, with this change in ownership, management goals are in many instances directed towards commercial timber production rather than indigenous use.

Common-property ownership is sometimes associated with another kind of 'tragedy of the commons' (Hardin, 1968). Such ownership is sometimes held to contribute to decay or degradation of the resource as each individual strives to maximise his or her personal benefit, with scant regard for the common good and sometimes in the absence of adequate checks and balances. Privatisation is sometimes advocated in order to avoid such degradation. There are cases, however, where communal ownership has been judged to have contributed to forest conservation rather than to destruction. The white pine forests of Guatemala offer one example. Here the pattern of forest use has been more conservative than in other privately-owned forests of Highland Guatemala (Veblen, 1978).

Some remnants of common-property ownership still survive in various parts of the world. For example over 5 million hectares of forest land in the United States is managed by the Bureau of Indian Affairs on behalf of the owners, who define the broad objectives of management (Sassaman and Miller, 1986). In Guyana, around 15 per cent of the forest belongs to Amerindian communities (compared with 84 per cent in state ownership and 1 per cent in private ownership (Prats Llaurado and Speidel, 1981). In Colombia, the government has now recognised that more than 12 million hectares of Amazonian forest is the collective and inalienable property of Indian communities (Bunyard, 1989). In Papua New Guinea, the imposition of European-based tenurial systems did not survive independence, and customary tenure, under which forest land cannot be sold, has now been brought back (de Saussay, 1987).

Common-property ownership does not fit well with modern exploitation of the forest by commercial logging. It is often replaced by state or private ownership prior to such development. If not, governments may enter into agreements with the customary owners and acquire rights to exploit commercial timber. These rights may in turn be granted to companies (Adeyoju, 1976). In Papua New Guinea, the Office of Forests buys rights to timber for a period of perhaps 40 years. Felling permits are then issued, and royalties are disbursed on ratios of 50 per cent to provincial government, 25 per cent to national government, and usually 25 per cent to the land owners. Up to 100 landowning groups may be involved in negotiations leading to timber-rights purchases (Bell, 1982).

Such complex arrangements are relatively unusual. More usually the transition from communal ownership to state control (with or without private exploitation through concessions) is abrupt and disruptive. Episodes of destructive exploitation frequently coincide with the transition in ownership, and reflect a breakdown in local control. Common-property ownership certainly did not ensure the complete conservation of the forest resource. In New Guinea, the use of fire brought about a reduction in the forest area as early as 10,000 years ago (Flenley, 1988), while both forest extent and composition in North America were modified by Indian agriculture and fire (Williams, 1989a). In general terms, however, the rate of attrition of the forest resource under communal control was usually very modest compared with that at the time of ownership transition. Destructive exploitation at the time of this transition in ownership was, in addition, frequently aggravated by the beginnings of rapid growth in population and by a breakdown in traditional lifestyles and social structures.

Phase 2: state ownership

Traditional indigenous ownership has now largely died out, and ownership of the forest resource is dominated by the state. State ownership dates back to the time of the Pharaohs in Egypt, and the royal forests of countries such as England, France and Prussia represented an extensive area of state ownership in the medieval and early modern periods. These royal forests, especially in the cases of France and Prussia, proved to be extremely important as the seed beds of modern forest management.

Nevertheless, the prominence of state ownership stems from the growth of the state in modern times. As has been indicated, the colonial period witnessed a tremendous expansion of state ownership, while many states also acquired or appropriated forest land in their home territories in the nineteenth and twentieth centuries. As a consequence of colonialism in many developing countries, forests belong to the state. As a further consequence, serious conflicts can arise between the needs of the local populations and the objectives of national policy (Fontaine, 1986).

State ownership (in its various guises) almost certainly accounts for over 70 per cent and perhaps as much as 80 per cent of the forest area. Data collected by the FAO for the 1963 World Forest Inventory cover over 3,000 million hectares, or about three-quarters of the estimated forest area (FAO, 1963). These data indicated that 77 per cent of the forest area covered was in public ownership. The previous World Forest Inventory in 1958 achieved a 46 per cent coverage and indicated that 80 per cent of the area covered was in the public sector. More recently, OECD (1989a) indicates that 72 per cent of world forests are in public ownership.

Table 5.1 gives a breakdown of the 1963 data, and shows that state or public ownership is dominant in areal terms in all the major areas except

Table 5.1 Ownership of forest land c. 1963 (areas in million hectares)

	Public area	%	Private area	%	Data coverage % of area
North America	476	73	173	27	87
Central/South America	362	55	295	55	68
Africa	250	79	68	21	40
Europe	67	47	77	53	29
USSR	910	100	—	—	100
Asia	283	92	25	8	56
Pacific area	21	25	62	75	86
World	2369	77	700	23	75

Source: FAO (1963)

Table 5.2 Forest ownership in selected countries and areas, early 1980s

	Total area (million ha)	Publicly owned (%)	Privately owned (%)
Canada	342	94	6
USA	298	39	61
Japan	25	42	58
Nordic countries*	60	26	74
EEC 10	33	38	62
Southern Europe	52	73	27
Eastern Europe	28	93	7
USSR	93	100	—

* Norway, Sweden and Iceland

Sources: UNECE/FAO (1985); Tsay (1987)

Europe and the Pacific: it accounts for about half of the forest area in OECD countries. The fuller coverage of data now available indicates that it also exceeds 50 per cent of the forest area in Europe. Table 5.2 sets out more recent and more detailed statistics for much of the developed world, and underlines the domination of public ownership. Public ownership accounts for more than 90 per cent of the forest area not only in eastern Europe and the Soviet Union, but also in a diverse range of countries including Canada, Greece and Turkey. In Asia, 80–90 per cent of the forest is under state ownership: in Malaysia, for example, 95 per cent of forest lands are owned by the respective state governments (Kumar, 1986). Overall, 50–60 per cent of forest land in Latin America is publicly owned, and there is over 80 per cent state ownership in Brazil, Colombia, Venezuela and a number of smaller Latin American countries (Lanly, 1982). Private ownership, on the other hand, accounts for the greater part of the forest area in a number of countries including the United States,

Japan, some Latin American countries such as Paraguay, El Salvador and Haiti, and, in Europe, most of the Nordic and EEC countries. Private ownership of forest land is generally limited in tropical Africa, being almost non-existent in French-speaking areas but rather more extensive in some former British territories, especially in southern Africa (Lanly, 1982).

The central state and its agencies account for most of the publicly owned area, but local government bodies (and collectives) are also involved in forest ownership in some countries. In detail the composition of the public sector is highly variable. In Canada, 67 per cent of the forest area is owned by provincial governments and a further 27 per cent by the federal government (Dunster, 1988). In China, 52 per cent of the forest land is owned by the state, with most of the remainder under the control of various forms of collectives (Li Jinchang et al., 1988). Within the European Community, state ownership ranges from close to 100 per cent of the public-sector area in Britain and Ireland to 25 per cent or less in Belgium and Italy. In central Europe, the state component varies from 82 per cent in Austria to 8 per cent in Switzerland. Perhaps one of the characteristics of state ownership of forests in some countries is its variability over time. In Britain, for example, state forest ownership grew from a negligible level at the beginning of the twentieth century to around 50 per cent by the early 1980s, as programmes of state afforestation were implemented. Since then, however, substantial areas of state forest have been sold to the private sector, in accordance with the prevailing political climate (e.g. Mather and Murray, 1986).

To a large extent, state and other public ownership correlate respectively with central and local control. In parts of the United States, for example, up to 25 per cent of the forest area is owned by non-federal government bodies. Such land enters the public domain through various means such as tax forfeiture, and uncertainty about future ownership may pose problems for long-term management (e.g. Lothner, 1986). On the other hand, some of the communal forests in mainland European countries have long been in that form of ownership, which in a sense is a partial survival from the stage of common-property ownership. In parts of West Germany and Switzerland, some areas of common land were divided into individual peasant woodlots, but many remained intact and became the basis for modern municipal forests (Ciriacy-Wantrup and Bishop, 1975). In West Germany, for example, sizeable areas of forest amounting to 47 per cent of the total forest area in Rheinland–Palatinate and 15 per cent in North Rhine–Westphalia remain in this form of communal ownership (Hachenberg, 1985). In some cases, however, such ownership came to an abrupt end. At the time of the French Revolution, for example, many communal forests were shared out amongst local inhabitants, often with the result of rapid deforestation (de Montgolfier, 1989).

The initial phase of common-property ownership, therefore, may be replaced directly by ownership by the central or local state, in the form of government agencies or municipalities. In the case of the latter, control may be both close and local, but in the case of the former it is more likely to be loose and remote. Ownership by the central state is often associated with private use under a system of licences or concessions, and may in turn be followed by outright transfer to the private sector.

Phase 3: private ownership

In some parts of the world, private forest ownership developed directly from common-property ownership, but elsewhere it arose from the alienation of land previously under state control. Such alienation occurred in much of the United States, except in the west, but has been resisted to a much greater degree in Canada. In the United States, the alienation of forest land in the nineteenth century was associated with settlement policy and agricultural development. In practice the same process operates in parts of the developing world today. In parts of Europe, huge areas of state forest were transferred to the private sector in the face of rising demand for timber during the nineteenth century. For example, the state forests of Austro-Hungary were reduced in extent by 60 per cent between 1800 and 1884 (Johann, 1984). In northern Sweden, privatisation of the forest was the first step towards a more intensive exploitation of timber resources (Gaunitz, 1984). In Finland, a similar process, involving land enclosure, proceeded rapidly from the late eighteenth century in the south of the country, while in the central and northern parts vast forests were allocated to the state (Astrom, 1988).

, A process of privatisation is continuing today in some parts of the world, and the transfer of state-owned forests to private ownership is a feature of the privatisation policies in some countries with 'new Right' goverments, such as Britain. In Japan, for example, one version of this process is the offering of part ownership of 0.25 hectare forest blocks to individual citizens for 500,000 Yen (Essman, 1985). In parts of the United States, extensive areas of public forest land have been transferred to the private sector in recent times: for example in Minnesota over 200,000 hectares passed into private ownership between 1964 and 1974 (Ellefson et al., 1982). Where control of the resource passes into private hands, the implications for management and use are profound.. These implications stem especially from the nature of the objectives of private owners, and these are discussed in a subsequent section.

These objectives depend on the type of private ownership. Many different forms of private ownership occur, and many classifications of private forest owners have been attempted. Private owners may be subdivided into corporate and individual types, with the former being further subdivided into industrial (forest-products companies), financial and investment institutions, and a miscellaneous category including companies whose forest holdings are incidental (for example mining companies). In Australia, for example, three main groups of private individual owners have been identified: 'genuine' farmers, hobby farmers and investors (Byron and Boutland, 1987). In the United States, a more refined sixfold classification has been suggested: 'custodial' owners who may have acquired their holdings by default, for example through inheritance; 'sideline' owners (for example those whose forest is an appendage to a farm); speculators; 'hobby' owners, to whom silviculture is a pleasurable interest rather than a means of earning a living; and 'true' investors (Yoho, 1985). An alternative classification suggested by Cunningham (1982) reflects the diversity of types of private individual owners: it includes commercial farmers, part-time farmers, rural non-farm residents, absentee business/professional owners, absentee retired owners, and absentee wage-earners. In France, seven main types of private forest enterprises have been recognised, ranging from large lowland estates of broad-leaved forests belonging to urban residents, to small mountain forest holdings of conifers, belonging to local farmers (Normandin, 1987).

Each type of owner has its own objectives: for example forest-products companies may seek security of supplies of raw materials, while 'hobby' owners may wish to maximise technical skill in management and 'true' investors aim to maximise profit.

Much of the privately owned forest area traditionally consists of farm forests. In much of Europe and the United States, this sector has contracted: the percentage of commercial forest land in the hands of farms declined from 35 to 25 per cent between 1952 and 1970 (Cunningham, 1982). Nevertheless, in some countries such as Norway, Sweden and Finland, the private sector is still dominated by farm forests. In Finland, for example, over 60 per cent of the closed forest area is farm forest (based on data in UNECE/FAO, 1985). In West Germany, 87 per cent of forest holdings belong to farmers (Harou, 1981). In Austria, half of all forests are farm forests (Eckmüllner, 1986). In other countries such as Britain and Ireland, farm forests are almost unknown. In Japan, on the other hand, 78 per cent of the 2.5 million private forest owners are farmers (Imamura, 1982). Traditionally farm forest-owners pursued a dual occupation, divided on a seasonal basis. Such duality was associated especially with Scandinavia, but it has now largely broken down, with many farmers migrating to the cities and retaining their forests as absentee owners, while increasingly mechanised forest work became a full-time occupation (e.g. Gaunitz, 1984).

The contrasting pattern of private ownership reflects contrasting forest histories and social and political climates. Similarly, the role of industrial companies as forest owners is varied. In some countries it is almost non-existent, but in others it comprises substantial proportions of the forest areas. For example industrial companies account for over 30 per cent of the forest area in Sweden and around 15 per cent of that in the United States. In terms of average size of forest holding, major contrasts frequently exist between company and farm forests. For example, the respective average sizes (closed forest) are 400 and 9 hectares in Denmark and 500 and 6 hectares in Spain (UNECE/FAO, 1985).

Two contrasting trends can be discerned in many parts of the world where there is substantial private forest ownership. On the one hand, industrial and/or financial company ownership is increasing. In the case of Scotland, for example, it grew from a negligible level in the 1960s to over 20 per cent of the private sector by the mid-1980s (Mather, 1987): most of this ownership is associated with financial rather than industrial companies.

Table 5.3   Structure of private forest ownership (percentage of forest holdings)

Size (ha)	France	Norway	Austria	Switzerland
5 or less	85.7	14.9	67.2	95.4
6–10	6.1	26.7	15.9	2.5
11–20	6.2	23.8	9.3	0.8
21–50	1.0	15.3	5.1	0.4
51–100	0.5	10.8	1.2	0.3
101–500	0.5	7.7	1.0	0.5
501–1000	—	0.5	0.3	0.1
Over 1000	—	0.5	—	—

Source: Compiled from data in UNECE/FAO (1985)

In the United States, a number of large forest-products companies have acquired substantial tracts of forest land, in pursuit of self-sufficiency in timber supply (Cox et al., 1985). Forest-industry ownership in the United States increased by 16 per cent between 1952 and 1970, mainly through acquisition from farmers and other private owners (USDA, 1982). One company amassed a holding of around 1 million hectares in the Southeast (Gammie, 1981).

On the other hand, much of the privately owned area has been fragmented into numerous tiny holdings, as Table 5.3 suggests. In some countries, such fragmentation has resulted especially from laws of land inheritance which result in repeated subdivision of properties. In France, for example, there are 2.8 million forest holdings of 5 hectares or less in extent (UNECE/FAO, 1985), while in West Germany half a million private owners have forest tracts averaging 6 hectares (Oedekoven, 1981). In Belgium, the 330,000 hectares of forest is divided amongst 106,500 owners, 69 per cent of whom own less than 1 hectare (Jadot and Sernsiaux, 1987). In Japan over 60 per cent of the holdings do not exceed 1 hectare and 90 per cent extend to not more than 5 hectares (Tsay, 1987). As much as 95 per cent of the units are under 10 hectares. In the United States, 71 per cent of the 7.8 million non-industrial private forest owners have less than 4 hectares of forest land (e.g. Birch, 1986).

Other forms of private ownership exist in some areas. For example in Britain a substantial and growing proportion of the forest area is owned by private or corporate investors who cannot be categorised either as farmers or as industrial companies. This trend is also apparent in other countries such as the United States, where the proportion of commercial forest land in the hands of non-farmers increased from 25 to 35 per cent between 1952 and 1970 (Cunningham, 1982). Also in the United States a small but increasing area of forest is owned by limited partnerships involving investment companies or forest-products firms (e.g. Howard and Lacy, 1986). In short, investment ownership, or ownership by financial capital in various forms, is becoming increasingly important in a number of countries. Such ownership is likely to be associated with commercial management, geared especially to timber production.

The category of private ownership, therefore, embraces diverse forms ranging from forest-products industries to private and corporate investors and personal owners of varying scales. Industrial and investment ownership are usually characterised by profit maximisation and maximum timber production. Small-scale private owners, on the other hand, are likely to be less interested in timber production and may place greater emphasis on considerations such as amenity, wildlife and recreation. Both these broad categories of ownership have attracted government concern or intervention in various parts of the world. Sub-optimal timber production from small privately owned forests is perceived as a problem in some countries, while some regulation of forest practices has also been introduced for environmental reasons in various countries around the world. These issues are discussed later in this chapter.

Ownership: general trends and national patterns

While state ownership dominates the forest resource in general terms, the detailed pattern is complicated by conflicting trends and contrasting patterns. Overall, common-property ownership has been largely displaced by state ownership, which in turn has partly given way to private ownership. In some cases, however, the 'state' stage of this simple model has been omitted, and in others there has been at least partial reversal of the sequence.

Within a country, there may be a distinct and significant geographical pattern of ownership. In the United States, for example, the federal government owns 34 per cent of the total forest area, but most federal forests are located in the west. On the other hand, most private 'industrial' and 'non-industrial' forests are in the south and east respectively. In Canada, most of the federal forest is on poor land in the north: the federal forest accounts for 27 per cent of the Canadian forest area but only 4 per cent of the wood volume (Dunster, 1988). Distinct contrasts may exist between the ownership classes in terms of the nature and potential of the resource as well as its management: in Quebec and Ontario, for example, the private forests make a larger contribution to industrial production than their relative size would suggest, because of their better soils and climate (Lortie, 1983). Such contrasts make inter-sector comparison of management difficult to carry out meaningfully: for example in the United States industrial owners have usually taken the lead in intensifying forest management and use, but this has been facilitated by factors of land quality, access and proximity to markets (Bingham, 1985).

The significance of ownership is profound. Different ownership classes usually have contrasting characteristics of size and composition: for example in the (ten) European Community countries, the average holding sizes for private, communal and state forests are respectively 4.5, 119 and 910 hectares. In Sweden, state forests are typically subject to large-scale clear felling operations combined with replanting with native species, whereas in company forests similar large-scale fellings are followed by replanting with both native and exotic species such as Lodgepole pine (*Pinus contorta*). The much smaller private forests are characterised by felling and replanting on a much smaller scale, combined with an emphasis on the production of valuable saw logs rather than pulp wood (Gaunitz, 1984). In short, the way in which the forest resource is used and managed depends to a large degree on its ownership.

Management

The primary significance of ownership lies in the control of the resource and in the potential for its management and use. The significance of management, at a time of rapid contraction in the extent of the forest resource, is obvious. Unfortunately, however, the availability of meaningful and reliable data on the extent and nature of management is even less than that for ownership. The reasons for this state of affairs are readily understandable. For example, management can take an almost infinite variety of forms, and can variously include the control and regulation of logging, protection against fire and disease, and silvicultural treatments. Furthermore, management plans may be prepared but not implemented. In short,

> Existing management systems vary so much that it is quite impossible to press them into a couple of main categories and believe that this says much about the truth. It is important to remember that a large proportion of the forests in many regions are officially under working plans or legal control and are reported as such, while in reality the different plans and laws are not followed. (Persson, 1974)

In recent decades, therefore, few attempts have been made to collect world-wide data on forest management.

Nevertheless, a number of firm conclusions can be reached about the nature of management control. First, it is clear that state ownership does not necessarily correlate with state management, nor indeed with any form of management. Second, it is apparent that much of the world forest area remains unmanaged in any formal sense. Third, there is disquieting evidence that the extent of forest management has actually decreased in much of the world forest area in recent decades.

Although most countries with significant forest areas have national forest services, the staffing, funding and general influence of these services are often extremely limited in relation to the extent of forest for which they have responsibility. Even if an ownership basis for management exists, in practical terms effective management and control of the resource may be impossible. Furthermore, in some countries state ownership of the forest is spread across a number of government departments and other agencies and is not necessarily concentrated solely in the state forest service. In the Soviet Union, for example, which is characterised by almost complete state ownership, 92 per cent of the forest is administered by the central forestry authorities but the remainder is in the hands of various ministries and agencies together with state and collective farms (Holowacz, 1985). Similarly, in China most of the state-owned forest land is administered by the Ministry of Forestry, but other ministries such as those for water conservation, land reclamation, railways and light industry also have their own forests or plantations. Where management does occur, therefore, its goals may vary according to the nature of the responsible body. In many countries the state-owned forest may be divided between the national forest service and conservation agencies, each of which is likely to have different objectives.

A relatively small proportion of the world forest area receives any kind of formal management. Data collected by the FAO for the 1963 World Forest Inventory indicated that 0.975 million hectares out of a total forest area of 4.229 million hectares were under management plans. World-wide, therefore, around 23 per cent of the forest area was subject to such plans, but this figure conceals major contrasts from region to region. In Europe and North America, the proportions of the forest area under management plans were respectively 55 and 67 per cent, but in Latin America and Africa, on the other hand, the proportions were under 2 per cent (FAO, 1966).

There is no directly comparable source of data for more recent years, but it has been concluded by the World Resources Institute from a variety of FAO data that less than 25 per cent of the world's forests were actively managed in the early 1980s (WRI, 1986). At first sight, this figure may seem to indicate that the relative extent of management has at least been maintained in recent decades. On closer examination, however, it emerges that over three-quarters of the total reported 'managed' area lies in the Soviet Union, and that most of the apparent increase in the extent of management in the areas included in the data contained in Table 5.4 is accounted for by the Soviet Union alone. The table contains a salutary reminder of the sensitivity of conclusions about management to the nature of definitions and reported areas. If the Soviet Union is excluded from the table, a very different conclusion is reached, with an apparent decrease in the extent of management in Europe, Africa and Latin America, combined with a very modest increase in Asia.

In Europe, the decrease is likely to reflect changing definitions and accuracy rather than real changes. In Europe, most of the publicly owned forest is covered either by plans or by controls. In the EEC (10), for example, just over 75 per cent of the publicly owned area is covered by management plans and the remainder is subject to controls (UNECE/FAO, 1985). Of the privately owned forests in the same region, however, only 6 per cent are covered by management plans. As will be discussed subsequently, the management of small, highly fragmented private forests has emerged as a major issue in parts of Europe, the United States and Japan.

In Africa, the area subject to management plans has fallen from over 10 million to under 2 million hectares, or less than 1 per cent of the closed

Table 5.4   Management of forests in selected areas

	Total area (closed forest)	(000 ha) Area under management plans 1963	1983
Europe	145 486	93 010	83484
Soviet Union	791 600	299 965	791600
United States	195 256	84 378	102362
Tropical Asia	305 510	37 370	39790
Tropical Africa	216 634	10 610	1735
Tropical America	678 855	2 444	522

Source: Based on data in WRI (1986)

forest area. Furthermore, much of the managed area is concentrated in a small number of countries. In the early 1980s, two-thirds of the managed area in Africa was in Ghana (Lanly, 1982) and three-quarters in Ghana and Uganda (WRI, 1986). Political turmoil in the latter has severely reduced the extent and effectiveness of management, and illegal agricultural encroachment and increases in unlicensed exploitation of forest produce have followed (Hamilton, 1984). In former Belgian and British colonies, working plans, often complemented by silvicultural treatments for forest regeneration and enrichment, were introduced early, and intensive forest management in these areas amounted to 4–4.5 million hectares of closed forest by 1960. Thereafter, management plans were abandoned in many countries, as a result of population pressure on forests and staff shortages in forest services.

In Latin America there has been a similar decline, and in Asia there is a similar pattern of concentration to that in Africa. India alone accounts for 80 per cent of the managed area (WRI, 1986). Furthermore, while the extent of management in Asia may not have declined as it has in Africa and Latin America, its intensity has decreased in some areas. For example silvicultural treatment in Sabah in effect stopped after 1977, and in practice thereafter the forest was treated as a wasting resource (Gillis, 1988b). In many areas management plans have been drawn up but never implemented, and in the tropics as a whole the proportion of the forest under management is tiny. Less than 5 per cent of the productive closed tropical forest, for example, was managed around 1980 (Lanly, 1982).

In the face of population pressure on the forest and inadequate funding and staffing of forest services, management plans have been abandoned or have not been followed up in many areas, and even if the technical ability to prepare and implement a management plan exists, the political will to do so may not always be present. In a number of countries such as Nigeria, Zaïre and Tanzania, the extent of management has contracted considerably in recent decades, and Lanly (1982) concluded that intensively managed forests no longer existed in these countries. In these and other countries, forest services and forest management (in at least some form) date back to colonial times, but the robustness of the management institutions has been inadequate in the face of subsequent social and political pressures. The fact that many of these institutions have colonial origins may also have hindered their survival and development in the face of modern pressures.

The extent of forest management is therefore limited, and it is clear that its development is not keeping pace with the growth of pressures on the forest resource. In particular, large areas of state-owned forest in the tropics are now subject to forest utilisation contracts between government and logging company, and the nature and enforcement of these contracts (or concessions) is an issue of fundamental importance to the future of the tropical forest in particular.

Forest utilisation contracts

In many countries part of the state-owned forest is used privately (at least for timber production) under various agreements usually known as forest utilisation contracts or concessions. In the absence of the capability or will to utilise the forest resource themselves, governments use such arrangements as an alternative to alienating the state-owned forests to the private sector. Utilisation contracts concede to private users, often in the form of corporations, the right to harvest timber under prescribed conditions and in return for payment. Some provision for management, for example in the form of replanting, is usually included in the terms of the contract.

Such concessions are associated especially with the use of the tropical forest, and also with problems of distribution of benefits and of conservation. They are not confined to the tropics, however, nor are their associated problems confined to that zone. Much of the Canadian forest, for example, has been subject to this form of private use under public ownership, and serious problems of resource conservation have arisen. By the 1960s, both government and the forest industry recognised that regeneration on cutover lands was inadequate. Companies claimed that they could not reasonably be expected to regenerate the forests themselves when they had no title to the land (Suffling and Michalenko, 1980). Thirty years' experience of one licence in one Canadian province was characterised by a failure of regeneration, less attractive species composition of the second crop, poorer annual growth rates than expected, and smaller projected volumes per unit area (Reed, 1983).

In recent decades there has been a major expansion in the extent of concession agreements, as well as considerable development in their terms and robustness. In the early 1960s, their total extent may have been little more than 30 million hectares, or less than 1 per cent of the forest area (based on FAO (1963)). By 1980, concessions had been granted to approximately 120 million hectares of tropical forest over the previous two decades (Gray, 1983). Around 50 million hectares of forest are under utilisation contracts in Africa, 40 million hectares in the Far East and 10 million hectares in South America (Prats Llaurado and Speidel, 1981).

Much of the rapid growth in logging in the tropical forest in the 1960s and 1970s was based on these concessions. In the Ivory Coast, two-thirds of the productive forest area became subject to contracts between 1965 and 1972 (Gillis, 1988a). In western Malaysia, 424,000 hectares of logging concessions were handed out in 1972, compared with 60,000 hectares in 1970 (Hurst, 1987). In the Philippines, the area under concession agreements increased dramatically from 4.5 to 10.5 million hectares between 1960 and 1970 (Repetto, 1988), and timber production increased from 3.8 million cubic metres in 1955 to 11 million cubic metres in 1968 (Boado, 1988).

Contract lengths
Utilization contracts occur in various forms, ranging from short term (one to three years) through medium term (five to ten years) to long term (fifteen to twenty-five or more years). Short-term contracts are usually granted to small-scale operators involved in local wood supply. Those of intermediate length are more likely to be geared to sawmill operations developed by logging companies, while long-term contracts may be linked to large, integrated forest industries drawing on a forest area of up to 200,000 hectares (Schmithusen, 1976). One of the persistent problems of concessions has been their length, and in particular the relationship between concession length, regrowth and cutting cycles. For example, Indonesian logging regulations prescribe that thirty-five years should elapse between cuts, but the standard concession agreements are for only twenty years (Walker and Hoesada, 1986; Repetto, 1988). Contracts that are much shorter than cutting cycles are unlikely to encourage good conservation practice. On the other hand, long concessions have not always meant that the value of the forest has been carefully conserved (Gillis, 1988c): they may be necessary but not sufficient for this objective.

Prior to the Second World War, long-term concessions for up to 100 years were granted to logging companies, but newly independent governments sometimes viewed such arrangements as vestiges of colonialism, and concession periods were shortened in the hope that more frequent renegotiation would produce better terms. By the 1980s, concessions were typically for periods of only five to ten years, even for large forest tracts, and few exceeded twenty years. In Sabah, for example, one and five-year licences covered 50 per cent of the total concession area in 1980 (Gillis, 1988b). Countries such as Ghana and Nigeria already used long-term contracts in the period between 1945 and 1955: indeed, in Ghana, prior to independence, concessions were granted for periods of fifty and sometimes for as long as ninety-nine years, but in 1971 their lengths were set at a minimum of five and a maximum of twenty-five years (Repetto, 1988). Long-term contracts were introduced more recently in French-speaking countries such as the Ivory Coast (Schmithusen, 1976). There, contracts of variable lengths of up to fifteen years were introduced between 1965 and 1968, but normal length reverted to five years in 1969. A general problem is that contracts may have been agreed and the forests opened up to exploitative use before the forest service was in a position to work out either the technical concepts on which long-term usefulness could rest or suitable means of enforcing the contract terms. Ivory Coast is cited as a particular example where the former point applies (Schmithusen, 1979). In some countries the disadvantages of both long and short agreements may be at least partly avoided by granting rights for periods of twenty or twenty-five years, with renewal occurring every five years if performance has been satisfactory (Dunster, 1988).

The significance of concession lengths in particular and the security of tenure in general extends beyond cutting cycles and forest managment to investment in forest industries. The nature of tenure may be an important factor in the investment decisions of forest-products firms, which may be understandably reluctant to invest in costly plant in areas where they have only short-term tenure. By relating tenure to the economic life of industrial plant, governments in countries (such as Canada) with very extensive state (provincial) ownership could regulate capital investment by forest-product companies (e.g. Nautiyal and Rawat, 1985), and hence exert an indirect as well as a direct influence on forest management.

Concession holders

The classic forest utilisation contract is drawn up between a foreign logging company (sometimes part of a transnational corporation) and a national forest service. Foreign interests are often prominent in tropical forests, but they are not confined to these latitudes. For example American and Japanese companies have interests, through local subsidiaries or joint ventures, in Canada and Brazil as well as in south-east Asia (Atkins, 1983).

Large proportions of forest investment in many tropical countries are typically foreign. In Ivory Coast, for example, the proportion is 79 per cent, whilst it is 85 and 89 per cent respectively in Congo and in the Central African Republic (Contreras, 1987). Especially in Africa, much of the foreign investment has been oriented towards exports of tropical hardwoods to European markets. In south-east Asia, much of the orientation has been towards Japan and the United States. In the Philippines, for example, subsidiaries of large US forest-products companies such as Weyerhauser, Georgia Pacific, Boise Cascade and International Paper became major concession-holders in the 1960s (Boado, 1988), while the first two of these together with Unilever were awarded concessions in Kalimantan in 1970 (Gillis, 1988c).

Such arrangements with overseas or transnational companies have been widely perceived as disadvantageous to the host country: disproportionate shares of benefits are believed to go to the transnationals. In recent years many attempts have been made to tilt the balance of advantage towards the host country. One approach has been to outlaw wholly owned foreign ventures, and to secure greater involvement of local interests. In Malaysia, Malays and other indigenous groups are favoured in the granting of concessions, and direct participation by others is ruled out. This provision, however, is sometimes evaded by 'back-door' arrangements, under which the nominal concession-holder serves merely as a figure-head (Kumar, 1986). In Indonesia, foreign ventures were prohibited from 1975, and thereafter all investments from abroad had to be in the form of joint

Table 5.5   Forest concessions in Indonesia, 1981

Companies based in	Area (000 ha)	Number	Of which joint ventures
Malaysia	1753	16	14
Hong Kong	1465	16	11
Japan	1362	12	10
USA	1081	4	2
Philippines	988	8	7
South Korea	875	6	4
Singapore	420	5	5
France	260	1	0
Italy	236	2	2
Netherlands	100	1	0
Panama	85	1	0
Other overseas countries	215	3	3
Sub-total	8840	75	15
Indonesia	40019	433	
Total	48859	508	

Source: Based on Walker and Hoesada (1986)

operations with national or state companies (Walker and Hoesada, 1986). Joint ventures have not always been successful. Some transnational corporations have regarded such investments as necessary evils, and have paid little more than lip service to the concept, sometimes using obsolete equipment discarded from European mills after the Second World War (Contreras, 1987). Even when successfully established in technical terms, a joint-venture plant may function as a social and economic enclave, with few multiplier effects or links to the rest of the economy.

In some cases assets of foreign logging companies were in effect nationalised: for example, in 1973 the Ghana government required all multinational natural resource companies to surrender 55 per cent of their equity (Repetto, 1988), and fear of expropriation caused the withdrawal of US companies from Indonesia forest enterprises in the early 1980s (Walker and Hoesada, 1986). A prominent theme has been the growth of joint ventures involving foreign partners with local interests. Details of these in the case of Indonesia are shown in Table 5.5.

Foreign companies have been and are still prominent as concession holders both in the example of Indonesia shown in Table 5.5 and in the tropical world more generally. Initially after independence, many of these firms were linked to the former colonial power, but more recently Japanese and subsequently Korean and Taiwanese companies have become very active. In Papua New Guinea, for example, 50 per cent of the timber rights are held by Japanese companies (Contreras, 1987). More recently still, logging firms from Malaysia and the Philippines have obtained concessions in neighbouring countries. In Sabah, for example, companies from the

Philippines. India and Malaysia have become involved in joint ventures (Gillis, 1988b). Major multinational companies based in the West have now largely withdrawn, and have been replaced by smaller transnationals from the Third World and locally-based enterprises.

The geographical character of the concession-holders has therefore changed markedly in recent decades, and while foreign influences are still strong, domestic entrepreneurs have been taking an increasing share of concessions in many tropical countries. This in itself, however, does not necessarily ensure increased benefit to the people of the host country: in the case of the Philippines, for example, both the traditional landed élites and those who came to power with ex-President Marcos or the military succeeded in acquiring substantial logging interests (Boado, 1988).

Concession terms

The terms of forest utilisation contracts are both varied and controversial. The balance of advantage between host government (and country) and the logging company is delicately poised: terms too favourable to the latter result in a loss of revenue and perhaps a seriously damaged forest resource, while terms that are too stringent may deter investment and hinder the utilisation of the resource.

Numerous systems of forest charges and forest revenue arrangements have been devised, and some of the more common of these are summarised in Table 5.6. Concessions may be linked to licence fees or annual ground rentals, both of which are usually very low. For example in Ivory Coast an initial fee of around (US)$0.25 per hectare is levied, and in Liberia an annual ground rental of $0.25 per hectare per year is charged. Alternatively, fees may be based on the volume of the annual allowable cut.

In addition, charges are usually levied on the timber actually harvested, and may be on a per tree basis, on the basis of timber volume, or less commonly on an area basis. For example Ghana imposes charges ranging from $2.20 to $19.60 per tree depending on species, while the range in Thailand is from $2.00 to $5.00. Volume-based charges are common and are usually the most important source of revenue from the exploitation of the forest resource. The charge is usually at a fixed rate per unit volume, depending on tree species, and may be differentiated on the basis of the destination intended for the timber. For example in Indonesia, the charge for domestically processed logs was $8.00, while that for logs destined for export was $52.00.

Charges may be imposed on processed forest products in addition to or instead of volume-based charges. These may be administratively convenient, but they do not encourage efficiency of use since they are based on the output of sawnwood or other product rather than the harvesting or input of logs. Export charges on logs are a common forest charge and a major source of forest revenue in some companies. Such charges may be levied in order to encourage domestic processing, and may be differentiated according to species. Liberia, for example, imposes charges ranging from $2.00 to $50.00 depending on species. Lower export charges may also be imposed

Table 5.6   Types of forest charges and alternative forest revenue arrangements

On concessions	—licence fees —annual ground rentals —fees based on standing timber volume/annual allowable cut
On timber harvested	—per tree charges —volume based charges —area based changes
On forest products	—processed forest products —minor forest products
On forest trade	—export charges on logs and/or products
On companies	—income/corporation tax —royalties
Government participation	—joint ventures —full government ownership

Source: Based on Gray (1983).

on processed products, and these are usually differentiated according to degree of processing. Mandatory government participation through joint ventures is a further common means by which economic benefit can be derived by the host government. These arrangements draw on the technical, managerial and commercial skills of the private partners while retaining measures of control and economic benefits. In some instances such as Ghana where nationalisation occurred in 1972, the forest industries are state-owned and controlled.

The strengths and weaknesses of the various components of forest revenue systems are reviewed by Gray (1983). In general terms the degree of success with which host governments have captured the economic benefits from forest exploitation have been limited but variable. Problems such as transfer pricing in multinational companies and corruption in government circles have frequently been experienced. Other problems may also exist. For example, a logging company in Papua New Guinea had its application for lease renewal refused, on the grounds of non-compliance with the terms of the lease. Pressure for the government of the country from which the company originated was followed by temporary renewal (Wigston, 1984). According to Westoby (1989, p.157), 'It would be possible to fill a book with examples of the unsavoury aspects of the tropical timber trade.'

Illegal timber cutting and smuggling has denied some countries the full benefits of their timber production. For example, recorded Japanese log imports from the Philippines in 1980 amounted to 1.1 million cubic metres, but recorded log exports from the Philippines to Japan were only 0.5 million cubic metres (Repetto, 1988). Overall, Repetto concludes that the Philippines government managed to capture only 17 per cent of the available rents from concessions during the period from 1979 to 1982, compared with 38 per cent in the cases of Indonesia and Ghana. Illegal felling may be as great a problem to the concession-holder as it is to the host government. Along with the incursion of shifting agriculture, it may be detrimental to the interests of the concession-holder as well as to the government, and 'exclusivity' may be an important issue when a contract is being negotiated (McNeil, 1981). In the Philippines, the government in 1987 decided to reward informers with 30 per cent of the value of any illegally felled logs (MacKenzie, 1988).

The nature of forest utilisation contracts affects the state of the resource as well as the economic benefits to the government. In Canada, for example, the company securing the use rights accepts responsibility for protection against fire, pests and diseases and for the regeneration of the logged area (Dunster, 1988). Two different provisions for reforestation have been widely incorporated in contracts. These are an obligation on the concession-holder to carry out reforestation itself, and a requirement that a reforestation fee is paid to the forest service which then carries out the operation. Schmithusen (1976) concludes that contracts requiring direct reforestation have in many cases proved unsuccessful, while fee-based systems, such as employed in Liberia and some francophone African countries have been more effective. In 1980 Indonesia introduced a reforestation deposit of $4.00 per cubic metre harvested (in Kalimantan and Sumatra). It seems that this measure has not induced concessionaires to undertake significant reforestation activity, although it has discouraged logging on marginal stands and increased government revenues per cubic metre of log production by 14 per cent (Gillis, 1988c). Elsewhere there has been similar difficulty in achieving reforestation: it is reported, for example, that 90 per cent of concession-holders in the Philippines in the 1970s and early 1980s violated concession agreements by failing to carry out reforestation programmes (Boado, 1988). Since 1988, logging companies have had to deposit a sum of money equivalent to the cost of replanting (MacKenzie, 1988).

The understandable wish to retain a higher share of the benefits arising from the use of the forest resource by discriminating against foreign concession-holders may itself have had adverse effects. It is suggested that the more capital-intensive operations of foreign-based companies, involving the construction of all-weather roads, typically remove a higher proportion of the harvestable stems than those of smaller 'dirt-road' loggers. With a lower utilization rate, a greater area is harvested each year (Gillis, 1988c). In addition, foreign firms may be well suited in terms of capital, technology and management to invest in plantations in their concession areas, but without secure property rights and confidence of poliical stability will be unlikely to do so.

The overall level of forest charges is likely to have an effect on the way in which the resource is used and managed. Rents per cubic metre harvested in Ivory Coast have been much lower than those in Ghana, for example, and deforestation rates have been higher. Furthermore, the grading of charges according to size and species of tree can have an obvious effect on the way in which harvesting proceeds, as can the minimum utilisation standards written into the contracts. In many early concessions, these were often poorly defined (Schmithusen, 1976). In the Ivory Coast, for example, harvesting methods were not prescribed prior to 1972 (Gillis, 1988a). More recently these and other conditions have often been tightened and extended: in the case of the Philippines, for example, from 1979 each concession holder has been required to set aside 5 per cent of the concession area as a wilderness area not subject to logging (Boado, 1988). Governments have generally become more experienced and sophisticated in their use of forest utilisation contracts, and more recently have been more successful in areas such as the protection of customary rights to the forest and the provision of roads and services for public use (Pardo, 1985).

In addition to defects in the terms of contracts there have been major and widespread problems of enforcement. In the Philippines, for example, large transnational companies have been found generally to keep to the law, but few controls have been found to be effective on smaller firms (MacKenzie, 1988). Even after the prescription of harvesting methods in Ivory Coast in 1972, enforcement was so inadequate that in practice concession-holders were not required to follow any particular method of selection or cutting (Gillis, 1988a). In practice, enforcement may be very difficult to achieve, not only at the level of the relationship between the concession-holder and government but also at the forest level of the relationship between the former and its contractors or workers. In theory, state ownership, combined with controlled utilisation, might be expected to mean that the resource would be used for the benefit of the state's population, and that it would be conserved from generation to generation. In practice neither of these expectations is always fulfilled. All too often the state permits the benefits of forest use to be biased towards a small section of the population, such as the ruling class.

In many countries 'concession' forests have been impoverished or degraded: the granting of concessions has been followed by a phase of destructive exploitation. In terms of conservation as well as of economic and social benefits, the performance of many projects has been disappointing. In Papua New Guinea, for example, an integrated project producing sawn timber, veneer and woodchips was launched by a Japanese company in 1973. It took ten years for reforestation to reach its planned rate, and by 1983 36,750 hectares of forest had been cleared but only 4,755 hectares reforested (Seddon, 1984). In short, the natural resource was depleted. Leslie (1980) concludes that 'Forests, on the whole, are simply being mined, . . . without any real concern for what happens afterwards.' He considers that weaknesses in bargaining skills is a fundamental cause of unsatisfactory concession agreements. A reluctance to invest sufficient resources in the stewardship and management of the public forest resource has also been identified as a major factor (Repetto, 1988). As a result, the value of the resource has decreased and the people have failed to benefit as they ought from the utilisation of their resource.

This conclusion applies especially to many tropical countries where use of the forest resource is based on contracts or concessions. It is not peculiar to these latitudes, however. Much of the Canadian forest, for example, is used in the same way and similar trends and problems in the condition of the resource are found there, despite the existence of a long-established forest industry. Both in Canada and in many tropical countries, the forest industries have been blamed for the state of the forest which they have utilised. In the case of the former, however, Baskerville (1988) presents an alternative interpretation by attributing the blame to society in general for failing to carry out effective management and for failing to accept its costs, and to public ownership in particular for having been a major causal factor in the degradation of the forests. Whatever the merits of this argument may be, it is a reminder that public or state ownership is not a guarantee of forest conservation, especially where it is combined with private use. On the other hand private ownership and management may also give rise to serious problems, as the ensuing section indicates.

Management in fragmented, privately-owned forests

In countries such as the United States of America and Japan as well as in parts of Europe, the ownership of much of the forest is fragmented into tiny holdings. The nature of the property inheritance laws has contributed to this fragmentation in some countries such as France, while traditions of farm forests, where agriculture and forestry are combined on the same holding, are long-established in countries such as Finland.

The management of fragmented forest holdings is characterised by several problems. In some cases, there is a lack of clear objectives for ownership and therefore of clear goals for management. In this partial vacuum little or no management may take place. If it does take place, it may not be geared to timber production. In addition, the small scale of many forest holdings means that diseconomies of scale are experienced, and the resulting economics of timber production may mean that little harvesting takes place. This may mean sub-optimal supply of timber for processing industries, and can in turn lead to accusations of mismanagement on the parts of small forest owners and to attempts by both governments and wood-using industries to encourage greater levels of timber production.

The objectives of small forest owners
These may differ markedly from those of both industrial owners and public agencies. In particular, they may differ from the former in terms of the primacy of timber production as a goal, and they may contrast with the latter in respects such as environmental protection. As might be expected, active management is related to the underlying motivations and objectives (e.g. Kurtz and Lewis, 1981), and is associated with characteristics such as size of ownership, age, education, place of residence (resident or absentee) and income (e.g. Greene and Blatner, 1986; Romm, Tuazon and Washburn, 1987).

Traditionally, most small forest owners were farmers, and many still are, especially in Europe. In countries such as Finland, for example, attitudes

Figure 5.2   Distribution of private ownerships, by primary reason for owning forest land (a) in Pennsylvania, and (b) in Maryland

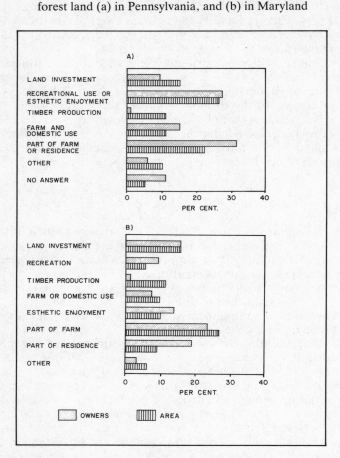

Source: (a) Birch and Dennis (1980) (b) Kingsley and Birch (1980)

to forest management contrast sharply between older farmers on small farms, who have a preference for the subsistence economy and minimum use of money, and more commercial farmers (Hahtola, 1973). The fortunes of agriculture may have significant implications for forest management. In Austria, for example, low profitability has driven many farmers to seek other employment, with the result that many farm forests are neglected (Eckmüllner, 1986). In Japan, some woodlots have been sold to forest companies when their traditional owners have given up farming, but in other cases they have retained their holdings and have run the woodlots on a part-time basis (Riethmuller and Fenelon, 1988). A large but decreasing area of forest land is still owned by farmers in the United States, but much has passed into the hands of non-farmer individuals. Constraints such as capital and time may limit the amount of forest management provided by farmers, while on the other hand factors such as absenteeism may affect that provided by non-farmer owners.

Timber production is rarely a primary reason for the small-scale ownership of forest land. Factors such as aesthetics, recreation, wildlife and increased land value may be equally or more important (e.g. MacConnell and Archey, 1986: see also Figure 5.2). In many instances the present owner has inherited or otherwise acquired his forest property by accident rather than design, and has given little conscious consideration to what he seeks from it. In many instances forest areas may be owned simply because they happen to be parts of farms or parts of residences. These were cited as the most important reason for ownership on 36 per cent of the privately owned commercial forest land in the state of Maryland, for example (Kingsley and Birch, 1980). Aesthetic enjoyment, recreation and land investment were other important reasons, and timber production was the main objective of only 2 per cent of the forest owners, who owned 12 per cent of the forest area. In the neighbouring state of Pennsylvania, only 1 per cent of owners held forest land primarily for timber production (Birch and Dennis, 1980). Many private non-industrial ownerships are short term. For example in nine Northeastern states, 53 per cent of the privately owned commercial timberland is held by the same owner for fewer than twenty-five years, and 30 per cent for fewer than ten years (USDA, 1982). A clear conflict exists with the time-scale of forest management.

Overall in the United States it has been estimated that only 5 per cent of private non-industrial owners manage their forests for timber production, using all or most practicable forestry practices. Around one-third have some interest in forestry practices geared to timber production, while nearly half have no interest in intensified practices but may from time to time sell timber grown without active management (Cunningham, 1982). When small owners do harvest timber, it is often for the purpose of raising cash to meet a financial crisis (Teeguarden, 1985), rather than on the basis of long-term planning. In Japan, 60 per cent of small woodlot owners grow trees as a store of wealth rather than to maximise timber production. Around 30 per cent have no special interest in timber production, using their lots primarily for recreation or for mushroom production (Riethmuller and Fenelon, 1988).

Generally similar findings on small-scale ownership and management are reported in other parts of the developed world. For example, Russell (1985) found that many woodlands in England and Wales are not managed primarily for financial gain, but for objectives such as recreation, and for landownership for its own sake or to maintain a family tradition.

In such circumstances it is not surprising that timber production is not maximised. In Pennsylvania, for example, only 25 per cent of private forest owners have actually harvested timber, but this proportion increases with size of holding. The average holding size for timber harvesters was found to be around twenty hectares; compared with an average of approximately ten hectares for all private forest holdings (Birch and Dennis, 1980).

Similarly, in eastern Oklahoma, a clear relationship was found between size of holding and management. Units of 4–20 hectares were essentially not managed commercially; those from 20 to 280 hectares had a significant amount of commercial management but suffered from size-related problems, while those of over 280 hectares were usually managed commercially (Thompson and Jones, 1981).

The existence of a relationship between size of forest holding and timber production had been widely confirmed, and has been explained in terms of factors such as economies of scale and marginal utility as well as objectives of ownership (e.g. Straka et al., 1984). Several other variables have also been identified as being related to timber production. In New Brunswick, for example, absenteeism and increasing income levels were found to be negatively related to timber harvesting (Jammick and Beckett, 1988). If the forest is owned for its amenity value and the owner is not dependent on it for income, then such relationships are readily understandable.

Assistance programmes
In many countries government incentives are offered in order to improve management in general and to increase timber production in particular. In the United States, for example, the tax legislation in many states is designed to encourage the management of 'non-industrial private forests': property tax relief is offered by assessing use-value rather than market-value, and various means of deferring timber taxes are available (Meeks, 1982). In Massachusetts, for example, the owner who practises forest management is rewarded with lower property taxes (Konrad and Harou, 1985). In addition, advisory or extension services may be used to encourage active management and timber production. Similar measures have proved effective in leading to increased frequency of timber sales and increased volume of production in Finland, for example (Jarvelainen, 1986).

Extension may be combined with cost-sharing, which is one of the most widely practised means of encouraging management and timber production. In the United States, the Forestry Incentives Program (FIP) was authorized by Congress in 1973, in response to concern about the low level of timber management on much of the privately owned forest area. Under FIP, the federal government shares up to 75 per cent of the cost of planting or treatment, on forest holdings of up to 400 hectares owned by private individuals. In addition, planting is encouraged by income tax regulations. By 1981, 0.5 million hectares had been reforested and 0.4 million hectares improved (Risbrudt et al., 1983), and in 1985 alone around 280,000 hectares were planted or seeded by private owners in the American South, mostly with assistance from FIP and/or tax credits (Royer and Moulton, 1987). In addition, some states introduced their own measures: for example the Californian forest improvement programme, introduced in 1980, initially offered up to 90 per cent of the costs of forest improvement (Romm et al., 1987).

Such incentives usually have different effects and different levels of uptake amongst different types of owners. In Texas, for example, the strongest interest was found in well-educated business and professional people with above-average incomes and urban residences (Hickman and Gehlhausen, 1981). Also the obstacles to forest management may vary, from lack of capital and lack of technical knowledge to incompatible goals of ownership (Worrell and Irland, 1975). Different forms of assistance may therefore be required in different circumstances, and in the light of the objectives of many small owners it has been suggested that programmes aimed at developing non-timber outputs such as grazing, wildlife and recreation might produce more management than programmes strictly geared to timber production (Greene and Blatner, 1986). There has been considerable debate about the economic effectiveness of cost-sharing and extension services (e.g. Boyd et al., 1988), and most of the debate has concentrated on the single criterion of timber production. Nevertheless, there are signs that performance on private non-industrial forests is becoming similar to that on other ownership classes in states such as Georgia (McComb, 1975) and North Carolina (Wallace and Newman, 1986). In Massachusetts, the percentage of owners harvesting timber increased from 19 to 29 per cent between 1963 and 1983 (MacConnell and Archey, 1986). Overall, the gap between small private and industrial forests in terms of volume of saw timber harvested per unit area has narrowed over the years (Cunningham, 1982).

On the other hand trends in timber prices may have a counter-effect: in the early 1980s, decreasing timber prices led to a waning interest in policies to stimulate timber production amongst small owners (De Steigner and Royer, 1986), while apprehension about prices and returns was a major factor discouraging the restocking of harvested timber land in the American South (Royer and Kaiser, 1983).

Although extension services and cost-sharing programmes may help to encourage some small-scale owners to produce timber, they are unlikely to do so in all cases. Timber production is perceived as environmentally disrupting by some owners with interests in wildlife or landscape conservation. If production is to increase, that association needs to be weakened and the one between timber production and increasing abundance of wildlife strengthened (Young and Reichenbach, 1987).

In addition to government programmes such as FIP, a number of other means can be employed to improve forest management and timber production in small, privately owned forests. In an effort to improve timber supply, private forest-products companies may themselves offer free management advice to small owners, without necessarily insisting on purchasing the timber in return (e.g. Meyer et al., 1986). 'Industrial' management has been extended over substantial areas of forest in the American South by means of increment contracts. Under these, the owner receives annual payments based on the average annual growth of wood that the land is capable of producing under management, and linked to prevailing prices (Zinn and Miller, 1984). Two means of overcoming the disadvantages of fragmentation are especially common: the setting-up of associations or co-operatives of woodland owners, and of organisations that undertake harvesting and marketing (or even entire management) of small woodlands. Co-operation amongst small owners may also lead to improvements in management and in marketing. In Quebec, for example, organisation in co-operative marketing dates back to the late 1950s, and in the 1970s management organisations were formed (Lortie, 1983). In Japan there are as many as 2,105 forest-owner associations, accounting for almost two-thirds of the individual forest owners and for nearly one half of the total forest area (Imamura, 1982).

Government assistance may encourage such initiatives, in the hope that increases in timber production will follow. In West Germany, for example, both federal and state governments offer direct financial aid to co-operatives, which represent more than half of the total area of forest in ownership units of under 100 hectares, and 19 per cent of the entire forest area. These co-operatives, which on average involve ninety individual owners and 1000 ha, have brought about improvements in management, and clear differences in technical skills and awareness are reported to exist between members and non-members (Oedekoven, 1981). Nevertheless, it may be difficult to achieve co-operation in some areas, since the attitude of individual owners towards co-operatives may vary depending on factors such as age (Hahtola, 1973).

Forest laws

State influence on the use of the forest resource is clearly greater than that of agricultural land because of the extent of state ownership of forests around the world. This influence, however, is not restricted to forest land under the ownership of the state. As has been shown by the assistance programmes offered to small forest owners in the United States, it may also extend indirectly to the private sector. Furthermore, many states have enacted numerous laws to regulate the use of the forest resource, irrespective of its ownership, within their territories. In many instances these laws have been introduced incrementally or on an *ad hoc* basis, and they may be neither comprehensive nor integrated. Nevertheless, they have a long history, and the general trend in recent decades has been for them to become wide-ranging and more extensive. The extent to which the use of the private forest is influenced or regulated by government has increased rapidly in recent decades.

The enactment of forest laws dates back for several centuries in some countries. The earliest forest ordinances and other administrative measures date in France to at least as far back as the fourteenth century (ONF, 1966). Numerous attempts were made in medieval Scotland to halt or retard the removal of the native forest, initially in order to protect hunting forests and subsequently to protect the forest as a source of shipbuilding timber. As early as 1504, a law was passed requiring landowners to plant at least 0.4 hectares of woodland around their houses, in areas where there was no significant forest (e.g. Caird, 1980). Such laws often proved difficult or impossible to enforce, and their effectiveness was usually very limited. In Russia, for example, the tsarist government in 1888 introduced a law to conserve the forest, but over the next twenty years 3 million hectares of forest were cleared in European Russia alone (Chapter 3; Barr, 1988). Nevertheless, although their effect may often have been limited, it is clear that forest laws long predate the emergence of the modern state, and their enactment is a salutary reminder that forest problems long predate the present century.

Much of the present body of forest legislation, however, is a product of the modern period. Two distinct but interrelated areas of legislation (and government influence in general) can be identified. These are concerned with the direct protection of the forest resource from over-use or neglect, and with environmental issues arising from forestry practices. General land legislation and the regulation of investment are also of significance for forestry in some countries.

The regulation of use and protection of the resource

This is the largest category, which as has been indicated dates back at least as far as medieval times. Most of its modern form, however, dates from the mid-nineteenth century, and reflects a growing concern about encroachment on the forest as a result of growing demand for timber and agricultural pressures. Concern became especially pronounced in parts of Europe where until now the forest resource had seemed adequate or abundant. In central Europe the growing concern was reflected in the Austro-Hungarian Forestry Act of 1852, which sought to ensure that land under forest in that year had to remain so in perpetuity (Johann, 1984). In theory, forest devastation was now prohibited and reforestation after harvesting became a legal obligation. Similar fears of degradation of the forest resource were felt in Finland around the same time: steps to regulate the use and mangement of Finnish forests began around 1860, and over-cutting was prohibited in a law of 1886, under which the police were made responsible for enforcement. A further Forestry Act in 1917 sought to keep the existing forest area unchanged (Raumolin, 1984). In Sweden, regeneration of harvested forest became mandatory in 1903 (Lofgren, 1986).

Similar measures, designed to prohibit or control the clearing of all forests or of forests in certain areas, are in force in many other countries. In France, for example, prior authorisation is usually required before forest clearance can take place (Prieur, 1987), and in countries as diverse as Switzerland and Rwanda a condition of permission to clear forest is to reforest an area equivalent in extent (de Saussay, 1987).

These measures originating in Europe were paralleled by developments in the United States, which although not seeking to preserve the existing forest area, led to the setting-aside of national forests in 1891. More recently zoning laws and a variety of other measures, usually implemented at the state level, have sought to protect the forest against conversion to urban and other land uses (Cubbage and Siegel, 1985; Hickman, 1987). Further north in Canada, the immensity of the forest resource meant that the need for protection was less obvious, and in British Columbia, for example, use was essentially unregulated by government up until 1945 (Young, 1984). This did not necessarily mean, however, that government influence was absent. A positive decision to retain forest land in public ownership was taken as early as the 1860s, and in 1891 the export of logs from public land was prohibited or at least severely restricted. In Latin America, Argentina was one of the first countries to introduce legislation relating to forest protection, in the late nineteenth and early twentieth centuries (Solbrig, 1984). In countries such as Argentina, Colombia and Paraguay, a licence or permit is required from the forest authority before an owner can change the use of his land, and often these licences are only granted on the basis of a working plan (Prats Llaurado and Speidel, 1981). In an effort to halt deforestation in the Dominican Republic, the forest agency was transferred to the army in 1967 and in 1969 a new measure was introduced whereby both a permit from the forest agency and the approval of the president were required before live trees could be cut (Ramm et al., 1987). This helped to slow forest contraction but did not halt it, and illustrates the basic problem of enforcement.

Attempts at regulation usually seek either to preserve the forest area at its existing extent, or to ensure that forest management is on a sustained-yield basis. Sustained-yield management was devised in the state forests of Prussia at the end of the eighteenth century and formalised and developed during the nineteenth century. It has proved difficult to translate the principle it embodies into legislation that can effectively ensure its adoption. Even when governments have decreed that all forests within their jurisdiction have to be subject to sustained-yield forestry, the official concept has often been overwhelmed by other priorities or practical realities. For example a German forest law of 1940 stated that all forests had to be subject to sustained-yield forestry, but in practice over-cutting was the norm during the war years (Rubner, 1984). Nevertheless, attempts to introduce sustained-yield principles have usually been more successful than those aimed at preserving the extent of the forest area.

In addition to measures intended to preserve the existing forest area and to ensure management on sustained-yield principles, straightforward controls on the harvesting of some forest products, and especially of timber, have been introduced by some governments. In British Columbia, for example, the era of unregulated exploitation of the forest resource came to an end in 1945, and thereafter regulation was imposed through the medium of annual allowable cut geared to sustained-yield principles (Young, 1984). In some cases, government has sought to regulate production in a positive, rather than negative, sense. In such areas (and especially in Scandinavia), the problem of encouraging private owners to harvest timber has been addressed in an attempt to overcome the chronic underutilization of the capacity of forest-products industries, many of which are publicly owned. As from 1983, private owners in Sweden are required by law to undertake thinning and felling operations as appropriate (Wunder, 1983). In Quebec a similar shortage of wood fibre gave rise in 1986 to provincial legislation combining sustained yield, allocation of timber supply and forest management (Paille and Deffrasnes, 1988).

In Britain a system of felling licences was introduced following the heavy exploitation of the country's limited forest resources during the Second World War. These licences, administered by the state forestry service (the Forestry Commission), were intended to regulate the use of the forest and hence to conserve its timber resources. More recently, the same instrument has been used as a means of achieving more general environmental conservation, and in particular the conservation of broad-leaved trees and woodland. A very similar trend is apparent in the United States, where forest-practice legislation was initially introduced for reasons connected with timber production and more recently has been extended to environmental protection (Kreutzwiser and Crichton, 1987).

Regulation for environmental protection

This switch in the use of the instrument of the felling licence from timber conservation to environmental conservation epitomises a major trend in recent years. During this period, greatly increased attention has been focused on the environmental repercussions of forest use, and on the need to control adverse impacts. Some of the earliest attempts to regulate the use of the forest for environmental reasons were set in the Alps, where forests were perceived to play important roles in relation to floods, torrents and avalanches. Strenuous efforts have been made over many decades to maintain the protective role of forests in this respect by regulating the ways in which the forests are used and managed. By the early nineteenth century, the Swiss cantons were attempting to restrict the cutting of timber and to prohibit timber exports, as well as encouraging tree-planting. In 1876 the first federal forest law was enacted in Switzerland, and amongst other provisions required that cleared and logged areas be reforested or alternative areas nearby be reforested. It also prohibited the sale or redistribution of use or property rights in state, communal and corporation forests (Price, 1988).

This environmental concern in Alpine lands, initially focusing on flood control or mitigation, has extended to the protective function of forests in many other parts of the world. In Latin America, for example, a provision exists in countries such as Argentina and Paraguay for the expropriation of forest land required for erosion control, and for its subsequent management for that purpose (Prats Llaurado and Speidel, 1981). A similar trend is apparent even in countries not traditionally associated with extensive forests. For example tree-cutting in Saudi Arabia was banned in 1977, and a programme of planting for environmental protection is now in process (Abo-Hassan, 1983).

The initial awareness of the protective function of the forest and of a need to safeguard it has also subsequently widened to embrace concern for nature conservation and the avoidance of pollution. In Sweden, for example, the Forestry Acts of 1975 and 1979 required that forest management should consider nature conservation (Eckerberg, 1985; Falk and Mortnas, 1984). Previous legislation between 1903 and 1975 was geared towards improving timber yield, and indeed this objective was still pursued. For example additions made to Swedish forest law in 1983 required forest owners to undertake thinning operations, to carry out fellings in mature stands, and to disclose working plans. These measures were prompted by the perceived need to maintain an increase in the timber supply, in order to utilise the capacity of the mainly publicly owned forest-products industries (Wunder, 1983).

There was a clear general tendency during the 1970s and 1980s for the control of forestry practices to be increased. By 1985, eighteen states in the United States had various laws and other measures regulating or influencing the practice of forestry on private lands. In some states such as California and Vermont, they are comprehensive and mandatory, with effective sanctions for non-compliance. In other states they are selective and voluntary, and are much less effective (Kreutzwiser and Crichton, 1987). Such measures typically seek to regulate cutting and harvesting methods, road construction and stream crossings, and the application of herbicides. In individual states, they deal with issues such as watershed protection, fish and wildlife conservation, recreation, and even air quality and scenic beauty (e.g. Cubbage and Siegel, 1985; Henly and Ellefson, 1986; Meeks, 1982). A careful balance between regulation or enforcement and influence in this area is required if successful environmental protection is to be achieved on private forest land. In Sweden, for example, 'top-down' and 'bottom-up' perspectives are combined under the Forestry Act of 1979. In order to gain the confidence of forest owners and thereby to influence their management, care is required to ensure that the role of law enforcer is not overdone on the part of district forest officers (Eckerberg, 1986).

These laws and regulations may lead to increased costs of management or to losses in timber production, on both private and public forest land: some examples are illustrated in Table 6.19 (p.198). For example, cutting restrictions resulting from nature conservation in Finland are estimated to amount to 1.2 million cubic metres annually, against a total allowable cut of 62 million cubic metres, while the 'loss' of wood production in Denmark for reasons of recreation and nature conservation amounts to around US $4 million annually (UNECE/FAO, 1985). In the state of Victoria in Australia, for example, it is estimated that environmental constraints in the form of prescriptions on operations such as logging and road construction increase costs by 5–8 per cent, while land-use constraints resulting from the classification of forests led to the 'loss' of 21 per cent of the area available for timber production (Greig, 1984). The latter arose mainly from the classification of forests as parks or recreation areas. In such areas, clear-felling is frequently perceived as undesirable or unacceptable. This is especially true in the United States, but also applies in other areas such as Hokkaido in northern Japan, where a new directive in 1973 resulted in a major reduction of areas to be clear cut, with corresponding large increases in selective-cutting and cutting-prohibited areas (Shimotori, 1984). In New Zealand, helicopter logging, which may cost two or three times as much as ground-haul or cable systems, is sometimes used in order to minimise environmental disturbance and the closure of recreational trails (Horn, 1986). In such ways the public service function of the forest, in terms of recreation and environmental conservation, comes into conflict with its timber-production function.

Such conflicts can arise on both private and state-owned forest land. In the case of the former, legislation and other measures often represent a compromise between private ownership and management and public control or oversight. In Norway, for example, the Forestry Act of 1965 provides that the owner should be free to manage his forest without government intervention, as long as this is done in accordance with sound forestry practice and with guidelines contained in the act. The government forest service can intervene if necessary, and more stringent rules apply in forests designated for purposes of environmental protection (Hosteland, 1989). In West Germany, the federal Forestry Law of 1975 seeks to ensure that woods and forests are protected and administered for the good of the community (Wegener, 1987). By a combination of constraints and subsidies, an attempt is made to strike a balance between the interests of the owners and the wider community.

Regulation of forest ownership and investment

The third major area in which government influence or control has been exerted is in forest ownership and investment. Various measures in this area can affect the extent, use and management of the forest resource. Measures to protect family farm holdings meant that bans on company ownership of forests were imposed around the turn of the century in Scandinavia, for example, although in Sweden companies were allowed to acquire forest again after 1965 (Gaunitz, 1984). In Finland, the acquisition of farm forests by forest industries, which had been permitted since the 1870s, was prohibited in a law of 1915 (Raumolin, 1984), with important repercussions for the management of small units of forest. Conversely, the redistribution of forest land and its division into small parcels in Mexico in 1934 exacerbated problems of forest management and conservation in that country (Crocker, 1984). Indeed the general nature of land laws and land policy is likely to have a major influence both on the survival of the forest and on its extent. Negative effects on the forest area may stem from the legal rights to title of land that may be claimed in some countries by persons who clear the forest and 'improve' or 'develop' the land. On the other hand, deforested public land has recently been transferred to private tenure in parts of China on condition that reforestation is undertaken (Li Jinchang et al., 1988). In some countries apparent safeguards are incorporated in land law to ensure at least the partial survival of the forest resource. In Brazil, for example, 50 per cent of the area of privately owned rural properties is now required to be left under its original vegetation cover (Browder, 1988). Whether this and similar laws can always be enforced is another matter.

In addition to the nature of land laws in general and forest laws in particular, specific measures may directly or indirectly influence investment in forests. For example the structure and activities of forestry investment companies have attracted attention in countries such as Australia and New Zealand. Legislation in the latter in 1934 cut the inflow of investment capital into companies, and brought private afforestation, which had reached a rate of 20,000 hectares per year, almost to an end (Roche, 1986; Jennings, 1980). Similarly, major changes in the regulations governing the taxation of forestry investments in Britain in 1974 and again in 1988 led to dramatic reductions in rates of afforestation.

Forest laws have been considerably modified and developed since the beginning of the 1970s, and have incorporated ever-increasing provisions on environmental protection and rational resource management, Schmithusen (1986) concludes that they can today be interpreted meaningfully only if considered within the wider framework of an expanding legal system for environmental conservation and social development. Despite their expansion, development and increasing complexity, however, many national sets of forest laws remain fragmented and uncoordinated (e.g. Mayda, 1986). Much legislation is incremental in nature, and is not always easily integrated into a comprehensive forest code. Perhaps it is not surprising that this is so, since so many fiscal, political and environmental issues impinge on the use and mangement of the forest resource.

6 THE USE OF THE FOREST RESOURCE

The use of the forest resource is as varied as it is controversial. It varies with the type and location of the forest; it varies in its ownership and status, and it varies through time. In turn the character and pattern of use have a strong influence on the nature and condition of the forest, and through time on its extent. They also have implications for the wider environment at scales ranging from the local to the global.

Forests world-wide have two main classes of functions: production and protection. In the former, timber and a variety of other commodities are produced. In the latter, the emphasis is on the provision of services such as watershed protection and nature conservation, rather than on material commodities. In practice the distinction between the production of commodities and the provision of services is not always clear or rigid. For example, the forest may be perceived or managed to 'produce' an equable flow of water. Nevertheless, the distinction between production and protection forests is manifested in official classifications in many countries, and is given spatial expression in the form of zoning systems. And in addition to this spatial dimension, a time dimension may also be recognised. This dimension is more apparent in terms of broad sequences than absolute dates, but it nevertheless has validity and utility as an integrating framework.

Three major stages of development of the forest resource, in terms of its use, may be recognised (see Figure 5.1, p. 90). The 'pre-industrial' forest is typically characterised by common-property ownership and by the production of a wide range of products, of which timber for construction and fuel is only one. The 'industrial' forest is usually subject to use by private individuals or companies (although it may remain under public ownership). In contrast to the diversity of products of the 'pre-industrial' forest, the product range is narrow and simple. Priority is usually given to timber production, sometimes to the exclusion of other considerations. In the 'post-industrial' forest, the provision of services such as conservation and recreation is accommodated alongside (or even to the exclusion) of timber production.

This sequential model is no more rigid than that sketched for forest ownership in the previous chapter. Some forests, for example, undergo a direct transition from the 'pre-industrial' to the 'post-industrial' stages on

123

Table 6.1   Uses of the forest resource

Traditional use and 'minor' products	Fodder, grazing, shifting cultivation Food—fruit, nuts, honey, game Medicines Fibres Latex gums, resins Building materials Wood for utensils and furnishings Fuelwood
Industrial use	Sawlogs Pulpwood Veneer logs Fuelwood and charcoal ('Minor' industrial products e.g. cork, turpentine)
Non-consumptive uses	Soil conservation Water conservation Nature conservation Amenity Recreation

classification as protection forests within a national system. And the model cannot at the global scale be calibrated in terms of years or dates. The forests of much of Europe and countries such as the United States and Japan may be regarded as collectively entering the post-industrial stage at present, although within these areas separate tracts of forest may be classified for production or for other purposes (in Europe more than 70 per cent of the forest area is managed primarily for wood production (Prins, 1987)). On the other hand, large areas of forest in the developing world are making the (sometimes difficult) transition from the pre-industrial to the industrial stage, as timber production and state/private control replace multi-purpose use and common-property ownership. Perhaps the key variable in the model is the primacy or extent of dominance of timber production. In many industrial forests the primary objective of management is timber production, and other goods and services, if acknowledged at all, are relegated to subsidiary positions. Value and utility are sometimes perceived by the managers to reside in wood alone, giving rise to the jibe that they 'cannot see the trees for the wood'.

'Timber primacy' is not to the same degree a characteristic of pre-industrial forests, nor indeed of post-industrial ones. Its relationship to a specific stage in the evolution of forest mangement is illustrated by the case of Austria, where it found expression in the Forest Act of 1852 and persisted until the Forest Act of 1975 was passed (Glück, 1987). While the details of this example may be peculiar to Austria, general parallels may be seen in many other developed countries, where in recent times multiple use or the provision of conservation or recreation services has been incorporated in forest management.

In this chapter the use of the forest resource will be discussed against the background of this model, and within the framework of Table 6.1. First, 'traditional' use and· use for 'minor' products are considered briefly, in relation to both indigenous consumption and to the introduction of market economies. The pattern of production of timber for industrial purposes and for energy (fuelwood) is then considered. Trends in this use are considered in the light of the resource potential. Finally, the role of the forest in the provision of services such as recreation and conservation is briefly outlined. It should be emphasised that there is no perfect or rigid correlation between model stage and nature of production and control. The relationship is an imperfect one and is complicated by the transitions that are implicit in a dynamic model such as this. The production of fuelwood, in particular, may span at least the first two stages of the model, although the nature of its organisation and the problems to which it gives rise change with 'progress' towards the second stage. For this reason, it is considered in a separate section.

Traditional uses and 'minor' products

Forests have traditionally yielded a great variety of useful products. The production of fodder, food and fibre typical of many African forests in recent times (Poulsen, 1982) also characterised forests in many other parts of the world in the past. Under common-property ownership, most products were consumed locally and never entered the market. In some parts of the world, however, the harvesting of 'minor' (i.e. non-timber) products has survived the transition to market economies and to state or private forest ownership.

In addition to providing the resource base for shifting agriculture, forests have provided food through the hunting of animals and the gathering of fruits, nuts and honey. They have also yielded products (or derivatives of products) that were or are perceived as useful as traditional or modern medicines, raw materials for domestic utensils and tools, and building materials and fuel. This traditional folk use of the forest characterised much of Europe until medieval times. In Scotland, for example, trees and woods even supplied the raw material for alcoholic beverages as well as for numerous more functional purposes. In Russia, the importance of the forest and its many functions was reflected in the language, which contained as many as 103 different words used to denote forest types and vegetation. The forest yielded wood for building, dead wood for fuel, fruit and berries, and honey and game (French, 1983).

Such use has largely died out in the industrial age in the developed world, but continues in many parts of the world. Forest-dwelling shifting cultivators may number as many as 500 million, and are believed to use around one-fifth of the tropical forest area (240 million and 170 million hectares respectively of closed and open forest) (Lanly, 1985). In addition to providing land for cultivation, the forest offers for these cultivators and other forest dwellers grazing and fodder, as well as fuelwood and direct sources of food such as nuts, berries and fruits. There may be a considerable indirect use through domestic animals that graze and browse in the forest. This use involves leaves and other green (as opposed to woody) material, but nevertheless is both important in the functioning of the local economy and significant in terms of amount of forest biomass consumed. In Nepal, for example, domestic animals may annually consume twice as much forest biomass as is used for fuelwood (Agarwal, 1986).

These uses may be continued in perpetuity if the intensity is modest, but the resource may be threatened – in terms of extent or productivity or both – if population pressures build up or when traditional systems of control break down. A shortening fallow rotation, perhaps combined with increased grazing pressures, may prevent the full recovery of the forest. Various modes of production may exist.

Forest dwellers may harvest products such as fruit and berries directly from the forest by simple gathering, or forms of management may be developed whereby plants perceived as useful are concentrated in special areas of the forest by human activity. Transplanting and selection amount to a semi-domestication of some plant species, and animal species of birds, fish, bees and mammals are also manipulated for use as food and game in areas such as Amazonia (Posey, 1985).

In both temperate and tropical forests, numerous plants and animals are utilised at present, or were utilised in recent times. In eastern Canada, at least 175 food plants and fifty-two beverage plants were gathered by native peoples, and over 400 plants were used in native medicine (Arnason et al., 1981). As in Russia and earlier in much of Europe, the forest was indeed the resource base for the needs and wants of its human inhabitants, and provided a huge range of useful materials as well as a living environment. Much of the tropical forest fulfils a similar role for its inhabitants today. In southern Venezuela, for example, the Yekuana Indians regularly use nine species of terrestrial mammals, nine species of monkeys, and eighteen species of birds (Linares, 1976). In eastern Ecuador, as many as 224 plant species are utilised, mostly for foods, but also for construction, tools and medicines, while in northern Bolivia 80 per cent of the forest's trees, shrubs, vines and herbs are used (Myers, 1986a). Elsewhere in the Bolivian Amazon, one hectare contains ninety-one species of which local Indians used seventy-five (85 per cent) in some way, while of 649 individual trees as many as 619 (95 per cent) were used (Prance, 1986). Around Iquitos in the Peruvian Amazon, one hectare of forest contains 275 species and 842 individual trees of 10 centimetres or more in diameter. Of these, 72 per cent of the species and 42 per cent of the individual trees yield products with a local market value (Peters et al., 1989). Diversity of products is a characteristic especially of the tropical moist forest, but it also applies to other tropical forests. For example over seventy tree and other species are listed by Persson (1986) as being used by village people in a savannah woodland area of southern Sudan. The uses of forest products in this area range from medicines and fish poisons through fruit, soap and cosmetic oils to ropes and constructional materials.

Although many non-timber products are consumed directly by forest dwellers, others do enter the market. Perhaps one of the most obvious is rubber. Prior to the establishing of large rubber plantations, the tropical forest was the main source of this commodity, and Amazonia experienced a rubber boom at the beginning of this century, and indeed the production of 'wild' rubber continues to the present. This boom was based on industrial demand from the developed world, and for the most part involved non-indigenous people but is usually characterised by a small scale of operation. The episode is a salutary reminder that the use of natural products of the forests is not necessarily geared to direct consumption, nor is it necessarily carried out by indigenous peoples; to this extent the 'pre-industrial' model is clearly an oversimplification.

Other products with commercial value include bamboos and rattans. (These, although woody materials, are not normally classed as timber.) Rattan exports from Indonesia have been reported to be worth $90 million per year (Myers, 1988). In East Kalimantan, a range of minor products including rattan and resins and even birds' nests and reptile skins have been an important source of income for the rural population. Some still are, and are continuing to expand; others have decreased in production with the rise of commercial logging (Priasukmana, 1986). In China, the area of natural and planted bamboo has increased rapidly in recent decades, in response to government encouragement of more intensive management of this widely used product, and it now accounts for nearly 3 per cent of the total forest area (Hsiung, 1987). In Tanzanian forests, wild bees provide large amounts of honey for export, representing a value many times that of timber (Westoby, 1989).

In many forest areas in the tropics, 'wild' meat constitutes a high proportion of the animal protein consumed by local people. In Nigeria, the proportion is around one-fifth and in Zaïre one-quarter; in Cameroon, Ivory Coast and Liberia it may be as high as 70 per cent and in the Ecuadorian Amazon as much as 85 per cent (Myers, 1986a, 1988). When this meat value is computed, and added to the potential harvesting of cayman hides and of primates for biomedical research, the potential value amounts to over $200 per hectare per year, in comparison with a return of a little over $150 per year from commercial logging (Myers, 1988).

The commercial value of each 'minor' individual product may be modest, but when aggregated the total value may be impressive and may indeed be not insignificant alongside logging values. The Indonesian tropical forest, for example, provides a range of products such as rattan, resin, sandalwood, natural silk and materials useful in the pharmaceutical and cosmetics industries. Exports of non-wood forest products from Indonesia in the early 1980s were worth around US$125 million annually, and had increased significantly over the previous decade, both in absolute terms and relative to total forest product export value. In 1973, for example, the share of non-wood products amounted to only 2.9 per cent of the latter, but it had increased to 11.2 per cent in 1981 and to 13.3 per cent by 1982 (Repetto and Gillis, 1988). Some estimates are even higher; Myers (1988), for example, puts the 1982 value at $200 million, compared with $28 million in 1973.

Compared with those from timber production, the benefits arising from 'minor' forest products are often relatively widely distributed. In Indonesia, for example, huge numbers of smallholders earn around $200 per year from non-timber products such as rattan and orchids (Myers, 1986b). In India, up to 30 million people depend on minor forest produce for some part of their livelihood (Agarwal, 1986). The production of local cigarettes, rolled in the leaves of the native tree *Dionspyros melanoxylon* contributes £200 million to the local economy and provides at least some income for 3 million part-time workers (Westoby, 1989). The total value of minor forest products in 1979–80 amounted to around 23 per cent of that of wood (Muthiah, 1987). It is reported that non-wood forest products accounted in the late 1970s for 40 per cent of the total net revenues accruing to the government from the forestry sector, and for 63 per cent of the exports. These figures exclude the estimated 60 per cent of such products that are consumed locally and do not enter the cash economy. Furthermore, the rate of growth of revenues from such products (including pharmaceuticals, gums and resins, bamboos and essential oils) was far higher than that from commercial timber, and non-wood products generated more than 70 per cent of the employment in the forestry sector as a whole (Myers, 1988).

The diversity and potential value of 'minor' products are perhaps greatest in the case of the tropical forest, but they are not confined to low latitudes. Further polewards, forests have traditionally supplied a variety of products for local economies, and in some cases there is still a considerable commercial value. In the Soviet Union, for example, huge areas of forests are (or can be) harvested for 'minor' products (Table 6.2). Non-timber products can contribute around 50 per cent of the economic value of the forest (Cherkasov, 1988) and in some areas even more; revenue from 'minor' products from Belorussian forests could reach 80 per cent of that from timber production (Sankovich, 1984). The full potential value is rarely realised, however, because commercial gathering of products such as berries and edible fungi is often laborious, and processing and marketing are often poorly developed. The harvesting of such products may depend on the pattern of ownership, amongst other factors. Where small, privately owned woodlots are owned by absentees, for example, there is less likelihood that mushrooms and berries will be gathered than if they are owned by resident farmers.

The significance and value of 'minor' products are often overlooked, for a variety of reasons. One is statistical coverage. It is almost impossible to achieve an adequate coverage of the production of a diverse range of products, many of which are consumed at or near the point of production and which do not enter domestic or overseas trade. FAO, for example, does not attempt to include coverage of such products in its *Yearbooks of Forest Products*. In the absence of such data, the value of the products can easily be overlooked, especially in comparison with that of timber, which can be relatively easily quantified. Timber enters international markets and

Table 6.2 Minor forest products: Soviet forests

(a)	Fruit-bearing area (000 ha)	Utilisation of yield (percentage collected)
Cedar nuts	30 000	5
Japanese stone-pine nuts	18 000	3
Edible chestnuts	72	25
Walnuts	46	50
Hazel nuts	1 700	50
Raspberries	10 000	3.5
Mushrooms	50 000	3.5

(b)	Production (000 tons, 1986)
All fruits and berries	167.3
Honey	22.9
Birch juice	42.7
Mushrooms	31.7
Nuts	10.5
Medicinal herbs, etc	15.7
Hay	338.3

Sources: Compiled from data in (a) Tseplyaev (1965); (b) Barr and Braden (1988)

brings in foreign exchange, whereas non-wood products are often sold locally, and are difficult to monitor and easy to ignore (Peters et al., 1989). For various reasons, therefore, timber production may be perceived to be of paramount importance, and this perception in turn may be reflected in national forestry policies which give priority to it and which conversely tend to neglect non-wood products.

Nevertheless, many of these products can be produced continually, and it has been concluded that 'It is not at all clear that the discounted present value of annual income (in perpetuity) per hectare from non-wood forest products must be less than the discounted present value of log extraction per hectare' (Repetto and Gillis, 1988, p. 65). On the basis of work on the Amazonian forest, Peters et al., (1989) have suggested that the annual collection of fruit and latex in perpetuity could have a greater value than sustainable timber harvest: the former could account for as much as 90 per cent of the total value, and the latter 10 per cent.

The harvesting of non-wood products is often non-destructive, especially when carried out in traditional ways, and may have minimal impact on the forest ecosystem. It does not, however, necessarily mean that the resource is always conserved. For example, the exploitation of fauna in the Peruvian Amazon in the 1970s proved to be exhaustive, and led to a ban on the commercial hunting of game. As recently as 1973 it generated an internal gross product comparable to that from timber. More recently, it has been suggested that active management could restore the wild fauna to former levels of economic and social importance, and at the same time eliminate the risks of extinction brought about by indiscriminate hunting (Douro-jeani, 1985). On the other hand, the development of logging, perhaps following the granting of logging concessions, can seriously affect the use of the forest for these traditional products, and obviously the removal of the forest effectively precludes it. Furthermore, external threats to the forest such as changing climate or acid rain (Chapter 7) can pose serious threats to the harvesting of minor products. For example a sudden increase in dieback in sugar maple in Quebec since 1982 has threatened a \$40 million industry and the livelihoods of 10,000 syrup producers (Hendershot and Jones, 1989). Both traditional use and the commercial use of minor products, however, are more usually jeopardised by the advent of commercial logging and the transition to the industrial forest.

Many examples of conflicts between the traditional use of the forest and logging and clearing have been reported. One of the most celebrated is that involving indigenous groups and small-scale rubber producers in the face of large-scale loggers and ranchers in Amazonia (e.g. Hecht and Cockburn, 1989; Schwartz, 1989), but there are many others that are less known. For example, the clearing of riverine forests in southern Somalia has resulted in the loss of an important resource for bee-keeping and honey production, as well as for timber for building and browse for livestock (Douthwaite, 1987). Much of the forest clearance in this case has resulted from donor-assisted refugee resettlement schemes, which have been carried out with scant regard for the interests of the local inhabitants. More generally, 'traditional' producers have frequently been poorly organised and poorly represented in conflicts with logging interests or with those who would clear the forests for other purposes. Furthermore, the harvesting of animal products is not always compatible with logging: in Sarawak, for example, heavy commercial logging is alleged to reduce the sustained-yield harvest of wild meat from 54 kg per local resident per year to about 2 kg (Myers, 1989). In 1987 several tribal groups in Sarawak set up barricades across logging roads to protest against the damage caused by timber companies (Apin, 1987). 'Traditional' use may be compatible with the common-property ownership which characterises many pre-industrial forests, at least unless and until rapid population growth occurs, but with the rise of industrial logging and private control it may suffer severe stress. Indeed the traditional users may be in effect dispossessed of both their land and of their traditional forest activities.

On the other hand, more intensive management of the forest for timber production is not always detrimental to other products. For example, while the yields of some berry species suffer from the lowering of water tables following the ditching of peatland forests in Finland, other species benefit from such treatment, and the application of fertilisers improves the yields of mushrooms and berries as well as the growth rates of trees (Veijalainen, 1976). Whether the increased yields are actually harvested is another matter.

The transition from the 'pre-industrial' forest, characterised by a diversity of products, to the industrial stage, distinguished by primacy of timber production, has occurred at different times in different areas. For example it was largely achieved in countries such as Sweden by the end of the nineteenth century (e.g. Stridsberg, 1984). More recently it is well illustrated by the case of Indonesia. As late as 1938, the value of trade in minor products amounted to as much as 13 million Dutch guilders, as compared with 16 million for timber. By the 1980s, the ratio had widened to 5:95 (Jacobs, 1988). There may be some signs that it is narrowing once again (see page 127), but there is no doubt that the transition has in general terms been difficult and painful. Part of the problem lies in the differing perceptions of traditional and small-scale producers on the one hand, and of logging interests on the other. It is all too easy for 'industrial' foresters to allege neglect of adequate forest management when traditional perceptions of the forest and its ownership and use encounter the modern economy. For example Kumar (1987) attributes damage to forests in Indian reserves in Alberta to the lack of management. Traditionally, such forests were used for hunting and for the small-scale use of various products. Common-property ownership suited such use, but could not cope with larger-scale logging for commercial purposes.

Superimposed on these contrasting perceptions are differences in influence and power. Traditional and small-scale users have usually lost out to commercial loggers, who are often backed by government. Various political factors contribute to the shift from the small-scale, multi-product use of the 'pre-industrial' forest to the large-scale timber production that characterises the 'industrial' forest. Several are listed by Jacobs (1988). They include the fact that logging may permit the extension of government power over remote lands, whilst economic development may be perceived as synonymous with large-scale exploitation. It may be difficult for governments to collect revenues arising from small-scale operations focusing on minor products, and these operations may not be attractive to aid agencies and their large-scale investments. Finally, small-scale collectors and other forest users have no significant power base from which to protect their source of income.

Formidable political and economic problems therefore underlie the shift from the 'pre-industrial' to the 'industrial' phase. In recent years there has been a growing awareness of the long-term benefits that may accrue from the use of the forest for minor products, and in at least some areas the value of output of these products is rising relative to that of timber. Nevertheless, major problems still confront the commercial exploitation of these products. The transition from local indigenous use to commercial harvesting has rarely been smooth. More often than not it has involved the growth of large-scale logging, and has been associated with both environmental and social disruption. Whether a smoother and less destructive transition can be made from the pre-commercial to commercial use in the remaining areas of 'pre-industrial' forest remains to be seen.

Wood production

A diversity of products, including timber for construction and for fuel, is characteristic of the 'pre-industrial' forest, but in the modern age timber has assumed primacy, and indeed in many instances an overwhelming predominance, in forest production. Many forests are now managed and used solely or primarily for timber production for industrial purposes, and in other cases the production of fuelwood has emerged as the dominant use.

The measurement of wood production, like that of the forest area and other forest attributes, is fraught with difficulty. Much production does not enter the market and cannot be precisely measured. In assembling statistics, therefore, bodies such as the FAO have to make assumptions about the level of use of fuelwood per head of population, for example, and even population totals may not be known with certainty or precision. Data for timber production should therefore be viewed in the light of these difficulties.

The *exploitable* or *operable* forest area is smaller than the total area of forest and woodlands since production in some areas is precluded by inaccessibility or management objectives of conservation or protection. The definition and measurement of the exploitable forest area are surrounded by uncertainty, not least because different types and orders of constraints may limit exploitation. Some are economic: the harvesting of some forests may not be economically viable at prevailing timber prices. This constraint may be linked to that imposed by transport or by costs of logging: new transport routes and new logging methods may radically alter perceptions of exploitability. And designation of forests for protection, conservation or recreation may also be an effective constraint.

Conflicting trends are probably operating in relation to the exploitable forest area. Some new areas are being opened up by new transport lines, whilst others are being designated for non-consumptive purposes. One of the potentially most spectacular examples of the former is the case of the forests along the Baikal–Amur railway in the eastern part of the Soviet Union. It is estimated by the FAO that an additional 40–50 million hectares of exploitable forest area will be added by this development (FAO, 1982a), and there are plans to develop wood-using industries along it (e.g. Eronen, 1983). (As yet, however, there has been little noticeable impact (Barr and Braden, 1988).) On the other hand large areas have been designated as non-production forests in countries such as the United States. Extent of exploitable area therefore changes through time, and also depends on definition. Unfortunately, estimates of this extent rarely specify date and definition.

Current estimates of the exploitable area are around 2,000 million hectares: a figure of 1,950 million hectares is quoted for exploitable closed forest by Kuusela (1987), while data assembled by Binkley and Dykstra (1987) indicate that the present exploitable area is around 2,150 million hectares. They estimate a total growing stock and net annual increment of approximately 300,000 and 5,200 million cubic metres respectively. (This

Figure 6.1 Trends in wood production (removals): softwoods (coniferous) and hardwoods (non-coniferous)

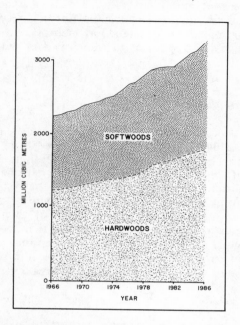

Source: Based on data in FAO *Yearbooks of Forest Products*

estimate of net annual increment is considerably higher than some previous estimates such as that of King (1975, Chapter 4).)

Total production or removals of wood from world forests has been around 3,250 million cubic metres in recent years (FAO, annually). Overall, therefore, recent levels of production may amount to little more than 60 per cent of the estimated net annual increment in exploitable closed forests. On the other hand they may exceed the net annual increment of the forest area, depending on which estimate is accepted. Recent volumes of production are equivalent to an average of around 0.65 cubic metres per person, and correspond to around 0.8 cubic metres per hectare of the (FAO) forest and woodland area and to approximately 1.6 cubic metres per hectare of exploitable closed forest.

Of the total production, around 40 per cent is softwood (coniferous) and the remainder hardwood (non-coniferous). These proportions approximate to the relative extents of these forest types, but the coniferous share has been decreasing slightly in recent years, having fallen from 42 per cent in 1975 to 40 per cent in 1986 (Figure 6.1). This trend has been evident for many years: in 1955, for example, production was divided almost equally between the two types, as indeed it was earlier in the century (Zon and Sparhawk, 1923). Furthermore, it seems set to continue, not least because hardwoods tend to be in surplus in the United States and many other developed countries (Bethel and Tseng, 1986), while softwoods are in shorter supply.

As will be discussed more fully later, around one half of the total production is used for industrial purposes (including construction and pulping) and the remainder is consumed as fuelwood or charcoal. These two sectors show marked contrasts in trends and in spatial patterns of production.

Trends in wood production

Wood production has increased rapidly in recent decades, especially in the developing world (Figure 6.2, Table 6.3). It rose from 1,823 to 3,252 million cubic metres between 1956 and 1986, representing an increase of around 75 per cent. On a longer timescale, the rate of expansion appears to be considerably slower: for example Zon and Sparhawk (1923) estimated total production at 56 billion cubic feet, corresponding to approximately 1585 million cubic metres. They emphasised that their figure was an estimate: for individual countries they considered that it was within 15–25 per cent of the actual production of saw timber but that it could be more than 50 per cent in error for fuelwood. Their figure, however, may well be an overestimate, and according to FAO (1946) the volume cut in 1937 was

Figure 6.2   Trends in wood production (removals) by world division

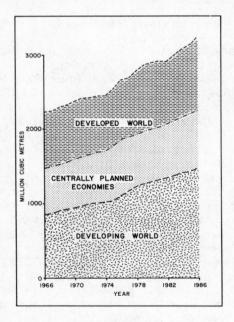

Source: Based on data in FAO *Yearbooks of Forest Products*

Table 6.3 Wood production (million 0^3)

	1950*	1960	1970	1980	1985
Total roundwood	1674	1901 (14)	2365 (24)	2927 (19)	3164 (8)
Developing			1118	1527 (37)	1743 (14)
Developed			1247	1348 (8)	1422 (6)
Fuelwood	866	872	1091 (25)	1476 (35)	1646 (12)
Developing			914	1241 (36)	1384 (12)
Developed			177	235 (33)	263 (12)
Industrial roundwood	808	1028	1274 (24)	1440 (13)	1518 (5)
Developing			204	327 (60)	358 (9)
Developed			1070	1113 (4)	1160 (4)

* Average 1950–2
Figures in brackets indicate percentage increase from previous date

Sources: FAO *The state of food and agriculture* (annual); FAO *Yearbooks of forest products* (annual); FAO *World forest products statistics 1954–63*; FAO Wood: world trends and prospects *Unasylva* 20 (1966) 1–135

1,500 million cubic metres, compared with 1,674 million cubic metres around 1950 (FAO, 1966). Whatever the precise levels of production in the first half of the century may have been, it is highly probable that they were less than half of present-day figures.

Fuller statistical coverage and better time-series data become available after the Second World War, although this improvement may bring its own problems. It is possible that part of the apparent trend in levels of production is statistical rather than real, and results from more comprehensive coverage and changes in procedures rather than from actual changes in levels of production. Statistics contained in FAO *Yearbooks of Forest Products* are sometimes revised (usually upwards) in successive volumes, posing problems for the assemblage of time-series data (and their graphical representation). For example, total production for 1975 was given as 2,452.7 million cubic metres and 2,579.2 million cubic metres respectively in the FAO *1976 Yearbook of Forest Products 1966–76* and *1986 Yearbook of Forest Products 1977–86*. The identification of the precise nature of long-term trends is therefore difficult, and there is a danger that real trends may be exaggerated by the more comprehensive coverage of recent years.

Nevertheless, the general trends are clear, and are dominated by a rapid rate of increase, especially since the 1960s (Table 6.3). During the ten-year period from 1977 to 1986 for example, production increased by 20 per cent, compared with an increase of 11 per cent during the previous ten-year period and one of 10 per cent between 1954 and 1963. During the 1970s and 1980s, annual rates of increase often exceeded 2 per cent and sometimes approached 3 per cent, although almost no growth occurred from 1980 to 1982. In the 1950s and 1960s annual rates of increase averaged little over 1 per cent.

Until recently, the rate of increase in wood production has been less than that of human population, but in the last few years the relationship has been reversed and growth in wood production now exceeds that of population. Between 1975 and 1985, population increased by 18.7 per cent, but total wood production rose 22.7 per cent. The increase in production of industrial roundwood (17.2 per cent) was slightly less than population growth, but the rate of increase in fuelwood production, at 28.3 per cent, was substantially greater. Over the longer term, however, there has been little change in per capita levels of production (and consumption): the average figures in cubic metres per person were 0.7 in 1937 (FAO, 1946) and 0.65 in 1985. Stagnation of levels of wood production in the early 1980s gave rise to a belief that the steady growth of consumption that had taken place since the Second World War was now slowing down (e.g. Kuusela, 1987), and that the flattened S-shape (logistic) curve that characterised growth in consumption of some other natural resource commodities such as oil and some minerals applied also to wood. The recent resurgence of rates of increase of production in the second half of the 1980s, however, may call such beliefs into question, and it is too early to reach definite conclusions. In many resource sectors, unusually high rates of growth in production and consumption during the third quarter of the present century fuelled fears of resource shortages, and prompted upward revisions of levels of production. In many instances, however, such trends have not been sustained, and the question arises as to whether the downturn in growth rates during the late 1970s and early 1980s was a temporary blip, reflecting the effects of the recession following oil-price rises, or the beginning of a new phase. A major complication in considering wood production is that different trends apply in different sectors, as is discussed subsequently. Projections of overall trends are therefore fraught with difficulty.

In the forest sector, as in many other resource sectors, the rate of growth during the late 1960s and 1970s was unexpected, and many forecasts and projections made in the 1950s and 1960s were exceeded by actual levels of production and consumption. Conversely, many more recent forecasts and projections have turned out to be overestimates, and in the last few years expected rates of increase have tended to be revised downwards. The significance of such forecasts and projections is profound, as they influence decisions on issues such as afforestation and investment in the forest-products industries.

Sectoral trends

Overall trends in wood production, however, conceal important contrasts between different sectors (Figures 6.1 and 6.3). The rate of increase in production of hardwoods or non-coniferous species has been greater than that of conifers. Between 1975 and 1985, for example, non-coniferous removals increased by 27.7 per cent, compared with 15.7 per cent for coniferous removals. Between 1960 and 1980, the estimated annual growth

Figure 6.3 Trends in production of industrial roundwood and fuelwood and charcoal

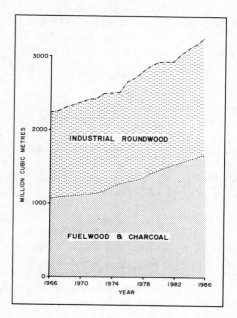

Source: Based on data in FAO *Yearbooks of Forest Products*

in softwood consumption (as industrial roundwood) averaged 2.4 per cent per annum, whilst the corresponding figure for hardwoods was 3.2 per cent (FAO, 1982a). These differential trends reflect a shift southwards in production, towards the tropical forests in particular.

In recent years the rate of growth in production of industrial roundwood has slowed down, while that of fuelwood has accelerated. Some uncertainty arises since the growth in fuelwood is relatively steady, whilst trends in industrial roundwood fluctuate considerably from year to year in accordance with the state of the world economy. The choice of study period therefore strongly influences the apparent rate. Between 1962 and 1974, annual growth rates averaged 3.0 per cent, while from 1974 to 1984 they fell to 0.6 per cent, prompting Kuusela (1987) to conclude that the steady growth in consumption since World War II was slowing down, and that a turning-point has been reached. The picture is complicated, however, by the stagnation that characterised demand for industrial roundwood during the recessions of the mid-1970s and early 1980s. Almost no growth occurred from 1974 to 1976 and from 1980 to 1982. Over the period from 1970 to 1982, annual growth rates averaged 1.0 per cent (FAO, 1986a). Since 1982, however, more rapid growth has been resumed, and during the ten-year period from 1977 to 1986, growth in production of industrial roundwood amounted to 14.0 per cent, compared with 13.9 per cent in the previous ten years. The slowing of growth that seemed apparent in the early 1980s is therefore called into question, and its significance in relation to long-term demand–supply relationships is debatable. Nevertheless, projected rates of increase in consumption for the period between 1980 and 2000 are substantially lower than those for 1960–80. Annual rates for softwoods are expected to average 1.8 per cent (compared with 2.4 per cent), while those for hardwoods are 2.3 as compared with 3.2 per cent (FAO, 1982a).

Whatever the long-term significance of apparently decelerating rates of increase in the industrial roundwood sector may be, however, it is clear that growth rates for the production of industrial roundwood have been slower than those for fuelwood. Annual rates of increase for industrial roundwood between 1963 and 1983 averaged 1.46 per cent, compared with 1.66 per cent for fuelwood. For fuelwood, there is a clear pattern of accelerating production, with increases of 9 per cent and 26 per cent respectively for 1967–76 and 1977–86. Fuelwood production has increased rapidly and steadily, while the production of industrial roundwood has grown more slowly and less continuously. These trends have been completely reversed since the 1950s and early 1960s. In the second half of the 1950s, for example, almost all the increase in total roundwood production was accounted for by an increase in the production of industrial roundwood. The net increase in fuelwood production of less than half a million cubic metres against a total of nearly 900 million cubic metres conceals the fact that the growth of fuelwood production in the developing world was counterbalanced by a long-term decrease in its use in Europe, the Soviet Union and North America (FAO, 1966).

Much of the recent growth in total production, therefore, is accounted for by the production of fuelwood. External factors such as the major increases in oil prices during the 1970s have had a major influence on trends in fuelwood production, not only in the developing world but to some extent also in the developed world. In Europe, for example, the downward trend in fuelwood consumption which began in the 1950s was reversed in the late 1970s. In the United States, the production of fuelwood increased fivefold between 1976 and 1981. On the global scale, a growing proportion of total production in the post-war period has been accounted for by fuelwood. For example in the mid-1980s (1984–6) its percentage was 51.7, compared with 49.7 per cent in 1975 and an average of 49.6 per cent in the early 1960s. In the mid-1950s, the proportion was 48.5 per cent. On a longer time-scale, however, the trend may have been different: Zon and Sparhawk (1923) estimated that 53.6 per cent of the removals at their time of writing were for fuelwood.

The spatial pattern of wood production

The spatial pattern of wood production is complex and varied. Disparate factors underlie it, including the extent and nature of the resource, environmental conditions in relation to tree growth, intensity of management and

Table 6.4 Area of forest and woodland and wood production 1986

	Percentage of world forest and woodland	wood production	Percentage of world industrial roundwood	fuelwood
Developing World	54.4	54.6	23.0	84.3
Developed World	45.6	45.4	77.0	15.7
Africa	16.9	13.8	3.4	23.6
North and Central America	16.8	22.2	36.1	9.3
South America	22.4	9.7	5.9	13.2
Asia	13.2	30.7	15.6	44.8
Europe	3.8	10.8	18.7	3.4
Oceania	3.8	1.2	1.9	0.5
USSR	23.1	11.6	18.5	5.2

Source: Based on *FAO Yearbook of Forest Products 1975–86* and FAO *Production Yearbook 1987.*

relative proportions of 'natural' and 'man-made' forests, forest classification (whether for protection or production) and accessibility. Production may also depend on the status and condition of the resource, and in particular whether sustained-yield management is being operated or whether the resource is diminishing as a result of over-exploitation. These factors operate on varying scales, and give rise to contrasting patterns of wood production at levels ranging from the continental to the local.

The pattern on the scale of continents and other major divisions is shown in Table 6.4. Just under half of the world area of forest and woodland lies in the developed world, and an almost identical proportion of wood production comes from that area. In general terms, tree growth rates in the non-tropical forests that make up most of the forest and woodland area in the developed world are slower than those in the developing world, but on the other hand the intensity of management is often higher. In general terms, however, a slow shift towards the developing world is apparent: in 1975, for example, its share of production amounted to 53.3 per cent, and it now has a large share of a larger total. In other words, the rate of increase has been considerably greater in the developing world than in the developed world.

In contrast to the accordance of shares of production and of the forest and woodland area at the scale of twofold division into developing and developed world, marked imbalances occur at the continental level. Relative shares of production and area rarely match at this level. The relatively intensively managed forests of Europe, for example, make up less than 4 per cent of the world's forests, but account for nearly 11 per cent of the production. Conversely, South America has more than one-fifth of the forest, but less than 10 per cent of the production. When total production is broken down into industrial roundwood and fuelwood,

Figure 6.4 Roundwood production (thousand m³, 1986)

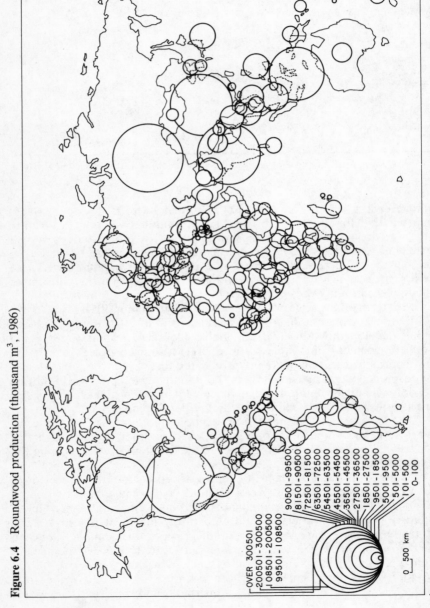

Source: Based on data in FAO *Yearbooks of Forest Products*

however, the distribution becomes very different, as Table 6.3 indicates. The developing world accounts for more than four-fifths of fuelwood production, but less than one-quarter of that of industrial roundwood. Nevertheless, its share of industrial roundwood production is increasing, having risen from 19.8 to 23.0 per cent between 1975 and 1985. Similar contrasts occur at the continental level, with Europe and North America in particular being characterised by contributions to industrial roundwood production that are far greater than their share of the world forest area. These two areas produce well over half of the world's industrial round-wood, from little more than one-fifth of the world's forest area.

The pattern of production at the national level is indicated in Figure 6.4. As the map suggests, production is strongly concentrated. Six countries accounted for 50 per cent of production in 1980, while eighty other countries collectively produced less than 5 per cent of the total (Styrman and Wibe, 1986). A small number of large, extensively forested countries such as the United States, the Soviet Union, Canada and Brazil stand out as major producers. In general terms, production is roughly proportional to the extent of the forest resource, but there are exceptions to this generalisation, and various qualifications need to be made. The productive potential of a national forest resource depends not only on its extent, but on environmental factors and intensity of management. Production levels also depend on accessibility, logging costs and trade: relatively cheap imports may discourage home production in high-cost countries such as Japan. Furthermore, in some countries little use of the forest has as yet been made for wood production, while in others the forest resource has been over-harvested (in relation to growth). Removals exceeded the potential cut in Finland in the 1960s and Sweden in the 1970s, prompting attempts to stimulate long-term wood supply (FAO, 1982a; Gamlin, 1988). More seriously, over cutting may reduce the extent and productivity of the forest resource on the long term. In Pakistan, for example, annual growth accounts for only 62 per cent of the annual wood harvest, and the forest resource is being eroded (Biswas, 1987).

Intensity of production

Harvesting intensity varies in terms both of growing stock and area. On the basis of an estimated total of 300,000 million cubic metres of growing stock, the overall harvesting intensity in the early 1980s was 0.8 per cent (Peck, 1984). This intensity was slightly higher in the developed world, at 0.9 per cent, where generally slower natural growth rates were offset by higher intensities of management, than in the developing world, for which the average was 0.7 per cent. There much of the forest was completely unmanaged. The highest harvesting intensities were recorded in Europe, where they averaged 2.2 per cent. Even there, however, removals were less than the net increment, and the standing volume is increasing. Indeed, it is expected that it will increase by around 8.5 per cent between 1970 and 2000 (FAO, 1982a). Growing stock is also increasing in the United States:

Figure 6.5 Average roundwood production per hectare of forest and woodland 1986 (m³)

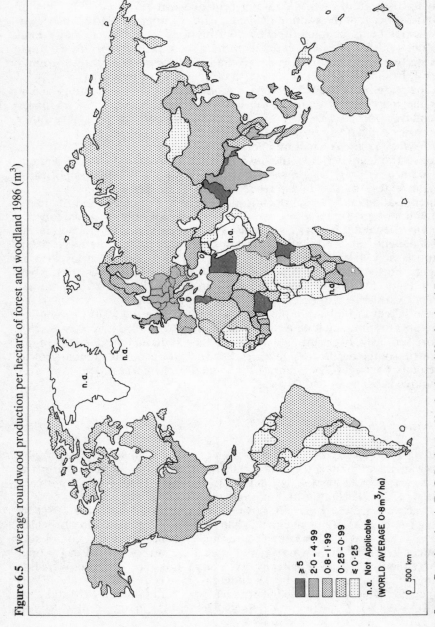

≥ 5

2·0 – 4·99

0·8 – 1·99

0·25 – 0·99

≤ 0·25

n. a. Not Applicable

(WORLD AVERAGE 0·8 m³/ha)

0   500 km

Source: Based on data in FAO *Production Yearbooks* and *Yearbooks of Forest Products*

between 1952 and 1977 the softwood-growing stock inventory increased by 7 per cent and that for hardwood by 43 per cent (USDA, 1982). In much of the world, therefore, the intensity of production is such that the wood resource is expanding, despite record levels of production. The pattern of intensity of production per unit forest area is shown in Figure 6.5. A small number of mainly low-latitude countries are shown as having very high levels of production in excess of 5 cubic metres per hectare of forest and woodland. This group contains a number of small countries such as Haiti, Costa Rica and Nepal, where the rate of deforestation is high, and also a number of countries such as Egypt and Libya where the forest area is very small. In contrast with the scattered pattern of very high-production countries, that of countries within the 2–5 cubic metres per hectare category is more compact. Most European countries lie in this group, and here there is a combination of moderate 'natural' growth rates and relatively intensive management.

Most of the large countries with large forest areas have production ratios below the world average. Both Canada and the Soviet Union are characterised by relatively low levels of production, resulting in large part from a combination of hostile climatic conditions which limit growth rates and inaccessibility which precludes the exploitation of much of the forest. Much of the tropical zone, however, also is in this group, and it is noticeable that many tropical countries in Africa and Latin America have low or very low levels of wood production per unit area. While climatic conditions are of course well suited to high ecological productivity in such areas, again the problem of inaccessibility has constrained the level of production to date.

If the forest is to be harvested on a long-term sustained-yield basis, the ultimate limit on removals or levels of production is net annual increment (NAI). Various natural and human factors determine NAI, including type and intensity of management. Climate is one of the main natural variables, and climatic gradients are clearly reflected in the spatial pattern of net annual increments per hectare, as reported by UNECE/FAO (1985). On the maritime margins of north-west Europe, for example, NAI values for exploitable closed forests are 8.51 and 7.29 cubic metres per hectare respectively for Denmark and Ireland. In the colder and more continental climates of Sweden and Finland, the values fall to 3.01 and 3.18, while in the Soviet Union and Canada they are 1.40 and 1.66 cubic metres per hectare respectively. For the Soviet Union, the average per hectare of forest-covered land (as opposed to exploitable closed forest) is quoted by Blandon (1983) as 1.15 cubic metres. This average conceals a marked contrast between the European part, at 1.58, and the Asian section with an average of 1.01. NAIs also decrease towards the drier areas of southern Europe and the Mediterranean, with values of 2.05 for Greece and 1.01 for Cyprus being reported. In the more arid areas, for example of Soviet Central Asia, average increments may be less than 0.1 cubic metres per hectare (Blandon, 1983).

The ratio of fellings to net annual increment depends not only on ownership, control, accessibility and forestry policy, but also on factors such as the age and maturity of forests, since very young forests are unlikely to be productive in this sense, irrespective of their growth rates. Fellings in most European countries usually amount to around 70 to 80 per cent of the net annual increment (UNECE/FAO, 1985). In the continent as a whole, removals have recently amounted to just under 70 per cent (Prins, 1987). In the United States, they amount to around 63 per cent (UNECE/FAO, 1985), whereas in 1920 wood consumption was more than four times the level of wood growth (Cox et al., 1985).

These national average ratios vary both spatially, as will be shown subsequently, and with ownership (Chapter 5). Much of the surplus of growth over removals in the United States, for example, is concentrated in non-industrial private forests owned by farmers and other small-scale owners (USDA, 1982). Comprehensive figures for other parts of the world are not available, but strong contrasts are likely to exist between the 'high' and 'low' producing countries. Many of the former are likely to be characterised with ratios well in excess of unity, and with rapid deforestation, while very low ratios obtain in the cases of lightly peopled countries, such as Surinam, which are still extensively forested and which have experienced relatively few and light pressures on their forest resources. In other instances such as Japan, production levels are relatively low because of the high costs of logging and extraction, competition from imports, and low-quality timber from some of the forests.

Within individual countries, strong variations may exist in both levels of production and in ratios of actual to allowable cuts. These variations reflect not only environmental conditions, but also forest classification and accessibility. Production may be inhibited by the classification of the forest for purposes of protection, conservation or recreation, and also by the need in some instances for harvesting to be incorporated within multiple-use frameworks. Remoteness and inaccessibility are also powerful influences, which are perhaps most clearly demonstrated in the case of large countries such as the Soviet Union. In 1975, for example, 70 per cent of its total wood production came from the European–Uralian section of the country, which contained only 18 per cent of Soviet mature timber. Conversely, only 30 per cent of the production came from Siberia and the Far East, which contained 82 per cent of the timber. In the former area, the cut represented 3 per cent of the growing stock: in the latter it amounted to only 0.3 per cent (Barr, 1984), while production as a percentage of defined allowable cut ranged from 91 per cent in the European part of the country to 29 per cent in Western Siberia and 32 per cent in the Far East (Blandon, 1983). The annual allowable cut is itself alleged to exceed the net increment by a factor of 2.5 for the country as a whole, and by ratios of 4 and 5 for the Ukraine and Lithuania respectively (Barr, 1988). In countries such as the Soviet Union and Canada, apparently low ratios for the country as a whole may therefore conceal the fact that some of the more accessible forests are over-utilised, while the more remote ones are almost unused.

Trends in the spatial pattern of production

The spatial pattern of production is characterised by some elements of continuity on the timescale of the present century but more especially by change during recent decades. Throughout the century, production has been dominated by the United States and the Soviet Union, but their degree of dominance has been weakening. In the early part of the century, these two countries accounted for 57 per cent of the total wood production (Zon and Sparhawk, 1923). In 1965 their share had fallen to 35 per cent, and by 1985 to just over one-quarter. In the 1920s the United States accounted for over 40 per cent of world production, its production being three times greater than that of the Soviet Union and nearly ten times that of the next largest producer, Canada. In the second half of the twentieth century, American production has actually been lower than it was in the 1920s. In the Soviet Union, on the other hand, production increased more than sixfold between 1922 and 1975 (Blandon, 1983): by then it was the leading producer although more recently it has been overtaken once more by the United States.

The weakening degree of dominance of the United States and the Soviet Union is accompanied by the rapid expansion of production in the developing world and especially in tropical countries. In the Philippines, for example, it has expanded from Zon and Sparhawk's estimate of just under 1 million cubic metres in the early 1920s to 35 million cubic metres in 1985: in Nigeria the increase was from 2.5 to 98 million cubic metres, while in Indonesia (Dutch East Indies) it was from 5 to 154 million cubic metres. Much of this growth has taken place within the last 20 years: in Brazil, for example, production increased from 148 to 238 million cubic metres between 1966 and 1986, while the corresponding rise in Indonesia was from 93 to 158 million cubic metres. In comparison, production in northern countries has been relatively static. In Sweden, for example, total production amounted to 52 million cubic metres in 1986, compared with 51 million in 1966. In some tropical countries, much of the rapid increase in recent decades is accounted for by commercial logging. For example, log production in Indonesia is reported to have increased from 2 million cubic metres in 1967 to 26 million in 1973 (Walker and Hoesada, 1986). In others, the production of industrial roundwood has actually decreased, but that of fuelwood has increased rapidly. In Ivory Coast, for example, industrial roundwood production fell from 5.5 to 3.6 million cubic metres between 1976 and 1986 (after increasing rapidly during the previous decade), while fuelwood production increased from 5.5 to 8.25 million cubic metres (Figure 6.6).

The detailed pattern of changes in total production at the national level is shown in Figure 6.7. Over the period from 1976 to 1986, large increases in production occurred in most of Africa and Asia, and in much of Latin America. Outside the tropics, countries showing an above-average increase include a group in north-west Europe (including Britain, Ireland and Spain) where twentieth-century afforestation is now being reflected in rapidly increasing production. Another group, including Finland and

Figure 6.6   Wood production in Ivory Coast and Indonesia

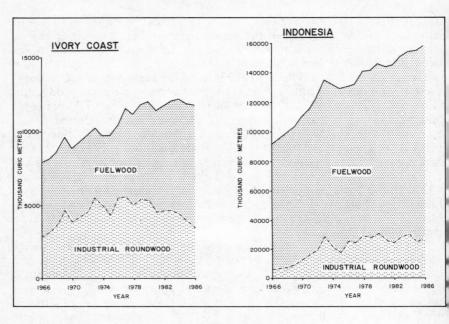

Source: Based on data in FAO *Yearbooks of Forest Products*

Canada, is characterised by a more stable forest area combined with more intensive management. Several European countries, on the other hand, have below-average increases, which in some cases may conceal the fact that both intensities of management and production levels were relatively high before the baseline of 1976. A number of neo-tropical countries, including Venezuela, Guyana and Surinam, also have production increases well below the world average: in these cases the tropical forest has been exploited much less than in neighbouring countries such as Brazil and Ecuador.

While the detailed spatial pattern of roundwood production at the national level is complex, the overall pattern on the global scale is very clear. Production from low-latitude areas in general and from the tropics in particular is rising relative to that from Europe, the Soviet Union and North America. On the basis of the production estimates of Zon and Sparhawk (1923) for the early part of this century, the three continents of Africa, Asia and South America accounted for 20 per cent of total world production. By 1965 that percentage had doubled, and by 1985 had increased to around 54 per cent. A clear shift towards lower latitudes is evident in roundwood production. With production levels in many northern countries already high in relation to growth rates (although still capable of some increase with more intensive management and with the use of exotic

Figure 6.7 Percentage change in wood production 1976–86

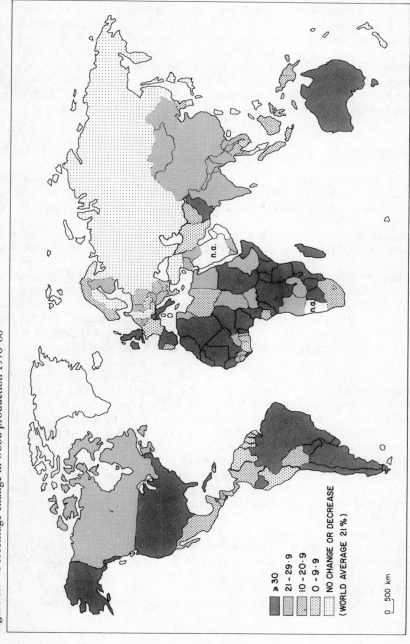

≥ 30

21 – 29·9

10 – 20·9

0 – 9·9

NO CHANGE OR DECREASE

(WORLD AVERAGE 21%)

0   500 km

Source: Based on data in FAO *Yearbooks of Forest Products*

species). With considerations of environment and amenity playing increasing roles in forestry policy and forest management in these countries, this trend is likely to continue, especially if high-yielding plantations are extensively established in tropical latitudes. Within Europe, a less obvious shift is likely as the century draws to an end. Maritime countries such as Britain and Ireland are likely to expand their production rapidly, as postwar plantations become productive, while rates of increase in central and northern Europe are likely to be slower. On both the global and European scales, therefore, there are likely to be signs of a shift towards the areas of high potential productivity as discussed in Chapter 2, while the dominance of the northern coniferous forest zone weakens in relative terms.

Industrial roundwood

Major contrasts exist between the industrial roundwood and fuelwood sectors in terms of composition, pattern and trends. While around 60 per cent of total roundwood production is from non-coniferous species, almost 70 per cent of industrial roundwood is coniferous. The extent of coniferous domination in this sector is slowly decreasing, as higher rates of annual increases in production characterise the hardwood sector of industrial roundwood as well as in fuelwood. Little change occurred during the first half of the century. According to Zon and Sparhawk (1923) three-quarters of the supply of industrial wood came from coniferous forests, compared with 76 per cent in 1955. By 1985, however, the percentage had fallen to 69, reflecting in particular the increasing exploitation of the tropical forest for this purpose. Nevertheless, the production of industrial roundwood is still strongly concentrated in the developed world (Table 6.4 and Figure 6.8).

The domination of industrial roundwood production by the United States and the Soviet Union is clearly defined and long established. Together, these two countries accounted for over 44 per cent of production in 1985, and if the contribution of Canada, the third major producer, is added, then the share amounts to 56 per cent. The same three countries were the largest producers in the early part of the century, accounting for around 74 per cent of the production of industrial timber (Zon and Sparhawk, 1923). The United States alone produced 53 per cent of the world's industrial timber at that time. Its share has decreased subsequently, to around one-quarter, as have those of the two other leading producers.

Although the United States and the Soviet Union remain dominant, their share of production is likely to continue to decrease, as production in tropical and other low-latitude countries increases. North America's share of softwood production, for example, is projected to decrease from 39 per cent in 1980 to 34 per cent in 2000, and Western Europe's share will also fall while those of Japan and Latin America are likely to increase (FAO, 1982a).

Brazil is now the fifth largest producer, whereas it was the seventh

Figure 6.8 Production of industrial roundwood (thousand m³) 1986

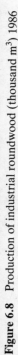

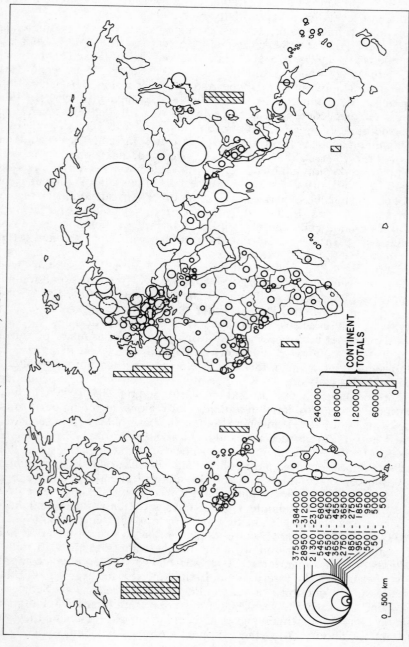

Source: Based on FAO Yearbooks of Forest Products

largest in 1975 and the eleventh in 1965. A number of other tropical countries are now major producers, including in particular Malaysia and Indonesia. In contrast to old-established countries such as Sweden where production levels have been relatively stable in recent decades, output from most tropical countries has expanded very rapidly. Commercial logging on a large scale began in many tropical countries in the 1960s and expanded in the 1970s. In Malaysia production rose by 49 per cent between 1975 and 1985, while in Indonesia it increased by 45 per cent. East Kalimantan (Indonesia) exemplifies the rapid expansion. Mechanical logging began in a joint venture with a Japanese company in 1960. In 1962 there were two concession-holders on an area of 400,000 hectares; by 1983 the number of concession-holders had grown to 106, working over 12.35 million hectares (Priasukmana, 1986). In some countries production rapidly grew to levels that could not be sustained, and soon dropped. For example, production fell by 46 per cent in the Philippines during the same period, and in Ivory Coast the decrease was 10 per cent. A similar trend had previously been experienced in some other African countries such as Nigeria and Ghana. In the latter, timber exports decreased spectacularly from 124 million cubic metres in 1973 to 11 million cubic metres in 1982 (WRI, 1985). In these countries the resource was over-exploited rather than husbanded, and the result was its erosion in the same way in which very different forest resources of countries such as the United States were damaged earlier in the century (see Chapter 3). Cycles of expansion and contraction reminiscent of the 'boom and bust' cycles of the Lake States and other parts of the United States a hundred years ago have been experienced in successive tropical countries over recent decades.

In the long term, the prospects of tropical countries as major producers of industrial roundwood are likely to depend largely on the successful establishment of a major plantation element in their forest resources. Table 6.5 illustrates estimates of potential returns to industrial plantations in representative schemes around the world. Sedjo (1984, 1986) concludes that these returns are large in a number of regions, including parts of the tropics and Southern Hemisphere, and on the basis of his figures such areas clearly outshine areas such as Scandinavia and the Northwest of the United States. On the other hand start-up costs may be high in some non-traditional locations, and both political and silvicultural risks may be high.

A number of countries, notably in subtropical latitudes, have been successful in establishing plantations to meet domestic requirements of industrial wood. For example, Chile, Kenya and Zambia succeeded in this respect over a relatively short time-scale of around twenty years (Spears, 1983). In Brazil, 4 million hectares of plantations now supply 60 per cent of domestic needs, compared with the 10 per cent from the 280 million hectares of Amazonian forest. At present industrial plantations comprise only 1 per cent of the forest area in Latin America, for example, but they already supply one-third of the continent's industrial wood (Sedjo and Clawson, 1984). By the year 2000, production from industrial plantations will be almost four times higher than in the mid-1980s, and they will account for about half of the continent's production (Sedjo, 1987). By

Table 6.5   Representative plantations: internal rates of return (1979 constant prices in perpetuity)

	Regime	
	Pulpwood	*Integrated**
South USA (*Pinus taeda*)	12.02	12.45
North-West USA (*Pseudotsuga menziesii*)	7.11	7.07
Brazil Amazonia (*Pinus caribaea*)	17.89	20.44
(*Gmelina* spp.)	27.53	23.54
Central (*Eucalyptus* spp.)	20.16	15.54
Chile (*Pinus radiata*)	23.39	17.50
New Zealand (*Pinus radiata*)	11.90	13.11
Australia (*Pinus radiata*)	10.68	10.06
Gambia/Senegal (*Gmelina* spp.)	18.42	17.52
Nordic countries (*Picea abies*)	4.61	5.57

* With sawtimber

Source: Based on Sedjo (1984)

2000, perhaps as much as one-third of all industrial roundwood removals in tropical countries will come from plantations, compared with 7 per cent in 1975 (USDA, 1982). In absolute terms, supply may increase tenfold between 1980 and 2000, reaching 100 million cubic metres per year (FAO, 1982a).

Composition of demand

The composition of demand for industrial wood has changed radically during the twentieth century. Demand for constructional timber and for pitprops has fallen, while that for wood for processing into pulp or board has increased. The trend is most apparent in old-established industrial countries such as the United States, for which the changing pattern of utilisation of wood is shown in Figure 3.3 (p. 45). In addition to the underlying trend of decreasing use of fuelwood, there is a clear shift from lumber towards manufactured wood products. Lumber consumption per capita has fallen to around one-third of its peak value at the beginning of the century, although the rate of decrease has slowed since around 1940. At the same time, both total and per capita consumption of pulp and plywood have risen steadily throughout the century. Worldwide, the ratio of production of sawlogs to that of pulpwood has decreased from around 4:1 in the 1940s (FAO, 1946) to little more than 2:1 in the 1980s. This trend reflects a steady decrease in the ratio of consumption of sawn wood to that of pulp and other highly processed products. Pulp and reconstituted panels accounted for around one-third of all industrial consumption in 1960, but by 1980 was almost 50 per cent and by 2000 may approach 60 per cent

(FAO, 1982a). This long-established trend reflects differential growth rates for different wood products. Consumption of fibre-based products has grown much faster than that of 'solid wood': the comparative annual rates of increase between 1960 and 1980 averaged 4.6 and 1.3 per cent respectively (FAO, 1982a). For the period from 1970 to 1982, annual growth in demand for industrial roundwood has averaged 1.0 per cent, compared with percentage rates of 2.0 for pulp, 3.2 for wood-based panels and 4.2 for paper for writing and printing (FAO, 1986a). The corresponding figure for sawn wood is around 0.5 per cent (Kuusela, 1987). In all these sectors, growth rates are much higher in the developing world than in the world as a whole or in the developed world.

In short, demand has been growing much faster for manufactured products than for sawn wood, and growth in the production of saw logs is now close to zero. These points are of fundamental importance in relation to prospects for the future adequacy of supplies of industrial wood. There are signs that coniferous sawlog resources that are economically exploitable are decreasing in traditional producing countries such as Canada and the Soviet Union, whilst the environmental lobby and conservation measures may limit the harvest from the remaining virgin coniferous forests of the United States. Potential supplies of wood for the more highly processed products are more plentiful and more widespread: these uses can draw on an increasing range of forest resources as wood technology develops. The perception of useful timber resources changes with technology (Chapter 1), and in practice each succeeding technological advance has been followed by an increase in the resource estimate.

In the early days of the wood pulp industry, spruce was the most suitable raw material, and early pulping plants were located mainly in areas such as northern Europe and the Northeast of the United States where spruce was abundant. Subsequently processes using pine were developed, initially for packaging materials and later also for fine paper. Thereafter, forests containing little or no spruce, which could previously be used only for lumber, became potential sources of paper-making fibre. New areas were therefore opened up, especially in the American South, where large areas of pine plantations were established on worn-out agricultural land (Clark, 1984), and more recently in Latin America and Oceania. This process of expansion has continued with the development of processes for pulping hardwood. The combination of technical developments and availability (and hence price) of hardwoods has led to a rapid growth in the use of broad-leaved species in pulping. This trend has been in operation even in traditional softwood areas such as the Nordic countries, where the proportion of hardwoods in pulpwood removals increased from 3 per cent in 1950 to 16 per cent by 1972 (Pringle, 1977). The trend, however, has been most spectacular in the case of Japan, where the contribution of hardwoods to pulpwood supply increased from 11 to 60 per cent between 1955 and 1970 (Shimokawa, 1977). This increase was accompanied by a rapid growth in imports of hardwood chips from the mid-1960s. These chips came initially from eucalyptus forests in Australia and from rubber and mangrove trees in Malaysia. During the 1970s, trade in chips of mixed tropical hardwoods ('jungle wood') developed between Papua New Guinea and Japan. While tropical rain forests still have limited industrial value (Ryti, 1986), in Papua New Guinea mixed forest containing 120 tree species has been used for the production of chips for export to Japan (Fenton, 1986). Such a change could revolutionise the use of the mixed tropical forest, where for long only a handful of tree species were considered commercially attractive (Whitmore, 1984). On a more modest scale, the same trend towards a widening of the range of species perceived as useful is evident in Indonesia. There the change in emphasis from log production for export to use for local plywood and sawmill industries has been accompanied by a widening of the range of harvested species.

The rise of the manufacturing sector has also been accompanied by an increase in the level of utilisation. While wasteful exploitation character-ised the American forest industry around the turn of the century, efficiency has since increased markedly. For example, in the United States the Weyerhauser Corporation reported that the level of timber utilisation per unit area increased from 21 per cent in 1950 to 79 per cent in 1975 (Cox et al., 1985). In Indonesia, almost one-third of the timber cut is regarded as waste because of rot or shattering (Schreuder and Vlosky, 1986), and logging waste, including damaged trees, amounts to 30–40 per cent of the timber harvested (Priasukmana, 1986). There is still plenty of scope for further improvement in efficiency, but in the United States, for example, the overall efficiency of wood utilisation has increased steadily at an annual rate averaging 0.8 per cent between 1950 and 1979 (USDA, 1982a).

World-wide, the use of mill residues has increased sharply in recent decades. Their contribution to total wood consumption rose from 5.7 per cent to 11.4 per cent in 1980, and may reach 12.7 per cent in 1990 (FAO, 1982a). It may amount to the equivalent of 300 million cubic metres of roundwood by 2000. Furthermore, waste papers can be recycled as inputs into some manufacturing processes, thereby reducing the requirement for roundwood. In the United States, the waste-paper recovery rate is around 25 per cent (US Statistical Yearbook 1987), while in Japan it has reached 50 per cent (Riethmuller and Fenelon, 1988), thereby achieving a major saving in primary raw material and in energy requirements in paper manufacture. In short, recycling and increased use of residues are likely to mean that net demand on the forest will increase less rapidly than consumption of wood products. In this respect, trends in the use of the forest/timber resemble those in other resource sectors such as mineral ores. With changing technology, perceptions of useful resources are revised, and increasing use is made of non-primary inputs (such as scrap metal). Both these trends tend to reduce pressures on the natural resource.

Trade in wood and wood products

A complex pattern of international trade in wood products has evolved, although less than 10 per cent of the total world production of wood leaves its country of origin (Gammie, 1981). Wood itself is a low grade and poorly

Table 6.6   Forest products: proportions entering international trade 1986

Product	Percentage entering trade (export)
Fuelwood and charcoal	0.1
Industrial roundwood	6.8
Saw logs and veneer logs	6.4
(coniferous)	5.0
(non-coniferous)	11.7
Pulpwood	10.2
Sawnwood	18.5
Wood-based panels	17.0
Wood pulp	16.1
Paper and board	21.2

Source: Based on statistics in FAO *Yearbook of Forest Products* 1986

transportable material, and only a small and decreasing volume of round-wood enters international trade. This volume amounted to around 3.4 per cent of total roundwood production in 1985, compared with 3.9 per cent in 1975. Almost all the roundwood entering international trade is intended for industrial purposes: trade in fuelwood is negligible. The proportion of production entering international trade increases with degree of processing, as Table 6.6 indicates. A marked differential exists between the shares of coniferous and non-coniferous saw logs entering international trade, reflecting the export of tropical hardwoods to the developed world. Nevertheless, the overall proportion of saw logs traded in this way is well under 10 per cent, while the corresponding proportions for several processed or manufactured wood products are around one-fifth.

The declining share of roundwood entering the international market is explained by the widespread wish to add value in the producing country, expressed in some cases in attempts to ban log exports. Furthermore, the trend in recent years has been for trade in more highly processed products such as paper, plywood and wood-based panels to grow faster than that in more basic products such as pulpwood or pulp, as Table 6.7 indicates. Between 1960 and 1974, for example, the proportion of paper production entering trade rose from 12 to 19 per cent, while that of pulp increased only slightly from 15 to 16 per cent (Pringle, 1977).

The overall pattern of imports and exports of forest products is very complex, as Figure 6.9 suggests. Many 'northern' countries are both importers and exporters, tending to import relatively basic products and to add value to these in industries developed initially on the basis of domestic wood production. Despite the complexity of the pattern, however, a number of general points stand out. First, a large proportion of trade in forest products comes from developed countries. These countries accounted for 90 per cent of the trade in 1963 and 86 per cent in 1985 (by value). North America and northern Europe have been the major exporters of

Table 6.7   Forest products exports: composition and trends 1975–85

	Composition by value (Percentage by total)		Percentage change in value 1975–85
	1975	1985	
Industrial roundwood	14.2	10.9	47.2
Sawlogs & veneer logs	10.2	8.3	55.6
Pulpwood	3.1	2.3	41.9
Other in, r'dwood	1.0	0.4	–28.3
Sawnwood	19.3	20.4	86.9
Wood-based panels	8.8	9.1	98.2
Pulp	20.7	15.8	46.7
Paper & board	36.7	43.6	127.3
Charcoal	0.1	0.1	102.6
Fuelwood	< 0.1	< 0.1	–46.4
Forest products			91.8

Source: Based on statistics in FAO *Yearbook of Forest Products* 1986

manufactured forest products, most of which have been based on softwoods, and account for over half the exports. Second, much of the trade is concentrated in a few major flows. Around half of world trade in forest products in recent decades has occurred in three main spheres: within North America, within western Europe, and between northern and western Europe (Kornai, 1987). In addition, Japan alone accounts for around 10 per cent of all imports, and is the focus of a rapidly expanding export trade from south-east Asia and the Pacific rim countries. On the basis of the gross value of imports of forest products, Japan is outranked by the United States, but it is the leading country in terms of net imports. In the United States, the huge value of imports is offset by exports. Japanese trade in forest products differs from that of the second largest net importer, the United Kingdom, in several respects. While the latter is poorly endowed with forest resources, Japan is one of the most extensively forested countries in the world. Paradoxically, it is also the largest importer. Japan also has a very different trading sphere centred in the western Pacific, while British supplies have traditionally come from North America and northern Europe. Furthermore, Japanese imports of saw logs and pulpwood are several orders of magnitude greater than those of the United Kingdom. Japan has favoured the import of primary products, while most of the forest-product imports into the United Kingdom are processed or manufactured. This policy of importing raw material rather than processed products has been supported by differential tariffs which discriminate against value-added products and which protect domestic industries. Such differentials are not unique to Japan, as Table 6.8 shows, although they are pronounced there. Tariffs on wood products generally increase with the level of processing, and the effect has been to favour the maintenance of processing industries in the 'traditional' forest-industry countries of the developed world, whilst discouraging the growth of

Figure 6.9 Trade in forest products

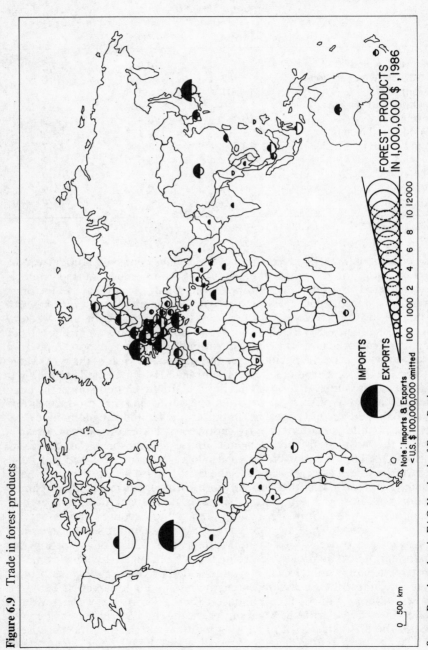

Source: Based on data in FAO *Yearbook of Forest Products*

Table 6.8   Tariff rates for forest products

(a) Japan 1986	Product	Percentage rate
	Saw logs	0
	Sawn timber*	0
	Woodchips	0
	Wood pulp	0
	Newsprint	3.1–4.6
	Printing & writing paper	3.1–4.6
	Finished timber	10
	Laminated timber	20
	Plywood (hardwood)	20
	(softwood)	15

* rate for pine under 160 mm is 7%

(b) EEC and Japan (Post Tokyo Round, concluded 1979)

	Product class	Percentage rate for imports from		
		Developing countries	Developed market ecs.	Socialist countries
Japan	wood in rough	0	0	0
	primary wood products	7.4	0.2	1.9
	secondary wood products	4.8	4.3	4.6
EEC	wood in rough	0	0	0
	primary wood products	1.9	0.8	0.8
	secondary wood products	1.5	1.7	3.2

Sources: (a) based on Riethmuller and Fenelon (1988); (b) based on Olechowski (1987)

manufacturing capacity in the developing world. At the same time, however, tariffs in developing countries are often even higher than in their developed counterparts, and also escalate with the level of processing.

For various reasons, this pattern of concentration of forest-product industries in the developed world in general and in Japan in particular is now changing. One reason is the general liberalising of trade and reduction or dismantling of tariff barriers. Another is the growing production of industrial roundwood from plantations in non-traditional locations such as Latin America, south-east Asia and the Pacific rim countries, at a time when there is little short-term scope for further expansion of production in traditional forest-product countries such as those of northern Europe. For example, Brazil by the mid-1990s is likely to produce quantities of pulp that are large in relation to world production, and is therefore likely to have a significant effect on world markets (Sedjo, 1980). National bans on log exports imposed by some countries in an effort to encourage the growth of domestic wood-using industries also encourage the trend. Also exports of logs from North America gave rise to much controversy from the 1960s

Table 6.9   Relative costs: pulpwood and paper production

(a) Growing and harvesting pulpwoods 1960s

Area	Species and growth (m^3/ha)		Growing US$/$m^3$	Logging US$/$m^3$
Chile	Pinus radiata	20	1.27	1.15
East Africa	Pinus spp.	17	1.90	2.00
SE USA	Pine	6.8–18.6	0.57–1.55	3.00
Sweden	Pine, Spruce	4.5	15.65	5.25

(b) Relative costs of major inputs in paper production 1984–5

	Pulpwood[1]	Fuel[2]	Labour[3]	
			Operator	Staff
Australia	30	130	27	38
New Zealand	20	170	20	30
Brazil	27	210	17	27
Japan	75	310	28	35
Canada (west)	37	175	50	61
United States (south)	47	180	52	69
Sweden	57	295	28	36

[1] Per cubic metre (under bark) at mill door, A$. [2] Per tonne oil equivalent, A$. [3] Per year, A$000

Sources: Based on Streyferrt (1968) and Riethmuller and Fenelon (1988)

and led to bans on exports of logs from federal forests (Cox, 1988). Furthermore, some forest-products industries may be perceived as polluting, and their expansion may be less than welcome by the environmentally conscious citizens of developed countries. In the case of Japan, for example, a preference is now being shown for expanding imports of pulp rather than woodchips, partly because of environmental concerns, partly because of instability in the supply of woodchips, and partly because of decreasing Japanese competitiveness in pulping. Much of the country's pulping and paper-making capacity is based on outdated machinery more than twenty years old. Rather than modernise such plant, several companies are actively seeking to develop overseas operations, including joint ventures in locations such as Tasmania (Riethmuller and Fenelon, 1988). Considerable advantages in terms of costs of raw materials, as well as in fuel, labour and management may also be enjoyed in countries such as Australia, New Zealand, Brazil and Chile, compared with Japan and other countries more traditionally associated with forest-products industries. Some examples of these advantages in terms of timber production and other costs are illustrated in Table 6.9. In short, the global structure of the wood-processing industry is being reshaped. 'Traditional' forest-product countries such as Finland have responded by becoming increasingly

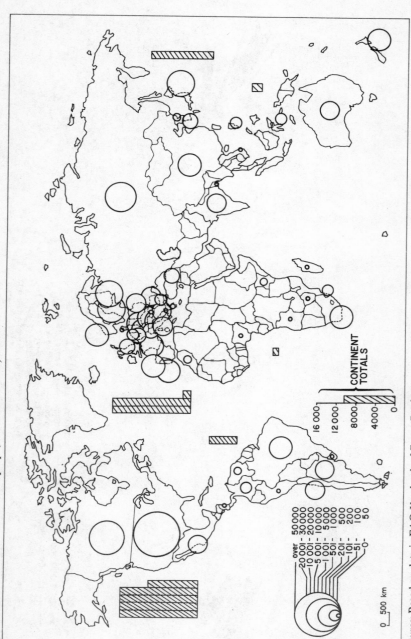

Figure 6.10   Production of wood pulp (thousand tonnes) 1986

Source: Based on data in FAO *Yearbook of Forest Products*

Figure 6.11 Directions of trade (exports): coniferous sawlogs, 1985

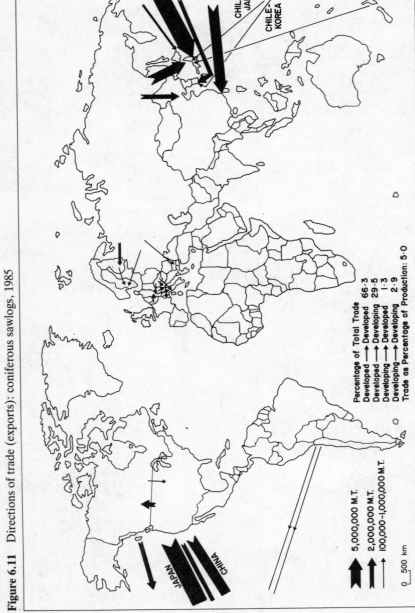

Percentage of Total Trade

Developed ➞ Developed   66·3
Developed ➞ Developing   29·5
Developing ➞ Developed   1·3
Developing ➞ Developing   2·9
Trade as Percentage of Production: 5·0

5,000,000 M.T.
2,000,000 M.T.
100,000–1,000,000 M.T.

0   500 km

Source: Based on data in FAO *Yearbook of Forest Products* 1986

Figure 6.12 Directions of trade (exports): non-coniferous sawlogs and veneer logs, 1985

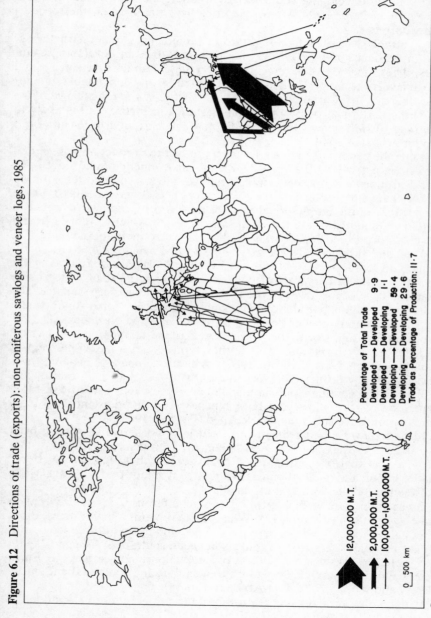

Percentage of Total Trade
Developed ⟶ Developed   9·9
Developed ⟶ Developing   1·1
Developing ⟶ Developed   59·4
Developing ⟶ Developing   29·6
Trade as Percentage of Production: 11·7

12,000,000 M.T.
2,000,000 M.T.
100,000-1,000,000 M.T.

0 500 km

Source: Based on data in FAO *Yearbook of Forest Products* 1986

specialised in higher-value products in which wood costs are relatively less important. As recently as the early 1960s it was the leading exporter of roundwood. This role has since passed to less developed countries, and the emphasis has switched to wood-based panels and then paper (Kiljunen, 1986). Some developing countries have undergone similar changes, and have switched to panels as new countries have emerged on the scene as log exporters.

Nevertheless, several factors retard or inhibit this global restructuring, and in particular the growth of woodpulp industries in developing countries. These include requirements of very large capital investments and a high level of technical skill, as well as substantial and dependable supplies of timber suitable for pulping (Bethel and Tseng, 1986). On balance, however, the pattern of pulp production as shown in Figure 6.10 is likely to continue to shift away from its traditional concentration in the northern coniferous forest zone.

While the pattern of trade varies from product to product, it is in general terms characterised by a high degree of involvement of the developed world. Collectively, the developing countries have accounted for no more than 16 per cent of total exports of wood products (Laarman, 1988). Large proportions of the international trade of most forest products are between developed countries, and the main foci, in North America, northern and western Europe and Japan, all lie in the North. Examples of the pattern of flow of one product – saw logs – are shown in Figures 6.11 and 6.12. Japan and to a lesser extent (South) Korea and China stand out as by far the main centre of imports of coniferous sawlogs, most of which come from the Pacific Northwest of the United States and western Canada. The major areas with exportable surpluses of softwood are North America and the Soviet Union: smaller flows occur from Chile and New Zealand. The export of logs and saw timber from New Zealand to Japan began in 1958 and 1967 respectively, and by 1972 they represented some 25 per cent of roundwood removals (Fenton, 1985). While the Japanese economy was growing rapidly during the 1960s and early 1970s, it seemed that export growth could continue indefinitely. Such expectations led to the rapid expansion of plantations, but both Japanese consumption and New Zealand exports have subsequently declined (Fenton, 1986).

In contrast with the Pacific theatre, which includes significant flows from the Soviet Far East to China and Japan, the European system (consisting of flows between western Europe countries and between the (western) Soviet Union and its neighbours) is a relatively minor one, as is also trade between the United States and Canada.

International trade in hardwood (non-coniferous) logs is different in scale and pattern (Figure 6.12). While Japan remains a major focus, more than half of the trade flows between the developing and developed world. By far the major direction of trade is between south-east Asia and Japan, but there are also distinct systems of interaction amongst western European countries (mainly from France to neighbouring countries) and, more clearly and simply, from west Africa to Europe.

Perhaps the most striking feature of international trade in wood is the remarkable growth in exports of tropical hardwoods over the last few decades. In the early part of the century, much of the trade consisted of dyewoods and tannin woods, and Latin America was the leading exporter. Pre-war, most of the exports from south-east Asia were of teak. Between 1946 and 1980, the volume of trade increased by twenty-four times, and the cumulative volume of trade during the 1970s exceeded that of the previous seven decades. This great increase reflected changes in both demand and supply. Growth in income and population, combined with a dwindling availability of certain species and grades of temperate hardwoods, led to greatly increased demand. On the supply side, mechanized logging and transport after the Second World War permitted the harvesting of species and areas that were previously considered unexploitable. Furthermore, improved technology for producing veneer and plywood from tropical hardwoods such as lauan and meranti opened up new markets for products such as doors and panels, whilst there have also been improvements in the technology of pulping. Although tropical hardwood logs comprise only 4 per cent of all trees harvested world-wide, production has been growing far more rapidly than that of other forms of timber. During the period from 1961 to 1980, annual growth in production averaged 4.8 per cent, compared with 1.2 per cent for softwood logs and 0.7 per cent for temperate hardwoods (Takeuchi, 1983). Much of the growth is attributable to Japan, which accounts for approximately half the world volume of traded tropical hardwood, compared with only 4 per cent in 1950 (Laarman, 1988).

The growth of exports of tropical hardwoods was accompanied by shifts in the pattern of production. In the early post-war period, the main source was Africa, but by the mid-1950s the Far East had become dominant and maintains that position to the present. Latin America accounts for only a very small proportion of exports. Within both Africa and the Far East, shifts have occurred from country to country, as production reached unsustainable levels and as bans have been imposed on log exports. The pattern of growth and decline experienced in the various forest regions of the United States in the late nineteenth century (Chapter 3) has been repeated, on a larger spatial scale if in a more subdued form, over the last thirty years. In Africa, log exports from Ghana and Nigeria peaked around 1960 and then declined, while those from Ivory Coast, Gabon and Cameroon increased. There have been similar trends in the Far East. The emphasis has moved from the Philippines to Indonesia and then to Malaysia, and in particular to Sabah and Sarawak. In the late 1970s, Indonesia and Malaysia accounted for nearly half of the production and three-quarters of the exports (Pringle, 1979): the latter alone was the source of 36 per cent of hardwood logs exported and 25 per cent of the sawn wood (Kumar, 1986). Thailand, which was once a major exporter of hardwood, is now a net importer. In the same way that log exports from individual countries within south-east Asia have risen and fallen, so also are they likely to do so from the region as a whole. Exports from the Far East are expected to decrease from 18.6 million cubic metres in 1980 to 9.2 million cubic metres by 2000 (FAO, 1982a).

Table 6.10 Log production, plywood production and sawmilling in East Kalimantan, Indonesia

	No. of concessions	Area (1000 ha)	Log production (1000 m³)	Workers
1969–70	13	1866	2527	2878
1971–72	34	4951	5537	9495
1973–74	65	7025	8411	12103
1975–76	70	7355	7260	19246
1977–78	86	8311	9883	23079
1978–79	93	8659	10159	26378
1979–80	99	9353	8809	26460
1980–81	101	9465	5634	15556
1981–82	104	9985	3150	10251
1982–83	104	9985	3418	11269
1983–84	104	9985	4174	9822

Year	Mills	Plywood Production (1000 m³)	Workers	Mills	Sawmill industry Production (1000 m³)	Workers
1978–79				61	87.3	1588
1979–80	8	18.7	3368	63	155.7	3685
1980–81	5	52.4	6034	287	277.0	6962
1981–82	7	172.6	7460	315	361.2	6678
1982–83	13	266.0	10816	318	122.5	6703
1983–84	22	602.7	19018	339	365.0	7499

Source: Compiled from data in Priasukmana (1986)

Concurrent with the growth in production and trade in tropical hardwoods there have been changes in the composition of exports. Whilst most exports from individual countries are initially in the form of logs, the emphasis then moves towards processed products such as plywood. In the case of Indonesia, for example, hardwood sawlog exports dropped to negligible levels in the early 1980s in response to a log export ban imposed from 1 January 1985, while production of plywood took off. In 1973 Indonesia had two plywood mills with an estimated output of 9,000 cubic metres but by 1986 the industry had grown to 108 mills producing more than 4.5 million cubic metres (Sinduredjo, 1986). Exports of plywood rose dramatically from 1,000 cubic metres in 1975 to more than 3.75 million in 1985. By 1982 Indonesia was the world's third largest producer of plywood, after the United States and Japan but ahead of Canada and the Soviet Union (see Figure 6.13) (Schreuder and Vlosky, 1986). Sawmilling also expanded dramatically, as Table 6.10 indicates: the clear trend in Indonesia, as in many other countries, was towards the production and export of manufactured wood products rather than logs.

Transit processors such as Singapore, which built up large-scale exports

Figure 6.13 Plywood production (thousand m³) 1985

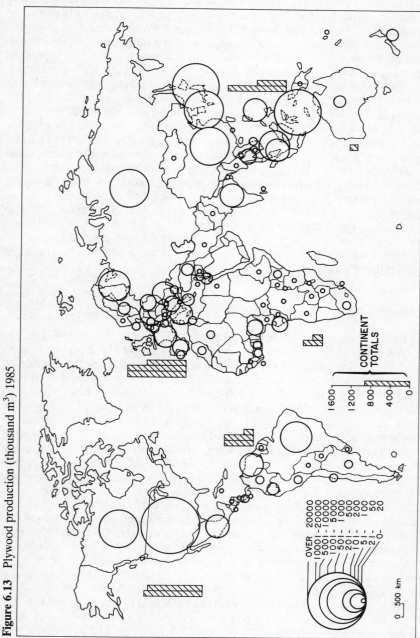

CONTINENT
TOTALS

1600
1200
800
400
0

OVER 20000
10001 - 20000
5001 - 10000
1001 - 5000
501 - 1000
101 - 500
51 - 100
21 - 50
1 - 20
0 - 20

0   500 km

Source: Based on data in FAO *Yearbook of Forest Products* 1986

of plywood on the basis of log imports, are very sensitive to such changes. In the long term, it seems probable that the trend will continue to be towards processing in the country of production, rather than in importing or transit countries such as Japan or Singapore. Transit processors in particular face serious problems as log export bans take effect.

In general terms, a slow and gradual shift is taking place in the forest-products industry. This shift is following that in the production of industrial roundwood, namely towards the parts of the world with high productivities. Different sectors of the industry are displaying this tendency at different rates and with different degrees of clarity. One important variable is the cost of wood relative to other inputs: another is the relative costs of transport of raw materials and of finished products. In some respects the shift is almost imperceptible: large degrees of inertia result from the capital investments in existing plant and skilled labour forces, and radical shifts are unlikely to occur in the short term. As constraints of wood supply and of environmental controls become increasingly significant in some of the traditional forest-products areas such as the Nordic countries and eastern North America, then much of the industry's expansion is likely to be set in areas such as the American South and tropical countries such as Brazil and Indonesia. These areas have already experienced major developments in forest-products industries: further expansion in these and similar areas can confidently be expected.

Prospects for industrial roundwood

For decades shortages of industrial roundwood have been predicted. At the beginning of the century, for example, the spectre of a timber famine haunted the United States (see Chapter 3). In mid-century, FAO asserted that a 'world-wide wood shortage exists and threatens to become critical' (FAO, 1946, p. 68). Most of these dire predictions have failed to materialise, as supply has greatly increased and as demand has changed or grown less rapidly than predicted. Growth in demand for industrial roundwood in particular has frequently been overestimated. For example in 1966 FAO estimated that the world would require 1,500 million cubic metres of industrial wood per year by 1975 (FAO, 1966) while actual production in that year was under 1,300 million cubic metres (incidentally forecast fuelwood requirements and actual production were very close (1,200 and 1,180 million cubic metres respectively). Similarly, many national forecasts have exceeded actual consumption, for example in countries such as Japan, the United Kingdom and the United States. Part of the reason for such overestimates is that the rate of increase in demand for saw timber for each unit of increase in per capita income has decreased. This has been especially true in Japan (e.g. Nomura, 1986). As a result many projections for national and global consumption have been revised downwards. On the global scale, demand for wood fibre is now expected to rise at an average rate of 1.8 per cent annually between 1980 and 2000, compared with an average of 2.4 per cent for the period from 1960 to 1980

(FAO, 1982a). At the same time as forecasts of growth in demand have been revised downwards, the prospects for supply have at worst not deteriorated. Inventories have continued to increase in a number of countries such as the United States, and in many countries removals have been less than net annual increments.

The changed perception of prospects for industrial wood is exemplified by that of FAO. In contrast to its earlier views, FAO concluded in 1982 that 'The world's supply of industrial roundwood is considered adequate to meet its growing fiber needs throughout the balance of this century' (FAO, 1982a, p. 197). This does not imply that no problems of supply will be encountered. On the contrary, it is expected that a shortage of high-quality hardwood logs will be encountered as supplies from the Far East forests diminish (and the small supplies expected from plantations will fall far short of compensating (Grainger, 1988). There may also be a strain on supplies of softwood logs and pulpwood. Furthermore, all types of wood may be scarce in some regions, such as western Europe and Japan (FAO, 1982a). Nevertheless, regional or sectoral scarcity is quite different from global scarcity. Furthermore, some of the expected shortages are offset by relative abundance in other sectors, or by continued expansion of plantations. For example mixed tropical hardwoods could physically contribute more, in terms of quantities, to industrial wood requirements, and the potential supply of hardwood fibre logs is abundant, especially in countries such as the United States and France where they are currently under-utilised. Much of the projected growth in demand for hardwood supplies is for pulp and reconstituted panels, rather than for 'solid wood' products. And the annual afforestation of the 1–2 million hectares of land that would be required to match an annual increment of up to 20 million cubic metres of softwood supplies is feasible (FAO, 1982a). Wood volumes equivalent to projected industrial needs for the year 2000 could in theory be met by production from 100–200 million hectares of plantations, or 3.7–7 per cent of the closed forest area (Sedjo and Clawson, 1984).

In short, the prospects for the adequacy of supplies of industrial wood, are largely if not invariably bright. Those for the fuelwood sector are another matter.

Fuelwood

Fundamental contrasts exist between fuelwood and industrial wood in terms of patterns and trends of production, ownership and management of the resource, and adequacy of supply. Much of the fuelwood supply comes from woodland or farm trees rather than closed forest. The greater part of it comes from hardwood trees, and its production is centred in low latitudes. Supplies of industrial wood are likely to be adequate to meet demand to the end of the century and beyond, while severe shortages of fuelwood already exist. The so-called fuelwood crisis has emerged as a major issue, and fuelwood is one of the most problematic sectors of natural resources in terms of adequacy of supply and resource destruction.

Like industrial wood, fuelwood is used in a variety of ways. Direct consumption as firewood for domestic cooking and heating is usually by far the largest use. Some fuelwood is converted to charcoal, which may then be used for domestic or for industrial purposes. Substantial quantities are used in industry, and although domestic use represents the larger sector, industrial consumption remains significant in many parts of the world.

Unlike industrial wood, fuelwood is usually obtained by self-collection by households, and only relatively small quantities enter the market. This mode of procurement prevails in the developed and developing worlds alike. In the United States, only one-quarter is purchased (Skog and Watterson, 1984), while in India the proportion is under 13 per cent (Agarwal, 1986). It does not follow, of course, that no costs are incurred in acquiring supplies, but these costs are not necessarily of a monetary nature.

The analysis of the fuelwood sector encounters especially severe data problems, since much of the production does not enter the market. In compiling statistics on fuelwood, FAO relies heavily on assumed per capita rates of consumption, which themselves vary with a number of factors including the relative availability of the material. Some imprecision and uncertainty are therefore likely to exist, especially in relation to trends in production. Nevertheless, it is clear that the production of fuelwood is increasing more rapidly than that of industrial wood (Table 6.1 and Figure 6.3). It is also clear that the pattern of production is very different from that of industrial wood (compare Figures 6.8 and 6.14).

Pattern of production: the global scale

The production of fuelwood is overwhelmingly concentrated in the developing world. Around 85 per cent of annual production in the mid-1980s was located there. In this respect, production of fuelwood is the converse of industrial wood. The composition of supply also strongly contrasts with that for industrial wood, with over 80 per cent coming from hardwood sources. Although significant quantities of fuelwood are produced in many parts of the developed world, the northern coniferous forest is much less significant in this sector than it is for industrial roundwood. A striking feature of Figure 6.14 is the degree of dominance of low-latitude countries in the pattern of production. As might be expected, large countries such as Brazil, China and India are the leading producers, accounting between them for just over one-third of total production. The production of fuelwood is less concentrated than that of industrial roundwood, for which top two producers account for around half of the world output (p.148).

Less immediately obvious from Figure 6.14, but equally or more significant, is the scale of production from countries with modest forest resources. Large volumes of fuelwood are produced from the savannah or *miombo* woodland (Chapter 2) of African countries. In many of these countries both the volume of growing stock and of net annual increment per unit area are low, but the pressures of demand for fuelwood are very

Figure 6.14   Production of fuelwood and charcoal (thousand m³), 1985

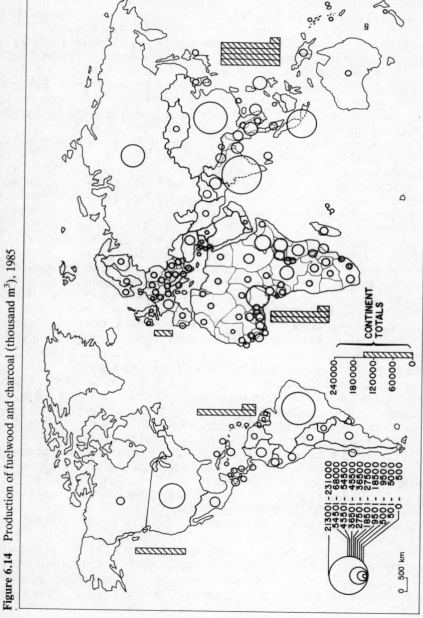

Source: Based on data in FAO *Yearbook of Forest Products* 1986

high. The consequence of such pressures on a limited resource is all too frequently resource depletion and fuelwood scarcity.

At the same time, however, fuelwood production cannot be considered solely in relation to forest resources, and indeed much of it comes from non-forest sources. For example, in Thailand during the 1970s some 57 per cent of fuelwood came from outside the forest or from wood residues. In Sri Lanka over half came from coconut and rubber plantations, while in Tunisia four-fifths came from shrubs and tree crops (Arnold and Jongma, 1977). Much of the fuelwood produced in many countries comes from farms, and 2–5 per cent of the farm area can usually grow trees for fuel (and for other purposes) without loss in agricultural production. In eastern Java, for example, 63 per cent of the fuelwood consumed by farmers comes from farm trees: as few as six coconut palms can supply the fuelwood requirements of a family of five (Ben Salem and van Nao, 1981). In Kenya and neighbouring areas of east Africa, almost all fuelwood requirements can be supplied by a combination of sources including dispersed farm trees, hedgerows around homesteads and field boundaries, and small woodlots on soils unsuitable for cropping (Winterbottom and Hazlewood, 1987). Furthermore, fuelwood is regularly available in areas where fallow systems of agriculture are practised. The clearing of fallow areas provides considerable amounts of woody material (Foley, 1987). In Mali, for example, a cropping cycle of four to five years is followed by eight to ten years of fallow, from which 30–50 per cent of the fuelwood consumption of small-scale farmers can be met. In addition, an average of seven trees per hectare, representing the remnant of the original vegetation, survives on field and fallow and also contributes to the fuelwood requirements (Ohler, 1985). It is concluded by Bailly et al. (1982) that the integration of trees into agricultural systems is the most worthwhile solution to the fuelwood problem. Plantations are expensive, while the improvement of the natural forest is cheap but inadequate.

The supply of fuelwood therefore depends on the nature and condition of the agricultural land resource and not only on the forest resource. Nevertheless, the forest resource is itself contracting in the face of pressures of fuelwood demands in many countries, including for example Pakistan (e.g. Biswas, 1987). Dead trees and branches have traditionally supplied much of the fuelwood requirement, and the cutting of livewood usually becomes a threat to the forest area only when a stress factor comes into play. This stress factor may take the form of rapid population growth, urbanization, or restriction of access for wood gathering as parts of the (previously common-property) forest become privatised or nationalised (Goodman, 1987; Arnold, 1987a). In addition, the clearance of forests may bring new pressures to bear. For example in Kenya, the removal of forests for military reasons in the 1950s and for cash crops had a profound effect on local communities (Ngugi, 1988), and one result was the fuelwood 'crisis' that developed as pressures were focused on the remaining resources of woods and trees. A similar process operated over a longer time and on a larger scale in India. Following the passing of the India Forest Act in 1865 (see Chapters 3 and 5), large areas of forest were reserved for commercial

Figure 6.15 Production of fuelwood and charcoal as a percentage of total roundwood production, 1985

 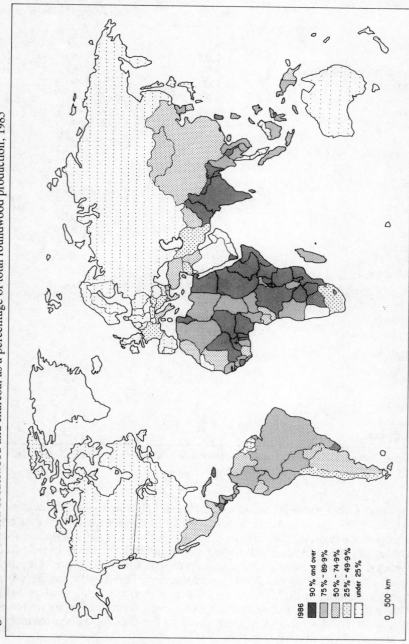

1986

■ 90 % and over

▓ 75 % – 89·9 %

░ 50 % – 74·9 %

· 25 % – 49·9 %

□ under 25 %

0 500 km

Source: Based on data in FAO *Yearbook of Forest Products* 1986

Table 6.11 Woodfuel consumption

Country	Consumption per capita (cubic metres)	Woodfuel as percent of total energy consumption
Angola	0.96	71.7
Benin	1.05	89.8
Central African Rep.	1.06	89.4
Chad	1.62	96.2
Ethiopia	0.83	89.9
Ghana	0.60	61.9
Ivory Coast	0.78	47.6
Kenya	1.48	82.8
Madagascar	0.59	74.7
Malawi	0.90	85.8
Mali	0.58	86.8
Niger	0.58	80.2
Nigeria	0.84	60.0
Senegal	0.55	47.8
Sudan	1.75	87.4
Uganda	1.77	95.9
Zaïre	0.91	81.5
Zimbabwe	0.96	33.6
Brazil	1.25	37.2
Chile	0.50	15.6
Colombia	0.50	15.8
Honduras	1.03	59.5
Bangladesh	0.32	68.5
China	0.16	8.2
India	0.29	32.5
Indonesia	0.74	51.1
Malaysia	0.50	14.4
Pakistan	0.21	23.3
Philippines	0.55	35.6

Sources: Compiled from data in Agarwal (1986) and FAO *Yearbooks of Forest Products*

purposes. Other areas were set aside to meet the needs of the local rural population for fuelwood and fodder. Many of these forests have suffered disproportionately in the face of growing population, and most of them have either been converted to agricultural land or have been totally degraded (Shyamsunder and Parameswarappa, 1987). Rural development projects may themselves lead to problems. The development of an irrigation scheme in the Tana basin of Kenya, for example, resulted in the trebling of the local population and severe impacts on the floodplain forest. Inadequate consideration had been given to the fuelwood requirements of the increased population (Hughes, 1987).

The relative importance of fuelwood production, compared with that of industrial roundwood, is illustrated in Figure 6.15. This map is a reminder that few individual countries conform to the overall pattern of production on the global scale, which is approximately evenly divided between fuelwood and industrial wood. Many developing countries use 80 per cent or more of their wood production as fuelwood, and in some cases the proportion is as high as 90 per cent. In some countries, such as those of the Sahel, fuelwood provides around 90 per cent of total energy consumption, as Table 6.11 shows.

Most of the biggest producers in absolute terms, including Brazil, China and India, are characterised by a much lower fuelwood share in energy supply, although fuelwood share in total wood production remains high. In much of the developed world, fuelwood accounts for under 10 per cent of wood production, and supplies a very minor or even negligible share of energy requirements.

The relative importance of fuelwood production in this respect is greatest in a number of African countries. Here the forest resource has not attracted development geared to large-scale production of industrial wood, but it has been intensively exploited for fuelwood. A notable feature of Figure 6.15 is the fact that the fuelwood sector remains very large or even dominant even in countries such as Indonesia and Ivory Coast, where the forest resource has been used for commercial logging for industrial purposes in recent decades.

Pattern of production: the local scale

The growing scarcity of fuelwood in parts of the developing world means that supplies have to be drawn from increasing distances. This tendency has to some extent characterised the use of the forest resource for the production of industrial wood as the world economy has expanded in recent centuries, but in the fuelwood sector it is especially apparent. Distances of several kilometres have frequently to be travelled to obtain firewood even in rural areas, while supplies for urban centres may have to be transported over distances of several tens of kilometres. The depletion of forests around cities is not new. In south-east Brazil, for example, removals for wood and charcoal constituted a demanding and extractive use of the forest around towns and cities by the nineteenth century (Dean, 1983), while concentric circles of deforestation were becoming evident around the cities of the Sahel by 1935 (Thomson, 1988). The extent and scale of depletion around cities have, however, greatly increased in recent decades.

In rural areas substantial and increasing parts of the day are now occupied for many people in the developing world by firewood-collecting. In parts of Sudan, for example, fuelwood collectors by the 1970s had to walk for one to two hours from their villages, whereas ten years previously adequate supplies were available within ranges of fifteen to twenty minutes (Digerness, 1979). In some areas of the developing world, women and children may spend up to 40 per cent of their daylight hours in scavenging for fuelwood (Goodman, 1987). In central Tanzania, it may take 300 man-days (or more usually woman-days) of work per year to provide the fuelwood for an average household (Grainger, 1982). In the Kigoma region of that country, villagers now have to walk 10 kilometres for firewood whereas twenty years ago they had to go only 1 kilometre (Fergus, 1983). In parts of India, collecting distances in some localities increased from 1.5–2 kilometres in the 1970s to 8–10 kilometres in the 1980s (Agarwal, 1986). In parts of Nepal, the collecting of fuelwood, which might have taken an hour or two per day in the previous generation, by the 1970s was taking a whole day (Eckholm, 1975).

The problem of diminishing resources and increasing distances is especially severe around some of the Sahelian cities. By the 1970s, fuelwood for Ougadougou mostly came from a belt lying from 50 to 100 kilometres from the city (Ki-Zerbo, 1981), while almost all woody growth had disappeared within a 70-kilometre radius of Niamey (Agarwal, 1986). In the case of Dakar, fuelwood and charcoal are supplied from as far as 400 kilometres (UN, 1977). 'Islands' of depleted fuelwood resources therefore occur at various scales around both villages and cities. In many instances the resource has been impoverished at the very time when rapid growth in population has occurred, giving rise to numerous local shortages of fuelwood. Increasing scarcity around the urban centres especially is directly reflected in rising costs of fuelwood. In the Sahel and also in parts of east Africa, up to 40 per cent of salaries may be taken up by the purchase of fuelwood (Ki-Zerbo, 1981; Mnzava, 1981). In parts of Tanzania, almost half of the income of families on minimum wages may go on fuelwood (Fergus, 1983). In Addis Ababa or Maputo, a family can spend up to half a week's wages in buying enough fuelwood or charcoal for survival (Goodman, 1987). Even if fuelwood does not have to be purchased, there is an indirect or opportunity cost as a result of the time taken to procure supplies. Substantial parts of the day may be given over to obtaining fuelwood, and this cost falls especially on women, whose responsibility fuelwood supply has traditionally been in many parts of the developing world.

Significant differences exist between patterns of production for rural and urban consumption. For rural consumption, production is largely from dead trees, bushes, farm trees and other non-forest sources. Much of it is in the form of twigs, small branches or roots. The scale of production is usually small, and it is carried out for and by the household. Firewood collection of this type is unlikely to cause serious deforestation. Production for urban or industrial use, however, may be quite different. Its scale may be far greater, it may be organised commercially, and it is far more likely to result in deforestation. If a market exists, there may be a strong incentive to cut live trees, and organised gangs of woodcutters, perhaps operating illegally or in collusion with forest guards, may plunder even nominally protected forests. This can happen not only around cities, but also at greater distances, if the wood is converted to the more easily transportable charcoal (Eckholm et al., 1984). The switch from fuelwood to charcoal which often accompanies the migration of rural dwellers to the city is potentially destructive of the resource. The loss ratio on conversion of wood to charcoal is around 2.5:1. A poor family moving to an urban area may therefore require two and a half times as much wood (assuming that their fuel requirements remained constant) and may therefore exert two and a half times as much pressure on the resource (O'Keefe and Kristoferson, 1984).

The use of fuelwood in cottage industries and for rural processing activities such as tobacco-curing and tea-drying can have similar results in terms of forest removal. These activities are estimated to account for between 11 and 25 per cent of the fuelwood used in the developing world (Agarwal, 1986). In Tanzania salt production through brine evaporation in Kigoma region over a thirty-year period consumed a quantity of fuelwood equivalent to the clear felling of 2200 square kilometres: the surviving area of forest in the region amounts to only 9,000 square kilometres (Fergus, 1983). In the same country, the wood from one hectare of savannah is required to cure the tobacco crop from a similar area (Mnzava, 1981). During the early 1970s tobacco-curing consumed more than 1 million cubic metres per year (Arnold and Jongma, 1977). With rapid expansion of cash crops such as tobacco, there has been rapid contraction of parts of the savannah woodlands. The production of 'industrial' fuelwood in dry areas in particular may have long-term detrimental effects. For example, in Australia the environs of some nineteenth-century mining towns are surrounded by a zone up to 50 kilometres wide from which fuelwood was collected and within which regeneration has not occurred (UN, 1977).

Consumption levels and resource adequacy

A feature of fuelwood use is the widely varying level of per capita domestic consumption both between countries and within countries. Consumption levels vary greatly even between countries where wood constitutes the main source of energy, as Table 6.11 indicates. In many countries, per capita consumption is around one cubic metre per year, a figure which, incidentally, is similar to that for the consumption of industrial wood in many developed countries. Considerably higher levels characterise some African countries such as Sudan and Uganda, while much lower rates are typical of many Asian countries. As a very broad generalisation, per capita consumption levels correlate with the extent of forest and woodland and with the availability of the resource. In parts of the developing world where fuelwood is plentiful, 2,000 kilograms or more may be used per person per year, while in areas of scarcity only one-quarter of that amount may be used (Eckholm et al., 1984). Economic factors are also, of course, a major influence on levels of consumption. They tend to reach a maximum in developing countries in the middle range of income (Laarman, 1987). As income rises, more fuelwood is initially consumed, but beyond a certain level its use decreases as other fuels such as oil are substituted. According to Foley (1985), price influences the amount of fuel that is consumed, but does not have a great influence on choice between fuels. As he acknowledges, however, this conclusion leaves unanswered the question of what determines the transition from wood to other fuels as a country becomes richer. 'Real income and an index of commercial energy prices are significant factors in relation to demand, but adjustments in consumption in response to these factors tend to be very slow and slight (Laarman and Wohlgenant, 1984). These workers also found that a contracting forest area was a significant variable in terms of supply, but that it had a stronger braking effect on fuelwood consumption in middle-income than in low-income developing countries.

Since levels of consumption appear to depend on the availability of the resource and on income, it is not surprising that consumption levels also vary greatly within countries. In Tanzania, for example, household consumption in villages near wooded areas is three times higher than in villages with little or no woodland (Agarwal, 1986). Similarly in Nepal, people moving to the well-wooded plains, where firewood is relatively abundant, consume twice as much as those remaining in the forest-depleted hills (Earl, 1975). In essence, people use more wood when it is readily available than when it is scarce.

This truism may partly explain the enormous range of estimates of per capita consumption reported for countries such as Nepal. A factor of 67 separates the highest and lowest estimates (6.67 and 0.1 cubic metres respectively) reported by Thompson and Warburton (1988). Even when the extreme highest figures were excluded, a range factor of 26 remained. Amongst the possible reasons cited for such variation are confusion (not least over units of measurement) between local people and visiting consultants or researchers, and misstating of actual levels of consumption as a result of suspicion or apprehension of tax collection or forest regulations. Levels of use of fuelwood also, of course, depend on the availability and price of alternative fuels, and therefore vary through time. Much uncertainty therefore exists over the concept of fuelwood 'needs', and this uncertainty is matched in some areas by that surrounding the availability of fuelwood. In Nepal, for example, estimates of forest productivity (the ultimate determinant of fuelwood supply) range from 0.2 to 15 or even 30 cubic metres per hectare per year (Thompson and Warburton, 1988). When both consumption and potential supply are so variable or uncertain, therefore, it is extremely difficult to quantify the dimensions of the fuelwood crisis.

Perhaps the best-known of the assessments of these dimensions is that produced by FAO (1982b). It is summarised in Table 6.12, 'Acute scarcity' is defined in terms of the depletion of fuelwood resources to the point where sufficient fuelwood cannot be obtained even by over-cutting, and consumption is below minimal needs. Approximately 100 million people lived in such areas in 1980, approximately half of them in Africa (Figure 6.16). A further 1,000 million lived in 'deficit situations', where minimal needs could be satisfied only by over-cutting and depletion of the resource. In 1980 almost 1,400 million people lived in areas of acute scarcity or deficit, and by 2000 that number may increase to close on 3,000 million.

Table 6.12a Populations involved in fuelwood deficit situations (millions)

	Acute scarcity	*Deficit*	*1980 Prospective deficit*	*2000 Acute scarcity or deficit*
Africa	55	146	112	535
Near East & North Africa		104		268
Asia Pacific	31	832	161	1671
Latin America	26	201	50	512
Total	112	1283	323	2986

Table 6.12b Fuelwood situation in Africa south of Sahara, 1980

	Population depending mainly on fuelwood (millions)	*Fuelwood Needs*	*Availability m³/inhabitant/ year*	*Balance*	*Total balance million m³*
Acute scarcity					
Arid & sub-arid areas	13.1	0.5	0.05–0.1	–0.45	–6
Mountainous area & islands	35.7	1.4–1.9	0.5–0.7	–1.1	–40
Deficit					
Savannah areas	131.4	1.0–1.5	0.8–0.9	–0.5	–66
Prospective deficit					
Savannah areas	65	1.0–1.5	1.8–2.1	+0.7	+45
High forest areas	36.5	1.2–1.7	1.8–2.0	+0.5	+20
Satisfactory					
High forest areas	6.2	1.2–1.5	5–10	over 4	+50

Source: FAO (1982b)

It does not necessarily follow, of course, that each of these persons will directly suffer from a shortage of fuelwood, as higher-income groups can subsitute oil. Nevertheless, around 57.7 per cent of the 2,000 million persons dependent on fuelwood in the developing countries in 1980 did not have access to sufficient supplies, and the proportion may rise to 89 per cent by 2000 (Montalembert and Clement, 1983). The problem is by any standard a major one, and as Figure 6.16 indicates, a striking feature of its spatial pattern is its widespread occurrence. While little scarcity occurs or is expected to occur in the equatorial zone (except for parts of Andean Ecuador and of east-central Africa), several separate areas of acute scarcity occur in locations ranging from the Andes and Caribbean through

Figure 6.15 Fuelwood supplies

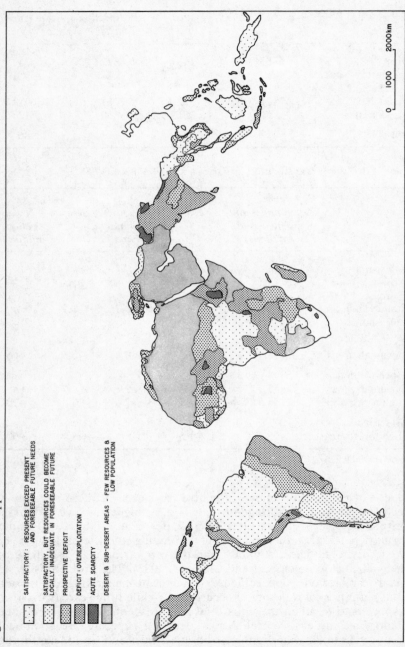

SATISFACTORY : RESOURCES EXCEED PRESENT
     AND FORESEEABLE FUTURE NEEDS

SATISFACTORY, BUT RESOURCES COULD BECOME
LOCALLY INADEQUATE IN FORESEEABLE FUTURE

PROSPECTIVE DEFICIT

DEFICIT : OVEREXPLOITATION

ACUTE SCARCITY

DESERT & SUB-DESERT AREAS - FEW RESOURCES &
        LOW POPULATION

0 1000 2000km

Source: FAO (1982b)

Sahelian Africa to the flanks of the Himalayas. Huge tracts of eastern Brazil, the savannah lands of Africa, and India also face actual or prospective deficits. The crisis indeed has international if not global dimensions, and as such represents one of the most notable resource problems of history.

The fuelwood shortage

Fuelwood has become increasingly scarce over the last twenty years. Since 1970 fuelwood and charcoal have increased in price relative to other goods at an annual rate of 1.5–2 per cent. Prior to 1970 there was a similar rate of decrease (Wardle and Palmieri, 1981). The resource has been depleted as a result of the pressures exerted on it. Various interrelated factors have contributed to the degradation: urban growth, the spread of charcoal production and the transition of fuelwood from a free good available to all into a commercial commodity (Montalembert and Clement, 1983).

As a major resource issue, the fuelwood shortage has attracted much attention and has generated some controversy. The effects of the shortage have proved to be almost as controversial as possible solutions. The woodland resource has undoubtedly been severely depleted in many parts of the world, and in addition to the ensuing economic and social problems, various environmental problems such as accelerated soil erosion have been reported. Furthermore, it has frequently been suggested that a fuelwood shortage initiates a vicious downward spiral in the welfare of some rural communities, whereby increased walking distances to supplies lead to a greater use of dung as an alternative fuel, and hence less use of it as a fertiliser for crops. The loss of dung as manure has been estimated to amount to a loss of as much as 20 million tons of grain production annually (Agarwal, 1986). In short, depletion of the woodland resources leads to a deterioration of farmland and hence to an increasing shortage of food as well as fuel (e.g. Eckholm et al., 1984). As indicated in Chapter 4, the general truth of this relationship has been questioned by commentators such as Bajracharya (1983a), who report that in Nepal at least, dung is used as an alternative to fuelwood in winter, when it is not required as a fertiliser. Nevertheless, there is little doubt that many communities have suffered greatly because of shortages of fuelwood.

Numerous problems are encountered in the search for solutions. To many governments of developing countries, investment in fuelwood resources has been perceived as a retrograde step in the pursuit of progress. Furthermore, state forestry services have traditionally been oriented towards the protection of forest reserves and the commercial production of industrial timber, rather than towards fuelwood (Noronha, 1981). These perceptual and institutional factors have been major handicaps.

It is apparent that simple single solutions are not available. The use of more efficient wood-burning stoves may help to alleviate the problem in some areas, whilst in others a variety of measures, including agro-forestry

and more intensive management of the existing resource, fuelwood plantations and the use of charcoal, may help. Agro-forestry systems may help to
increase household production of fuelwood in some rural areas, but even
here rapid population growth may be a serious constraint. In Kenya, for
example, it has been established that the intensity of management of farm
woodlands increases with population density: planted and managed woody
biomass increases as a percentage of total on-farm woody biomass as
population density increases. And the amount of land devoted to the
production of woody biomass also increases with population density
(Bradley, 1988). Nevertheless, population densities may be so great in
some areas that large deficits are experienced, despite these trends.
Despite these local problems, however, agro-forestry probably remains the
most promising solution to the problem of fuelwood shortage. Around 300
million hectares of agro-forestry could (in theory) supply the fuelwood
needs of 2,000 million people on a continuing basis, assuming a yield of
5 cubic metres per hectare per year and an annual requirement of 0.75
cubic metres per person per year (Goodman, 1987).

Population pressures may also militate against more intensive and
effective management of existing resources. Such management becomes
more difficult, as well as more necessary, as the traditional institutional
systems and structures suffer increasing stress. Common-property land
constitutes a particular problem in some areas. The rural poor are heavily
dependent on fuelwood from such land: in parts of India, for example, 90
per cent of the landless labourers and small farmers rely on it (Agarwal,
1986). The extent of common land contracts as private ownership becomes
established, and over-harvesting and rapid depletion become almost
inevitable as population pressures increase. The poor, as well as the
women, therefore tend to suffer disproportionately.

Fuelwood plantations and the use of charcoal imply the monetisation of
fuelwood production. In many areas fuelwood has been regarded as a free
good, and farmers therefore are not readily persuaded to plant it, and are
even less inclined to view it as a cash crop. The perceptions of both
consumers and potential producers may therefore have to be altered if a
successful transition is to be achieved. Furthermore, production from some
plantations, for example in the Sahel, has proved to be disappointing and
far below the projections employed in investment appraisal (e.g. Eckholm
et al., 1984). In the Philippines yields from plantations established under a
'dendrothermal power' programme have been far less than expected:
annual growth rates of 75–100 cubic metres per hectare were predicted but
some yields have been less than 100 cubic metres over entire four-year
cycles of growth (Durst, 1986). Enormous sums of money have been
devoted to forestry products in the Sahel in particular, but there has been a
decline in the availability of fuelwood. Most of the projects have involved
plantations: few have been directed at managing and utilising existing
forests, although these would also contribute food, fodder and a range of
'minor' products (Gritzner, 1988).

Nevertheless, the combination of fuelwood plantation and charcoal
production offers many attractions. For example, this mode of production

could be freed from proximity to the market, and located with greater consideration for climate and soil (e.g. Kelta, 1987). Use of high-value, relatively transportable charcoal, as opposed to wood, could mean that plantations could be located in areas with optimal growth potential or alternatively on poor land with minimal impact on agriculture, and not necessarily in optimal location with respect to the market. While 30–50 per cent of the heat value of wood is lost on its conversion to charcoal (Arnold and Jongma, 1977), the use of charcoal rather than fuelwood has clear advantages in some instances. In addition to permitting the development of 'remote' fuelwood plantations, it can be produced from wood residues and from non-commercial species available, respectively, from wood-using industries and from land-clearing.

Fuelwood plantations have been established for many years in a few areas. For example, farmers on coastal saline soils around Madras grow casuarina trees on short rotations, maintaining a tradition dating back to the nineteenth century (Foley, 1985). And energy plantations consisting mainly of eucalyptus were established around Addis Ababa in the 1890s in response to a severe wood shortage (Eckholm et al., 1984). More recently small commercial fuelwood plantations designed for supplying local urban markets have been expanding rapidly in parts of India (Arnold, 1987b). In Gujarat the rate of private planting increased fourfold between 1975 and 1979, doubled again by 1981 and yet again by 1983. By then the equivalent of more than 150,000 hectares had been planted. This rapid expansion was stimulated by very attractive rates of financial return (Arnold, 1983; WRI, 1985).

In India some attempts have also been made to integrate fuelwood production in industrial plantations. Degraded land is offered to industry for planting, on condition that up to 30 per cent of the biomass, in the form of top, lop and bark can be removed free of charge by local people, and also that a proportion of fodder species be grown (Shyamsunder and Parameswarappa, 1987). As yet only a very small area is committed to such schemes.

These examples of fuelwood and multi-purpose plantations, however, are on small and localised scales. South Korea offers an example of a much more spectacular scale of reforestation oriented to fuelwood. Under a village fuelwood programme launched in 1973, more than 1 million hectares of land were planted. In addition, 600,000 hectares of existing fuelwood plantations and more than 3 million hectares of other forest land were brought under more intensive management (WRI, 1985). This scale is most unusual, and its community basis is, with the possible exception of China, unique. Extensive establishment of community plantations elsewhere has proved very difficult, especially where there is no surviving tradition of community forestry.

An enormous expansion of plantations or other supplies will be required if significant inroads are to be made into fuel shortages. It is estimated that around 48 million hectares of fuelwood plantations would have been required to meet the tropical fuelwood deficit in 1980, and 105 million hectares that are expected in 2000. In Africa the requirement to supply the expected shortfall in 2000 would correspond to a 6,000-kilometre belt extending from Senegal to Ethiopia, and averaging 34 kilometres wide (Grainger, 1986). Against such requirements achievements to date are modest almost to the point of insignificance. Attempts to create community plantations for fuelwood on the degraded Jos Plateau of Nigeria, for example, began just after the Second World War, but by 1987 covered only 0.5 per cent of the area (Buckley, 1987). In Africa as a whole, the annual rate of establishment of non-industrial plantations averaged around 40,000 hectares per annum around 1980: a forty-fold increase would be required to meet the expected shortfall in 2000 (Grainger, 1986).

Fuelwood in the developed world and large-scale 'industrial' use

The scale of the domestic fuelwood shortage in the developing world has overshadowed the whole of the fuelwood sector. As a result, relatively little attention has been focused on the use of wood as an energy source in other parts of the world or even for industrial purposes within the developing world. In particular, the fact that the use of fuelwood has increased far more rapidly in the developed world than in the developing world in recent years has been largely overlooked. Nevertheless, between 1976 and 1986 it rose by 57 per cent in the former compared with 23 per cent in the latter. Wood now provides 2–3 per cent of energy requirements in the United States, and is thus of the same order of importance as nuclear and hydro sources (e.g. Schreuder and Vlosky, 1986). In Europe it accounts for around 2 per cent of energy consumption (Prins, 1987).

Most developed countries at some time in their history have been as dependent on wood as an energy source as many countries in the developing world are today, and indeed many have experienced similar wood shortages or famines. As recently as mid-century, the developed world accounted for over half of world consumption of fuelwood, while at the beginning of the century the proportion was two-thirds (Tillman, 1978). In the United States in the latter part of the nineteenth century, wood was the primary energy source, and most of the wood produced annually was used as firewood. In earlier centuries, the same was true of countries such as England, where fuelwood was used for both domestic heating and cooking and for industrial purposes such as iron-making. By the seventeenth century, severe problems of supply were being encountered, and this early fuelwood crisis stimulated the transition to coal (Nef, 1977). A similar transition to coal and oil duly occurred in the United States at the turn of the present century even although an acute shortage of firewood was not encountered. During the nineteenth century, firewood was cheap and abundant, especially where the forest was being cleared for agriculture, and its use was profligate. By the 1960s, the use of firewood in the United States had fallen to a negligible level, and consumption had also fallen rapidly in many European countries and in the Soviet Union.

Since then, however, there has been a partial revival, not least because of rises in oil prices in the 1970s. In Europe, fuelwood removals by 1986 had increased by around one-fifth compared with those of the mid-1970s. The revival has been spectacular in the United States, with a fourfold increase between 1975 and 1980. It remains to be seen whether this renewed interest is permanent, and it is noticeable that many countries have experienced temporary increases in the use of firewood when other fuels were scarce, for example during and after wars. Nevertheless, it seems that the higher levels of use of the 1970s have been at least maintained during the 1980s in many developed countries.

While the amounts used remain modest compared with industrial use, the production of firewood is a significant element in the use of the forest resource in many developed countries. In the United States, for example, around half of the 7.8 million private forest owners cut firewood from their own forest land (Birch et al., 1982). Firewood production may therefore be at least one of the objectives of numerous small owners, not only in the United States, but also in European countries and Japan. It may be a management objective in a far greater area of forest than its apparently small-scale use would suggest. Rising oil prices may therefore stimulate increased levels of intensity of management of farm woodlands in the developed world, as well as imposing additional stress on fuelwood supplies in the developing world.

Increasing demand for firewood in the developed world has had little effect on timber markets. Firewood prices are usually very low compared with those offered by industrial consumers, and much of the firewood comes from trees that are unsuitable for industrial purposes. In the United States, for example, only a quarter of the firewood cut by households comes from trees suitable for pulpwood or saw logs (Skog and Watterson, 1984). In any case, much of the firewood comes from small private (non-industrial) forests, rather than from larger industrially owned or managed ones. These small forests are often viewed as providing various services as well as goods. The collecting of firewood may be perceived by households as an enjoyable activity in itself, and in at least some North American, European and Australasian countries may be at least partially seen as a form of forest recreation and not just as a chore (e.g. Trotmann and Thomson, 1988).

While it is unlikely that forests will be greatly expanded in the developed world to produce domestic firewood (except perhaps on farms), there is a greater likelihood that sizeable plantations will be established for commercial energy production. Rises in oil prices during the 1970s led to renewed interest in alternative energy sources, including short-rotation forests geared to producing fuel for power stations. The feasibility of producing woody biomass for energy has been investigated especially within the European Economic Community (e.g Hummel, 1988), and it has been shown that systems based on coppiced hardwoods with short cutting cycles may have some potential. For example, it has been shown that energy plantations of sycamore on cut-over peatland can have attractive returns in parts of Ireland (Lyons and Vasievich, 1986). Such systems may have some attraction as alternatives to conventional agriculture in times of food surpluses, but their viability will ultimately

Table 6.13   Wood as an energy source in Europe around 1980

Total removals (million cubic metres)	342
Fuelwood	72
Wood and bark residues	40
Forest products after original use	11
estimated wood equivalent of pulping	44
liquors burnt in chemical pulping	
Total	167

Source: Based on Prins (1987)

depend on the prices of other energy sources.

More conventional use of wood for energy for transport and industry is, of course, long established in some parts of the world. In the United States in the nineteenth century, for example, large tracts of forest were harvested on a rotational basis in order to produce charcoal for iron-making, and a number of metal smelters and refineries were still fuelled by wood in the 1970s (Tillman, 1978). Perhaps the largest-scale industrial user of fuelwood, however, is Brazil, where charcoal was used in the production of around 30 per cent of the annual output of pig-iron during the 1970s (Tillman, 1978). The projected expansion of iron production in Brazil has major implications for the forest resource (Fearnside, 1989b). To feed the proposed expansion of smelting capacity at Carajas in eastern Amazonia, the charcoal from either 700,000 hectares of eucalyptus plantations or from the clear-cutting of some 50–70,000 hectares of dense native forest annually would be required. On the other hand, the use of wood as a fuel in some other industrial applications is much less significant in relation to the forest resource. Much of this use involves wood residues or wastes, rather than material removed from the forest as fuelwood. In Europe, for example, fuelwood represents less than half of the total volume of wood used for energy (Table 6.13). Around 40 per cent of the volume of wood removed annually is eventually used as a source of energy (Prins, 1987).

The forest-products industry is the biggest single industrial user of fuelwood in most countries. In the United States, the forest-product sector accounts for 50 per cent of all the wood used for energy (Schreuder and Vlosky, 1986). Up to half of the energy consumed in the course of manufacture of plywood or pulp and paper may be supplied by wood, and much of that comes from mill residues and other waste material. The growth of wood-using industry in the developing world may offer some potential for increasing production of charcoal from waste, and hence facilitate the use of woodfuel in cities remote from forests. In Malaysia and Indonesia, for example, charcoal production increased by an estimated 26 and 21 per cent respectively between 1976 and 1986, and charcoal exports from the former increased almost fourfold in the same period. World-wide, exports almost doubled between 1975 and 1985, but much of them were destined for the developed world or for oil-rich but forest-poor countries in the Middle East, rather than for the areas of greatest need of domestic fuel.

Non-consumptive functions

The forest has traditionally been regarded as fulfilling two major types of functions. On the one hand, it is a source of wood and in some instances also a variety of other products. On the other hand, it may provide a variety of services such as soil and wildlife conversation, general environmental protection, and recreation. This function is sometimes described as non-productive, in the sense that physical products (such as wood) are not involved. Here the term 'non-consumptive' is preferred to 'non-productive', as it may have fewer negative connotations.

In practice the distinction between the production of goods and the supply of services is not always sharp, and in particular the frequently used classification into 'productive' and 'non-consumptive' or 'protective' functions is sometimes inaccurate or misleading. Recreation, for example, may be as valuable a 'product' of the forest as wood, while the economic value of watershed protection may in some instances be as real as that of wood production, although it may be far more difficult to estimate.

As Chapter 7 indicates, the forest is of major environmental significance. The existence and nature of forest cover has a strong influence on the hydrological characteristics of an area, and this influence may extend far beyond the forest. Similarly, the forest has traditionally been perceived as protecting land from soil erosion. Environmental protection may therefore be a major function of the forest, and indeed in some instances the primary or sole one. The interaction between the forest resource and the environment issue is discussed further in Chapter 7: in this section the focus is on the relative extent of the function (in so far as it can be established) and on the management issues involved.

Since this protective function does not yield revenue in any direct sense, it has rarely been associated with private ownership. Similarly, the use of forests for informal public recreation rarely involves payment at the forest gate, and is more typical of publicly owned forests than of those in private ownership. In short, non-consumptive uses are often associated with public or state forests, while management for wood production is equally associated with private ownership. This correlation, however, is by no means perfect, and in the long term it is probably becoming weaker. This trend perhaps characterises the transition from the 'industrial' to the 'post-industrial' forest. In the former, wood production is the primary or indeed sole objective. In the latter, wood production, wildlife conservation, recreation and various other functions are combined as multiple objectives, to which varying priorities are ascribed. The trend is apparent in both private and public forests in some parts of the world, and indeed one of the features of the 'post-industrial' forest is perhaps the blurring of the distinction between public and private ownership as government influence and regulation increase (Chapter 5). This is not to say that all forests are now subject to multiple use, or that management under private and public control is identical. Huge areas of single-purpose forests remain, as do major contrasts in management objectives. In some parts of the world, however, and especially in Europe, there has been both diversification of use and convergence of management. Private forest management has been increasingly influenced by a combination of regulation and incentives, while in at least some countries the management of state forests has become more commercial in outlook and orientation. At first sight forest privatization and other developments in some countries raise questions about the strength of government influence and the continuation of the long-term trend of growing government involvement. On closer examination these measures may turn out to be less a reversal of the long-term trend than a turning-point in how government influence is exerted.

The extents of non-consumptive uses

Non-consumptive uses of the forest are almost impossible to quantify meaningfully in terms of areas and extents. Recreation, for example, may range from high-intensity, primary use to low-intensity occasional use for which no management is provided. To attempt to quantify such use in terms of hectares is not necessarily helpful, and even when estimates are based on official classifications of forests and management objectives their value may be limited. In some instances recreation may be the sole or primary use, whilst in others it is a subsidiary activity. Estimates of the extent of non-consumptive uses should therefore be viewed with the greatest of caution. The problem is further exacerbated by differing international definitions and procedures, which mean that the simple addition of national statistics (assuming that they are available) is unlikely to produce a meaningful global estimate. A particular problem arises over the terms 'protection' and 'protected'. Some forests are managed primarily for forms of environmental 'protection' such as soil or water conservation. Some forests are 'protected' as national parks or other reserves. Some forests may be both protective and protected, while some may be one or the other. The semantic confusion is sometimes increased by the use of statistical categories such as 'protection etc'. Furthermore, forests may be classified for protection against very different hazards. In Bavaria, for example, woods and forests may be separately classified for protection against soil erosion, avalanches, air pollution and noise (especially along motorways) (Woodruffe, 1989).

Around half of the world forest area is considered to be 'exploitable' (which term, incidentally, reflects the perceived primacy of wood production) (p. 132). 'Unexploitable' forest is characterised by low physical productivity, by inaccessibility and high transport costs, or by classification for special (non-wood or non-consumptive) purposes such as conservation. These characteristics may overlap in many areas, and it is not therefore always possible to identify the relative importance of forest designations in

Table 6.14 Forest proportions by recognized main functions (percentages of respective areas)

	Total forest and other wooded land			Exploitable closed forest	(unexploitable closed forest)	
	Wood production	Protection etc.	Recreation	Wood production	Protection etc.	Recreation
Nordic Countries	90.5	7.5	2.0	96.6 (—)	3.3 (45.1)	0.1 (54.9)
EEC	89.0	10.6	0.4	98.8 (44.1)	1.1 (53.4)	0.1 (2.5)
Eastern Europe	80.3	12.4	7.3	85.3 (16.1)	10.7 (49.7)	4.0 (34.2)
Southern Europe	55.2	43.7	1.1	98.4 (6.5)	1.6 (83.1)	<0.1 (10.4)
USSR	65.1	32.9	2.0	100.0 (27.3)	— (65.4)	— (7.3)
USA	89.5	10.5	—	100.0 (100.0)	— (—)	— (—)
Canada	95.7	4.3	—	100.0 (–0)	— (100.0)	— (—)

Source: based on data in UNECE/FAO (1985)

rendering a forest 'unexploitable'. In any case, classifications are not necessarily permanent, and although increasing areas in many parts of the world are being designated as reserves of one kind or another, the designations are not always immutable. Nor does official designation of a forest as a nature reserve or other protected area always mean that wood production does not take place.

Despite these problems and provisos, some indication of the relative extents of different functions can be obtained for at least some parts of the world, and variations in the relative significance of different functions can be identified at the national level. Table 6.14 shows estimates of the relative extents of 'recognised major functions' for Europe, the Soviet Union and North America, representing most (in areal terms) of the developed world. In this area, wood production is the 'recognised major function' in approximately three-quarters of the area of forest and woodland, while recreation has that role in around 1 per cent of the area. In the 'unexploitable closed forest', of course, the relative proportions are very different. Protection and recreation are classed as 'recognised major functions' in 52 per cent and 6 per cent respectively. Together, these two functions are therefore likely to constitute the main reason for 'unexploitability'. In terms of the total area of closed forest, however, they represent only 15 per cent although they amount to 25 per cent of the total area of 'forest and other wooded land'. Wood production is clearly the primary function, in terms of area, in both the closed forest and in the category of 'forest and other wooded land'. Protection-related functions are next in importance in terms of area, while recreation is a 'recognised major function' on around 1 per cent of total area of 'forest and other wooded land' and 0.1 per cent of 'exploitable closed forest'.

In Europe, wood production is the major function on 78 per cent of 'total forest and wooded land', while protection and recreation account for 19 and 2 per cent of the area respectively. These continental percentages, however, conceal a distinct gradient of increasing importance of the protective function from north to south, and a corresponding reduction in the relative importance of wood production. In some countries such as the United Kingdom and Ireland, protective functions are of negligible significance in terms of area, while in others they are as important as wood production. In Turkey, for example, protection is a 'major recognised function' in two-thirds of the total area of forest and woodland, and in Spain in almost half of that area. In the case of Spain, much afforestation has been carried out over the last half-century in areas affected by or prone to soil erosion. In general terms, the relative areal extent of the 'protective' function increases towards the south and east of Europe, and is generally low in the more humid areas of the north and west.

Outside Europe, the relative extent of protective forest is very variable. As Table 6.14 indicates, around one-third of the forest area in the Soviet Union has a protective function, but the inevitable problems of definition need to be borne in mind in interpreting this figure alongside that of just over 10 per cent (31 million hectares) shown for the United States, where a complex variety of sometimes overlapping designations apply to forest land. In the Soviet Union, around 100 million hectares of forest fulfil a 'predominantly protective' function. In addition, more than 5.5 million hectares of protective forest stands have been established, mainly on previously agricultural land (Pavloskii, 1986). In Japan, around 8 million hectares of the total forest area of 25 million hectares are defined as protection forest (Hebbert, 1989). Three-quarters of the former area is protected or the conservation of headwaters and the remaining one-quarter for soil erosion. In Chile, over 60 per cent of the forest area is either protective or protected (WRI, 1985). In Malaysia, around one-third of the intended permanent forest area is classed as protective (Tang, 1987), while the corresponding proportion in Indonesia is 27 per cent (Haeruman Js, 1988).

Protected forests

While large areas of forest have environmental protection as a 'recognised major function', the relative extent of protected forest, lying within designated national parks and nature reserves, is much smaller. Around 4 per cent of the closed forest and 17 per cent of the open forest are thus designated: overall approximately 8 per cent of the area of forest and woodland is protected (Table 6.15).

Proportions of protected closed forest area do not differ greatly between the developed and developing worlds, but a much higher percentage of open forest is protected in the former than in the latter. This means in turn that the protected extent of the overall forest and woodland area is nearly three times greater in the developed world than in the developing world. In

Table 6.15   Protected forests

| | Percentage of forest area in protected forest | | |
	Closed forest	Open forest	Total
Tropical Africa	4.3	8.6	7.3
Tropical America	2.1	1.0	1.8
Tropical Asia	5.8	1.9	5.4
Tropical countries	3.4	6.1	4.4
Europe	1.3	58.3	12.3
USSR	2.5	100.0	17.0
North America	7.9	na	4.9
ECE Region	4.2	35.4	11.7
Total	3.8	17.2	8.0

Source: Based on WRI (1986)

the United States, around two-thirds of the forest area is classed as commercial timberland (capable of producing at least 20ft^3 (0.566 cubic metres) of industrial wood per acre per year), and approximately 5 per cent of the area thus capable has been withdrawn by statute or regulation as national park or wilderness area (USDA, 1982). Overall, in addition to 32 million hectares of national parks (WRI, 1986), over 30 million hectares of land, most of which is forested, are offically defined as wilderness (Daniels et al., 1989), in which lumbering is not permitted. Most of this area is remote and inaccessible, and indeed two-thirds is in Alaska.

This case illustrates the general tendency in many countries for highest environmental and timber values to be non-coincident in spatial terms. In much of Alaska the costs of harvesting timber would exceed its returns, and hence there may be no opportunity cost involved in designating the forests for conservation purposes (Hyde and Krutilla, 1979). Similarly in New Zealand, where around 10 per cent of the land surface lies in various reserves where the prime concern is the preservation of flora and fauna, most of the protected area lies in upland forests or alpine areas where the threat from agriculture or exotic afforestation is unlikely to be great (Halkett, 1983). Perhaps it is not surprising that protected forests often tend to be those of lowest commerical value. This tendency raises the questions of the purpose of designation if few threats exist, and also the problems of establishing protected status in the commercially (and sometimes ecologically) more valuable areas.

On the other hand, in the Soviet Union much of the 'Protection etc' area indicated in Table 6.14 consists of highly accessible forest where thinning and sanitary and regeneration cuts are permitted (Holowacz, 1985). Of the approximately 300 million hectares of protected forest indicated, around 20 million hectares are in national parks (WRI, 1986). In Japan, over 3 million hectares of national parks, most in forested country, overlap with the protective forest area, and thereby exemplify the problems of functional definitions. In Australia, national parks and similar areas from which log production is precluded amount to around 8 million hectares, compared with a native forest area of 42 million hectares (South, 1981). The relative extent of protected forests in the developing world tends to be smaller (but not invariably so), although the definitional problems are as great if not greater than in the developed world. In tropical Africa, America and Asia, less than 5 per cent of the combined open and closed-forest area was 'protected' around 1980 (WRI, 1986). Around 3 per cent of the closed tropical forest is safeguarded, at least on paper (FAO, 1986c). The relative extent of protected closed forest is not dissimilar to that in the developed world, and indeed each of the three major tropical continents has a higher proportion of their closed forests in protected areas than has Europe (Table 6.15). On the other hand the relative extent of open forest with protected status is very much smaller, at 6 per cent compared with 35 per cent. Protected forests are most extensive in relative terms in Africa, where some game and forest reserves date from the early part of this century, and least extensive in Latin America.

A characteristic of the tropical continents is the degree of concentration of protected forests in a few countries. For example, Zaïre accounts for 60 per cent of the reported area of protected closed forest in Africa, Indonesia has over 50 per cent of the corresponding area in Asia, and Brazil and Venezuela together account for over 50 per cent of that in South America (based on data in WRI, 1989). The apparent degree of concentration partly reflects the different rates and degrees of progress made in classifying forests as a basis for management policy. In the case of Indonesia large absolute and relative areas have been assigned functions of protection or conservation (Table 6.16). Concentration applies also at the intra-national scale as well as at the international level. In Indonesia, for example, more than three-quarters of the forest area in Bali has been zoned for protection and nature conservation, while only around 10 per cent is designated as production forest (McTaggart, 1983).

Zero or negligible areas (less than 500 hectares) are indicated for around 5 per cent of countries for which protected forest areas are listed by WRI (1989). Most of these cases are in Europe, and include countries such as Belgium, The Netherlands, Ireland and the United Kingdom, where surviving remnants of native forest are of negligible extent. The fact that the relative extents of protected forest in some developed countries are so small is to some extent understandable in terms of the limited surviving areas of 'natural', unmodified forest. It does little, however, to strengthen their case when trying to persuade some developing countries to adopt more conservation-minded policies towards their forests. On the other hand the stark breakdown of forest classes in cases such as Finland may be misleading: nature conservation and recreation are also given some priority over one-quarter of the area of 'timber production forests' (Table 6.16). Just as 'protected' status may have different meanings in different settings, so also classification as production forest may have very different significance for nature conservation (and recreation) in different countries.

Small though the relative extent of protected forest areas may be, there

Table 6.16   Forest classification: examples of Indonesia and Finland

Indonesia		(million ha)
Permanent production forest		33.6
Limited production forest		30.4
Protected forest		30.3
Nature conservation forest		18.7
	Total	113.0
Finland		
Timber production forests		18.2
Nature reserves		0.4
Preserved high latitude/altitude forests		0.6
Recreational areas		0.1
Private forests used for recreation		0.5
Other		0.3
	Total	20.1

Sources: Indonesia—Schreuder and Vlosky (1986); Finland—OECD (1988)

is a clear trend towards expansion. Globally, the extent of all kinds of protected areas has grown rapidly, with an approximately fourfold increase between the mid-1960s and mid-1980s. In Central America, for example, the number of national parks and other protected areas increased from 25 to 149 between 1969 and 1981, with a corresponding expansion of the protected area from under 200,000 to over 600,000 square kilometres (Neumann and Machlis, 1989). In Costa Rica the national-park system inaugurated in 1970 now extends to around 8 per cent of the country's land surface (Green and Barborak, 1987). Financial assistance from American conservation bodies has aided this expansion.

Numerous other instances of increases in the extent of protected forest areas could be quoted. Two examples from contrasting countries will suffice. In Australia, the native forest area from which log production is precluded following designation as national parks or similar areas increased from 1.8 to 8 million hectares between 1971 and 1981 (South, 1981). In the very different setting of Bulgaria, protection forests, national parks and other special-purpose forests increased from 400,000 to 1 million hectares between 1965 and 1985, when they comprised some 29 per cent of the total forest area (Nedelin and Gulev, 1987). Almost world-wide, increasing areas of native forest have been designated for some form of conservation, but formidable obstacles have been encountered in some areas. In Papua New Guinea, for example, the nature of forest landowner-ship (Chapter 5) has meant that it has proved very difficult for the government to acquire land for parks and similar purposes, and the need to select areas representative of all altitudinal bands is an additional problem (Diamond, 1986).

The expansion of designated areas reflects the emergence of environ-mental issues and environmental pressure groups. In countries such as Australia and New Zealand in particular, the role and future of native

Table 6.17   Protected forest areas by biomes and realms 1985

Biome/Realm	No. of areas	Total area (million ha)
Tropical humid forests	280	39.1
Afrotropical	44	8.9
Indomalayan	122	5.0
Australian	53	7.8
Neotropical	61	17.3
Subtropical/temperate rainforests/woodlands	275	18.5
Nearctic	18	4.3
Palaearctic	48	1.7
Australian	26	0.9
Antarctic	145	2.8
Neotropical	38	8.8
Tropical dry forests/woodlands	581	65.5
Afrotropical	240	48.7
Indomalayan	238	10.4
Australian	10	0.9
Neotropical	93	5.5
Temperate broadleaf forests	483	11.5
Nearctic	82	1.9
Palaearctic	400	9.6
Temperate needle-leaf forests-woodlands	175	38.8
Nearctic	53	30.3
Palaearctic	122	8.5
Evergreen sclerophyllous forests	475	12.0
Palaearctic	122	3.4
Afrotropical	41	1.6
Australian	301	6.9

(Realm areas of less than 0.5 million ha omitted)

Source: Based on IUCN (1985)

Note: Biome type is not synonymous with habitat type: a protected area within a tropical humid forest biome, for example, may not necessarily contain tropical humid forest. Furthermore, the total area of each biome in each realm has not yet been determined with sufficient precision to assess percentage coverage. Biogeographical realms are as defined by Udvârdy (1975)

forests have emerged as a major issue, and this is reflected in the designation of increasing extents of the surviving forest under some form of protection. In Australia, for example, opposition on the part of environmentalists to woodchip developments in native forests led to the setting-aside of forest reserves (Conacher, 1977). Similarly, in New Zealand, increasing extents of lowland forest on the west coast of South Island have been reserved in the face of environmentalist pressures (Tilling, 1988). Previously, in the 1970s, similar pressures led to the adoption of sustained-yield use of such publicly owned forests in place of clear felling. While the issues may be sharply defined and the controversies especially heated in these countries, they are present in some form in almost every developed country and are increasingly emerging in many developing countries.

While a standard response to environmentalist pressures in many countries is the designation of protected forests, the process of designation is itself likely to have implications for non-designated forest areas. On the west coast of New Zealand's South Island, for example, the earlier failure to manage the native forests on a sustained-yield basis has alienated environmentalists. In response, more and more of these forests have been protected, and the reduced area available for timber production has curtailed efforts at promoting sustained-yield management in the remaining production forests (Tilling, 1988). In short, protected forests may be subject to single 'use' in the same way as timber production may be the single use on non-protected, exploitable forests, and an increase in the protected area can simply lead to an increase in the intensity of management of other, non-protected forests for timber production.

Furthermore, the granting of protected status does not necessarily guarantee the effective conservation of the protected area. Full legal support for the status of strict natural reserves is rare, and even when it exists it does not necessarily guarantee full protection (Hall, 1983). Illegal felling is often a major threat, whilst the collection of forest produce may also conflict with the objectives of reserve management (e.g. McKinnon et al., 1986). Local people may be as alienated or disaffected by their exclusion from the forest for reasons of conservation as they are for reasons of commercial exploitation of timber. In Thailand, for example, nearly half of the virgin forest area is now formally protected, but the loss of the forest through activities such as poaching and opium growing has not been halted (Ewins and Bazely, 1989). In Brazil, a fairly comprehensive system of protected areas has been established, extending to over 3 per cent of Brazilian Amazonia, but protection remains inadequate in practical terms (Johns, 1989).

Despite the disparity that may exist between designation and practical protection, protected status is of fundamental importance in relation to the conservation of habitats and species, and therefore it is important that an adequate coverage of forest types is achieved. Table 6.17 shows the distribution of protected areas by biome and biogeographical realm, but as the note to the table indicates, percentage coverage cannot yet be determined and hence adequacy of coverage cannot be assessed.

Recreation

If increasing area of protected forest is a feature of recent decades, so also is increasing recreational use. While recreation in the form of hunting has been a forest use since time immemorial, the use of the forest for informal recreation such as walking, hiking and camping is a characteristic of the twentieth century, and more especially of the period since the Second

World War. In much of the developed world, levels of recreational use have generally grown rapidly in recent decades, usually at rates far surpassing those of timber production. In the United States national forests, for example, there was a thirty-fold increase over the forty-year period from the late 1920s (Clawson, 1976). In the state of Victoria in Australia, the number of visitor-days at the mainly forested national parks was increasing at a rate of 11 per cent per annum in the early 1980s (Algar, 1981).

Rapidly growing recreational use is a characteristic of almost all accessible and state-owned forests in the developed world, and increasingly it is also taking place in less accessible and privately owned forests. In the United States, for example, recreational use in national forests amounted to around 188 million visitor-days per year by 1970 (Clawson, 1976). In the state forests of the United Kingdom, the annual number of recreational visits is estimated at around 24 million (Willis and Benson, 1989). In Ireland, recreational access to state forests was actively discouraged until as late as 1968, but by the early 1980s around 1.5 million visits were being made annually (UNECE/FAO, 1985). In West Germany, visits to forests for informal recreation may number as many as 1.2 billion per annum (UNECE/FAO, 1985). In Denmark, 90 per cent of the adult population visit the forest at least once a year, compared with 79–85 per cent in Sweden and 92–96 per cent in Norway (Koch, 1984).

While recreational use is often strongly associated with publicly-owned forests, it is by no means confined to that sector. In the United States, although only 4 per cent and 1 per cent respectively of non-corporate and corporate private owners have commercial recreation as a primary management objective, 29 per cent and 54 per cent of the non-corporate and corporate forest land is open to the public for some form of recreation. In addition, large areas that are not open to the public are available to family members, friends, or employees (USDA, 1981). Over much of the private area recreation is permitted because it would be too difficult to prohibit, but on the other hand more positive attitudes such as 'good neighbour' policies or profit-seeking prevail. Furthermore, as private ownership changes and non-farmer owners become increasingly common in some countries, so a shift in the perceived value of the forest holding takes place, with timber production being accorded less significance and recreation value more importance. Such shifts may have implications for levels of timber production, especially in countries such as Finland (OECD, 1988).

While recreational use and protected status are not necessarily mutually exclusive (for example in national parks and wilderness areas), protected forests and recreational forests often have different locational characteristics. The former are often in remote areas, where relative inaccessibility has afforded at least partial protection from inroads by lumbering and agriculture. The most heavily used recreational forests, on the other hand, are usually to be found in more accessible locations, especially around large cities. In small, densely populated countries such as The Netherlands and England, recreation may be the principal function of some forests around urban areas, and indeed forests have been and are being created primarily for recreation in such settings. In The Netherlands, for example, the 1984 Forestry Plan aimed at expanding the forest area by around 10 per cent by the end of the century, and one-third of the expansion was to be close to the main cities (van den Berg, 1989). In general terms, highly accessible forests may have high values in terms of both timber and recreation, and hence conflicts in management objectives are sometimes encountered.

Intensive recreational use may also be found in some remoter areas, but there it is usually highly localised in a few prime landscapes such as national parks. In such settings the revenue generated by forest camping, for example, may far exceed that from timber production. In some of these areas timber values are low in both absolute and relative terms. Around the northern timber line in Finland, for example, timber-cutting is restricted for environmental reaons, and the value of tourism and recreation is twice that of timber production (Saastamoinen, 1982).

Recreational use of the forest may conflict with timber production in a number of ways, such as impairment of tree growth through soil changes resulting from trampling, or as a result of management decisions involving choice of species, silvicultural systems and rotation lengths. It may also conflict with nature conservation, through, for example, disturbance. And there may be internal conflicts within the recreational sector, especially between hunting and informal recreation. In West Germany, for example, this conflict arises from the disturbance of game by other recreational activities, while conflicts between hunting and timber production result from damage caused by game and disputes as to the choice of tree species that are optimal for timber production or game (e.g. Lang, 1986).

Forest recreation is not usually associated with tropical areas, but there are signs that the perception of tropical forests as a resource for recreation and tourism is growing. The recreational use of Malaysian forests, for example, is growing as the population becomes more urbanised (Hamzah et al., 1983). In Indonesia, around 0.5 million hectares have been designated as recreational forests (Haeruman Js, 1988). In Bali some areas have been earmarked as forest reserves accessible to tourists, in order to assist with the development of tourism (McTaggart, 1983). In Costa Rica, forest national parks have begun to attract foreign exchange through tourism (Green and Barborak, 1987). In the past, tropical rain forests were perceived to have little tourist or recreational value, and this is one reason why few national parks were established in lowland forest areas in Africa (Pullan, 1988). The growing perception of their value for tourism and recreation is a welcome step that may help to halt their loss. Perhaps it is significant that one of the factors contributing to the forest 'turn-round' in the United States at the end of last century was a growing awareness of recreational values and wilderness qualities (Chapter 3).

Table 6.18 Forest and woodland areas by importance of function (1000 ha)

| Country/category | Importance of function | Function | | | | | | Area | |
		Wood production	Recreation	Hunting	Protection	Nature conservation	Range	Total	Closed forest
Sweden (closed forest)	High	11800	5000	100	500	200	0		
	Medium	10000	12400	24000	1500	1000	2600	24400	24400
	Low	2600	7000	300	22400	232000	21800		
France (forest & other wooded land)	High	7140	1000	11600	738	95	0		
	Medium	5200	121000	2520	4500	12580	620	15075	13875
	Low	2735	1955	955	9837	2400	14455		
W. Germany (forest & other wooded land)	High	6395	293	–	4917	118	0		
	Medium	202	1133	–	0	1898	0	7207	6989
	Low	610	5781	–	2290	5191	7207		
Netherlands (closed forest)	High	120	270	92	5	40	0		
	Medium	130	30	104	15	0	0	300	300
	Low	50	0	104	180	260	300		
Spain (forest & other wooded land)	High	1800	100	6973	5433	60	750		
	Medium	2900	1000	2693	3770	40	350	12511	6906
	Low	7811	11411	2845	3308	12411	11411		
Soviet Union (forest & other wooded land)	High	548400	18900	754600	176300	–	138700		
	Medium	442900	304900	0	73600	–	110600	1185900	
	Low	194600	862100	431300	936600	–	936500		
United States (forest & other wooded land)	High	141288	80898	56634	87409	17300	30583		
	Medium	56933	103134	155000	44711	15030	143911	298076	195256
	Low	99855	114044	86442	165956	265746	123582		

Source: Compiled from UNECE/FAO (1985)

Non-consumptive functions and multiple use

Increasing recreational use and an increasing absolute and relative area of protected forest is a feature of recent decades, but a more distinctive characteristic of the 'post-industrial' forest is the incorporation of several or multiple objectives – including protection or conservation – alongside timber production. This trend is not easily quantified, and differences in definitions, procedures and management frameworks make international comparison difficult. Nevertheless, UNECE/FAO (1985) have attempted to assemble data on relative extents and relative importance from most of the developed world, and some examples are indicated in Table 6.18.

While qualitative terms such as 'high', 'medium' and 'low' mean that detailed interpretation requires great caution, some general points stand out clearly. Timber production is defined as a function in almost the whole of the forest area of the specimen countries listed in the table, but its relative importance varies greatly. In the small, densely populated Netherlands, for example, wood production is ascribed 'high' importance in less than half of the forest area, while recreation has 'high' status in 90 per cent of that area. In more sparsely populated Finland, on the other hand, timber production has 'high' importance on 90 per cent of the area, compared with a recreation ranking of only 3 per cent. In some Mediterranean countries such as Spain and Turkey, larger areas of forest are of 'high' importance for protection than for timber production, but in most of these cases nature conservation has low importance.

As Table 6.18 suggests, various combinations and priorities of functions of objectives exist, and large areas of forest are in practice subject to multiple use. In many if not most cases, wood production was the original function, to which others have been added incrementally and chronologically. In state forests in New Zealand, for example, management for soil and water conservation was added in the mid-1950s, recreation in the early 1960s, nature conservation in the early 1970s, landscape conservation in the late 1970s and provision of educational opportunities in the early 1980s (Tilling, 1988). Non-consumptive objectives are now firmly incorporated into national policies, and indeed the concept of multiple use (at least for state forests) is explicitly adopted in countries such as the United States (under the Multiple Use-Sustained Yield Act of 1960) and New Zealand (under the Forest Amendment Act of 1976). Multiple use may also be encouraged in various indirect ways in private forests, especially in European countries, through guidance and encouragement if not by strict enforcement.

While concepts of multiple or balanced use are widely espoused, they bring with them various problems. As Zivnuska (1961) observed, multiple use means multiple problems. If a forest is managed for purposes such as recreation, hunting or nature conservation, there is likely to be a cost in terms of wood production foregone. This cost may be expressed in a variety of ways ranging from straightforward damage resulting from recreation (for example through fires) or from game to the choice of species, techniques or rotation lengths that are sub-optimal from the

Table 6.19   Losses in wood production or increased costs due to recreation, protection or nature conservation

	Species	Rotation periods	Non-Optimal Techniques	Silvicultural measures	Cutting restrictions
Canada					+
Denmark	+	+	+		
Finland					+
France	+	+	+		(+)
Hungary	+	+			
Ireland					+
Italy				(+)	(+)
Netherlands	+	+			+
Poland		+	+	+	+
Sweden	+				+
Turkey					+
United Kingdom	+	+			

+ indicates that losses occur: (+) losses occur in some areas only
Source: Compiled from UNECE/FAO (1985)

standpoint of timber production. Some examples of such costs are illustrated in Table 6.19. These costs can be expressed in timber volumes or monetary values. In Sweden, for example, the present species composition in 100,000 hectares of broad-leaved forest is to be preserved, with a potential annual loss of around 0.5 million cubic metres of wood, while in Finland cutting restrictions will lead to a reduction of the total allowable cut by about 2 per cent. In France, restrictions on cutting and on choice of species are estimated to 'cost' FF 200 million: in Denmark to 100,000 cubic metres of wood worth around $US 4 million annually. In the United Kingdom it is claimed that recreation and conservation functions cause losses amounting to an estimated £1.8 million per year, as a result of sub-optimal rotation periods and species (UNECE/FAO, 1985). On the other hand, clear-felling causes recreational use to decrease (e.g. Kardell, 1985), and recreation itself has a value whether or not it produces revenue at the forest gate. In short, in multiple use a trade-off occurs between wood and other goods or services offered by the forest.

Some of these other goods or services may generate revenue directly – for example, forest campsites or hunting licences – but most of them have values that are very difficult to quantify in monetary terms. Numerous attempts have been made to estimate the value of informal recreation, but that of species conservation is much more difficult to quantify, although perhaps no less real. One obvious value is in the role of the native forest as a source of species or provenances suitable for planting elsewhere. One indirect indication of this value is the fact that 4 million hectares of eucalyptus plantation have been established outside Australia (Algar, 1981). The fact that benefits may accrue far beyond the immediate area of forest greatly adds to the problems of evaluation in monetary terms. Using a travel-cost method of evaluation and grossing-up from a small number of accessible forests. Willis and Benson (1989) have estimated that the recreation 'value' of state forests in Britain amounts to between £14 and £45 million per annum, compared with timber sales of around £60 million (these will rapidly increase as the young forests mature). Impressive as such figures may be, however, they are difficult to interpret. Since access to the forest for informal recreation is not normally charged, the values are notional or at best indirect. Furthermore, since no charge is usually made for recreational access to state forests, private forests owners are rarely in a position to charge for recreational access to their forests. Nevertheless, the relatively easily quantified 'losses' of wood production resulting from management for recreation or conservation need to be viewed against the 'gains' from these other functions.

Problems of multiple-use policies

The formal adoption of multiple-use policies for the management of state forests is a recognition that forests have values that extend beyond wood production, and is a reflection of growing pressures from environmentalists who perceive high value in the continued existence of native forests in particular. While an official endorsement of environmental and recreational values is widely welcomed, multiple-use policies are not without their problems. Since different units or currencies apply to the various uses, it is difficult to optimise total 'output', and the relative weights or priorities have still to be ascribed to the various functions. Most multiple-use policies are rather vague about priorities. In New Zealand, for example, clear guidelines about the roles and places of different uses in forest management were not given (Tilling, 1988), and in the United States, the Multiple Use-Sustained Yield Act evaded the issue of priorities entirely (Bonnicksen, 1982). Multiple use 'has all too often meant a little of everything everywhere' (Clawson, 1976, p. 766).

This vagueness does not mean that the adoption of such policies has been without effect or meaning. On the contrary, it has provided an arena where competing single-use groups come together and a means whereby goals other than timber production can be promoted by interest groups or pressure groups. In the United States, for example, the clear-felling of forest stands (with its association with the destructive forest exploitation around the turn of the century) was strongly opposed by environmentalists during the 1960s and 1970s. This led to the passing of the Forest Management Act of 1976 which confirmed that all management decisions had to be in accord with multiple-use policy. Selective cutting was encouraged, and while clear-cutting was not prohibited it was made subject to guidelines (Cox et al., 1985: see also Chapter 9). The very vagueness and lack of specificity of the concept of multiple use may have made such policies politically acceptable to governments and to conflicting parties and pressure groups such as timber producers and environmentalists, but at the cost of presenting almost insurmountable problems for the forest managers.

For example, since the adoption of 'balanced-use' policies for state forests in New Zealand in 1976, the 'highest-attainable goal for managers . . . [has been] a state of moderate dissatisfaction among all client groups – hardly inspirational or motivating and virtually guaranteed to reinforce any latent tendency to fortress mentality' (Kirkland, 1988). Under such conditions, priorities amongst objectives are likely to be ordered according to the effectiveness of client or pressure groups, and their relationship to the prevailing political philosophy and government of the day, rather than on more rational or popularly based criteria. It is therefore perhaps not altogether surprising that the decision was taken in New Zealand in 1985 to separate commercial and non-commercial forest management, with the Forest Service having responsibility for the former while most of the native forests were transferred to the Department of Conservation.

It remains to be seen whether this separation in New Zealand will set a trend and whether it marks the beginning of a reversal of the trend towards multiple use and non-consumptive functions that characterise the 'post-industrial' forest. Paradoxically, it comes at a time when increasing regulation is being imposed on the management of private forests in much of the developed world, to the extent that the distinction between private and public forests is being blurred. This trend is more apparent in some countries than in others, and indeed in the case of the United States, for example, in some states than in others. In is manifested especially in terms of constraints on management practices, especially in relation to environmental protection, and in some cases also in public recreational use of private forests. In West Germany, for example, public entrance to private forests is permitted under the Federal Forest Law of 1975. Forest owners must allow the forest authority to install trail-marking signs, and visitors have the right to pick flowers and berries (for non-commercial purposes) (Lundmark, 1986). In Britain, grants towards the costs of establishing private forests are now given only where certain environmental criteria are fulfilled. In short, government influence is exerted on the design and use of private forests, and is certainly not restricted solely to state-owned forests. As the means of exerting such influences increase, the perceived need for continued state ownership may decrease. Under such circumstances, the privatisation of publicly owned forests may accelerate.

If a blurring of the distinction between the management objectives of state and private forests is in prospect, perhaps a similar trend may become apparent between native and exotic or man-made forests. Whilst nature conservation values will remain highest in native forests, man-made forests may increasingly be designed, under the influence of a combination of government 'carrots and sticks', to provide for nature conservation as well as timber production. Similarly, man-made forests may be designed to cater for recreation, and for some types of recreation may do so very effectively, as for example in countries such as Britain and The Netherlands. Even in countries such as New Zealand where sizeable proportions of native forest remain, exotic forests accommodate a wide range of informal recreational activities, and indeed these activities are there practised in private and state forests alike (Trotmann and Thomson, 1988).

7 THE FOREST RESOURCE AND THE ENVIRONMENT

Environmental issues are of fundamental importance in the use of the forest resource at the present day. The fate of the tropical rain forest, for example, has emerged as a major issue on the global scale, and attracts the attention and concern of both citizens and governments far removed from tropical latitudes. Similarly, symptoms of forest decline in central Europe and parts of North America give rise to much concern, not least because of the symbolic significance of dying forests as indicators of environmental malaise. This significance is heightened by the image of the forest as a clean environment, yielding equable flows of pure water, protecting against soil erosion, and providing wildlife habitats and recreational settings. Such an image has for long been promoted by forest services and proponents of forestry: it is an image that suffers badly when the reality is seen to be marred by unhealthy trees, muddy streams and the loss or impoverishment of wildlife.

During much of the present century the forest has been perceived in very positive terms, and any attempt at afforestation or reforestation has usually been welcomed as an environmental improvement. In recent years, however, environmental groups have begun to oppose the expansion of forests in countries such as Britain and Denmark, because of the perceived environmental effects of the type of afforestation and the way in which it is carried out. Both the use of the forest resource and changes in its extent attract widespread attention on environmental grounds, and environmental issues are now taking their place alongside economics and politics as major influences on forestry policies.

The relationship between the forest resource and the environment is of the utmost complexity, and some aspects of it are characterised by uncertainty. This short review can outline only a few of its main features. First, the nature of the effect of some general environmental trends on the forest resource will be considered. Second, the environmental effects of the use and management of the resource will be reviewed. Finally and very briefly, some of the environmental effects of afforestation will be outlined.

Environmental trends and forests

While timber harvesting and other forms of resource use often have significant effects on the forest environment, the forest itself is affected by changes in climate or other elements of the wider environment. As we near the end of the twentieth century, two issues in particular are attracting much attention. The first of these is the increasing content of carbon dioxide in the atmosphere, and the resulting increase in temperature through the 'greenhouse effect'. Forest growth and distribution may be affected by this warming effect, while tree growth-rates may be directly modified by changing concentrations of carbon dioxide. Second, acid precipitation and other forms of atmospheric pollution have been suspected of being responsible (wholly or partly) for the symptoms of forest decline reported from the forests of parts of Europe and North America. Both these issues have important implications for the future of the forest resource – the former on the long-term and the latter on the medium-to-short time-scale.

Climatic warming

The distribution and extent of forests are not static, as might be implied by maps such as Figure 2.1, but have undergone major changes in response to climatic fluctuations in recent (geological) times. During glacial periods, the forest belts have migrated equatorwards, only to move polewards again during inter-glacials. Such shifts may seem irrelevant on the human time-scale and in the context of resource use, but they are reminders of the dynamic nature of forest patterns and distributions. It is possible that current climatic trends may give rise to comparable changes in forest distributions over the next few decades and centuries.

The role of deforestation

The much-publicised 'greenhouse effect' results from the role of carbon dioxide and other 'greenhouse' gases in absorbing long-wave terrestrial radiation, with consequent warming of the atmosphere. Carbon dioxide (CO_2) is only one of several 'greenhouse' gases, but it is the most important and accounts for at least half of the 'effect'. As is well known, concentrations of CO_2 in the atmosphere have been rising steadily, and are likely to continue to do so in the foreseeable future. Most of the increase in CO_2 comes from the combustion of fossil fuels, but substantial amounts also result from the clearing and burning of forests. Estimates of the relative importance of forest clearance and other biotic sources compared to fossil fuels vary greatly. For example, a 'deforestation' output of between 0.4 and 2.5 billion tons of carbon is reported by Houghton and Woodwell (1989), as compared with an output of approximately 5.6 billion tons from the combustion of fossil fuels. Using FAO/UNEP data on deforestation rates in 1980, Houghton et al. (1985) concluded that the net flux from non-fallow forests was between 0.7 and 1.4×10^{15} g of carbon, compared with a release of 5.2×10^{15} from the combustion of fossil fuels. Lower estimates of at least 0.4 but not more than 1.6×10^{15} of carbon in 1980 are suggested by Detwiler and Hall (1988). Of their estimates, between one-third and one-quarter comes from decreases in soil organic matter, while the burning and decay of cleared vegetation account for the remainder.

Some disagreement exists about the nature of the flux of carbon from the clearing of forest vegetation. Combustion is frequently incomplete, resulting in conversion of biomass into charcoal and soil organic matter and hence functioning as a carbon sink rather than carbon source (Seiler and Crutzen, 1980). More generally, the fate of wood cut from tropical and other forests determines how rapidly that organic matter is returned to the atmosphere as CO_2. While fuelwood is quickly returned, industrial wood products are usually broken down much less rapidly. Paradoxically, even some deforestation may create carbon sinks, if it is followed by a vigorous regrowth with rapid uptake of CO_2, and if a proportion of the initial biomass remains on site (Lugo and Brown, 1980).

Considerable uncertainty therefore surrounds the contribution of forest removal to rising levels of CO_2, but deforestation may account for around 20 per cent of the total increase in CO_2 (Brünig, 1987). It is a minor, but nevertheless significant, contributor to the total output, and hence to the 'greenhouse effect'. Furthermore, the use of woodfuel is an additional source of CO_2, over and above that resulting from forest fires associated with forest clearing or arising from natural causes. Its contribution is estimated to amount to around one-tenth of that from the fossil fuels (Rotty, 1986).

Deforestation (and other biotic sources such as the cultivation of grassland soils and the drainage of wetlands) and fossil fuel combustion have both increased rapidly over the last 150 years. For areas such as south-east Asia, for example, it has been suggested that the current flux of CO_2 is much larger than at any time in the past, because of the growth and density of the population, reflected in increasingly extensive and intensive land use (Palm et al., 1986). Conversely, however, a change in forest trends can lead to a reversal of function in terms of carbon budgets. Temperate forests now function as CO_2 sinks, whereas in the past they have been sources, like the tropical forests of today (Lugo and Brown, 1980). The Southeast of the United States, for example, was a net source of carbon from around 1750 to 1950, as the forests were cleared for agriculture. Since 1950, it has become a sink (albeit a minor one) as reforestation has proceeded (Delcourt and Harris, 1980). This North American example may be repeated in other areas where the forest area has been increasing, and perhaps even for non-tropical forests as a whole. Afforestation has been suggested as a possible tool for moderating global warming (e.g. Sedjo, 1989). Furthermore, the recent case of the American power company which agreed to plant 500 square kilometres of forest in Guatemala gives rise to some hope for the future. This forest will absorb at least as much CO_2 as its new power station in Connecticut, using fossil fuels, will emit (Tyler, 1989). On the other hand, differences in biomass between natural and planted forests mean that reforestation can never completely offset the carbon losses to the atmosphere resulting from initial deforestation (Delcourt and Harris, 1980).

Whatever the detailed role of forest trends may be, the role of tropical forests is crucial. The rapid rates of carbon recycling in tropical rain forests in particular mean that their conservation, together with the upgrading of already degraded tropical habitats, is potentially the most effective demand-side means of dealing with the global CO_2 problem (Goreau and de Mello, 1988).

The greenhouse effect results not only from increasing concentrations of CO_2, but also from changes in concentrations of other gases such as methane. The burning of tropical rain forests may indirectly lead to increases in such gases, as well as in CO_2. It has recently been suggested that the burning of tropical forests and savannahs generates at least as much carbon monoxide (CO) as does the burning of fossil fuels, and that this in turn leads to the accumulation of methane as well as ozone, which can be toxic to plants (Newell et al., 1989).

The effect on forest patterns

Atmospheric CO_2 concentrations have increased by almost 25 per cent over the last hundred years. They are rising (at a rate of around 10 parts per million during the 1980s, against a level of around 350 ppm at the end of the decade) and are likely to continue to do so in the foreseeable future. By one hundred years from now, they may have risen to between 500 and 600 ppm. By then global average temperatures could be several degrees higher. Such increases in temperature are unlikely to be evenly distributed around the globe, but are likely to be relatively small in the tropics and much higher (of the order of several degrees) in high latitudes.

On the basis of temperature changes resulting from projected CO_2 concentrations, major changes in forest extent and distribution could result. One well-known model, based on a doubling of CO_2 and on Holdridge Life Zones (indicating the type of vegetation expected from climatic parameters) was developed by Emanuel et al. (1985). Its results are spectacular: forest zones would shrink from 58 to 47 per cent of the land surface, and there would be some expansion of the tropical forest zone and a dramatic contraction of the boreal coniferous zone (Table 7.1; Figure 7.1). Much of the present boreal zone would be replaced by cool temperate forest or steppe, and its poleward migration would be impeded by the relative paucity of land in polar latitudes.

The main value of such a model probably lies in its indication of the possible scale of impact rather than in the detailed pattern of forest changes. Possible changes in precipitation, which would be of major importance at the forest–steppe boundary, were not incorporated, nor were the effects of altitude or of soils. Furthermore, changes in mean annual temperature were employed, and it has been suggested that the seasonal distribution of temperatures would be more relevant (e.g. Harrington, 1987). More recent work has drawn attention to the roles of other factors such as soil moisture in determining the detailed pattern

Table 7.1   Climatic change and possible changes in forest ecosystems

Forest	*(10⁶ km²)* Base case	Elevated CO_2 ($\times$ 2)
Tropical	19.004	24.965
Sub-tropical	11.998	8.689
Warm temperate	15.951	15.540
Cool temperate	11.226	12.230
Boreal	17.375	0.835
	75.554	62.259

Source: Emanuel et al, (1985)

of response, and also factors such as the changing availability of soil nitrogen, which may be both a cause and an effect of changing vegetation (e.g. Pastor and Post, 1988). Even with these qualifications, however, the results of the work of Emanuel et al. are startling, and there is agreement that large reductions in the extent of boreal forests, together with a poleward shift in their boundaries, is a distinct possibility (e.g. Shugart et al. (1986)).

The effect on forest growth
In addition to these shifts in the forest belts, dramatic changes in forest productivity could occur, especially in the boreal forest zone. In absolute terms, the greatest increases in growth would be expected in the warmer, southern parts of the zone, but in relative terms the increases would increase northwards (Kauppi and Posch, 1985). Figure 7.2 shows an estimated increase in potential productivity resulting from the CO_2 levels expected to exist in the middle of next century, compared with present conditions (Kauppi, 1987). Productivity would more than double in some areas. Potentially significant increases are not confined to the boreal zone. In theory, sizeable increases might be expected over much of Australia, for example, but in practice other limiting factors, such as availability of water or nutrients, may come into play (Pittock, 1987).

In practice there would be a time-lag between climatic change and biological response, and the response indicated in Figure 7.2 would certainly not be immediate. Such a time-lag would also, of course, characterise distributional changes in forest area.

On the other hand there is some indication that changes in growth rates and in forest boundaries are already occurring. Under laboratory conditions, an increase in the CO_2 level is usually found to increase the rate of photosynthesis, and changes in growth rates may therefore result directly from this 'fertilization', as well as from climatic warming. In the western United States sub-alpine conifers have been found to have had increased growth since the middle of the nineteenth century (La Marche et al., 1984). This increase exceeds that which would be expected from climatic trends, but is consistent with global trends in CO_2. In high-level forests in the

Figure 7.1   (a) and (b) Ecological zones (Holdridge classification)
(a) base case (b) elevated CO_2

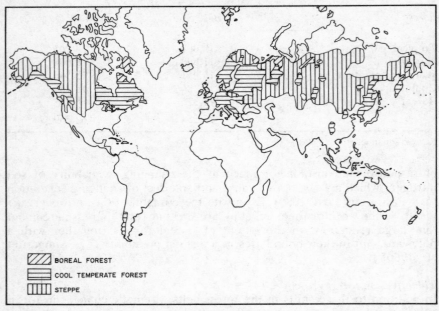

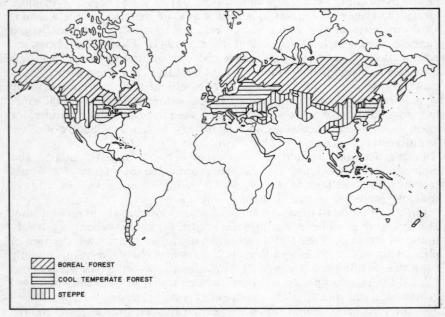

Source: Modified after Emanuel et al. (1985)

Cascade Mountains of Washington, net primary productivity at a number of widely separated sites has increased by up to 60 per cent during the present century, but it has been concluded that changes in summer temperatures, rather than direct CO_2 fertilization, are responsible (Graumlich et al., 1989). Elsewhere in North America, increased tree-ring widths and/or advancing forest margins are reported from Alaska, sub-Arctic Canada and Quebec (e.g. Garfunkel and Brubaker (1980) and Payette et al. (1985)). It has also been suggested that similar changes resulting from climatic warming (with or without CO_2 fertilization) have occurred in Europe. For example, in southern Finland an increase in volume increment has been observed between successive inventories, and its magnitude could not be explained in terms of climatic conditions or improved silviculture. The tentative conclusion is that the increase is due to rising CO_2 levels and/or nitrogen deposition (Arovaara et al., 1984).

While changes in growth rates and forest boundaries in high-altitude or tundra-margin forests may be of little significance in practical terms of resource use, those in areas such as Finland may be more important. Also the possible ramifications of increasing CO_2 levels extend well beyond growth rates and forest boundaries. Changing climate could mean changing frequencies of climatic events such as gales or severe frosts, and could thus have implications for the choice of species, as well as possible effects on growth and yield (Cannel et al., 1989). In Canada, for example, fast-growing species, including some hardwood and weed species, may be favoured, and a mismatch may develop between the present forest types and the climatic regions that they occupy (Pollard, 1985). Under such conditions, pest outbreaks and fire damage may intensify, and in addition operational problems, for example in winter logging, may be encountered. In short, rising levels of CO_2 may well have both positive and negative effects: in the words of Hoffman (1984, p.166) '(it) presents neither an unmitigated blessing nor a disaster for forestry'. Nevertheless, the changes in high-latitude forests such as those of Canada are expected to be considerable, and commentators such as Harrington (1987) have urged the responsible agencies to devise appropriate strategies to deal with them, especially since the lifetime of current plantings will extend well into the period of expected climatic change.

Forest decline

While growth rates in some forests may already be increasing as a result of changing CO_2 concentrations, other forests are showing signs of decline and even of death. One of the major environmental issues of the 1980s was the forest decline reported from much of Europe and from parts of North America. Forest decline is not a completely new phenomenon. Local-scale damage to forests from air pollution has occurred widely, both in the past and at present, and is associated especially with metal-smelting industries. Furthermore, periodic declines have been reported from a number of areas and for a number of species in the past. The forest decline that became so

Figure 7.2 A scenario of the possible forest effects of warming. Estimated increase in the potential productivity of boreal forests resulting from mid-twenty-first century CO_2 levels (a) in m³/ha/yr and (b) in percentage terms. Note that there is likely to be a time lag between climatic change and forest response

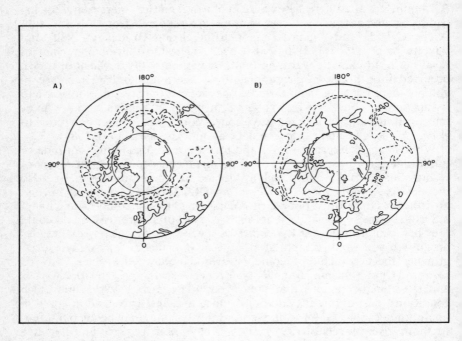

Source: Based on Kauppi :1987)

apparent in the 1980s, however, is of a different scale. While local pollution effects such as those around Sudbury, Ontario, extended to an area of nearly 20,000 hectares (Smith, 1985), the scale of the forest decline of the 1980s is regional or even continental, extending to millions of hectares. And while the pollutants responsible for local declines in the past have usually been readily identified, the causes of recent forest decline remain uncertain. Symptoms include discolouration and loss of needles and leaves, decreased growth rates and abnormal forms of growth, and in some instances death of trees. The effects are in due course transmitted throughout the forest ecosystem. In the Netherlands, for example, a deteriorating quality of eggshells of some hole-nesting birds, attributed to acid precipitation and hence insufficiency of calcium, is reported (Drent and Woldendorp, 1989). In Hungary, a decline in oakwoods, believed to be related to soil acidification which in turn is related to air pollution, has been accompanied by a disappearance of mushrooms (Jakucs, 1988).

During the 1970s, signs of decline were observed in white/silver fir (*Abies alba*) and then in Norway spruce (*Picea abies*) in West Germany. By

Table 7.2   West German forest damage surveys 1982–4

Tree species	Per cent of forests damaged		
	1982	*1983*	*1984*
Spruce	9	41	51
Pine	5	44	59
Fir	60	75	87
Beech	4	26	50
Oak	4	15	43
Others	4	17	31
Total	8	34	50

Source: Based on WRI (1986)

the early 1980s, the symptoms were observable also in pine, larch and a number of broad-leaved species. By 1983, up to 75 per cent of the area of fir in West Germany was affected, while over 40 per cent of pine and spruce, 26 per cent of beech and almost 15 per cent of oak were also identified as damaged in 1983 (CEC, 1987). In 1982, 8 per cent of West German forests showed signs of damage: by 1985 the proportion had increased to 55 per cent (WRI, 1986). Very rapid increases in the extent of damage were reported for some species between 1982 and 1984 in particular, as Table 7.2 indicates: in the *Land* of Baden Wurttemberg the percentage of healthy fir trees fell from 62 to under 5 between 1980 and 1982, whilst that of spruce damage increased from 6 per cent in 1981 to 94 per cent in 1983 (CEC, 1987). The extent of damage appeared to stabilise in the second half of the 1980s (Figure 7.3). While forest decline or *Waldsterben* is usually associated with West Germany, other countries in western, central and eastern Europe have also suffered serious damage. The extent and progress of this damage in one instance – part of Czechoslovakia – is shown in Figure 7.4.

Various species in North America have also displayed symptoms of decline. These include sugar maple in the Northeast of the United States and the south-east of Canada, white pine and high-altitude red spruce in the eastern United States, and Ponderosa and Jeffrey pines in California (e.g. Chevone and Linzon, 1988). A sudden increase in dieback of sugar maple was observed in Quebec in 1982, and since then symptoms of defoliation, dieback and mortality have worsened and spread to other species. The heaviest mortality corresponds with localities suffering severe insect attack, seasonal climatic extremes, low soil nutrient status and highest fallouts of wet acid sulphate and nitrate (Hendershot and Jones, 1989). Annual growth of red spruce in New England increased consistently from 1910–20 to 1960, and then fluctuated around a generally declining trend. By the early 1980s, it was 13 to 40 per cent below its peak levels (Hornbeck and Smith, 1985). Uncertainty exists as to whether the observed declines in growth rates are natural or anthropogenic (Zedakaer et al., 1987). Defoliation by spruce budworm, climatic change, increasing maturity

Figure 7.3   Forest decline in West Germany: results of forest-damage surveys
1983–87

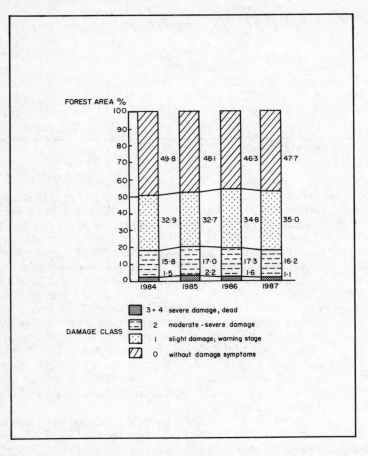

Source: Blank et al: reproduced from *Nature*, 336: 27–30, Macmillan Magazines Ltd. (1989)

of the forest and acid deposition have all been identified as possible
explanations.

Various hypotheses have also been advanced to explain forest decline in
Europe. These include soil acidification, accelerated by the deposition
of acid substances from precipitation or directly from the atmosphere,
leading to aluminium toxicity and possibly magnesium deficiency; gaseous
pollutants such as ozone, sulphur dioxide and ammonia; excess nitrogen
from the atmospheric deposition of nitrogen compounds (especially from
automobile engines); organic compounds; and general stress, perhaps from
multiple pollutants, which expose the trees to increased risk of damage

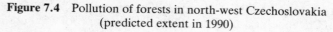

Figure 7.4   Pollution of forests in north-west Czechoslovakia
(predicted extent in 1990)

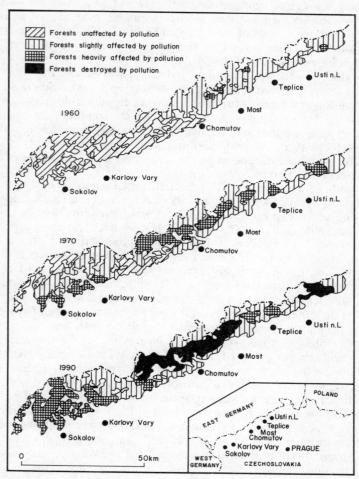

Source: Based on Carter (1985)

from drought or pests (see, for example, Hinrichsen, 1986). Different
causes may be responsible in different areas: for example, local effects
result from high levels of ammonium sulphate around intensive livestock
units in the Netherlands and around industrial plants and power stations in
countries such as Czechoslovakia and Poland (Pitelka and Raynal, 1989),
but other, larger-scale factors must be responsible in areas such as
the German and Swiss mountains. Ozone, produced by photochemical
reactions involving emissions of nitrogen compounds and hydrocarbons
from power stations and motor vehicles, is believed to be at least a

contributory factor in West Germany (Ashmore et al., 1985) and North America (Chevone and Linzon, 1988). Rigorous proof of cause has been established for ozone damage in eastern white pine and in southern Californian forests, while there is circumstantial evidence of causality in the sugar maple forests of New England and neighbouring areas and in low-altitude coniferous forests in the eastern United States from New England to Florida (Cowling, 1989).

While ozone is the only regionally dispersed pollutant that has been rigorously proven to cause detrimental effects on forests, others such as acid deposition (especially in rainfall and from cloud and fog) are strongly suspected of being damaging. In Canada, the opinions of surveyed scientific experts are that acid deposition has already significantly reduced forest productivity in the east, and may soon do so in the west (Fraser, 1985). The estimated decline in productivity may be of the order of 5 per cent (Crocker and Forster, 1986).

Soil acidification is widespread, especially under conifer crops, and while it may be a natural process, there is also evidence that it has accelerated. The strong and deep-reaching acidification which is widespread on all except limestone soils in Germany is traced back to acid deposition (Ulrich, 1986). In Sweden it has been established that the rate of acidification between the 1920s and 1980s was higher in the south than in the north, and the most likely explanations is the larger load of acid deposition in the south (Tamm and Hallbacken, 1988). In southern Sweden soil acidification of up to one pH unit has occurred (Anderson, 1986). On the other hand, however, the geographical pattern of symptoms of forest decline in Scandinavia is not correlated with levels of gaseous pollutants (Pitelka and Raynal, 1989). Nor is there a close correlation between acid deposition and forest decline in West Germany (Rehfuess, 1985). Despite the synchronous appearance of symptoms of decline across different regions and species in Europe, it seems that no single cause is responsible. In the case of Norway spruce, for example, several different diseases and causes may be responsible, and the synchroneity of onset of symptoms is perhaps due to climatic stress. Climatic conditions are also considered to be the key factor underlying changing growth rates in the Vosges Mountains of France, although regional air pollution may have had an exacerbating effect (Becker, 1989).

While it has been concluded that, at least in some areas such as parts of West Germany, 'it has been proven through complementary circumstantial evidence that air pollution is the determinative factor causing the forest decline' (Schöpfer and Hradetzky, 1984, p. 248), the occurrence and severity of the decline are not correlated with any specific pollutant. Probably no single casual factor is responsible (Klein and Perkins, 1987). In this state of uncertainty, the prognosis is obviously unclear. Climatic warming may itself impose stress on some species, and predispose them to attack by pests or disease, and various other factors may also contribute. One may be the structure of the affected forests. Uniformly structured European plantation forests are compared by Mueller-Dombois (1987) with similarly structured natural forests in New Zealand and Hawaii.

Extensive die-back occurs in the latter when they enter the senescing life-stage, even in the absence of air pollution. The underlying basis of the process in Europe may therefore be natural, and factors such as air pollution may simply accelerate it. Another factor may be land-use history, especially in relation to observed reductions in growth rates in pine stands in the south-eastern United States. Many of the stands planted between 1945 and 1965 were on abandoned farmland, while many of the more recent plantings have been on cut-over timber land, giving lower growth rates (Sheffield and Cost, 1987). This trend, combined with other social and institutional factors, may lie behind the recent downward turn of net annual growth of softwood in the region, following a long climb (Knight, 1987).

Whatever the causes of forest decline may be, the potential practical significance in terms of lost timber production is enormous. In North America, if it is assumed that the effect of acid deposition is to reduce forest productivity by 5 per cent, then the annual losses to the commercial timber industry would be around $197 million (1981 dollars) in Canada and $600 million in the United States (Crocker and Forster, 1986). Estimates of the annual costs of *Waldsterben* to the West German timber and related industries amount to hundreds of millions of dollars per annum and may eventually amount to a billion or more dollars (WRI, 1986). One study suggested that the total direct and indirect monetary cost, based on loss to the forest industry, reduced recreational value and additional costs arising from the increased need for protection against avalanches could amount to a staggering $200 billion between 1984 and 2060 (Blank et al., 1988). In Bavaria, where the loss of annual increment was estimated at 17 per cent in 1984, the cost was believed to amount to over DM 200 million per annum (Kroth, 1985). Behind these aggregate figures lie serious consequences for numerous owners. For example, it has been estimated that a model farm-forest enterprise in Bavaria, consisting of 80 hectares of forest and 7 hectares of grassland together with tourism and hunting, could witness a decrease in gross annual income from DM 114,400 under damage-free conditions to DM 48,400 under a scenario of constant-damage intensity and to DM 8,400 with a moderate increase of damage (Netsch, 1985). Any increase of damage would seriously jeopardize the viability of the farm forest. On a wider scale, fears have been expressed that a general collapse of the forest-products industries in West Germany could occur unless strict controls are imposed on air pollution (Jäger, 1985). In addition to the obvious economic costs, indirect losses will be incurred in terms of reduction of intensity or quality of recreation in damaged forests. Further-more, protected forests (Chapter 6) will be affected as much as production forests in the regions in question.

Perhaps the biggest cost, however, is the alarm and concern generated in the minds of the population: if the supposedly pure forest environment displays symptoms of decline, what does this indicate about the health of the wider environment? The fact that the causes of the decline have not been fully identified makes it seem even more ominous and sinister. On the other hand the rapid increase in symptoms of decline observed during the first half of the 1980s has not continued through the second half of the decade (Figure 7.3). While damage has increased in some areas, others have shown some signs of recovery. And the predicted financial disruption to the timber market resulting from unplanned salvage fellings has not materialised (Blank et al., 1988).

External environmental changes are of major significance in relation to the use of the forest resource. On the one hand, climatic warming may lead to a reduction in the forest area and a shift in the forest belts. On the other hand it, in combination with CO_2 fertilization, may enhance growth rates and necessitate changes in cultivation practices. Little can be done to halt these trends, as the output of CO_2 is so huge and widespread, but uncertainty remains as to their strength and pattern. Their effect will probably be increasingly felt in the future, while the symptoms of forest decline are already all too apparent in parts of Europe and North America. While regional-scale air pollution is suspected as a major cause or predisposing factor, the details of the mechanisms involved are imperfectly understood. Whilst in theory emission levels of ozone and acid deposition could be reduced more easily than that of CO_2, in practice it will be many years before regional controls become effective. The outlook for the boreal coniferous and cool temperate forests, therefore, is uncertain.

Forest resource use and the environment

While the growth, extent and health of forests may be affected by air pollution and changing atmospheric composition, the use of the forest and changes in its area can also affect the wider environment. Some of the impacts arising from resource use are well known, but in other cases there is greater confusion or uncertainty. One of the main problems is that resource use can take various forms, ranging from complete removal of the forest to more modest and benign operations such as the harvesting of 'minor' forest products (Chapter 6). Deforestation itself may take various forms, ranging from sudden and drastic clearance to a slow and gradual attentuation of the forest. Furthermore, the same operation carried out in different ways can have very different effects. For example 'recovery' from forest clearance in areas such as Amazonia may take only a few years if the clearing is carried out manually, but thousands of years if it is done mechanically.

Hydrology

The forest has been widely perceived as supplying equable flows of pure water and linkages between forest cover and rainfall have been widely believed to exist. For example, in the United States in the nineteenth century it was thought that afforestation on the Great Plains would lead to increased rainfall (e.g. Williams, 1989a). Myth and fact are difficult to separate in this area, and relationships that are well established in some areas cannot necessarily be extrapolated to other situations.

Forest and rainfall

On the local scale, it has usually been assumed that no definite connection exists between forest cover and rainfall, and allegations of declining rainfall following forest removal have rarely been supported by convincing evidence. More recently, however, some evidence has accumulated from places as different as India, Peninsular Malaysia, the Philippines, Ivory Coast and the Panama Canal area to support the hypothesis that deforestation may be followed by lower and/or less reliable rainfall (Myers, 1989), or at least a reduced availability of water. The actual mechanisms by which rainfall might be reduced are uncertain, although it has been suggested that changed surface roughness may be involved. One special case is that of high-altitude cloud forests and forests in coastal fog belts. Occult precipitation (from fog and cloud) may be of very significant amounts on the large surface areas of leaves, needles, stems and branches. In Hawaii, for example, occult precipitation in such forests contributed an extra 760 millimetres compared with 2,600 millimetres in a similar non-forest area (Hamilton, 1988). It follows that removal or attentuation of cloud forests will be followed by a reduction in rainfall.

On the larger scale, there is also some uncertainty about the relationship between rainfall and forest cover. It has been speculated that extensive deforestation in areas such as Amazonia could result in significant reductions in rainfall. It has been shown that the Amazonian forest plays an important role in recirculating water to the atmosphere: about half of the incoming precipitation is returned to the atmosphere as evaporation, and the rainfall intercepted by the forest canopy is a significant component of this evaporation (Shuttleworth, 1988). A reduction in this recirculation could therefore lead to a reduction in rainfall. Salati and Vose (1984) conclude that continued large-scale deforestation could lead to reduced precipitation, which in turn could adversely affect climate and hence agriculture in south-central Brazil. Furthermore, it has been asserted that

> total annual rainfall will decrease considerably when a certain percentage of Amazon forest has been destroyed and the seasonality of rainfall will become more pronounced. This will probably have a disastrous effect on the survival of spared forest areas which are intended as 'nature reserves' or the like. (Sioli, 1985 a and b)

Henderson-Sellers and Gornitz (1984) have attempted to simulate the climatic effects arising in changes in albedo resulting from tropical deforestation. They simulated the effects of removing almost 5 million square kilometres of forest (the current global rate continued for thirty-five to fifty years) from Amazonia, and replacing it with a grass/crop cover. This extreme scenario yielded a decrease in rainfall of only 0.5–0.7 millimetres per day (annual rainfall is 3,000 millimetres or more in much of the basin). Earlier work by Potter et al. (1975) in modelling the climatic effects resulting from albedo change following removal of the entire tropical rain forest indicated slight decreases in precipitation in tropical and high latitudes and a slight increase in the subtropical zone. (They also suggested that the albedo effect would result in slight global cooling.)

While the general direction of the changes in rainfall indicated by such modelling is the same as that alleged in much popular and environmentalist writing, the modest dimensions of change contrast with many of the more extreme predictions of withering droughts following tropical deforestation. Furthermore, the climatic effects of deforestation in a continental area such as Amazonia will not necessarily be replicated in other parts of the world with different situations and climatic regimes.

Water yield and river flow
Similar uncertainty and disagreement characterise the role of the forest in relation to water yield and river flows. The forest and its soil have frequently been claimed to function like a sponge, absorbing rainfall and releasing it gradually in equable flows (e.g. Myers, 1988). The corollary is that the removal of the forest will result in decreased and less equable flows, and hence tend to lead to droughts and floods. Both of these components of this belief are open to question, qualification or refinement.

Whatever its effects on rainfall may be, the removal of trees and forests usually reduces losses through evaporation and transpiration, and hence increases water yield. Cloud forests may represent a special and exceptional case, but there is widespread evidence to suggest that an increase in water yield is the normal response to a decrease in forest cover. For example the conversion of tropical forest in the high rainfall belt of Zambia to agricultural use had resulted in an increase in streamflow (Mumeka, 1986). On the basis of a review of ninety-four catchment experiments around the world, Bosch and Hewlett (1982) found that the increase in yield was greatest in areas of high rainfall, that it was proportional to the reduction in the forest canopy, and that for every 10 per cent reduction in forest cover there was an increase in water yield equivalent to about 40 millimetres of rainfall in the case of coniferous and eucalyptus forests and around 25 millimetres for deciduous types. In other words, deforestation is more likely to increase water yield than to decrease it. Conversely, afforestation is likely to reduce streamflow. In a study of ten large river basins in Alabama, Georgia and South Carolina, where the forest area increased from 10 to 28 per cent between 1919 and 1967, annual stream discharges were found to decrease by amounts varying between 4 and 21 per cent (Trimble and Weirich, 1987). A change in the type of forest, and hence in its functions of rainfall interception and evapotranspiration, may also result in changes in streamflow. For example, in the southern Appalachians, annual streamflow decreased by around 20 per cent following the conversion of a mature deciduous hardwood forest to white pine (Swank and Douglass, 1974). Young, rapidly growing eucalyptus plantations in the humid tropics have been found to consume more water than natural forests (FAO, 1986b), and decreases in water yield of as much as 28 per cent have been reported from cases in India (Mathur et al., 1976).

Some evidence exists to support the popular belief that forest cover helps to regulate river flows, especially in comparison with crops. In the Ivory Coast, for example, the dry-season flows of rivers are much higher from primary forest than from coffee plantations: the ratio of flow varies from approximately 2:1 during mid-season to 3–5:1 at the end of the dry season (Dosso et al., 1981). In Malaysia, it was found that low flows of rivers from primary rain forest were roughly double those from rubber and oil-palm plantations (Daniel and Kulasingam, 1974). To this extent, then, the 'sponge' theory is supported, and has been invoked to explain the problems of water availability for the Panama Canal which first became evident in the late 1970s. Destruction of the forest by peasant cultivators was believed to be responsible (Simons, 1989). On the other hand, the relationship between deforestation and flooding is complex. There is a long-held belief that forests prevent or reduce floods: large areas of land were planted for this reason in the Tennessee Valley and elsewhere in the United States during the 1930s, for example. Rates of run-off may be much higher from cropland than from natural forest, but it does not necessarily follow that allegations that major floods in rivers such as the Ganges and Brahmaputra are 'caused' by deforestation or the harvesting of fuelwood in the Himalayas (see, for example, Guppy, 1984; WRI, 1985; Myers, 1983c; Jacobs, 1988). According to Myers (1983c, p. 66), for example, over the last thirty years 'forest cover in the upper catchment territories (of the Ganges) has been reduced by 40% . . . with the result that monsoonal flooding now causes appreciable damage'. Other commentators, including Hamilton (1987) and Hamilton and Pearce (1988), however, conclude that it is simply not defensible to attribute major floods in the rivers of the lower parts of the Indian subcontinent to fuelwood harvesting in the Himalayas. Indeed, Ives (1988, 1989) asserts that claims that deforestation in the Himalayas has caused serious impacts on the plains and deltas of the Ganges and Brahmaputra must be challenged at all levels.

While deforestation may intensify downstream flooding by increasing the frequency of small floods, it is unlikely to have much effect in terms of major floods. The storage capacity of the forest 'sponge' is limited, and once exceeded, especially in high-rainfall, mountainous areas such as the Himalayas and New Zealand, it will have little effect in preventing major floods or even in reducing their magnitude. Nevertheless, even if upstream deforestation is not responsible for disastrous floods in areas such as Bangladesh, there may be a significant effect in terms of the heights and frequency of small floods. For example, it has been suggested that agricultural colonisation in Peruvian Amazonia has increased flooding downstream, to the detriment of human settlements and crops along the rivers. The height of the annual flood crest of the Amazon at Iquitos is reported to have increased markedly during the 1970s, when the population of Peruvian Amazonia doubled but rainfall patterns apparently did not change (Gentry and Lopez-Parodi, 1980). This claim, however, has been disputed by Nordin and Meade (1982) and by Sternberg (1987). The latter found no clear statistical evidence to support the allegations of an increasing height of annual flood, and even if such a change had occurred, it was not necessarily due to deforestation.

While it is appropriate that the 'sponge' theory has been subjected to critical review in recent years and that allegations of a direct relationship between deforestation and major floods be treated with some scepticism, there is perhaps a danger of over-reaction. In theory grassland and scrub may provide as much storage and protection as forest, but in practice that protective role may be greatly reduced by overgrazing or burning (Smiet, 1987). Quite apart from any other benefits it may yield, the maintenance of the protective forest may well be justified by hydrological reasons, although the effectiveness of the protective function depends on the type of forest. Eucalyptus plantations, for example, have been found to regulate flow less well than natural forests (FAO, 1986b).

The macro-scale climatic and hydrological effects of extensive deforestation in areas such as Amazonia have attracted much popular attention, but other forms of impact also occur, as do impacts arising from smaller-scale operations carried out as normal parts of forest use and management. An example of the former is a rising water table following clear-felling of indigenous forest. With forest removal there is a reduction in evapotranspiration, and in addition to the increases in river flow that have already been discussed, there may also be a rise in the water table. Resulting problems of salinity have been encountered in areas such as south-west Australia, where native sclerophyll forests have been felled for wood chips (Conacher, 1983).

Clear-felling of small areas usually results in an increase in streamflow (e.g. Likens et al., 1978). Following the clear-felling of two small catchments in central Sweden, run-off increased by 119 and 75 per cent respectively, but these results are more dramatic than those reported from other Scandinavian investigations (Rosen, 1984). Over larger river catchments, the nature of the effect may be both small and complex, depending on, amongst other factors, the size and location of the coupes. For example, in central Sweden the total effect on peak flow of a 10 per cent clearcut in a large basin is small compared to the effects of extreme weather conditions. The locational pattern of cuts, however, has a differential effect which is greatest in spring because of its influence on the pattern of snowmelt (Brandt et al., 1988).

On the scale of small clear fells or coupes, these hydrological effects are likely to be exceeded in significance by those of sediment transport, and numerous reports from around the world confirm that both forest removal and timber harvesting are likely to lead to increased rates of sedimentation.

Soils

The relationship between forest vegetation and soils is close, and any change in forest vegetation – for example through clearance or selective felling – may be followed by changes in the physical or chemical characteristics of the soil. Harvesting and other mechanical operations may also lead to changes in soil conditions, and these changes may have off-site consequences – for example, in increased sediment loads downstream – or on-site consequences such as reduced growth rates in subsequent rotations or cycles.

Forest clearance, soils and water budgets

When natural forest is cleared, the nutrient and water budgets of the soil are fundamentally altered. With the removal of trees and shrubs, evapotranspiration is reduced, and hence both water tables and water yields may rise. Circulation of nutrients from soil through trees and shrubs and back through plant litter to the soil is disrupted. The practical significance of these consequences varies with climate and ecological situation. In cool temperate regions such as the maritime fringes of north-west Europe, for example, increased waterlogging following the initial forest clearance thousands of years ago led to the development of peat bogs which have persisted ever since. In addition to the direct hydrological effect of reduced losses from evapotranspiration, the removal of deep-rooting trees meant that the soil surface was no longer enriched by nutrients brought up from the deeper layers of the soil, while increased leaching of the surface layers meant impoverishment of their nutrient status. In both physical and chemical terms, therefore, the soil deteriorated, and might become incapable of supporting forest growth, or at least growth of the kind typical of the original forest. Such changes are not confined to cool, maritime areas. In the Mediterranean zone, for example, a comparison of soils under cultivation and under oak forest in the south of Spain has shown that removal of the forests has resulted in a decrease in organic matter, in cation exchange capacity, and in available water. Deforested soils have undergone physical and biological degradation, as well as water erosion (Delgado-Calvo-Flores et al., 1985).

While such deterioration has undoubtedly occurred in some parts of countries such as Scotland and Ireland as well as in the Mediterranean world, the soils of most of the long-cleared forests of the temperate zone have been transformed by cultivation, drainage, and enrichment by fertilisers as they have been converted to agricultural use. In the tropics, however, the effects of forest clearance may be more dramatic and more serious. In some instances hard crusts of laterite may form on the soil surface, following the transformation of the micro-climate and drying out of the soil. Crusts of indurated material of around 2 metres in thickness are reported to have developed in areas such as the Cameroons in less than a century (Goudie, 1981). These crusts are by no means inevitable consequences of forest clearance in the tropics, and their frequency of occurrence has perhaps sometimes been exaggerated. Nevertheless, serious deterioration of the soil is a widespread consequence of forest removal.

In addition to the transforming of the micro-climate, clearance of the tropical forest disrupts nutrient cycling. A characteristic of the tropical rainforest is the fact that the biomass contains a very high proportion of the total nutrient content of the ecosystem. With the removal of the forest, much of the nutrient content will be lost. Despite the luxuriance of the forest, the nutrient status of the soil may be modest, and down through the years numerous forests have been cleared in the hope that their apparently fertile soils could be equally productive under agriculture or plantation crops. Initially the nutrients contained in the ashes of the burned biomass may help to maintain the illusion, but all too often a marked deterioration

Figure 7.5 The influence of timber-harvest activities on hydrological and erosional processes in a watershed

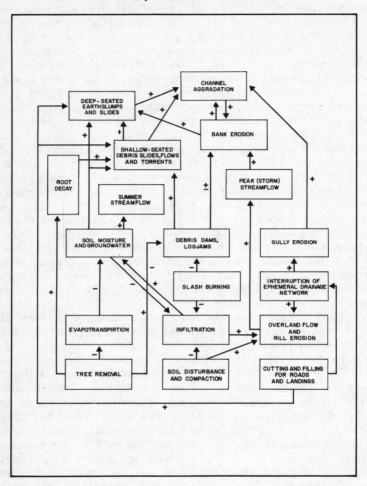

Source: Based on Coats and Miller (1981)

in productivity has set in within a very few years. The 'export' of nutrients in products such as timber or beef may simply accentuate the trend, and represents a major change from the tight and closed nutrient cycles of the original forest. In one example from Amazonia, it is reported that the carrying capacity of pastures created on former forest land fell from 0.9–1 head per unit area to 0.3 head within six years (Sioli, 1985 a and b). Such land is then likely to be abandoned, and forest regeneration may begin. Where abandonment has been almost immediate there is little depletion of total nutrient stocks and a 25 per cent recovery of mature

Figure 7.6   Suggested pathways of ecosystem degradation and recovery following deforestation

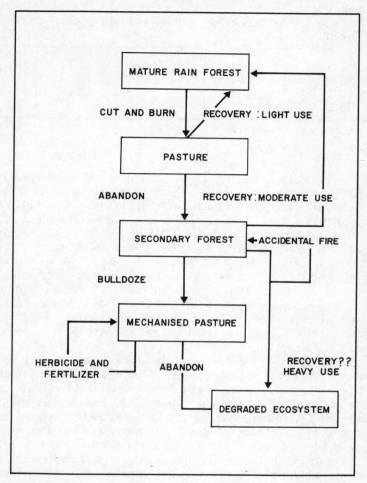

Source: Based on Uhl et al. (1988)

rain forest biomass may occur within eight years. The regrowth forest, however, will not necessarily have the same species composition as the original one.

The nature and significance of these effects of forest clearance depend on how the land is used after conversion as well as on the original ecological characteristics. They may also depend on how the clearance is achieved (Figure 7.6). In Amazonia, bulldozing, herbicide applications and chronic fire disturbance may effectively prevent forest recovery on about 10 per cent of the land cleared for pastures and then abandoned (Uhl et al., 1988).

Table 7.3   Forest clearance and physical effect on soil

Dry bulk densities Soil depth (cm)	Virgin forest	'Slash and burn' clearance	Bulldozer clearance
0–5	0.79	0.84	1.31
5–10	1.04	1.06	1.25
10–15	1.12	1.13	1.17
15–20	1.11	1.12	1.18

Source: Based on Nortcliff and Dias (1988)

Physical effects

A body of evidence is building up to show that large-scale mechanised clearance is likely to have greater effects than small-scale clearance by 'slash and burn'. Clearance by tractor in Africa has been reported to result in a more than fivefold increase in erosion compared with traditional manual methods (Lal, 1986). Table 7.3 compares some of the physical characteristics resulting from different modes of clearance of virgin tropical forest. Soil bulk density, reflecting soil compaction, is considerably higher where the forest has been cleared mechanically, while infiltration rates are much lower, indicating higher rates of run-off and higher probabilities of soil erosion (Nortcliff and Dias, 1988). At the same time, the protective canopy of the forest has been removed, exposing the soil surface to the kinetic energy of raindrops and hence to the initiation of soil erosion by impact splash.

The removal of the forest may therefore have a double effect in terms of soil erosion, and any modification of the forest canopy can lead to altered rates of soil loss. Under primary rain forests, sediment yields are usually very low not only because of canopy protection, but also because of the protective litter layer and dense root mat. If the forest is converted from its original form to one of high tree cover with bare ground underneath, then bare soil splash may increase by up to 6.6 times its value under the primary forest (Brandt, 1988). Thus while annual erosion rates under undisturbed natural tropical forest are usually very low, they may increase dramatically under plantations, as Table 7.4 indicates. Different types of forests mean different rates of erosion, and some types may have little beneficial effect in reducing erosion rates. For example, eucalypts are not effective means of erosion control under dry conditions, since the ground vegetation cover is suppressed by root competition (FAO, 1986b). In plantations of *Eucalyptus globulus* in Portugal, 66 per cent of the ground surface was found to be exposed soil without vegetation or litter, compared with percentages of 1.9 and 27.4 respectively in plantations of pine (*Pinus pinaster*) and oak (*Quercus suber*) (Kardell et al. (1986).

Modification of forest vegetation, whether in the form of complete removal and replacement by pastures or crops or of conversion into plantations or managed forests, may therefore be accompanied by changes

Table 7.4 Forest soil erosion: annual rates (tons/ha/year)

Undisturbed natural forest	Teak plantation widely spaced mixed understorey	Teak plantation closely spaced no undestorey
0.2–10	2–10	20–160

Source: Based on Brünig et al. (1975)

in soil characteristics. Processes of forest management, such as timber harvesting, may also have significant effects. Adverse effects resulting from logging operations have been reported from almost all types of exploited forests, from the tropics to the sub-Arctic.

The effects of logging
Low-technology logging in the tropical forest, using human and animal power combined with river transport, may have little lasting environmental impact (e.g. White, 1978). In contrast, mechanised logging in the tropical forest causes extensive baring and compaction of the soil, even although only a few trees are extracted per hectare. The extraction of only eleven trees per hectare in East Kalimantan, for example, was found to leave around 30 per cent of the ground surface bare and compacted, with a reduced rate of water infiltration and hence an increased rate of run-off (Rochadi Abdulhadi et al., 1981). In the same area, selective logging at a rate of twenty trees per hectare resulted in the development of skid tracks over 30 per cent of the logged area. On these tracks, water infiltration rates were found to be very much lower than in undisturbed primary forest (0.63 centimetres/minute compared with 4.62 centimetres/minute) (Kartawinata et al., 1981). In the tropical forests of Ecuador, the haphazard development of skid trails, combined with skidding during wet weather, was found to result in very high levels of ground disturbance, with up to 75 per cent of the surface under trails (DeBonis, 1986).

The magnitudes of such effects depend to a large degree on the way in which the operations are carried out. For example, the avoidance of skidding during wet weather in the Ecuadorian example is advocated as an effective means of reducing damage. In the Queensland rain forest of northern Australia, a marked reduction in sediment yields occurred after a few simple conditions were imposed on the loggers (Gilmour, 1971). These included a prohibition on hauling through streams, and a requirement that the loggers should construct and maintain drains along their roads. A major problem, however, is that of communication between the concession-holder, feller and skidder operator (e.g. Boxman et al., 1987). General instructions from the former may be modified in the course of transmission to the latter, and much unnecessary damage may be done by the skidder in searching for the logs to extract. In short, the environmental consequences of exposed soil and increased rates of erosion depend to a

Table 7.5   Sediment production from forests: representative rates

Forested slopes	$4-10 \text{m}^3/\text{km}^2$ road per year
Logged slopes	$16 \text{ m}^3/\text{km}^2$ road per year
Roads during use	$10\ 000-15\ 000 \text{ m}^3/\text{km}^2$ road per year
Roads, first year	$1\ 000-2\ 000 \text{ m}^3/\text{km}^2$ road per year
Abandoned roads	$100-500 \text{ m}^3/\text{km}^2$ road per year

Source: Compiled from data in Roberts and Church (1986)

large extent on the way in which management operations are conducted, rather than on the type of use of the forest resource.

These effects of soil compaction and erosion are not confined to the tropical zone, but have been reported from numerous types of forests around the world. The complex physical consequences following tree removal in temperate latitudes are illustrated in Figure 7.5, while Table 7.5 illustrates the dimensions of increases of sediment production related to forest operations in one major forest area, the Pacific Northwest. Growing environmental awareness during the late 1960s and 1970s led to greatly increased attention to logging effects in this area in particular, and has subsequently spread to some other parts of the world, including countries such as New Zealand where forests in steep country are being logged (e.g. Carson, 1983).

Extraction roads and stream crossings are especially susceptible to high rates of sediment yield. In a Quebec broad-leaved forest, for example, a two hundredfold rise in sediment concentrations was found following the skidding of logs across streams (Plamoudou, 1982), while the construction of extraction roads in an Idaho forest increased sediment production by a factor of around 750 compared with the 'natural' rate (Megahan and Kidd, 1972). It follows that the avoidance of stream skidding, the maintenance of buffer strips along streams and the design of roads can greatly reduce sediment yield in temperate forests as in the tropics. For example a 24 per cent reduction in sediment yield could have been achieved if conventional engineering methods had been employed in the construction of roads in a Californian forest (McCashion and Rice, 1981). In the Pacific Northwest of the United States, which has been one of the main settings for research on sediment yield related to forest operations, a paved road surface was found to yield less than 1 per cent of the amount of sediment yielded by a heavily used road with a gravel surface (Reid and Dunne, 1984). Intensity of use and road design have a major influence on sediment yields. The problem is one of implementation: methods of erosion control on forest roads are well known but frequently are not employed (Patric, 1980).

Although the effects may be greatest on roads and skid trails, they are not confined to such extraction routes but extend to some degree over much of the harvested area. While erosion rates, in the form of debris slides, were a hundred times higher on roads and landings than in undisturbed areas in Oregon forests, they were seven times higher in harvested areas (Amaranthus et al., 1985). In New South Wales, a hundredfold decrease of water infiltrability was found on roaded areas, while a fivefold decrease was recorded on clear-felled areas (Riley, 1984). The more modest changes in logged areas, compared with roads and skid trails, are usually also more short-lived. In Oregon, overall values of infiltration capacity and erodibility measured three to six years after logging did not differ significantly from those on unlogged areas (Johnson and Beschta, 1980). Similarly, differences in sediment yield between harvested and control areas faded to insignificance by the fourth year in a study in the Ouchita Mountains reported by Miller (1984). On the other hand extraction tracks on sandy soils under *Pinus radiata* forests in Australia were found to be still compacted fifty years after use (Greacen and Sands, 1980).

Therefore, while some physical effects of timber-harvesting on the soil (for example surface erosion) may be short-lived, others can be delayed or semi-permanent. The decay of roots after timber-cutting may lead to slope failure after a number of years, and slope stability may thus be adversely affected (Ziemer, 1981). In the case of *Pinus radiata* forests in New Zealand, for example, the most susceptible period ranges from about two years after harvesting, when the root systems are in an advanced state of decay, to about seven or eight years when the root systems of the replacement crop begin to provide substantial reinforcement to the soil (O'Loughlin and Owens, 1987). The potential significance of this effect is obviously greatest on steeplands, into which forest exploitation may begin to move after the more accessible and easily worked lowland forests have been fully utilised. Slope failure in such situations may add to the problems of soil disturbance at the time of logging, and the net effect may be a sizeable reduction in soil depth. In a comparative study in virgin beech-podocarp forest and logged forest in South Island, New Zealand, Laffan (1979) found that soil depths were 20 centimetres or less in 33 per cent of observations in the former, but in 56 per cent in the latter.

Sediment yield from timber-harvesting depends on the techniques used as well as on the nature of the site. The method of logging is of primary importance. Soil disturbance, which in turn is correlated with sediment yield, is directly related to logging method, with ground-skidding systems usually giving rise to much higher percentage rates of ground disturbance than cable-based systems. In British Columbia, the extent of disturbance from the former was found in one study to be 40–45 per cent, compared with 22–30 per cent from the latter (Krag et al. 1986). In the Pacific Northwest, Swanston and Dyrness (1873) found that with the use of tractors for extraction, 35 per cent of the ground surface was bare soil, while the figure fell to 12 per cent when cable extraction was employed. Average values for percentage soil disturbance reported by Megahan and King (1985) for the United States and Canada range from 35 per cent for tractor systems to 23 per cent for ground cable systems, and to 9 and 5 per cent respectively for skyline and aerial (balloon/helicopter) systems. Unit erosion rates may be as much as 3.7 times greater from tractor-logging than from cable-logging systems.

Different types of ground extraction machine, as well as different numbers of loaded passes, have been found to give rise to different severities of damage (Murphy, 1982). Even apparently minor details of the extraction method can have an influence on the extent of disturbance. Power requirements are much higher for whole-tree skidding than for the skidding of tree lengths, and also vary depending on whether the logs are skidded butt-end or small-end first (Wingate-Hill and Jakobsen, 1982).

Logging has various effects on the soil, including 'scalping' of the soil surface and shallow roots, the formation of ruts, and beating and compaction (Rotaru, 1985). Its consequences, and hence its significance, may be manifested in various ways both in the locality in which it is undertaken and sometimes also downstream. The consequence of greatest direct concern to the forest manager is a reduction in tree growth rates. Both accelerated erosion and soil compaction lead to reduced growth rates. The height growth of Douglas fir on landslide scars in Oregon was found to be reduced by 62 per cent compared with that on similar sites, and in addition substantial proportions of the scars were incapable of supporting tree growth because of instability or impenetrability of the surface (Miles et al., 1984). Stand volumes of the same species thirty-two years after tractor logging were found to average 34.1 cubic metres/hectare on skid roads compared with 128.9 cubic metres/hectare on undisturbed areas, and the corresponding densities were 693 and 1,180 stems per hectare respectively (Wert and Thomas, 1981). Growth of Ponderosa pine on compacted soils along skid trails was found to be reduced by 6 per cent on moderately impacted areas and by 12 per cent where the impaction was heavy (Froehlich, 1979). More generally, Greacen and Sands (1980) conclude that compaction by harvesting machines may reduce current and future growth of trees, but that it is difficult to predict the extent of such reduction because of the complex interactions involved.

In addition to possible reductions in tree growth and timber production, disturbance from logging may have other adverse effects. If the forest has a primarily protective function, any increase in sediment yield resulting from logging, forest conversion or other operations may be undesirable, and the functions of production and protection may be difficult to combine. Furthermore, increased sediment yield means increased turbidity of forest streams, and in addition to potential problems of downstream river pollution there may be effects on fisheries or marine life. Such effects have been reported from New Zealand by Johnston et al., (1981), and contamination of coastal fishing grounds as a result of logging-induced erosion is alleged to be a serious problem for the Philippines and many other tropical countries (Hodgson and Dixon, 1989). Coarse sediment may also be delivered to stream channels and remain there semi-permanently, giving persistently poor aquatic habitats (Roberts and Church, 1986). Again, however, the magnitude of the effect of sedimentation following logging can be greatly reduced by precautions such as the maintenance of buffer strips along the streams. For example, in New Zealand Graynoth (1979) found that suspended sediment concentrations were respectively 8, 188 and 27 milligrams/litre in a control area, in an area logged with no protection, and in an area logged with riparian protection.

These off-site effects may focus attention on forest operations and in some instances lead to controls being imposed. In the United States, for example, federal water-pollution legislation is concerned with non-point sources of pollution (such as forest and farm land) as well as with point sources. In addition, some states such as California have introduced forest-practice acts (Chapter 5). In the case of California, a forest owner wishing to harvest timber must first lodge a timber-harvest plan prepared by a registered professional forester. Logging must be carried out in accordance with regulations and standards established by the State Forestry Board, and violations are subject to criminal penalties.

Both practical and theoretical problems, however, are encountered in attempting to achieve regulation and control. In addition to problems of policing, there are more basic difficulties of design of regulatory frameworks. One problem is the nature of cumulative effects in a catchment: harvesting practices on individual sites may give rise to only limited effects off-site, but cumulatively the effects could be more serious. The duration of effects is also problematic. Short-term impacts (such as surface erosion) may be mitigated by dispersing timber harvest in space and time, but long-term effects are less easily alleviated by such approaches (Coats and Miller, 1981).

Although most research work on the effects of forest use and management on soil erosion and compaction has been concentrated in only a few parts of the world (such as the Pacific Northwest of the United States and to a lesser extent in New Zealand), there is convincing evidence that significant effects can arise both on-site and off-site. While it may be asserted that forest land can be managed so that there is little or no increase in soil erosion (Patric, 1976), it is clear that increases have occurred in numerous management regimes around the world. Some situations are more susceptible than others, depending on factors such as slope and climate, while management practices vary greatly in their damage potential. On-site effects may be of direct concern to the forest user, if reductions in tree growth rates result. Off-site effects are attracting increasing attention from the wider public and their representatives in central and local government, resulting in at least some areas in the imposition of controls and regulatory frameworks relating to logging and other management practices.

While timber-harvesting has been the focus of concern about forest use and its effects on the soil, it should perhaps be borne in mind that other uses may also have similar effects. Recreational use may, through compaction resulting from trampling along trails and around campsites, also cause reductions in tree growth rates. For example growth reductions of 20–40 per cent are reported from around campsites in 60–110-year-old Scots pine stands in southern Finland (Nylund et al., 1980). Finally, it should perhaps also be borne in mind that alternative land uses such as agriculture may have erosion rates as high or higher than those characteristic of the forest. Typical sediment yields of around 0.25 tons per acre per year from minimally disturbed forest land in the eastern and western parts of the United States (excluding the Pacific Northwest) are contrasted by Patric et al. (1984) with yields of 2–5 tons that are considered tolerable for agricultural land. The natural forest usually has very low sediment yields. These are likely to increase overall on conversion to managed forest, and to increase dramatically on conversion to agricultural land and following harvesting. The magnitude of the increase, however, can to a large degree be controlled by the means of conversion and the technique of harvesting.

Forestry and nutrient budgets

Forestry practices may have important chemical effects on the soil as well as physical effects such as accelerated production of sediment. In particular the extraction of plant nutrients in timber harvest has been suspected of impoverishing the soil under some management regimes, and hence of leading to declining growth rates in subsequent rotations. By its very nature, this long-term process is less obvious than accelerated sediment yield, and is characterised by a greater degree of uncertainty. This uncertainty stems partly from conflicting results from studies that have been undertaken, and partly from the relatively sparse research effort that has been devoted to the subject.

In Australia, second-rotation planted stands of *Pinus radiata* have been found to have lower productivities than first-rotation crops on the same sites (Keeves, 1966). Declines in productivity in second and subsequent rotations have been tentatively linked to losses of soil organic matter and of certain nutrients such as phosphorous (Blyth and McCallum, 1987). Declines in productivity in teak have also been observed in India after the first rotation, and teak productivity is also likely to decline in Venezuela, especially on highly productive sites (Hase and Foelster, 1983). On the other hand, no evidence of any decline in site productivity has been found after several rotations of pine, eucalyptus and wattle monocultures in South Africa (Schutz, 1986), while both better and poorer rates of growth have been reported from some forests, for example in Swaziland (Evans, 1982). A second-rotation decline in productivity in eucalyptus plantations has been reported from India, and conflicting reports exist from Portugal. One account suggests that the third successive coppice of *Eucalyptus globulus* yielded only 80 per cent as much wood as the second (Wadsworth, 1983), while another states that a decline of this type has not been observed (Kardell et al., 1986). Nevertheless, the upper mineral soil horizons under *E. globulus* plantations show a clear depletion of calcium at the end of each rotation, and the soils show an increase in compaction and decrease in aggregate stability compared with those under native vegetation (Madeira, 1989). The cropping of eucalyptus on short rotations has been found to lead to rapid depletion of nutrients in the soil, and other species grown in similar regimes will probably have a similar effect (FAO, 1986b). In Britain a parliamentary inquiry concluded that the effects of plantation forestry in respect of nutrient reserves were uncertain (House of Lords, 1979–80).

In managed and man-made forests, nutrient cycles are usually much more open than those in natural forests where the uptake of nutrients in the biomass is largely compensated by the release of nutrients on decomposition. In forests from which timber is produced, the 'leakage' of nutrients in timber and sometimes from the burning of slash is much greater. The significance of this leakage depends partly on the frequency with which it occurs. With logging at intervals of 70–120 years, the clear felling of New England hardwoods, for example, is not likely to have a significant adverse effect on site-nutrient capital (Hornbeck et al., 1986). The short rotations typical of tropical plantations may give rise to problems of nutrient reserves under some conditions (e.g. Cornforth, 1970). Also with shortened rotations geared to 'biomass' or 'wood energy' plantations, the risks of nutrient depletion increase, and deficiencies may appear after repeated harvests (Anderson et al., 1983). Short rotations mean not only frequent removal of nutrients in biomass, but also the loss of nutrients as a result of accelerated erosion during the harvesting–replanting part of the cycle (Raison and Crane, 1986). Nutrient loss through soil disturbance on harvesting may be a greater problem than nutrient depletion *per se* (Van Hook et al., 1982). Dyck and Beets (1988) conclude that the displacement of nutrients by the piling of logging slash and the disturbing of topsoil can result in a substantial decline of *Pinus radiata* plantations in New Zealand, in addition to any effect arising from nutrient export in harvested material.

Whole-tree harvesting also increases the magnitude and significance of nutrient loss, and raises the spectre of soil impoverishment on many forest sites (Kimmins, 1977). Nutrient exports may be increased by a factor of two or more (van Hook et al., 1982). Whole-tree harvesting usually removes one and a half to four times more nutrients than bole-only harvesting (Borman and Gordon, 1989). Work on nutrient budgets in Nova Scotian forests, for example, suggests that one or several whole-tree harvests of hardwood stands on rotations of around fifty years would be unlikely to result in important depletions of site nutrient capital overall, but calcium removals would be a cause of concern as they would amount to a large percentage of total site capital (Freedman et al., 1986). And some problems of nutrient availability have been encountered even in less intensive management regimes, involving manipulation of the forest from its natural form to even-aged stands of one or more preferred species, rather than clearance followed by replanting. One case where problems of unavailability or inadequate cycling of nutrients has been experienced is in jarrah (*Eucalyptus marginata*) forests in Western Australia (Hingston et al, 1981). The mode of management appears to have an important bearing on the nature of effects on soil chemistry: soil acidity has been found to decrease following clear-felling on northern coniferous soils, but the removal of slash was associated with decreased pH values compared with sites where slash was not removed (Nykvist and Rosen, 1985). In more general terms, various techniques may mitigate the adverse effects of short-rotation energy forests. For example, practices such as fertilization, dormant-season harvesting, cable logging, harvesting on frozen ground or snowpack, and buffering stream channels are advocated by van Hook et al., 1982.

Increasing concern about the sustainability of modern resource processes, combined with changes in forestry practice involving shortened rotations and whole-tree harvesting, has led to heightened concern about nutrient budgets. While nutrients lost through soil erosion or biomass extraction can be replaced by artificial fertilisers, this practice may be undesirable on economic or environmental grounds. Fertiliser application may not be financially viable, and even where it is there may be objections because of its ecological effects, especially on aquatic ecosystems. Usually less than half of applied fertiliser is utilised by trees (van Hook et al., 1982). Some may be washed or leached into the drainage water, especially when applied to ploughed surfaces at the time of planting, and hence lead to nutrient enrichment downstream.

Ecological effects

The use and management of the forest resource have a variety of ecological effects in addition to physical effects. These extend from changes in the species composition of the forest to less direct effects on wildlife, and occur in a range of intensities varying from a complete loss of habitat (when the forest is removed or destroyed) to minor disturbance. In general terms, the removal of forest cover is likely to result in a loss of species of plants, animals and invertebrates, and similar effects may result where forest management is directed solely or primarily at timber production. Much of the popular concern about the nature of forest resource use stems from these ecological effects, and especially from the consequences for wildlife in general and for bird life in particular.

Forest management and wildlife

In temperate latitudes the effects result mainly from the intensification of management and the drive for increased wood production, rather than from the complete destruction of the forest habitat. Most of the forests are managed primarily for timber production, and to that end the species composition has been altered and habitats modified by drainage or by treatments with fertilisers or chemicals. Such management has had significant effects on the forest ecology. In southern Sweden, for example, the managed forests consisting mainly of spruce and pine contrast with the mixed natural forest of deciduous and coniferous species. Comparing natural and managed areas of similar age, Nilsson (1979) found that bird densities were three times higher in the natural forests, and that the number of species represented was also much higher than in the managed forests. Bird densities in young spruce plantations were only one-ninth of those in the natural forest. The width of this ratio is probably at least partly a function of the age of the plantation as well as of its design. In France Blondel (1976) found that most of the woodland bird communities around Mont Veloux were as rich and well balanced in the man-made forests as in the natural ones, but confirmed that the diversity of the forest structure and its richness in bird life were directly related.

The intensification of forest management in Sweden has included not just alterations in the structure of natural forests, but also the use of drainage, fertilisers and exotic tree species. Many species have been threatened by this drive for increased timber production. It is believed that forty species of vertebrates are now seriously endangered, while fifty species of fungi, lichens and flowering plants are on the verge of extinction and a further 220 are in some danger (Gamlin, 1988).

The expansion of plantations of exotic tree species in countries such as Australia and New Zealand, and in particular the replacement of native forests by exotic plantations, has also generated much controversy. Although the coniferous plantations in Australia are not the 'wildlife deserts' alleged by some opponents, they lack some of the species of plants, birds and mammals found in native forests, and their proportion of introduced species tends to be higher (Friend, 1980; 1982). On the other hand, exotic afforestation on degraded grasslands and other habitats may lead to an increase in species diversity (Zobel et al., 1987). Similarly, short-rotation energy forestry involving, for example, willow coppice, can lead to an increase in habitat diversity in regions dominated by coniferous forests or in intensive agricultural areas (Gustafsson, 1987). The nature of the ecological effect will be determined by the management system, and especially by factors such as rotation length and the use of herbicides.

The design and structure of the forest are important variables, with species numbers and population densities varying not only with age of stand but also with location in relation to native forest. Declining wood production from forests in the European Community in recent years may mean that they become of increasing ecological significance, as most mixed and deciduous forests become ecologically richer as they age (CEC, 1987). Richness and density tend to be highest alongside native forests, and in inliers of native forest. In New Zealand, long-rotation pine forests are claimed to provide useful habitats for some but not all native animals, and again faunal diversity has been found to increase with age. Nevertheless, it rarely if ever becomes as high as in unmodified native forests on similar sites (Bull, 1981).

Tropical deforestation and extinctions
Similar trends to those in temperate latitude are now in evidence in much of the tropical zone, and in addition there is widespread loss of forest habitat as the tropical forest area shrinks. The nature and magnitude of the resulting ecological effects depends on the initial forest environment, the way in which it is used and managed, and the purposes for which it is cleared.

In Kenya, for example, the clearance of indigenous forests to make way for plantations of exotic conifers has severely impoverished the native bird fauna in terms of both species and densities. On the other hand, the new pine plantations may extend the wintering range for some Palearctic migrant species of birds (Carlson, 1986). The clearance of the native forest for purposes other than plantations is likely to have a similar or greater effect on bird and animal species. In Puerto Rico this clearance has proceeded further than in most low-latitude areas. During the development of human settlement from the early sixteenth century, the island was deforested at an increasing rate, until less than 1 per cent remained by 1900 (although a further 9 per cent consisted of coffee plantations shaded by trees remaining from the native forest). At the same time as deforestation was proceeding, the island's inhabitants selectively persecuted some of the larger bird species. The avian extinction rate resulting from these factors was at least 11.6 per cent: deforestation was an important ultimate factor behind this loss of species, although humans were the proximate cause (Brash, 1987).

The possibility of a similar or greater extinction, on the scale of the tropical world as a whole rather than that of a small island, lies behind much of the current concern about the fate of the tropical moist forest. The ecological richness of these forests is well known: they contain 40 to 50 per cent of all species but occupy only 7 per cent of the land surface (Myers, 1980b). It is asserted that one or more species become extinct every day as a result of the clearance, conversion, or disturbance of tropical forests (Myers, 1983b). In the projection prepared for the *Global 2000* report, Dr Thomas Lovejoy of the World Wildlife Fund (as it then was) estimated that between 15 and 20 per cent of species would become extinct as a result of deforestation by the end of the century (Barney, 1980). Assuming that the tropical rain forest is being cleared at a rate of 1 per cent per year, Wilson (1989) estimates that 0.2–0.3 per cent of all species in the forest are lost each year. On the basis of a further estimate that the forests contain a total of around 2 million species, he concludes that this rate corresponds to a loss in absolute terms of 4,000–6,000 species per year. During the last quarter of the century, according to Myers (1979), an 'extinction spasm' accounting for one million species will be witnessed. This is roughly equivalent to one species per day.

Both the reliability of such estimates and their potential significance are difficult to evaluate. Much uncertainty surrounds the total number of species world-wide, which may amount to anything between 5 and 30 million (WRI, 1986). As yet fewer than 2 million have been identified, although the identification rate for mammals, birds, fishes and plants is far higher than that for invertebrates. Confusion is sometimes engendered because some estimates of numbers and percentages relate only to plants, birds and animals, while others refer to all species. Some focus on deforestation alone, whilst others include other forms of human impact. The confusion and flimsiness of basis for the estimates of Myers and Lovejoy have been attacked by commentators such as Simon and Widalsky (1984) and Simon (1986). They regard them as little more than exaggerated guesses, and also question their perception of the significance of extinctions. Such perceived significance depends on value judgements of the intrinsic worth of a species, as well as any material benefits that may flow from it, and it is perhaps not surprising that disagreement exists.

Some firmer evidence exists, however, for current rates of extinction. On the basis of a recent study of extinctions of birds and flowering plants in the neo-tropical moist forests, the continuation of current trends would mean a loss of 12 per cent of the bird species and 15 per cent of the plant species by 2,000 (Simberloff, 1986). These rates would correspond to losses of around 15,000 plant species and 100 bird species, but numerically would not be comparable to the major mass extinctions of the geological past. If deforestation were to continue unabated through the next century, until the tropical forests of the New World were reduced to those currently projected as parks and reserves, extinction rates would reach 69 and 66 per cent respectively for birds and plants. Such rates would be similar to those experienced in episodes of mass extinctions in the geological past.

Ecological effects of logging

While the prospects for such mass extinctions remain controversial, evidence has begun to accumulate in recent years about some of the immediate effects of the exploitation of the tropical forest, although much remains unknown. In Peninsular Malaysia, for example, the forest cover contracted from 84 per cent of the land area in 1958 to 51 per cent in 1975. This was accompanied by reductions of between 23 and 56 per cent in populations of six primate species (Aiken and Leigh, 1985). The same authors concluded that selective logging did not necessarily result in a very depauperate fauna, and indeed some large mammals were found to be more common in logged-over areas than in undisturbed forest. Much depends on the availability of undisturbed refuges to which animals may move during logging, and from which they can subsequently return. Many species with large territories move away while logging is in progress and return afterwards, but others do not adapt well to logged-over forests. After logging, there is a major change in the species mix, and then a gradual return. There is disagreement, however, about the rate of this return and the degree to which the logged-over forest biota can approach those of the virgin forest (e.g. Shelton, 1985). On the basis of work in East Kalimantan, Wilson and Johns (1982) concluded that logged forest could be successfully recolonised providing that adjacent areas of undisturbed forest remain to provide a population pool for re-colonisation, and that hunting levels are low. Species diversity was found to be similar in undisturbed forest and in forest selectively logged three to five years previously, although densities were lower in the latter. Selective logging may mean a drastic reduction in the overall availability of food sources because of the high levels of damage. The extraction of 3.3 per cent of the trees from a Malaysian forest, for example, meant that a total of 50.9 per cent were destroyed (Johns, 1988). In Amazonia, the monkey *Chiropotes satanas* was found to be eradicated by the removal of two or three trees per ha, and resulting damage to 50–60 per cent of the stand (Johns, 1989). In Malaysia, the extraction of 11 trees per ha was found to cause damage to 40 per cent of the residual trees, and to result in a decrease in both tree species and densities (Abdullah et al., 1981).

Selective logging of this kind may have a significant effect on the usefulness of the resource, as well as consequences for wildlife. Its main impact is argued by Estève (1983) to be on economic value, rather than in biological or ecological terms. Future timber-producing value is reduced, even if the forest extent is not reduced.

In theory, selective logging on a rotational basis is an environmentally benign form of utilisation. It creates gaps in the canopy, akin to those resulting from natural disturbance, and natural regeneration may be rapid. Furthermore, only the logs are removed. These usually have low nutrient contents, and the more nutrient-rich leaves are left behind. In practice, however, the way in which selective logging is carried out can mean that the resource deteriorates. Poorly controlled logging has meant that some species that are useful sources of timber or 'minor' products such as rattans, gum and latex have effectively disappeared over large areas in the tropical uplands, and in regions such as the Amazon (Siebert, 1987; Fox, 1976). The same process that affected North American forests in the nineteenth century is therefore in operation in many areas of tropical forest today. In addition, the selectively logged forest may become more prone to fire. While the undisturbed rain forest is usually too wet to burn, logged-over areas may burn much more readily. Human disturbance dramatically increases the risk of fire. Combustible material in the form of tree debris is left on the ground, and the forest floor becomes drier as the canopy is opened out (Uhl et al., 1989). In Amazonia, fires set to control weeds on degraded pastures commonly spread onto logged forest, but not to undisturbed forest (Uhl and Buschbacher, 1985). Thus the effects of selective logging and of pasture-burning interact to produce more detrimental effects than either operation acting separately.

While selective logging is closely associated with the tropical forest today, it was carried out in huge areas of the temperate forest in the past, especially in the nineteenth century. Even in areas where the forest was not completely removed, the long-term ecological effects may be considerable, and the net effect may be a reduction in the usefulness of the forest as a resource for timber and other products. Some of these effects in the Great Lakes forest of Michigan have been recorded by Whitney (1987). Prior to settlement, the Great Lakes (pine) forest was conditioned to fire at intervals of 130–260 years. Selective logging of white pine, and later of hemlock and hardwoods transformed the forest (Table 7.6). Waves of fires, following logging in quick succession, upset the equilibrium of the forest. The result was a poorly stocked forest of oak and aspen, which had previously played a subordinate role in the pre-settlement forest. A reduction in the frequency of fires after control measures were imposed from the 1920s allowed the oak and aspen to mature, and set the stage for a new pulp-oriented industrial forest in the 1950s. More generally the very extensive removal or modification of the Midwest forest has apparently resulted in few tree species being eliminated completely, but the relative abundance of the more common species has shifted significantly (Whitney and Somerlot, 1985). A reduction in species diversity or general ecological impoverishment is a frequent result of the use of the forest. One recent example is reported from southern China (Young and Wang, 1989). Here the original broad-leaf evergreen forest has been replaced by a secondary forest of pine, which is characterised by a lower bio-diversity and density.

Ecological changes of this type can have significant 'knock-on' effects. In the forests of eastern Canada, for example, until recently only the best

Table 7.6 Pre- and post-settlement extent of various forest types in Crawford County, Michigan

	Percentages of land area (i.e. of 145 630 ha)		
	1836–59	*1927*	*1979*
Hemlock–white pine–northern hardwoods*	16.4	3.7	4.5
Aspen–birch	0	12.0	18.9
Pin cherry	0	2.2	0
Mixed pine	27.4	0.3	7.8
Pine–oak	22.3	0	0
Oak	0	24.2	19.5
Jack pine	24.4	23.7	28.2
Jack pine openings†	0.5	–	–
Lowland conifers and alder swamps	8.2	6.2	6.1
Grass land and upland shrubs	<1.0	20.6	8.0

* predominantly sugar maple after 1920
† probably included under poorly stocked jack pine forest after 1920
Source: Whitney (1987)

timber was taken, leaving impoverished stands of less desirable species. Balsam fir, which readily colonises disturbed sites, is often a major component of the modified forest. With protection against fire provided by forest management, stands develop to maturity and become susceptible to attack by outbreaks of budworm. Whilst in theory it would be possible to harvest the most susceptible stands before or during an attack, the resulting accelerated harvest rate is feasible only if the market can absorb a sudden influx of timber. One alternative to this strategy is to use insecticide sprays as a control measure (Dunster, 1987), and these may in turn have their own 'knock-on' effects on the forest ecology, as well as giving rise to adverse popular perceptions of forest management. In short, any modification of the forest ecosystem such as the harvesting of the most valuable timber species may have far-reaching and unforeseen effects, which may extend both to the nature of the forest resource itself and to the wider environment.

The environmental effects of afforestation

Although the forest is widely perceived as environmentally benign and as a provider of protective services, paradoxically the creation of forests is increasingly seen in some quarters as undesirable for environmental reasons. This paradox may perhaps be partly explained by a negative reaction to dramatic landscape change of the kind represented by afforestation, and partly by the way in which afforestation is carried out. The use of exotic species, such as, for example, Sitka spruce in Britain, Radiata pine in New Zealand and eucalypts in countries as diverse as Portugal and India, attracts particular attention and opposition. Deeper-seated reasons, however, also exist for the antipathy that exists in some quarters to continuing afforestation in countries such as Britain, Denmark and Ireland, and which to some extent matches the opposition to the conversion of native forests to exotic plantations in Australia and New Zealand. This antipathy is based on various grounds, including social issues such as employment as well as on environmental concerns. These concerns, however, are often expressed vociferously and many of them have been shown by recent research to have a factual basis.

Physical effects
Ground preparation, including ploughing and ditching, in advance of planting leads to major increases in sediment yield. In Scotland, the analysis of lake sediments has shown an increase in sedimentation rates as a result of afforestation of some catchments (Battarbee et al., 1985). Sediment loads in streams may increase by orders of magnitude (e.g. Robinson and Blyth, 1982), and although this scale of effect is usually short-lived the effect itself is long-lasting. In one study area in the north of England, for example, suspended sediment concentrations were found to stabilise at double the pre-planting level (Blackie and Newson, 1986).

Increases in sediment loads may do damage to aquatic life and to anglings, as well as posing problems of sedimentation in reservoirs and creating difficulties in filtration systems in public water supplies. Sediment loads can be greatly reduced by terminating furrows and ditches back from stream courses, and codes of practice have been introduced in Britain in order to achieve this objective. Field supervision, however, does not always match the quality of design of the operation (in this sphere any more than in, for example, the logging of tropical forests). The combination of this effect with the reduction in water yield which usually follows afforestation may mean that the water industry will oppose afforestation schemes. The effects – and opposition – are likely to be greatest in small catchments undergoing complete or extensive afforestation, but they may also extend to larger scales. For example in the 906 square kilometre Tarawera catchment in central North Island, New Zealand, 250 square kilometres were afforested between 1964 and 1981, and the mean river flow was reduced by 13 per cent as a result (Dons, 1986).

Water chemistry may be affected as well as water quantity. Streams draining afforested catchments in Scotland have been found to be more acid than those in open moorland, and to have lower fish stocks (Harriman and Morrison, 1981). This effect may be partly due to the direct effect of the coniferous afforestation, and partly to the effect of the coniferous trees in filtering dry acid deposits from the atmosphere. These pollutants are then washed from the trees by subsequent rainfall, and the drainage system provided by the pre-planting ditching means that the water runs off before it can be buffered by the deeper and less acid horizons of the soil. Fertilisers may be applied at the time of planting, and large proportions of the applications, especially where falling on furrows and bare ground, find their way into the streams during the first year, and losses continue for up to three years. Phosphate concentrations, for example, may be ten times higher than the original levels for several months after treatment (Binns, 1986). In some instances this effect may be perceived as beneficial in increasing stream productivity, but in other cases leaching into ponds or lakes could have ecologically undesirable effects (Harriman, 1978), especially if nature conservation sites were affected. Again, the method of application influences the strength of the effect. If the fertiliser is applied before ploughing or to established crops, less will be lost to the streams.

In addition to effects on water quantity and quality, afforestation may also result in acidification of the soil. Soil acidification is associated with afforestation with conifers such as the extensively used Sitka spruce in Britain, for example (Hornung, 1985). In Canada, the soils under coniferous plantations in abandoned farmland showed a significant increase in acidity over a period of forty-six years (Brand et al., 1986). Soil acidification may be especially pronounced if an entire catchment carries the same age of fast-growing stand. The rate of acidification, which at first may be rapid, is likely to slow down later in the rotation (Nilsson et al., 1982). On the other hand, some species such as birch may reduce the acidity of heathland or moorland soils (Miles and Young, 1980). And afforestation may induce physical changes such as reduced waterlogging and improved aeration in wet soils (Pyatt and Craven, 1978).

Ecological effects
Ecological effects may also result, in addition to these physical ones. Pre-afforestation vegetation is transformed as the forest canopy develops, and the heavy shade cast in many plantations means that vascular plants on the forest floor are largely eliminated. The extent of this elimination depends on the choice of species and design of the forest. In the new habitat, bird life is also transformed. Compared with open moorland, songbird densities are found to be around three times greater in young plantations, and four to six times higher in thinned plantations (Moss, 1978). But this increase in numbers is accompanied by a change in species, with birds of the open moorland being replaced by those of woodland. The former may be much more rare than the latter, and be perceived to have a much higher conservation value. This issue lay at the heart of a major conflict between forestry and nature conservation interests over the afforestation of moorland in the far north of Scotland during the 1980s (Ratcliffe and Oswald, 1986), and in practical effect reduced the area available for afforestation in that part of the country.

While the image of the forest may in a general sense be one of beneficence, it does not follow that afforestation will be welcomed on environmental grounds in all situations. Environmental interests are now seen as major obstacles to afforestation in Britain, and indeed commercial afforestation using conifers is now to all intents and purposes outlawed in England. The roots of opposition perhaps lie more in the way in which afforestation has been carried out and the types of forest that have been created than in antipathy to afforestation *per se*. (Small-scale broad-leaved plantings are still welcomed in England.) Many of the forests created in recent decades have been designed primarily or exclusively as industrial or production forests, with scant regard for either the provision of other goods or services or for the environmental consequences of the mode of afforestation. The reactions have been strong, and now strongly influence the amount and type of afforestation that is permitted and the way in which it is carried out. At present such opposition is largely restricted to a small number of countries: it remains to be seen whether it will become a major factor elsewhere and whether it may yet have a significant influence in a possible transition from contracting to expanding forests on the global scale.

The environmental effects of afforestation in countries such as Britain are usually perceived in terms of wildlife, landscape and amenity, but the new forests may themselves be at risk from biological hazards. Plantations of exotic species in particular can suffer attack from pests and pathogens, whilst native trees species in neighbouring areas remain unscathed. In Scotland, for example, plantations of Lodgepole pine have been affected by larvae of the Pine Beauty moth, which pose few problems in Scots pine forests. They have been treated by aerial application of a pesticide, which in turn has given rise to concern about wider ecological effects although no evidence of resulting bird mortality has been found (Spray et al., 1987). Monterey (Radiata) pine has been attacked by pine needle blight in settings as far apart as Chile, New Zealand and southern Africa. In some instances spectacular outbreaks of pests have resulted as local insects have adapted to exotic tree species. This process of adaptation can take several decades, and it may still be under way in parts of areas such as Africa and Latin America where plantations of exotic softwoods have been established in recent years (Perry and Maghembe, 1989). And unexpected consequences can result from the creation of plantations. Dieback in an area of tropical rain forest in Uganda has recently been reported from the vicinity of conifer plantations. While the cause of the dieback remains unclear, it has been suggested that any one or several factors such as fungal pathogens, toxins or hydrological effects may be involved (Struhsaker et al., 1989).

Forest and environment

Environmental interests now have a major influence on deforestation and on forest utilisation world-wide. The environmental consequences of forest use are the focus of unprecedented interest and concern. Whereas in the past the protection of the timber resource was usually the main motive for government intervention in forest management, today it is equally likely to be environmental protection. The forest is perceived not only as a source of timber, but also as a valued environment in its own right. This perception is held more strongly in some parts of the world than in others, but the emergence of environmental groups in countries such as Brazil and Malaysia suggests that it is widening in spatial terms as well as intensifying through time.

Much uncertainty still exists about the nature of physical and ecological effects arising from the use or conversion of the forest: myth and fact are not always clearly distinguished. Nevertheless, environmental issues and interests affect the use of the global forest resource as never before. Previous episodes of deforestation and destructive utilisation, such as in medieval Europe and nineteenth century North America, failed to generate the volume of environmental interest and concern now associated not only with the tropical forests but also with more local forestry issues around the world. The significance and effectiveness of this state of affairs for forestry policy and management await evaluation.

Finally, the environmental effects of the use of the forest resource need to be seen within the context of cyclical phases and trends in the forest area. The effects of both deforestation and reforestation or afforestation tend to be concentrated in certain areas, rather than randomly distributed. For example, the environmental effects of deforestation are concentrated in the tropical world today, whereas in the nineteenth century they were mainly felt in higher latitudes such as those of North America, parts of Scandinavia and Russia, and in some of the more mountainous parts of western and central Europe. In the French Alps, for example, episodes of severe erosion occurred as a result of deforestation which in turn resulted from rapidly increasing population. As population pressure lessened and reforestation took place, this episode of erosion was succeeded by one of greater stability (e.g. Combes, 1982). Cyclical patterns of forest removal and replacement, therefore, are likely to be matched by cyclical patterns of environmental effects extending over wide areas.

8 THE TROPICAL FOREST

The fate of the tropical forest is one of the major environmental issues of the day. During the 1980s, it became a focus of attention and concern on the global scale. For the first time in history, trends in the extent and condition of the forest in one part of the world have become a matter of popular concern in other parts. It is sometimes assumed or implied that the trends currently affecting it are unique in type, intensity and significance. The alternative view is that the tropical forest is at the same phase of development or destruction as that previously experienced on a more localised scale in the eastern Mediterranean in antiquity, in western Europe in the Dark Ages, and North America in the nineteenth century. On the one hand, the conclusion is that a major environmental disaster is taking place and that a 'mega-extinction spasm' is about to happen: on the other, current trends in the tropical forest are perceived in terms of sequential stages of contraction and stability of forest area similar to those experienced in much of the temperate zone in the past.

How these trends are interpreted is less a matter of factual data, although statistics are sometimes simultaneously incomplete, confusing and unreliable, than of perception, which in turn depends on viewpoint and assumptions. If it is assumed, for example, that current trends of deforestation can reasonably be extrapolated indefinitely into the future, the inevitable conclusion is that the tropical forest will eventually disappear completely. On the other hand, if it is assumed that current trends in forest area are temporary and will soon give way to stability or expansion, the outlook is one of optimism and perhaps of complacency. Unless the mechanisms underlying the forest-area transition in the temperate zone are accurately identified, the grounds for assuming that they will automatically also operate in the tropics are flimsy. In any case, even if a tropical forest-area transition does occur on the temperate model, this in itself is no reason for complacency about current tropical trends. The history of use of the forest resource in Europe and North America is characterised by wastefulness and mismanagement. Even if the temperate forest has stabilised or expanded during the present century, many countries and regions have suffered from treelessness, and much of value has been lost. What happened relatively slowly and locally in the temperate zone (but with increasing intensity and expanding scale) is now occurring rapidly in the tropical zone. In short, while one view may be of an unique and unprecedented catastrophe, involving the irreplaceable loss of material

and non-material values and irreversible environmental change, an alternative view is that what is happening is merely the latest and largest chapter
in a long saga of destructive exploitation of the forest.

The disappearing tropical forest?

As Chapter 4 suggests, much uncertainty surrounds both the extent of the
tropical forest and its rate of change. The debate about the tropical forest
has been beset by apparently conflicting statistics, and there has been much
confusion over definitions both of the forest itself and of deforestation.
Statistical support has been readily found by both optimists and pessimists:
both complacency and alarmism have been engendered. Some statistics
have been for deforestation and others for disturbance or modification:
some have related only to rain forests or to the tropical moist forest, while
others have been for all tropical forests including those in drier areas.

A few well-publicised estimates extrapolated from limited data made a
significant contribution to the emergence of the tropical forests as a major
environmental issue during the late 1970s. The authors of these estimates
usually qualified them carefully, but unfortunately both the bases and
qualifications were often overlooked or ignored. For example, Sommer
(1976) concluded, on the basis of an analysis of data for thirteen countries,
that the tropical moist forest area of 935 million hectares was contracting at
an annual rate of 11 million hectares. This was duly translated into the
more memorable figure of 20 hectares per minute. Subsequent figures in
the *Global 2000* study suggested a deforestation rate of 18–20 million
hectares per year (Barney, 1980), or nearly twice Sommer's estimate, and
the Director-General of FAO stated in 1978 that conversion of all forms
accounted for 30 hectares per minute, but did not explain the basis of this
figure. Myers (1983b, p.14) considered that it was 'not unreasonable to
suppose that the earth is losing around 670 square kilometres of tropical
moist forest per day, or an area the size of Wales or Massachusetts each
month'. On the basis of some heroic assumptions, in the early 1980s he
estimated the annual rate of loss at around 245,000 square kilometres per
year, which would mean 'in theory' that the entire biome of 9.35 million
square kilometres could be eliminated within thirty-eight years (e.g.
Myers, 1983a, p. 296). The rate is equivalent to 46 hectares per day.

Expressed in other ways, these rates of 10 and 40 hectares per minute
amount to around 0.5 and 2.2 per cent respectively of the tropical moist
forest, and assuming constant rates would mean that the biome would
disappear between around 2020 and 2120. A straight-line projection of
Lanly's (1982) figures gives a date of 2057 for the final demise of the
tropical rain forest (e.g. Guppy, 1984). In a paper published in the early
phases of the recent emergence of the tropical rain forest as an issue of
international concern, Denevan (1973, p. 130) contended that 'within one
hundred years, probably less, the Amazon forest will have ceased to exist'.
The rather flimsy basis for such predictions is illustrated by the fact that in
the late 1970s, estimates of the extent of deforestation in Brazilian

Amazonia varied from 1.5 to 20 per cent (Giaimo, 1988), while as recently as 1988 they ranged from 8 to 12 per cent (Fearnside, 1989a).

Assertions about the demise of the tropical forest are of greater value in helping to focus attention on the issue than as accurate predictors. While their impact is indisputable, the careful distinctions drawn between projections and predictions are not always maintained, and stark and graphic illustrations of how serious the issue is can cause as much confusion as enlightenment. Confusion and uncertainty are compounded by the vastly different estimates of the relative extent of the tropical forest that had already disappeared before the growth of concern over the last twenty years.

An awareness of the wide contrasts between these estimates may give rise to a healthy scepticism and to an examination of the procedures and assumptions on which they are based. In the popular media, however, little attention is usually paid to the discrepancies in the data or to their authors' definitions, procedures and reservations. The result is that deforestation rates of 20 or 40 hectares per minute become established in the popular consciousness, and the perception grows of a tropical forest crisis.

The apparent conflict and confusion are exemplified by two of the frequently quoted statistics for disturbance in the tropical forests, dating to the early 1980s. The FAO/UNEP estimate of disturbance in *closed* tropical forests at that time was 7.5 million hectares (Lanly, 1982), while that prepared by Myers (1980a) for the (American) National Academy of Science seemed almost three times greater at 22.0 million hectares. The former figure, however, referred to deforestation, while the latter related to conversion, and included fallow areas within the closed broad-leaved tropical forest. If these fallow areas were excluded, then the deforested area shrinks to 7.5 million hectares. Myers' data, however, related to broad-leaved forests, while the FAO/UNEP one included all tropical forests. When adjusted for broad-leaved forests, the FAO/UNEP figure falls to 5.9 million hectares, thus leaving a difference of 1.6 million hectares as compared with the NAS study. Most of this difference arises from different estimates in deforestation rates in just four Asian countries, and while it is still substantial is of a different order from the apparent conflict between the original figures of 7 and 22 million hectares. Figure 8.1 summarises the deforestation trends as estimated by the two studies.

At first sight, the results emerging from two major studies may seem to lead to the conclusion that the fate of the tropical forest is less desperate than is perhaps first suggested by alleged disappearance rates of 20 or 40 hectares per minute. Deforestation rates of 6–7 million hectares per annum correspond to rates of 0.5–0.6 per cent per year. Low as these rates may seem, they would mean, in the unlikely event that they were to remain constant, that the tropical forest would disappear within 150 years. Conflicting estimates abound on how much of the tropical forest has already disappeared. On the one hand Matthews (1983) indicated that around 4 per cent of the tropical evergreen rain forest had been removed, using a basis of mid-century data (Table 4.5, p. 79). On the other hand Sommer (1976) contended that about 40 per cent of the tropical moist

Figure 8.1 Dynamics of tropical forest areas (million ha: total area bold)

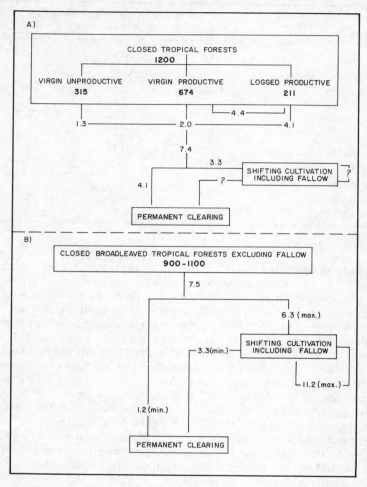

Source: Compiled from data in Myers (1980a), Lanly (1982) and Melillo *et al.*

forest area had already gone. His conclusion, however, was based on the extent of the area whose climate is capable of supporting tropical moist forest, and ignored factors of soil and topography that may have reduced that theoretical area. Nevertheless, similar figures of around 40 per cent have been widely quoted for the area of tropical moist forest that has already been cleared or degraded (e.g. WRI, 1985). Perhaps as much as 15 per cent of the extent disappeared between the early 1960s and early 1980s (National Research Council, 1982), in comparison with around 25 per cent throughout the remainder of history. Irrespective of the precise extent that

Table 8.1   Tropical deforestation c. 1980

| | Natural tree formations (million ha) | | |
	Closed	Open	Total
Area in 1980	1201	734	1935
Area cleared annually			
Tropical America	4.4	1.3	5.6
Tropical Africa	1.3	2.3	3.7
Tropical Asia	1.8	0.2	2.0
Total	7.5	3.8	11.3
Area cleared as percentage of total area	0.6	0.5	0.6
Transferred to			
(a) shifting cultivation	3.4	1.7	5.1
(b) other land uses	4.1	2.1	6.2

Source: Based on Lanly (1982)

has already disappeared, it is obvious that the rate of contraction has accelerated greatly in recent times.

These deforestation rates of around 7.5 million hectares or 0.5–0.6 per cent per year are for the tropical closed forest. In addition, tropical open forest of around 735 million hectares has been shrinking at a rate of around 3.8 million hectares per year, or 0.5 per cent per year. As Table 8.1 indicates, the tropical forest as a whole is therefore contracting at a rate of over 11 million hectares per year. The 'tropical forest' issue is not just one of the tropical rain forests or moist forests: the immediate consequences of the depletion of the *dry* tropical forest resource, for example in terms of fuelwood, may be far more serious from the viewpoint of local populations than the trends in the closed moist forest.

Closer examination of the trends in the closed moist forest, however, gives rise to more disturbing conclusions than might be reached at first glance. In addition to outright deforestation, large areas of forest have been modified by logging. As Figure 8.1 indicates, the area of 'virgin productive' forest disturbed by logging (4.4 million hectares) is more than twice that deforested (2.0 million hectares). Around 1 per cent of the 'virgin productive' area is therefore affected either by deforestation or logging each year (6.4 million hectares out of 674 million hectares). Extrapolation of this rate would mean that all virgin forests suitable for production will either be deforested or logged within a century. As Chapter 7 indicates, logging of the type carried out thus far has usually meant a modification of the forest environment and a depletion of its resource value. This kind of disturbance is likely to be most widespread initially in the more accessible lowland forests, where species diversity is usually greatest and hence the impact in terms of direct resource depletion and species loss highest. Subsequently it extends into more remote and

Table 8.2   Classification of areas of tropical moist forest by rate of conversion

Area	Nature of threat
Areas undergoing broad-scale conversion at rapid rates*	
Australian lowland tropical forest	Timber exploitation, planned agriculture
Bangladesh	Timber exploitation, forest farming, population pressure
India	Forest farming, population pressure
Indonesian lowland forest	Timber exploitation, forest farming, transmigration programmes
Peninsular Malaysian lowland forest	Timber exploitation, planned agriculture
Melanesian lowland forest	Timber exploitation, planned agriculture
Philippine lowland forest	Timber exploitation, forest farming
Sri Lanka	Timber exploitation, forest farming
Thailand	Timber exploitation, forest farming
Vietnam	Forest farming, timber exploitation
Brazil: Atlantic coastal strip	Timber exploitation, cash-crop agriculture
Central America	Forest farming, cattle raising, timber exploitation
Colombian lowland forests	Colonist settlement, cattle raising
Ecuador: Pacific coast forest	Plantation agriculture, some timber exploitation
Madagascar	Forest farming, timber exploitation
East Africa: montane forests	Timber exploitation, firewood cutting, forest farming
West Africa	Timber exploitation, forest farming

* 'little left' by 2000

Areas undergoing moderate conversion at intermediate rates	
Burmese lowland forests	Forest farming, some timber exploitation
Papua New Guinea	Timber exploitation, forest farming
Brazilian Amazonia	Colonist settlement, forest farming, cattle raising, timber exploitation
Colombia: Pacific coast forests	Timber exploitation
Ecuadorian Amazonia	Colonist settlement, forest farming, some planned agriculture
Peruvian Amazonia	Colonist settlement, forest farming, some planned agriculture
Cameroons	Timber exploitation, forest farming

(*Parts* of these areas are affected, and appreciable or extensive areas could be converted by 2000)

Areas apparently undergoing little change

Brazil's western Amazonia
French Guiana, Guyana and Surinam
Zaïre Basin (Congo, Gabon, Zaïre)

Source: Based on data in Myers (1980a)

Figure 8.2 Distribution of closed tropical broadleaved forest (thousand ha) and ratios of forest area to annual deforestation rates (c. 1980)

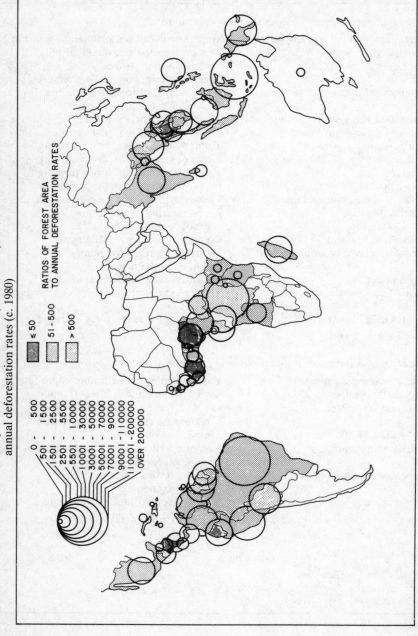

Source: Compiled from data in Grainger (1984a)

mountainous areas where resource values for timber production and species conservation may be lower, and potential impacts such as accelerated soil erosion higher.

Global average figures for rates of deforestation and disturbance conceal wide variations from place to place. Both the rates themselves and their significance are highly differentiated: in some parts of the tropics the forests have already disappeared; in others they are likely to do so within the next ten or twenty years, and in others again there is little immediate threat. Table 8.2 sets out a rough classification of areas by conversion trends, and Figure 8.2 attempts to depict both the extent of the surviving closed broad-leaved forests in tropical areas and the ratio of these areas to recent rates of deforestation. It should be emphasised that there is no logical basis for expecting the ratios to act as reliable predictors of the ultimate disappearance of the forest, but they may indicate the area under the greatest threat at present. Two main conclusions emerge.

First, tropical moist forest is under greatest threat (in the sense of complete deforestation) in insular and peninsular situations, and large tracts of west Africa, Central America and south-east Asia are likely to lose their native forests soon. Many of these areas are accessible and densely populated, and the pressures of both agricultural development and forest resource exploitation have been irresistible. Some have fragile, mountainous environments. In some cases, such as Madagascar, for example, the forests contain large numbers of endemic species.

Second, the areas under little immediate threat are few in number and are characterised by large tracts of forest and low population densities. They include the Congo basin, part of the western Amazon in Brazil, and a belt across the northern part of South America, including French Guiana, Guyana and Surinam. If it were to be assumed that recent deforestation rates would remain constant, then the forests of French Guiana, Guyana and Surinam would last for thousands of years, while those of central African countries such as Zaïre and Gabon would last for several centuries. While on the one hand the probable survival of large tracts of forest in such areas is welcome, on the other hand the loss of forest in numerous peninsular and insular areas, often with distinctive or unique ecologies, can only be lamented.

It is most unlikely that the tropical forest in general or the tropical moist forest in particular will disappear completely within the next century, even if the driving-forces behind recent deforestation were to remain unchanged. As the forest contracts to a few large, inaccessible areas such as central Africa and north-east South America, deforestation rates will inevitably slow down. It is therefore misleading to suggest or imply that the continuation of recent deforestation rates would be elimination of the forest by, for example, the middle of next century. At the same time, however, the loss in resource value implied by a continuation of recent rates of deforestation and disturbance could be enormous, especially if this value is perceived primarily in terms of species and genetic resources rather than timber. The disappearance of the forest from many islands and peninsulas has resulted and will continue to result in inestimable losses in this respect, even if core areas of forest in continental interiors not only survive but are also successfully protected from disturbance in the huge parks and reserves that have been established in countries such as Surinam and Zaïre (e.g. Myers, 1980s).

Can the tropical forest be saved?

There is widespread agreement that current rates of loss of the tropical forest are undesirably high, even if there is disagreement or uncertainty about the precise rates of loss. At the same time, there is a widespread tendency amongst commentators on the tropical forest issue to assume that the loss of the forest is an unique phenomenon, and that the projection of recent rates of loss into the future is a valid procedure. Conversely, a few commentators state or imply that the same type of forest transition (in terms of area and/or management) that characterised the American forest in the early twentieth century and the European forest much earlier will also take place in the tropics (e.g. Sedjo and Clawson, 1983). The prospects for the tropical forest depend to a large degree on the causes of its destruction and on the prospects for their amelioration. Different causes operate at different scales, and proximate causes may tend to conceal underlying pressures. One obvious example of a proximate cause of deforestation is the construction of new roads in previously inaccessible areas. The opening-up of forests in this way is not confined to the developing world. Pressures on the rain forest in north Queensland in Australia, for example, have greatly increased following the completion of a new road and the sale of blocks of land for retirement homes (e.g. Aiken and Leigh, 1987; Parker, 1987). On a grander scale the construction of the BR-364 highway in Brazil, and the system of roads leading off it, opened up the forest to colonists and gave rise to the striking pattern of deforestation depicted in Figure 8.3. The strong relationship between the pattern of forest clearing and the transport network reported for Costa Rica (Sader and Joyce, 1988) is probably typical of many other countries. Ease of access has influenced the order in which forest areas have been cleared, and is in turn related to slope. The result has been that the extent of forest clearance is inversely related to slope angle (Table 8.3). The last areas to be cleared are those in inaccessible steeply sloping country. While the protective function of forests in mountainous country may be invaluable, species diversity is often lower in such areas than in the earlier-cleared lowlands (Chapter 2) and hence the value for nature conservation may be limited.

However close the relationship between accessibility and forest clearance may be, roads are only the symptom of more basic factors. They merely give physical expression to some of the underlying structural causes such as demographic and political factors. They are a proximate rather than fundamental cause of deforestation. The conclusion reached by Hirsch (1988a) in relation to Thailand is probably of general applicability. He concluded that deforestation could not be explained by any single,

Figure 8.3   Deforestation patterns in Rondônia, Brazil (black)

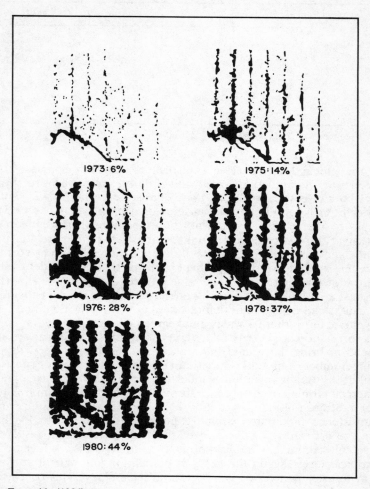

1973:6%

1975:14%

1976:28%

1978:37%

1980:44%

Source: Fearnside (1986)

isolated factor. As well as being perceived negatively as backward and inimical to development, the forest had suffered as part of the broader development of the national economy and polity over the last century. Two processes were of overriding importance: the expansion of the agricultural economy, and the political process of state formation, manifested in the linking of the national periphery to the centre, and the resulting increase in accessibility. If the spatial expansion of the world economy is substituted for state formation, then global deforestation can be seen to have similar driving-forces.

Table 8.3   Slope angle and forest loss, Costa Rica

Slope class (per cent)	Forest loss (per cent)
0–5	100
6–15	96
16–30	89
31–45	89
46–60	89
<60	69

Source: Compiled from data in Sader and Joyce (1988)

At the global level, a close statistical relationship appears to exist between rates of population growth and of deforestation. This relationship applies both cross-sectionally on the global scale at the present day, and historically or longitudinally within individual countries (Chapter 3). An example of the inverse relationship between trends in population and forest cover, for the case of Sri Lanka, is illustrated in Figure 4.6 (p. 74). Globally and nationally, high rates of deforestation seem to be correlated with rapid population growth, perhaps implying that rates of deforestation will slow down when rates of population growth also do so. An expectation that forest areas will stabilise with population, however, will be valid only if the causes and dynamics of deforestation are correctly identified.

In general terms there is widespread agreement that population pressure and deforestation are closely related, and that forests shrink as a result of the need to bring more land into cultivation in order to feed the ever-growing number of mouths. Quantitatively, land clearance for subsistence agriculture is usually regarded as much more significant than clearance for commercial farming or disturbance through logging. For example, Steinlin (1982) indicates that 0.6 per cent of the tropical forest is cleared annually for subsistence agriculture, while 0.2 per cent is disturbed by logging: in Africa, he estimates, 70 per cent of the forest destruction results from shifting cultivation. The implication is that the key to the safeguarding of the tropical forest lies in the fields of population and agriculture, rather than in forestry policies or in silvicultural technology. This conclusion is reinforced by the fact that small-scale cultivators occupy more than one fifth of all tropical moist forests, including large tracts of primary forest (e.g. Myers, 1983a). With growing populations, greater disturbance of primary forests, shorter fallow periods in secondary forests, and more rapid and complete clearance of surviving areas of forest, are to be expected. Myers estimates that at least 10 million hectares of forest are eliminated annually in this way, mostly in south-east Asia.

To 'blame' the destruction of the tropical forest on population pressure is, however, illogical, even if a close statistical relationship between forest clearance and population growth can be established. At one level, some densely populated areas have successfully retained relatively high levels of tree (if not forest) cover. In Java, for example, agro-forestry systems have evolved over a long period, and population growth has not been accompanied by a complete removal tree cover as might be implied by the converging curves of population and forest area (Figure 4.6; p. 74). At a more general level, the relationship between population and forest area needs to be viewed within the context of the prevailing social and political structures. In particular, questions need to be posed about the underlying reasons for forest colonisation by small-scale farmers. Is this process driven solely by population pressure, or is it an inevitable function of social and political structures? In some parts of the tropical world both informal, unplanned clearance and formal, planned forest colonisation projects may be alternatives to, or substitutes for, land reform (e.g. Westoby, 1989). Instead of carrying out major programmes of subdivision of the extensive estates of powerful landowners, governments may prefer to encourage or permit colonisation of the forest. In Panama, for example, a small number of wealthy farmers control the best farmland in the lowlands. As population grows and the land shortage becomes increasingly acute, peasant farmers (*campesinos*) face the alternatives of migrating to the cities or colonising the upland forests (Simons, 1989). The ensuing deforestation is likely to continue unless or until other land is made available through land reform. It is not surprising, therefore, that land reform has been identified by observers such as Lutzenberger (1987) as the first priority if the complete destruction of the Amazonian forest is to be averted.

Furthermore, small-scale cultivators are often displaced from their land by the advent of large-scale commercial agriculture, often directed to export markets. The problem is therefore one of *shifted*, rather than *shifting* cultivators. Cycles of displacement develop, with small cultivators clearing land which is subsequently appropriated by commercial interests. All too frequently, the latter have the active or tacit support of the political and legal establishment: the outworking of this structural bias and absence of natural justice is the progressive clearance of forest. Meanwhile, behind the forest frontier the land is given over to large-scale commercial production, rather than to satisfying the basic needs of small cultivators. In the words of Westoby (1987, p. 311),

> The main instruments of forest destruction are the disinherited of tropical forested countries: peasant farmers, shifting cultivators, rural landless. But these are the agents, not the causes. . . . This pressure will inevitably continue, until there is a more equal access to land and other resources. This is not a sufficient condition for saving the tropical forests, but it is a necessary one.

Social and political structures, and the mode of 'development' pursued in many developing countries, are therefore the driving-force behind deforestation, rather than population pressure *per se*.

Even if population growth is held to be the main driving-force of forest destruction, it does not necessarily follow that population control is the only solution. If agriculture could be intensified sufficiently, so that more mouths could be fed from the existing area of farmland, then much of the pressure on the forest could be removed. Indeed it has been argued by observers such as Huguet (1982, 1983) that the tropical forest can be preserved only in so far as a veritable agricultural revolution, within the reach of small farmers, takes place. Pressure on the forest would then be relieved, as has happened in most rich and temperate-zone countries.

To isolate population pressure and the growth of numbers of subsistence cultivators as the major cause of deforestation is, therefore, to simplify a complex scene. The causes of deforestation are in many countries as much political as demographic. Furthermore, the various causes of deforestation do not work in mutual isolation from each other, but rather than in combination. In particular, logging and agricultural colonisation are often directly linked. The initial opening-up of the forest for logging, and the accompanying construction of roads, allows the penetration of cultivators into previously inaccessible areas (as well as causing direct and indirect forms of impact on the forest environment, as outlined in Chapter 7). In the Ivory Coast, one hectare of forest has been found to disappear at the hands of the follow-on cultivator for every 5 cubic metres removed by the timber exploiter (e.g. Myers, 1983a). Extrapolating from this limited base, he calculates that tropical log production of around 150 million cubic metres would mean that 30 million hectares would be affected annually. This figure he states to be too high, because of differential impact in different parts of the world, but at the same time he considers the conservative figure of 10 million hectares could be 'decidedly too low' (p. 293). He therefore settles for an intermediate figure of 20 million hectares per year, which would mean that 1 per cent of the tropical moist forest would be accounted for by subsistence agriculture each year. This figure represents around 80 per cent of his estimated total conversion rate of 24.5 million hectares per year, the balance being made up, on the basis of rather sweeping assumptions, of further areas of 2.5 million hectares as a result of fuelwood gathering and 2.0 million from clearance for ranching. There is thus a difference amounting almost to an order of magnitude between the scales of significance of the causes of tropical deforestation. The conclusion that the tropical-forest problem is a problem of agriculture rather than forestry is thus in turn strengthened. If the needs of the subsistence cultivators could otherwise be provided, the pressure on the forest would thus be greatly reduced.

It does not follow, however, that forestry and the use of the timber resources of the tropical forest are irrelevant or unimportant. The role of logging as the precursor of clearance for subsistence agriculture has already been mentioned, and there are numerous examples of destructive exploitation that has either exhausted or degraded the resource. One recent case concerns the tree species *Ceiba pentandra* around Iquitos in the Peruvian Amazon. A plywood industry based on this species developed in the early 1970s. By 1983 uncontrolled exploitation had led to a total depletion of the resource base and to the collapse of the industry (Gentry and Vasquez, 1988). The cycles evident in forest exploitation in parts of the United States one hundred years ago, and in many other parts of the world at various times in the past, are still evident in parts of the tropical forest today.

There is also the question of the adequacy of the tropical forest as a timber resource, in the face of growing demand for tropical timber. Part of this growth in demand is from export markets, and measures that could be adopted in these developed-world markets could help to curb further growth and pressure in this respect. But demand for wood and wood products is also growing rapidly in the developing world, and hence direct pressures on the forest can only increase. Indeed there is doubt as to whether the tropical forest can satisfy this demand.

If it is assumed that a sustained yield of 3 cubic metres per hectare per year can be achieved from tropical rain forests, an aggregate demand of 1,500 cubic metres by around 1990 would mean that 5 million square kilometres of forest would be required (Wadsworth, 1983), or over half of the surviving area. By 2000 almost the entire area would be required. In short, the tropical forest in its natural form could not satisfy projected requirements, even if managed on a sustained-yield basis.

This conclusion further highlights the potential significance of plantations in meeting timber demand, and at the same time casts serious doubt on the ability of sustained-yield management to solve or ameliorate tropical-forest problems. And irrespective of this ability, the sustained-yield management of the tropical forest is itself associated with serious problems.

Sustained-yield management

The management of the tropical forest as a flow resource, on a sustained-yield basis, is often advocated as a preferable alternative to its 'mining' through destructive exploitation. Serious problems, however, confront the application of sustained-yield management. These problems include both technical difficulties and those of a social and political nature. And even if they can be overcome, serious doubts remain as to the extent to which such management can solve the current problems of the tropical forest resource. These doubts apply both to the priorities to be afforded to regeneration and silviculture, as compared with other measures, and to the relative merits of 'natural' management and the establishment of plantations. One view is that regeneration and silviculture should take lower priorities than surveillance and protection of the forest. For example Lowe (1984, p. 134) suggests that 'silviculture can be a way for tropical foresters to bury their heads in the sand while the forest melts away around them.'

At one level, the potential ability of 'naturally' managed tropical forests to meet current and future demands for wood is limited. As Chapter 2 indicates, the total biomass and productivity of the tropical moist forest ecosystem are high, but those of commercially useful wood species are more modest. Stem growth, which provides potentially useful timber, receives a small fraction of the gross productivity. And as much as 65 per cent of the total standing crop of woody species in a tropical high forest may consist of lower and middle storey species, which are not normally perceived as useful (Kio, 1979). There is much confusion between total primary productivity and wood production, and indeed wood production in natural tropical forests is not necessarily higher than that in natural temperate forests (Jordan, 1983). The luxuriance of the tropical moist forest is not fully matched by luxuriance of timber growth. In addition to this fundamental characteristic of the resource ecology, there are both technical and non-technical problems that combine to limit the potential of sustained-yield management of the tropical forest. Attempts have been made for more than a hundred years to practise such management in parts of the tropics, and especially in south-east Asia. Success has generally been greater in the Dipterocarp forests of south-east Asia than in other parts of the biome, but even here it has been limited. The great diversity of tree species, only some of which are or ever will be merchantable, has been a major stumbling-block. Where natural regeneration does take place, it may create a forest which differs from the original one and which is of lower economic value (Catinot, 1978). The nub of the problem is that in a forest where only 4–10 per cent of the tree species are commercial, the probability that a harvested tree will be replaced by another commercial tree species is also about 4–10 per cent (Jacobs, 1988). Even if only a very small number of trees are removed (for example two per hectare), they may represent 50 per cent of the population of that species. The great danger, therefore, is that the resource simply deteriorates in quality and value.

After the Second World War, the tropical forests began to be increasingly viewed as a source of timber for the developed countries. During the 1950s the development of suitable management techniques was a primary concern (e.g. Steinlin and Pretzsch, 1984). This concern was manifested in the application of management techniques in some countries, even before the main phase of forest development during the 1960s and 1970s. In general terms, however, experience with systems of sustained-yield management was disappointing, and it is patently obvious that such systems have not averted widespread destruction and degradation of the tropical forest resource.

The forests of Malaysia and neighbouring areas are more amenable to management than most other parts of the tropical moist forest, as they are characterised by having several dominant species of a single family (Dipterocarps), several of which, in turn, produce wood of commercial qualities. In the words of Whitmore (1984, p.98), the silviculturist working the lowland Dipterocarp forest from Sumatra to the Philippines 'is luckier than his counterpart anywhere else in the humid tropics': with relative ease the forest here can be manipulated to produce a higher stocking of commercial species than existed in the virgin forest.

After the Second World War, the Malayan Uniform System (MUS) was introduced in the face of increasing demand for wood combined with the use of mechanised logging. It aims essentially at converting the tropical lowland forest to a more or less even-aged forest containing an increased proportion of commercial species. In upland and mountainous areas, the Selective Management System (SMS) was subsequently introduced (Thang, 1987) (Table 8.4). Under SMS, a pre-felling inventory is undertaken, and on its basis one of three procedures is selected. Areas with

Table 8.4 Management systems

Malaysian Uniform System (MUS)	
Year	Operation
n – 1½	Linear sampling of regeneration, and enumeration of merchantable trees
n to n + 1	Exploitation, followed by poison-girdling
n + 3 to n + 5	Linear sampling of new crop, followed by cleaning climber cutting and poison-girdling as required
n + 10	Linear sampling of new crop, followed by treatment as required or 'passed' as regenerated
n + 20, n + 40, etc	Sampling and thinning as required

Selection Management System (SMS)	
Year	Operation
n – 2 to n – 1	Pre-felling inventory and determination of cutting regime
n – 1 to n	Climber cutting to reduce damage during logging, tree marking incorporating directional felling
n	Felling as prescribed
n + 2 to n + 5	Post-felling inventory to determine residual stocking and appropriate silvicultural treatments

Source: Based on Thang (1987)

inadequate natural regeneration of desired species are enriched by planting or replaced by plantations; the areas richest in adolescent trees of commercial species are identified for management on a polycyclic system (i.e. with the removal of selected trees in a series of felling cycles), whilst other areas are to be managed by MUS (Whitmore, 1984). The term 'selection' in this context applies to the selection of the appropriate procedure, rather than that of individual trees. Despite this relatively long history of natural forest management in Malaysia, the successful regeneration of forests is still fraught with uncertainty. One of the major problems has been the difference between the theory and practice of systems such as SMS: the former may be sound but the latter less so (Tang, 1987).

Derivatives of management systems first devised in south-east Asia have been employed in parts of Africa, and to a much lesser extent in America. In Nigeria, for example, the Tropical Shelterwood System (TSS) was introduced in the 1940s as an adaptation of the MUS. Under TSS, the forest canopy was gradually opened to induce regeneration by natural means and to guide the development of seedlings. Climbers were cut during the first year, while girdling and poisoning of uneconomic species were carried out in the second and third years, and mature uneconomic species were felled in the fourth and fifth years. This system, however, was judged to be unsatisfactory under Nigerian conditions. Compared with Malaysian forests, the Nigerian forest had a more diverse tree flora (with the density of commercial species rarely exceeding ten trees per hectare) and more irregular structure. Furthermore, the opening of the canopy to allow the penetration of more light increased not only the growth of desired species, but also favoured the increased growth of herbaceous weeds and climbers: the net result in some instances was to retard the growth of desired species (Kio and Ekwebelam, 1987). A total of 200,000 hectares was treated under TSS before the system was abandoned in the 1960s. Other attempts at management, such as enrichment planting, were also given up at around the same time.

In general there has been poor communication of information from south-east Asia and Africa to America (Wadsworth, 1987), and fewer attempts have been made to manage the natural forest in that continent. As yet, sustained management of the Amazonian forest is non-existent on a commercial scale, and is in its infancy in terms of research. Various systems are now under trial in Surinam and French Guiana, as well as in Brazil and Peru (Fearnside, 1989c). However successful they may prove to be in technical terms, it is doubtful whether they will be widely adopted as long as uncut virgin forest is available for exploitation. The additional costs incurred in sustained-yield management reduce the profits when the timber is sold, and unless a greatly increasd level of timber is produced or harvesting costs are greatly reduced, managed forests will be at an economic disadvantage. The traditional tendency to carry out financial assessments on the benefits of timber production alone, as opposed to more broadly based economic evaluations of the range of goods and services provided by the natural forest (see Chapter 6), is a further obstacle to adopting management of natural forests rather than replacing them with plantations. And in addition to problems of a technical and economic nature, there is a fundamental problem of political commitment, reflected in the provision (or all too frequently non-provision) of suitable legal and managerial frameworks and institutions, and of trained and motivated manpower.

A fundamental problem of sustained management, at least outside parts of south-east Asia, is that it represents a form of land use that is not sufficiently intensive to compete with arable or perennial crops. The tropical shelterwood system in Nigeria, for example, was abandoned in the 1960s for this reason (Lowe, 1977). In Ghana, it had a similar history, having been introduced in 1946 and abandoned in 1966 after failing to give the expected results (Asabere, 1987). In addition to the inherent technical problems of reconciling the need to open the forest canopy with the effective control of climbers and other undesired species, the economic performance simply could not normally match that of alternative land uses.

In some instances production in natural stands improved by silvicultural treatment can compare with that from artificial stands: Maitre (1986) for instance quotes the example of teak in Ivory Coast. More usually, however, a wide gap exists between the yields of managed natural stands and plantations. While rational management and simple operations in the tropical moist forest can treble the yield of merchantable timber to 6 cubic metres per hectare, plantations on the same soils can provide yields of 35 cubic metres or more (Westoby, 1989). Even if Westoby's figures are over-optimistic, the wide differential between the yields of managed natural and plantation forests remains. While WRI et al. (1985) suggest in *Tropical forests: a call for action* that with an average annual yield of 2 cubic metres per hectare from managed natural forests, the existing area of logged-over forest (around 210 million hectares) could be managed more intensively to supply 85 per cent of the industrial timber demands of the developing world by 2000, the outlook of other observers is more gloomy. For example, Wadsworth (1983) estimates that by 2000 the entire area of surviving tropical forest would be required to meet contemporary timber demands. He concludes that 'reliance on native forests for future wood requirements is a blind alley' (p. 287). In contrast, the conversion of 15 per cent of the existing logged-over area into fast-growing plantations, with an assumed yield of 15 cubic metres per hectare, could meet the demand (WRI, 1985). This is not to assume or imply that plantations are free from the technical and economic problems that have beset sustained management in the tropical forest. In Amazonia, for example, most of the attempts at industrial-scale plantation silviculture that have been made from the 1920s onwards have been unsuccessful (Rankin, 1985). A possible exception is the huge operation at Jari, 450 kilometres west of Belém, near the mouth of the Amazon. Here an integrated project, including plantations extending to 100,000 hectares, a pulp mill and agricultural developments, was initially financed by Daniel Ludwig, an American entrepreneur. The plantations, mainly established between 1968 and 1980, consisted of two-thirds *Gmelina* and one-third *Pinus caribea*, grown respectively on rotations of six and twelve years with yields averaging 25 and 15 cubic metres per hectare per year (Rollet, 1980). Initially, the native forest there was clear-felled and burned without timber salvage, and heavy machinery was used in clearance. From around 1980, however, between 60 and 90 per cent of the native timber on sites cleared for plantations was harvested for use as fuel or for pulp or sawmilling, and the use of heavy machinery was discontinued with it was found that the resulting soil compaction had an adverse effect on tree growth. The long-term viability of that much publicised project may hinge on the changes in soil fertility under plantation regimes, and on losses due to pests and diseases. Slight decreases in *Gmelina* growth rates have already been observed during the second rotation (Rankin, 1985). While biological productivity can be maintained by the use of fertilisers, the economics may be another matter. By the early 1980s Jari was experiencing difficulties with both biological success and economic health, and in 1982 was sold to a consortium of twenty-seven Brazilian companies. The project has experienced both successes and failures (Palmer, 1986), and its long-term biological and economic viability remains uncertain (Rankin, 1985). The fact that it was sold at a loss (Horrick et al., 1984), however, is significant.

Whatever the final evaluation of the Jari project may be, it is unlikely that it will be a widely-emulated model in the foreseeable future, and its performance will probably be of limited significance for the evaluation of the relative merits of plantations and sustained management in the tropics in general. Views on these relative merits differ widely. On the one hand, it is argued by some that fast-growing plantations divert attention from the necessity to apply sustained-yield management to the tropical forest (e.g. Jabil, 1983). Kio (1979) suggests that plantation forestry offers little more than an easy way out from the embarrassment arising from inadequate understanding of tropical forest ecology. On the other hand, plantations can play a vital role in reducing the emphasis on the wood production function of natural forests, thus making their natural regeneration and sustainability more attainable (Tang, 1987). It has been suggested that the conservation of the natural forest heritage of Papua New Guinea, for example, depends on the establishment of a number of large-scale planta-tions (Hilton and Johns, 1984).

The comparative evaluation of plantations and sustained-management forest is perhaps pointless, as they both suffer from limitations. In the tropical dry forests of Africa, for example, the management and improve-ment of natural forests is an economic but inadequate solution to the problem of wood needs, while plantations are very expensive and are therefore only a limited solution. Here the integration of trees into rural land management and landscape (in agro-forestry systems) may be argued to be the most worthwhile solution in the long term (Bailly et al., 1982). 'Natural' management and plantations are not necessarily alternatives, although they may compete for scarce resources. Tropical rain forests do not necessarily have to be cleared to make way for plantations: many tropical countries have extensive areas of degraded scrubland or grassland which can adequately support plantations. Indeed, most tropical planta-tions established to date are in areas of former scrubland or grassland, rather than rain forest. Furthermore, sustained-management may well have a major role to play in protective forests even if it cannot produce large yields of timber. Even if it is accepted that the prospects for natural management of the tropical moist forest for timber production are poor (Wyatt-Smith, 1987), sustained management may still have a crucial role to play in providing non-timber products as well as environmental services. 'Natural' management is appropriate when the forest is intended to fulfil purposes of conservation or is unsuited for other purposes, and it is appropriate when conversion to plantations is hindered by lack of capital or other obstacles (Vincent et al., 1987). In some countries such as Costa Rica, Nigeria and Vietnam, however, the reduction of the productive forest area to its present extent has severely limited whatever potential may have existed for extensive 'natural' management: the demands on the limited surviving areas are simply too great to be met by low-intensity management (Schmidt, 1987). Demand for forest products in Nigeria, for example, exceeds the ability of natural forests to supply it, and plantations must play a major role (Kio and Ekwebelam, 1987). On the other hand, conventional plantation silviculture focuses on timber production to the exclusion of most other functions, and if the total disappearance of useful non-wood components of the natural forest in West Africa, for example, is to be avoided, then plantation techniques will have to be modified (Nwoboshi, 1987).

If conservation and timber production are not fully compatible, then separate allocations of forest lands to these functions are required (Wyatt-Smith, 1987). Managed semi-natural forests are likely to become less important in the future (Whitmore, 1984), as plantations provide increasing proportions of industrial wood requirements and 'natural' forms of management are applied to upland and protective forests. If this is so, then it seems inevitable that the tropical forest will follow a similar path of development to that experienced in temperate latitudes. The multi-purpose 'pre-industrial' forest becomes more specialised in its functions as management (often combined with non-indigenous or non-local control) is applied. Many tropical forest areas, in short, may just be entering the 'industrial' phase at the same time as many temperate areas begin to make the transition from the 'industrial' to post-industrial' stages, as functions such as conservation and recreation are progressively added to timber production (Chapters 5 and 6).

However inexorable this trend may be, its implications are ominous for the welfare of the local people and indeed also for the forest itself. FAO (1985b) in its review of *Intensive multiple-use forest management in the tropics* concluded that as the intensity of management for wood production increases, so the ability to produce minor or traditional forest products is reduced. This trend towards the production of wood at the cost of other benefits is to the detriment of the poorest sectors of society. The almost inevitable result is alienation: if the local population derive few and decreasing benefits from the forest, it is scarcely surprising that it will perceive it as land to be encroached upon when more cropland is required. At the same time, the growing primacy of wood production may mean that the resource is degraded if not devastated, unless stringent controls are enforced and rigorous management applied. In short, modern trends in the use of the tropical forest resemble all too closely those in other parts of the world in earlier times. The parallels with the use and abuse of the Russian forest in the eighteenth and nineteenth centuries, as recounted by French (1983), seem especially close. Perhaps the real tragedy of the tropical forest is that the lessons of the past have not been heeded.

The tropical forest issue

The destruction of the tropical rain forest differs in one major respect from similar episodes of forest destruction in other parts of the world in the past. Whereas the destruction of the Russian and American forests in the eighteenth and nineteenth centuries attracted some attention and gave rise to some concern within the respective countries, it did not become a major global issue. Opponents of the destruction tended to be localised in distribution and few in number. Forest issues were essentially domestic concerns. Today, conditions are quite different. While opponents of destruction in some tropical countries may be no more numerous or influential than their American counterparts a century and half ago, they are far outnumbered by millions in other countries beyond the tropics. Since international concern about forest issues is such a new phenomenon, it is not surprising that its significance remains uncertain. It remains to be seen whether the focusing of world-wide attention on the tropical forest issue hastens a turn-round of areal trends and attitudes to the resource and its management. While it may well do so, it is also possible that changes will come about for other reasons, and that the phases and cycles identified in the use of the non-tropical forest resource will be completed far more quickly in relation to the tropical forest. In short, the significance of tropical forest issue is as difficult to evaluate as its reality as a global environmental concern is easy to recognise. What is clear, however, is that already that concern has given rise to a number of institutional innova-tions. It is still too early to evaluate these innovations, but it is obvious that comparable institutional initiatives were completely lacking in previous major episodes of forest destruction.

Tropical Forestry Action Plan

One major response to the data on shrinkage of the tropical forest that became available in the arly 1980s have been the Tropical Forestry Action Plans (TFAP), produced by FAO and the World Resources Institute. The FAO Committee on Forest Development in the Tropics recognised that not only was the forest contracting rapidly, but also that only tiny proportions were either managed or safeguarded. FAO (1985c, 1986c) estimated that in the early 1980s, less than 5 per cent of the productive closed forest was managed on a satisfactory basis for the production of timber, and that only 3 per cent of the closed forest was safeguarded in national parks or other protected areas. Much of that paltry proportion was protected on paper only, and not in reality. Certain forest types, such as the east-coast rain forest of South America and the forests of Madagascar, had almost disappeared. The Committee concluded that 'It is now generally recognized that the main cause of destruction and degrada-tion of tropical forests is the poverty of the people who live in and around the forests' (FAO, 1985c).

While the FAO committee were deliberating, a task force assembled by the World Resources Institute (WRI) and including representatives from the World Bank and the United Nations Development Programme also addressed the problem (WRI, 1985). In *Tropical Forests: a call for action*, the task force acknowledged that government policies had contributed to the depletion and destruction of tropical forests, and that unsustainable use of the forest had been fostered by lenient forest-concession terms and subsidies. It recognised that deforestation was a complex problem, whose underlying causes were poverty, skewed land distribution, and low agri-cultural productivity.

Table 8.5 Tropical Forestry Action Plans: priority areas

FAO Committee on Forest Development in the Tropics
Forestry in land use
Forest-based industrial development
Fuelwood and energy
Conservation of tropical forestry ecosystems
Institutions (administration, research, training, extension)

WRI Task Force
Rehabilitation of upland watershed and semi-arid lowlands
Forest management for industrial use
Fuelwood and agroforestry
Conservation of forest ecosystems

Sources: FAO (1985c, 1986c): WRI (1985)

The proposals of FAO and WRI were similar in many respects. Five priority areas were identified for attention in the former, and four in the latter (Table 8.5).

WRI estimated that the level of investment required to tackle the problem of tropical deforestation over the five years following the publication of its *Call for Action* would be around US$ 8 billion, with half coming from development-aid bodies and lending agencies, and the remainder from private investment and national governments. This rate of investment would represent around twice the then-existing levels. One of the main emphases of the WRI proposals was the need to increase development assistance to forestry. It was seen as very small, and furthermore was declining in relation to other sectors. The World Bank and Inter-American, Asian and African Development Banks allocated less than 1 per cent of their annual funding to forestry, and the UN Development Programme only 2 per cent (WRI, 1985).

The breakdown of investment proposed by the WRI Task Force is indicated in Table 8.6. One feature of the proposals is the apparently substantial sum of over US$ 1 billion to be devoted to the strengthening of institutions, and in particular to improvements in research, training and extension work. This sum amounts to around 20 per cent of the total, and it was recommended that approximately three-quarters should be devoted to national-level institutions and the remainder to regional and international activities. Another feature is that at least 30 per cent of the proposed investment would be related to agriculture, with the aim of relieving pressures of agricultural colonisation in the forest.

While this segment of the proposed investment is geared to the causes of the tropical forest problem as identified by both FAO and WRI, it is more doubtful whether the remainder is equally directed. Criticisms have been levelled in particular at the prominent role ascribed to industrial forestry. For example Caufield (1987) argues that this type of forestry, and the

Table 8.6 Tropical Forestry Action Plan: summary of needed investments 1987–91

	Fuelwood and agroforestry	Land use on upland watersheds	million US$ Forest management for industrial uses	Conservation of forest ecosystems	Total
Africa	507	191	210	130	1038
Asia	902	915	705	177	2699
Latin America	490	125	725	243	1585
Total	1899	1231	1640	550	5320
percentage	36	23	31	10	
Institutional component*	323	315	324	102	1064

* Included in sectoral totals
Source: WRI (1985)

investment that underlies it, will merely serve the interests of Western nations. The effect of the plan, it is claimed, could be to increase deforestation and impoverish further local populations. She dismisses the WRI plan as the product of the 'jet-set' environmentalists of the World Resources Institute and the World Bank.

Equally forceful criticism has come from numerous other commentators. For example Westoby (1989) observes that the plan seeks to encourage local people to farm in a way that does not destroy their environment, but ignores the circumstances which oblige them to do so. Similarly, Ross and Donovan (1986) conclude that neither plan focuses on the crux of the problem, which is wasteful, unplanned forest destruction, and that neither considers the potential role of natural forests in reducing rural poverty. In particular, they point out that the problem of deforestation is usually different from the need for reforestation. Programmes focusing on afforestation and reforestation divert attention from the problem of wasteful and unnecessary deforestation. Shiva (1987) offers even more scathing criticism, suggesting that the 'Tropical Forest Action Plan' should be retitled 'Action Plan for Tropical Forest Destruction'. He perceives it as exacerbating, rather than alleviating, the destructive processes presently operating in the tropical forest.

At the heart of much of the criticism is the emphasis on investment in general and on foreign aid in particular. If the causes of the tropical forest problem have been correctly identified by FAO and WRI as essentially social and political, it is not clear how the root of the problem – as opposed to some of the symptoms – can be solved by increased invest-ment. At one level, many developing countries are reluctant to increase their debt burdens by embarking on reforestation programmes that are unlikely to yield short-term benefits. At another level, the effects of foreign aid may be indirectly to increase pressures on the forest by promoting agricultural or plantation projects, which in turn involve either removal of the forest or the displacement of small-scale cultivators into previously little-disturbed areas. For example Shiva (1987) refers to TFAP's recommendation that US$400 million to convert natural forests in Brazil to plantations. In the same country, the World Bank has financed the Carajas iron-ore project in eastern Amazonia, whose demand for charcoal will lead to the destruction of large areas of forest (Rich, 1989). Similarly, the World Bank assisted with the construction of Highway BR-364. (Figure 8.3) (Fearnside, 1989a).

It is easy to be critical of the plans (and of international financing) but much more difficult to suggest alternatives. It is relatively easy to identify rural poverty as a major contributor to the problem, but to identify the cause is not to suggest a practicable solution, at least in the short term. Clearly the Tropical Forestry Action Plan is not a panacea, but this is not to say that it will not be a helpful contribution. It has helped to focus attention on the problem, and it may have beneficial effects in encouraging both co-operation amongst aid agencies and higher levels of investment in institutional infrastructure. It may even help to convince governments in developing countries that the problem is serious and that local and national action is urgently required. On the other hand, the gloomy conclusions of Westoby (1989, p. 165) may be well founded: '[the] history of efforts to halt the shrinkage of the tropical forest by inter-governmental action goes back nearly two decades', but 'that history can . . . be described as a series of loudly trumpeted non-events.'

Perhaps it is unrealistic to view either set of proposals as a plan in any specific sense: they amount to a proposed programme rather than a detailed blueprint. Implementation, involving the co-ordination of numerous bodies and agencies, encounters many difficulties. One important step in the WRI programme was the meeting of representatives of various government and other bodies in Bellagio in Italy in 1987. The statement issued after the meeting referred to various steps and measures to curb deforestation and promote sustainable use of the tropical forest, including, for example, fuller assessment of the costs of deforestation, national reviews to assess the extent of deforestation and to identify key areas for remedial action, and the fuller involvement of local peoples and non-governmental organisations (WRI, 1989). Perhaps the most useful role of such 'plans' is to act as catalysts for action and as integrators or co-ordinators of the activities of the various interested bodies, rather than as blueprints for action. Evaluation of the plans, viewed in this light rather than that of the detailed investment proposals, for example, is extremely difficult, and tangible results can be difficult to measure accurately. This does not necessarily mean, however, that no beneficial results are forthcoming. At the most basic level, the effects of the plans in helping to focus attention on the tropical forest problem are more likely to be helpful than harmful, even if serious issue can be taken with some of the detailed proposals.

International Tropical Timber Agreement

A second institutional innovation during the 1980s was the International Tropical Timber Agreement (ITTA). This agreement stems from the proposal in the 1970s of the United Nations Conference on Trade and Development (UNCTAD) to inaugurate an Integrated Programme for Commodities (IPC). Objectives of the IPC, and of the agreements for individual commodities, included the strengthening of the positions of producing countries (mainly in the developing world), and regulation of the fluctuations of the commodity markets. While this parentage serves as an useful reminder that timber is only one of several primary products on which the economies of many developing countries strongly depend, there are many differences between timber and other commodities such as sugar and coffee. Indeed ITTA differs from other commodity agreements, and in particular ascribes relatively less importance to market regulation than do most of the other commodity agreements. The maintenance of stability in prices and supplies, through intervention in world markets, is not attempted as a primary objective.

Although the primary aim of ITTA is to promote the expansion and diversification of international trade in tropical timber, it at the same time seeks to encourage sustainable use of tropical forests, the conservation of the resources that they constitute and of the environments in which they are located. The agreement was finally ratified in 1985, after years of negotiations and wrangling. By 1988 forty-two countries had signed the agreement and become members of the International Tropical Timber Organization (ITTO). These members, comprising twenty-four consuming and eighteen producing countries, account for 70 per cent of all tropical forests and 95 per cent of tropical timber exports (WRI, 1989). By 1989 the numbers had grown to thirty-three consuming and thirty-six producing countries, and international support, as indicated by both the number of signatories and financial support pledged to ITTO, appeared to be growing (Oldfield, 1989). Five main areas are identified for attention: improved forest management and wood utilisation, better market intelligence, improved marketing and distribution of tropical timber exports, the encouragement of processing in producer countries, and the encouragement of industrial tropical timber afforestation (plantation forestry).

The significance of ITTA and ITTO remains to be seen. Consumers and producers share related concerns: the former are worried about the rate of depletion of the resource, while the latter are aware that they were (or are) 'mining' their resource without renewing it. Nevertheless formidable problems and differences were encountered in the years of negotiation leading to the agreement. A particular problem was the allocation of voting rights, especially since shares of trade are not proportional to shares of forest area. The initial wrangling delayed the reaching of agreement and the setting-up of ITTO, and seemed to bode ill for its efficacy. By the late 1980s, however, the first specific projects aimed at improving forest management and reforestation were being implemented. One focuses on ways of rehabilitating some 3.5 million hectares of fire-damaged forest in East Kalimantan (WRI, 1989).

The long-term effectiveness of ITTO, like that of the Tropical Forestry Action Plan, remains to be seen. Initial attitudes were sceptical: one review, for example, questioned whether the agreement was a chimera or an opportunity (Johnson, 1985). It is unlikely that ITTA and ITTO will prove to be a panacea, any more than the Tropical Forestry Action Plan. This does not mean, however, that it will be unhelpful, and the growing support is a hopeful sign. Again one of the main effects may be in raising international consciousness and concern.

This growing concern is manifested in various ways. At one level, there are threats of boycotts of tropical timber products. For example, two large chainstores in Britain have stopped selling goods made from tropical wood which does not come from managed forests, and more than thirty local authorities have stopped using it. In the Netherlands, half of the units of local government have discontinued the use of tropical wood (Anderson, 1989). In West Germany, more than 150 towns and communities have imposed similar bans (Oldfield, 1989). In Switzerland, the use of tropical hardwoods for coffins has been rejected (Johnson, 1985). While most activity thus far has been at local government level, national and supra-national institutions are also becoming involved. The West German Ministry of Building, for example, has discontinued the use of tropical wood in government building projects (Anderson, 1989), while the European Parliament has called on member states to ban imports. As yet this call has not been sustained by the European Commission.

It is obvious that such measures and initiatives signal widespread concern about tropical hardwood logging, but their effectiveness in curbing tropical deforestation and forest degradation is another matter. Logging is, of course, only one of several threats to the tropical forest, and there is a risk that boycotts may antagonise producing countries and hence do as much harm as good. In particular, a decrease in demand for tropical hardwoods may result in a decrease in price, and hence in a further discounting of the value of the tropical forest as an economic resource.

During the early 1980s, the setting-up of an Organisation of Timber Exporting Countries (OTEC) was advocated by Guppy (1983). The proposed organisation would have had some similarities to the Organisation of Petroleum Exporting (OPEC) countries, which at the time was seen as being very effective in regulating supply and price. This proposal has not materialised, and it is debatable whether such an organisation would be as effective in relation to a diverse and heterogeneous product such as tropical hardwood as it appeared to be in relation to petroleum. An attempt by a group of countries including Malaysia, Indonesia, Philippines and Papua New Guinea to set up a loose cartel in the 1970s did not have a major effect in the face of a Japanese near-monopoly of imports and the urgent needs for revenue on the parts of Indonesia and the Philippines (Kumar, 1986). It is possible, however, that an effective regulation of supply by a group of exporting countries would lead to a rise in price and hence more careful husbanding of the tropical forest resource. Whether agreement over control of supply could be reached by the exporting countries is another matter, as is the question of whether any price rise would have significant effect on the perception of the resource.

Debt-for-nature swaps

Many developing countries are burdened by huge foreign debts. The need to attempt to service and repay international loans has encouraged drives to expand exports. This has in turn led to more and more land being given over to export crops, and has directly or indirectly led to increased pressures on the forest. Economic imperatives have, therefore, contributed to the destruction or degradation of forests.

During the second half of the 1980s, however, foreign debt has been used as a means of encouraging the conservation of some areas of forest. Conservation interests, usually located in the United States or other developed countries, acquire parts of a developing country's foreign debt, and in return the debtor country agrees to protect certain areas of forest. One of the first of these 'debt-for-nature' swaps was negotiated in 1987, when a conservation body – Conservation International – acquired US$650,000 of Bolivia's debt for the discounted sum of US$100,000. In exchange, Bolivia agreed to establish protected areas, amounting to around 1.5 million hectares around a major reserve. Under the agreement, the Bolivian government will manage the forests for sustainable development (Walsh, 1987; Palca, 1987). In another deal the World Wildlife Fund and the (American-based) Nature Conservancy acquired Ecuadorian debt amounting to US$9 million (at a discounted price of little more than US$1 million) (Dunne, 1989).

Such arrangements at first sight seem attractive and promising. Debt pressures that might otherwise have contributed to forest destruction are converted into a means of conservation. In addition, the international dimension of the value of the tropical forest, especially in terms of species conservation, is reflected by the contribution from developed countries. In a sense these countries are paying for conservation under the arrangements. The burden faced by the developing country in bearing the costs of conservation and foregoing the possible benefits of forest conversion is partly lifted. It remains to be seen how effective the conservation measures will be, and much may depend on the local infrastructure, and how well developed it is as a framework for effective management. Clearly it is very difficult to secure any guarantee that the agreements will be kept permanently. It is also true that the scale of 'debt-for-nature' arrangements is tiny in relation both to debt and to the extent of forest thus protected. For example, the sums involved in the case of Bolivia, amounting to some hundreds of thousands of dollars, are trivial in comparison with a foreign debt of US$4 billion. There is also a more fundamental weakness. While it is appropriate that international assistance is provided to conserve a resource of international value (such as plant and animal species), there is also at the same time the problem of payment or compensation for conservation, which, arguably, should be regarded as a normal form of management. This problem has been encountered on a small scale in a different setting in Britain, where land occupiers may be paid for *not* damaging the conservation interest of certain defined sites. Whilt it is appropriate that compensation or payment is offered in return for securing the management of the land in a way preferred by society rather than the occupier, the approach can also have its dangers. It is possible that the controller of the resource, be it a small conservation site or extensive forest, may threaten detrimental use or management unless payment is forthcoming. At least in theory, the pressures on the forest could be increased rather than alleviated by financial measures of this kind.

The emergence of 'debt-for-nature' swaps, alongside the International Tropical Timber Agreement and the Tropical Forestry Action Plan, gives some grounds for optimism. None of these measures is likely to be a panacea for present problems, but each represents the translation of international concern about the fate of the tropical forest into at least some kind of action. Past periods of forest destruction and degradation neither gave rise to the level of concern that has been focused on the tropical forest, nor experienced international attempts to curb the devastation. It remains to be seen how effective such measures may be, and to what extent they, and the international concern that they manifest, can hasten the transition of tropical forest trends to conditions of greater stability.

9 PEOPLE AND POLICIES

In this last chapter the focus falls on the social and political background to the use of the forest resource. Initially the popular perception of forest issues is considered as a basis for reviewing forest policies and their formulation. A number of themes emerge, including the general lack of involvement of the population at large in decisions about forest management, the roles of forests in social and economic development, and the formulation and significance of forest policies.

People and forest issues

Throughout history the forest has been a resource of primary importance to large numbers of people. Management and control of the forest, however, have usually been in the hands of a relatively few individuals, and the people of a country, for example, have rarely been consulted directly on how they would wish their forest resource to be used. As forestry has developed in technical terms, there has been a tendency for decisions about forest management to be seen as the prerogative of professionally trained foresters. This tendency has extended to decisions about what the forests should be used for as well as how they should be managed. Forestry issues have seldom occupied leading positions on the political agenda, and usually have been overshadowed by concerns such as economic policy, defence or agricultural matters. Furthermore, national policy-making has been prone to 'capture' by special interest groups, such as the forest-products industry or forest owners (e.g. Davis, 1984), and the views of members of such groups have often had a disproportionate influence compared with those of the rest of the population.

Popular opinion and forest management

As Chapter 1 indicates, the fate of the world forest resource is a major popular issue of the day, at least in the developed world. Around one-third of the population in the European Community, for example, appear to be concerned about it. Much of this concern is directed at the tropical rain forest, which has been promoted as a major issue by a number of international environmental groups. It also extends, in some countries at

Table 9.1 Forest issues and public opinion in Canada

(Percentage of respondents)	'Companies should be free to harvest without government regulation'	'Chemicals such as pesticides are necessary for taking care of forests'	'In recent years more trees were cut down compared to the number of trees planted'*	'The forests should not be exploited economically at all
Agree strongly	4	12	35	18
Agree somewhat	5	46	31	20
Disagree somewhat	17	24	16	39
Disagree strongly	73	15	6	20
Don't know	1	3	12	3

* 22 per cent of cut was replanted or reseeded in period 1976–80.

Based on survey of sample of 1960 respondents, 1981.

Source: Statistics Canada (1986)

least, to concern over domestic forest issues. This concern embraces, in varying proportions, environmental questions and issues such as control of the resource and the provision of employment and other social and economic benefits from it. Broadly-based surveys of popular attitudes to the forest and its management are conspicuous mainly by their absence, but one large-scale investigation in a country with huge forest resources – Canada – has yielded interesting results, which are summarised in Table 9.1.

One of the features emerging from the table is the apparent strength of feeling that Canadian forests should not be exploited at all. The forest-products industry is a major sector of the Canadian economy, and Canadian forests have a social and economic importance far greater than in most other countries. Yet a very substantial minority, amounting to 38 per cent of the people questioned, agreed strongly or 'somewhat' with the proposition that 'The forests should not be exploited economically at all'. Presumably this section of the population viewed the forest primarily as a non-material resource, of value for recreation, wildlife conservation and wilderness qualities rather than as a source of timber. The prominence of the 'non-exploitation' view as reported in this survey contrasts with the recent perception that 'within the general public [in Canada] there exists a view, undiminished by the years, that there are plenty of forestlands to be exploited and that technology will somehow keep on improving accessibility, growing methods and utilization' (Gillis and Roach, 1986, p. 259). Perhaps policy-makers perceive public attitudes on such issues inaccurately, and unless specific and particular issues emerge to provide foci for public attitudes to be expressed, will continue to base their policies on such misperceptions. It is encouraging, however, that *A national forest sector strategy for Canada* recommends that the forest sector should encourage public participation in developing the objectives for forest management (Canadian Council of Forest Ministers, 1987).

Another striking feature is the strength of opinion about the need for regulation of forest use. Of the persons questions in the survey, 90 per cent disagreed with the view that 'Companies should be free to harvest our forests without regulation'. While the resource quality of Canadian forests has not been maintained, at least the forest area has been conserved to a far higher degree than in most countries. It may therefore seem surprising that there should be such an overwhelming support for government regulation of forest harvesting.

Responses to the other two statements are perhaps less striking, but it is noteworthy that a substantial body of opinion (39 per cent) disagrees with the view that the use of chemicals is necessary in the forest, while a clear majority accurately perceive that replanting does not match harvesting. More than one-third of the respondents agreed strongly with the statement, and the pattern of response suggests that the population at large had at least a general awareness of the forest trends in this respect. The table does not indicate directly whether this awareness is matched by concern, but the high proportion agreeing 'strongly' may suggest that concern is indeed present.

Three important conclusions may be surmised, if not logically deduced, from Table 9.1. First and on the basis of the admittedly limited evidence, it seems that the population at large accurately perceives the nature of basic characteristics such as the ratio of cutting to planting. If this is indeed so, then the argument that the population in general has neither an awareness of nor interest in forest issues in untenable. In turn, the view that forest issues are matters to be reserved for professional and technical personnel is untenable. Second, there is strong support for public or government regulation of the use of the forest. Third, almost two-fifths of the population consider that the forests should not be exploited economically *at all*. Presumably a larger proportion place value or utility on non-consumptive uses of the forests. In short, popular demand for the 'post-industrial forest' appears to be running ahead of any actual shift in the nature of use and management of the forest, and professional forest managers and policy formulators may be lagging far behind that demand.

Whilst it would be wrong to place too great emphasis on the results of one survey in one country, the indications they provide are of considerable interest. They deserve further testing in other countries, both in the developed world where many forests may be in transition from the 'industrial' to 'post-industrial' stages, and in the developing world where the transition is more likely to be from 'pre-industrial' to 'industrial', and where a completely different set of public opinions may be encountered.

The fragmentary evidence that is available suggests that Canadian perceptions are not atypical, at least of the developed world. For example, the proportions of respondents indicating concern about the use of insecticides and pesticides in American forests in the early 1980s were respectively 37 and 36 per cent (Hendee, 1982) – figures comparable with those from Canada. Hendee concluded that the public distrusts many of the methods used by the forestry profession, and in particular considers that forestry managers fail to consider properly the non-commodity, environmental and human aspects of forestry.

Specific issues: clear-cutting and native forests
Clear-cutting, with its historical associations with destructive exploitation, is one particular manifestation of conflict over forest resource values. According to Hendee, it was identified by 43 per cent of respondents as subject to widespread abuse. Clear-cutting has been a major source of conflict in the United States, resulting in court action between conservation interests and the US Forest Service, which was perceived by the former as giving priority to timber production (e.g. Bonnicksen, 1982; Culhane and Friesema, 1979). In Australia clear-cutting has attracted opposition even when used within ecologically based regimes for the management of fire-climax species, and followed by even-aged regeneration (Bartlett, 1988).

In the United States, the clear-cutting issue that came to a head in national forests in West Virgina and Montana in the late 1960s and early 1970s gave rise to the most widespread discussion of forest management since the beginning of the century (Dana and Fairfax, 1980). Whereas in the early 1900s there was widespread public support for government management of forest resources, the US Forest Service was now seen as being excessively influenced by the timber industry, and as neglecting its multiple-use mandate. Clear-cutting symbolised a perceived overemphasis on timber production and underemphasis on other products and services. Eventually limits were imposed on the areal extent of individual clear-cuts, and these maximum sizes varied according to forest location.

Another specific issue, which perhaps emerges more widely around the world, is the fate of native forests (and their replacement in some instances with plantations). This issue is epitomised by the case of the California redwoods. Since the late nineteenth century, the preservation of some of these woods was vigorously advocated, in the face of threats from logging. The preservation movement continued through the twentieth century, culminating in the 1970s with extensive purchases of surviving redwoods stands for preservation. By then, however, most of the old redwoods had disappeared, except for the few per cent protected in public parks (Schrepfer, 1983).

This issue is not confined to North America. In Australia, for example, a survey of 5,000 members of the Australian Conservation Foundation showed native forests to be seen as the top priority for action, amongst a list of eighteen environment issues (Florence, 1983). In the same country, intense controversy has been generated by a policy of expanding wood production from native forest areas, with the consequence of severely modifying the native forests or replacing them completely with plantations. In the course of the sometimes bitter conflict between the holders of different resource values, the public were not consulted, and indeed it was alleged that conversion plans were kept secret (Routley and Routley, 1974). It was alleged by the same authors that the role of the forest service was primarily as a servant of the wood-using industry, and that non-commodity values are generally overlooked or discounted by the forestry 'establishment'. In support of this view, they calculated that over 80 per cent of the articles in the journal *Australian Foresty* between 1956 and 1971 had been solely concerned with wood production or associated matters, and that only 2 per cent were on aspects of forest ecology not directly affecting wood production.

Whilst the native-forest issue may have generated more heat in countries such as Australia and New Zealand than in many other parts of the world, the basic nature of the conflict, lack of consultation with the public and perceived orientation of the forestry profession towards wood production are common to many other parts of the developed world. It remains to be seen whether native-forest issues develop domestically (as opposed to internationally) to the same extent or intensity in developing countries as they have done in much of the developed world.

Popular opinion: the transition to the 'post-industrial' forest

Many native forests remain under public ownership, and therefore few obstacles might be expected to impede their transition towards 'post-industrial' status. Indeed concrete indicators of this transition exist, including for example the designation of areas as national parks or designated wilderness. In the United States, the net transfer (or 'loss') of timberland to non-timber purposes has averaged around 2 million hectares per decade in recent times (Bonnicksen, 1982).

Where forests are under private ownership, the transition might be expected to be less smooth, and the relevance of popular opinion might be thought to be less direct. In practice, however, increasing state influence has been brought to bear by means of a combination of regulation and incentives such as grants (Chapter 5). The public is consulted as seldom over the nature of these influences as on the management of forests on public land, but environmental interest groups may have considerable effect on the policy objectives underlying these measures. For example, environmentalist concern about the dwindling broad-leaved forests in Britain in the early 1980s led to the emergence of a new broad-leaved policy encompassing favourable planting grants and presumptions against the 'coniferisation' of existing broad-leaved woodlands. In this and most other comparable cases, however, the outcome was the result of campaigning by interest groups, rather than the product of any systematic attempt to base policy on public opinion. It was concluded by Douglas (1983) that forest services in developing countries are highly conservative and traditional, lacking mechanisms for meaningful reference to the broader economic and political perspectives of society. Perhaps his conclusion also has some validity in the developed world.

In the classical 'industrial' forest, policy objectives are solely or primarily utilitarian. The classical view was well expressed by the first director of what was to become the US Forest Service: 'The main service, the principle object . . . has nothing to do with beauty or pleasure. It is not, except incidentally, an object of aesthetics, but an object of economics'

(Fernow, 1896, quoted in Kennedy, 1981). Such views are, of course, deplored by environmental interest groups and perhaps by the wider public in many countries today. Nevertheless, powerful inertial factors have retarded their modification. One of these was (and is) the difficulty in incorporating non-material and non-economic values into decision-making. This difficulty was related in turn to a cultural problem: professional foresters, reared in a system in which priority was accorded to timber production, tended to discount concern for outdoor recreation, landscape or (non-game) wildlife as peripheral or as 'weak', emotionally based and generally unprofessional (Kennedy, 1981). Attuned to an utilitarian tradition and lacking clear and direct channels of contact with changing popular attitudes and values, they tended to react defensively at first. In the United States, for example, the Forest Service and the Society of American Foresters either resisted or failed to support legislation such as the Wilderness Act (1964) and the National Environmental Policy Act (1970), despite strong support from Congress. In Australia, most foresters were taken unawares by the vehemence of the criticism levelled at the first proposals to reduce native eucalyptus forests to woodchips for export to Japan. For the foresters the discovery that certain eucalypts were suitable for chipping provided an opportunity for a long-standing dream to convert these 'unproductive' forests into productive ones (Carron, 1979). This opportunity was quite consistent with the traditional 'production' orientation of the profession, though it conflicted head-on with the changing resource values of the day.

According to Kennedy (1985), part of the problem has been that foresters, like engineers and physicians, do not welcome advice and criticism from persons not trained in their discipline. He also considers that many students entering the forestry profession are attracted by the perceived simplicity and tranquillity of the production forest, and that they do not welcome a role as conflict manager adjudicating between different interests and values. Furthermore, many professional foresters have looked upon themselves as the custodians of the community interest in forest management, and as the appropriate judges of where that long-term interest lies (Husch, 1987). In short, the age of the industrial forest fostered an outlook in which objectives, as well as the techniques of management, were assumed to be the prerogative of the professional forester, and in which timber production was paramount. It is understandable, therefore, that the challenge represented by the changing values, aspirations and attitudes of the public should encounter some resistance, and hence that obstacles should be encountered in the transition from the 'industrial' to the 'post-industrial' forest.

Popular opinion: the 'pre-industrial' and 'industrial' forest

Popular opinion may play a limited part in forest management in the developed world, but it has nevertheless been successful in effecting a partial transition from the 'industrial' to the 'post-industrial' forest.

By comparison, it has probably had less effect in the developing world. The transition from the 'pre-industrial' forest, with communal control and use of the forest for a variety of purposes such as production of fuel, food and fodder as well as timber, to the 'industrial' forest with external control and an emphasis mainly or wholly on timber production, is often abrupt. It is more often imposed on local people than sought by them. The opinions of local people are rarely taken into account, and in less sophisticated societies it is more difficult for interest groups to form and function effectively.

As Chapter 5 shows, this transition has frequently met with opposition, and it (or aspects of it) have often had persistent, long-term effects. One of these is resistance to conservation measures imposed by colonial governments, often with little or no reference to traditional patterns of rights and use. Post-independence governments in Africa, for example, have found it difficult to overcome these negative perceptions (e.g. Anderson, 1987). Another example is the case of India where resistance has been manifested in the form of forest *satyagraha*. The Chipko movement that evolved in the early 1970s was a reaction against the management and use of forests for wood production to supply non-local needs. Its demand for the Himalayan forests to be seen as protection rather than production forests was ultimately at least partly successful (e.g. Bandyopadhyay and Shiva, 1987; Shiva and Bandyopadhyay, 1988). Examples of successful attempts to halt the transition to the 'industrial' forest have been rare, but the last decade has seen the emergence of social or community forests as alternatives. Here the emphasis of production is on fuelwood, poles and various other 'minor' products, rather than on industrial wood.

During the 1950s and 1960s, many national forest services concentrated on industrial forestry in accordance with theories and policies of industry-led development, with a corresponding neglect of other aspects of forest use and management. This orientation is unsurprising: many post-independence national forest services were descended from former colonial services, and in addition many of their personnel were trained and educated in Western institutions. The forestry schools in many of these institutions were probably strongly geared towards timber production, and indeed many of them were probably strongly influenced by timber companies through grants and other means. In short, the Western, 'industrial' view of the forest was widely inculcated. Furthermore, the attempted segregation of land uses, as commonly practised in temperate-zone forestry, has often led to detrimental effects and confrontation in the tropics (von Maydell, 1985). Eventually in the 1970s widespread interest emerged in agro-forestry in reaction to this.

By the 1970s the growing realisation of the importance of fuelwood and other non-industrial products led to growing interest in social and community forestry. In the view of Kennedy (1985), who is himself a forester, the fact that the concept of social forestry had to be invented in order to emphasise broad and varied social needs is an indictment of the narrow value focus of 'traditional' forestry and its close association with wood production and market prices. In addition, there is the problem of social friction or conflict arising from the fact that the forester has had both an industrial orientation and an association with powerful industrial or landed interests, rather than with the local population. A widely held view is that 'down through the ages, the forester has usually been looked upon as the gendarme of landed property and rich forest owners' (Westoby, 1989, p. 80), and that forest administrators have often been insensitive to the needs of local communities (Husch, 1987). This view is largely shared by Filius (1986, p. 191): 'The needs of the local people have almost always been ignored in forest planning. This has mainly been oriented towards the prime or classical goal of forestry, which is the production of industrial wood.' He goes on to emphasise that the socio-economic and cultural systems of the local population must be studied if social forestry is to be successful, and not only physical site characteristics and the wood market.

The outstanding and oft-quoted example of successful community forestry is the Republic of Korea (Chapter 6). Here more than 1 million hectares of fruit, fuel and timber trees were planted in five years in the 1970s by a network of over 20,000 village forest co-operatives supported by the government, which provided legislation to make land available, as well as free planting stock and extension services (Arnold, 1987b). The resulting forests to some extent resemble typical 'pre-industrial' forests, with community involvement and multi-purpose use, but they are of course man-made rather than natural and their creation was to a considerable extent a 'top down' rather than 'bottom up' process. Whilst some success was subsequently achieved with this style of community forestry in a few other countries such as Nepal, collective approaches of this kind generally have enjoyed at the best only slow progress. Projects involving individual rather than group approaches have often been found to enjoy greater success. Perhaps the re-creation of the 'pre-industrial' forest in its typical, communally-controlled form, can be achieved only rarely, irrespective of whether the driving force is government or people. If the forest resource under communal control has almost disappeared in a locality it is not surprising that it is difficult to re-establish it in that original form.

The transition from the 'industrial' to the 'post-industrial' phase may be driven by public opinion and that from the 'pre-industrial' to the 'industrial' stage is usually imposed by government or external would-be exploiters of the timber resource. The re-establishment of 'pre-industrial' forests seems to require strong external stimuli such as government or aid agency. It remains to be seen whether direct transitions from 'pre-industrial' to 'post-industrial' stages will occur widely. If they can and do, then perhaps far more of the tropical forest will survive than if the transition can be effected only through the intermediate stage of the 'industrial' forest. Perhaps an encouraging, if very tentative indicator is the nationwide logging ban imposed in Thailand in 1989, imposed in response to a combination of pressures from rural villagers, conservationists, and widespread public reaction against a series of damaging mudslides perceived to be related to deforestation (Lohmann, 1989).

Forests and employment

One of the main foci of public interest in forests, and in some national forest policies, is in the employment they offer either directly or in wood-using industry. Forest employment is widely seen as a significant issue both in countries with extensive forest resources, and in those with continuing afforestation programmes. In comparison with the attention focused on it, however, forest employment is relatively limited in scale. It also suffers from a number of characteristics that limit its usefulness as a means of encouraging rural development. Nevertheless, the creation of employment is identified by FAO (1986d) as one of the main contributions that forest industries can make to socio-economic development. It goes on to assert that small-scale forest industries provide the principal employment for between 20 and 30 per cent of the rural labour force in many developing countries.

On the national scale, the contribution of forests and forest-based industries to total employment is usually very much less. In many countries it amounts to only 2 per cent or less. It is under 5 per cent even in most countries with extensive forest resources and well-developed forest industries. In the United States, for example, the proportion of employment attributed to timber in the 1970s was 4 per cent of all civilian employment, and of this proportion only 10 per cent related to timber management and harvesting (USDA, 1982). The remainder was in primary and secondary manufacturing (13 and 27 per cent respectively), construction (24 per cent) and transport and marketing (26 per cent). In Chile, where there has been a rapid growth of a plantation-based forest industry in recent years, forest-based activities (including transport) employ 3 per cent of the active population (Solbrig, 1984). The overall proportion is similar in Malaysia, which has one of the most highly developed forest industries in the developing world. Here the forest sector absorbs only 3 per cent of the total labour force, and logging accounts for less than one-third of that proportion (Rauf, 1983). Small as the overall contribution is, however, it has grown markedly in Malaysia as the forest industry has developed, with an increase of 46 per cent occurring between 1972 and 1976 (Kumar, 1986). On the other hand the forest-dependent labour force has generally declined through time as forest operations have become increasingly mechanised. In Canada, for example, almost half of the adult male population were involved in the timber and lumber industry in the late nineteenth century (Gillis and Roach, 1986), while now only 7 per cent of the labour force is forest-dependent (Environment Canada, 1989). The long-term trend is almost invariably and inevitably downwards, because mechanisation and improvements in labour productivity mean loss of employment after the stage of maximum sustainable yield has been reached. In Sweden, for example, forest-sector employment reached a peak at the end of the 1930s. Since then, it has decreased at a rate of around 2 per cent per annum, although wood removals increased by about 1 per cent per year until the early 1970s (Lönnstadt, 1984).

The mechanisation of forest operations and decreasing labour requirements pose serious problems in areas where the economy is poorly diversified and opportunities for alternative employment are few. Forest-based employment is often of greatest relative importance in such areas. Ever-increasing areas of forest are required to maintain or provide one job, and conflicts arise between the wish to manage the forest on a sustained-yield basis and the desire to maintain stability of employment in the forest and in wood-using industries. These problems are of long standing in Scandinavia and parts of North America. In addition in countries such as Canada current forest management and harvesting practices threaten long-term sustainability of production and hence of employment, and in addition their environmental effects may adversely interact with employment in other resource sectors such as fisheries (Environment Canada, 1989). Similar problems are likely to become increasingly prominent in the developing world. Even if the worst excesses of destructive exploitation, and of resulting instability of communities, are avoided, it may still be difficult to reconcile social, commercial and sustained-yield objectives.

In addition to the secular trend of decreasing demand for labour, problems are also caused by cyclical fluctuations in demand for timber. In order to help to stabilise logging-dependent communities during periods of downturn in demand, timber sales from national forests have at times been maintained by the US Forest Service (e.g. Repetto, 1988). This practice may, in turn, merely destabilise logging activity on private forests.

There is a long tradition of using mobile or transient labour in the forest, rather than settled workers. In many parts of the developed world today, as in North America in the past, this labour is housed in camps rather than in permanent communities. Such a mode of labour is understandable in terms of cyclical exploitation of the forest resource, but it can mean that few social and economic benefits accrue locally. For example, one study in East Kalimantan in Indonesia revealed that only 12 per cent of the total jobs provided in logging camps were taken by local people, and that local foods accounted for only 5 per cent of camp expenditures on consumable goods (Kartawinata et al., 1981). In short, few benefits from logging were retained locally. Furthermore, the overall intensity of employment creation is very limited: in Indonesia, for example, 53 hectares were logged for each job created, including jobs in industrial processing (Repetto, 1988).

Secular changes in labour requirements and fluctuating demand depending on the age or stage of development of the local forest are world-wide problems that impair the usefulness of the contribution that the forest can make to socio-economic development. They limit that contribution in the developed and developing worlds alike, as they do irrespective of whether the forest is a natural one, whether it has been managed for many decades, or whether it is a recently established plantation.

The initial stages in establishing plantations in countries where the forest resource is expanding through afforestation have a relative high labour demand for ground preparation and planting. Thereafter the need for labour drops to very low levels, and remains there until thinning begins or clear-felling occurs. Peatland afforestation in Ireland, for example, typically requires seven workers per thousand hectares during years 1–5, but only one during years 6–17 (Gallagher and Gillespie, 1984). Such a strongly fluctuating requirement does not fit well with the characteristics of typical areas of afforestation, which are often remote and lightly populated. Nor does it make a substantial contribution to socio-economic development in such areas in the short term, although in the longer term some benefits may be provided by wood-using industry.

Fluctuating labour requirements associated with afforestation are frequently met by mobile squads or migrant workers rather than local residents. In addition to providing limited or minimal local benefits, such patterns of provision sometimes appear to lead to social friction. A rise in petty crime, for example, is reported from Northland, New Zealand (Farnsworth, 1983). On the other hand, the same author indicates that forest development programmes there have helped to arrest and reverse trends of rural depopulation, and have led to greater diversity of community structure and higher proportions of young married couples in local communities. In contrast, afforestation has apparently not helped to stem rural depopulation in areas such as North Wales (Johnson and Price, 1987).

Although labour requirements may fluctuate, they are often at least as great as for previous or alternative land uses. In Otago in South Island, New Zealand, for example, direct employment in forestry and pastoral farming is similar, but when downstream employment is included, forestry employs more than four times as many workers per unit area as does agriculture (Aldwell and Whyte, 1984).

Whilst forestry may have employment densities similar to or higher than those in pastoral farming, the conversion of land to forest plantations by no means always results in increases in employment. In Portugal, for example, employment densities in eucalyptus plantations are lower than in previous land uses involving olive groves and vineyards: the creation of 5,000 hectares of plantation means a loss of 2,000 man-years of employment (Kardell et al., 1986). Similarly, while a typical small farm in Latin America can sustain several labourers, a typical 100-hectare eucalyptus plantation provides jobs for only two or three (Joyce, 1988).

Regardless of whether forests or alternative land uses provide more employment, there appears to be a widespread tendency to overestimate the number of jobs that forestry and forest-products industries can provide. Employment potential is frequently an important element in forest policies or in justifying individual forest projects, and exaggerated or over-optimistic estimates have often been made. For example, it was forecast in the early 1970s that employment in forestry and the wood industry in Australia would rise substantially: in fact it has declined (Dargavel,1982). In Scotland the chief minister in promoting a programme of forest expansion in the 1940s looked forward to a day when forestry would employ workers as many as agriculture and coal-mining (around 150,000) (Johnston, 1952). In fact it now employs little more than 10,000.

Advocates of forestry expansion have frequently used arguments of social and environmental benefits in support of their case. Objectives incorporating these benefits have often been included in national forestry policies and programmes. Unfortunately the way in which the expansion has been implemented or carried out has not always meant that the benefits have materialised in the ways expected. This in turn has on occasion led to disappointment and disillusionment.

Forests and development

This disappointment and disillusionment have been felt at a variety of scales, ranging from local projects to the international level. Nowhere are they better reflected than in the changing views of J.C. Westoby, who was a forestry official in FAO. These changing views are chronicled in a series of papers and books published between the early 1960s and the 1980s, culminating in the publication of his collected papers under the title of *The purpose of forests: follies of development* (Westoby, 1987). Initially, both he and FAO believed that forest industries in the developing countries could look forward to very bright prospects. In terms of resource endowment and environmental potential they were well placed to meet the growing timber needs of the developed world. Linkages between the forest sector and other industries and other branches of the economy would mean that the sector could make a special contribution to the overall development process. In short, the forest sector deserved special consideration in development strategy: 'industrialization based on the forest can both contribute to and promote the general economic development process' (Westoby, 1962, p. 200).

By 1973, doubts were creeping in: 'progress has not been as rapid as we thought we had a right to expect' (Westoby, 1987, p. 207), and with them the realisation that the world's industrial wood needs could be met from plantations which would amount to only a tiny percentage of the world forest cover. By 1978 the gloom was deepening: 'as yet, forest industries have made little or no contribution to socio-economic development in the underdeveloped world – certainly not the significant contribution that was envisaged from them a couple of decades ago' (p. 246). By this time he had concluded that forest development projects, like parallel developments in food and agriculture, were geared primarily to the needs of the developed world, and that they thus served to promote socio-economic *under*development. According to Westoby, the forests in developing countries and in tropical latitudes were exploited primarily for the benefit of the developed world, and the 'development establishment' (including international agencies) had assisted in this process or colluded with it. In his view, international aid in forestry has helped to identify, for the benefit of foreign capital, forest resources suitable for exploitation, and it has helped some irresponsible governments to alienate and eliminate substantial parts of their forest-resource endowment. In particular, almost every country now had a forest service, but many forest services in developing countries were woefully understaffed and underpaid: 'because they exist, exploitation is facilitated; because they are weak, exploitation is not controlled'

(p. 248). He went on to conclude: 'the basic forest products needs of the peoples of the underdeveloped world are further from being satisfied than ever. . . . The famous multiplier effects are missing. Few new poles of development have been created' (p. 248).

Linkages between the forestry sector and other parts of the economy proved harder to forge than had been expected. Policy-makers have usually overestimated employment benefits from forest-based industries, as they have from afforestation programmes, and benefits in terms of regional development have also been overestimated (e.g. Repetto and Gillis, 1988). In short, the bright hopes of the 1950s and 1960s that the forest resources of developing countries could offer a springboard to socio-economic development have not been fulfilled. The same phases of destructive exploitation that characterised the use of the forest resource in eighteenth-century Russia and nineteenth-century North America have all too often been repeated, and perhaps even facilitated or promoted under the guise of development aid. Local resource values have been submerged under those of the developed world: the 'pre-industrial' forest has given way to the 'industrial' forest in many areas, and to one that has been rapidly degraded.

In a few developing countries the forestry sector has made a significant contribution to socio-economic development. One example is Malaysia, where the forestry sector has made significant contributions in both overall development and in terms of distributing the benefits of this development (Douglas, 1983). In peninsular Malaysia, forest utilisation has been relatively well integrated with rural development and the growth of a export-oriented processing sector. Value is added through sawmilling and plywood manufacture, and government has attempted to control rates of harvesting, to improve management and utilisation, and to expand planta-tions. The scene there does not quite conform to the gloomy picture or model sketched by Westoby, nor does it wholly do so in the case of Sabah and Sarawak. Whilst the emphasis in these areas is still on logs (rather than on processed products), control of forest clearing and of land allocation for agriculture has been retained by the Malaysian government, although this has not prevented conflict with indigenous peoples (Chapter 5). The rate of growth of forest-products exports during the 1960s surprised even government economic planners, and by the mid-1980s the forestry sector contributed around 5 per cent of Gross Domestic Product compared with under 3 per cent in 1960 (Kumar, 1986). Douglas (1983) concludes that the overall performance of the forestry sector can be interpreted in a favourable light because control over forest exploitation has been main-tained, rural development has to some extent been achieved, and forestry-industry activities have been specialised in areas of comparative advantage.

Such examples, however, are rare, and do not invalidate the Westoby view. Until the mid to late 1970s, most of the development effort was focused on large-scale industrial forestry. With widespread disenchant-ment about the results of such effort, attention then began to swing towards a recognition of the importance of forestry in rural (as opposed to industrial) development (e.g. Guess, 1981). With this shift came a re-evaluation of the financial characteristics of forest projects geared to objectives of rural development rather than to wood-using industry, and with it new problems of funding and of co-ordinating the various institutions that provide the infrastructure within which the projects can be carried out. This shift is reflected in the dramatic change in the nature of funding of forestry projects by the World Bank. Prior to 1977, around 85 per cent of funding from this source went to industrial aspects of wood production and utilisation: only four out of seventeen projects funded between 1953 and 1976 were specifically intended to benefit rural people (World Bank, 1978). Since then the share of a greatly increased volume of funding has fallen to 35 per cent. The other 65 per cent is now allocated to projects concerned with fuelwood and timber for domestic (as opposed to industrial) use, environmental functions, rural development, and the management of natural forest ecosystems (e.g. Brünig, 1984). Over half of the forty projects in the Bank's forward lending programme at the end of the 1970s were regarded by it as 'people-oriented' as opposed to 'industry-oriented' (World Bank, 1978, p. 9).

While the significance of involvement of bodies such as the World Bank in relation to forest destruction and forest conservation is debatable (Chapter 8), there is little doubt that some reorientation away from industrial forestry projects has occurred.

The role of forest policy

The form and content of forest policy are enormously variable. Forest laws and institutional arrangements have a bewildering complexity and diversity. In some countries, specific laws and codes date back for centuries, relating for example to matters such as ownership and control (Chapter 5). Many of them relate, literally, to the trees rather than to the forests, and in many countries they have been added sporadically and incrementally. They are often fragmentary and piecemeal, lacking integration into coherent policies. Few countries have coherent, consistent and comprehensive policies, and where such policies do exist they are almost invariably the product of the twentieth century. The nature and content of forest policies may reflect something of the character of the state. This character and role are of fundamental importance. Whilst ideally the state may function as the trustee of its peoples, and manage the forest and other resources on their behalf, in practice it has often functioned in a way favourable to sectional interests. In varying degrees it still does so. A popular (*sensu stricto*) basis to forest policy has generally been lacking.

Forest policy seems at first sight to be the key to effective management of the resource. It seems to be self-evident that the objectives of the management of the forest resource need to be clearly defined, and effective means of achieving them require to be identified. Yet many countries, including large countries such as Canada and Australia, have found great difficulty in formulating and implementing forest policies. During the 1970s, the Seventh and Eighth World Forestry Congresses urged that all countries devise and declare national forest policies, and that existing policies be updated. By no means all countries yet have forest policies, and '. . . there is scarcely a country which has a formal, thought-out and declared forest policy' (Westoby, 1989, p. 215).

If they exist at all, national forest policies are often characterised by vagueness, confusion, or uncertainty. They may attract much attention, but less agreement and even less commitment. In a paper entitled 'National forest policy – myth, manifesto, mandate or mandala?', Carron (1983) chronicles the sorry saga of national forest policy in Australia, which has extended over a period of more than seventy years. He concludes:

> Anyone reading the mass of material on and around the subject might well be pardoned for not being sure whether we have one: whether we had one but don't have it any longer; whether we think it would be nice to have one but it isn't practicable. (p. 261)

It is true that particular problems are encountered in federal countries such as Australia (and many others including Malaysia, Canada and the United States). Different provinces or states pursue different policies: for example, in Australia, New South Wales allows woodchipping for export, while Victoria does not, and Tasmania places tight controls on the management of private forests while the other states do not (Bartlett, 1988). And the Commonwealth government is keen to protect the Queensland rain forest, while the state government proposes to have it logged on a sustained-yield basis (MacDonald, 1989). Under such conditions, broad forest strategies, rather than precise national policies, may be the most that can be expected.

This Australian example reflects the peculiar problems faced by federal countries, as well as the common and basic problems of will, commitment and agreement. It illustrates something of the general problem that arises from the distribution of power between different levels of government. This problem is experienced in unitary as well as federal countries, and difficulties in formulating national policy are encountered under both types of political structure. These difficulties include, amongst many others, the position of forestry issues on the political agenda, and the simultaneous requirement for long-term consistency in defining policy objectives and for flexibility in the face of changing pressures and concerns. Policy statements are sometimes regarded as stereotyped and irrelevant, because of their rigidity and failure to keep pace with changing conditions. It is sometimes argued that policy-making should become a continual process in order to keep pace with changing conditions (e.g. Gane, 1983). If too flexible, on the other hand, they may be overwhelmed or overshadowed by emphemeral or transient issues, and may fail to convey the impression of long-term commitment that forest management requires.

Part of the problem is that forestry issues have rarely had a sufficient degree of immediacy or urgency to ensure them a high priority on the political agenda. Even today, when interest and concern are widespread, it does not necessarily follow that forestry issues are the leading concerns: matters such as defence or social policy are likely to occupy more prominent positions in the agenda. Forestry issues rarely emerge prominently at general elections, and when they do attract much attention it may be at local or regional rather than national levels, or from relatively small interest groups rather than the population at large. Major influences, disproportionate to the numerical strength of the membership involved, may be exerted by groups representing forest-industry and environmental interests in particular.

The evolution of policy

It seems that forest policy rarely evolves gradually in response to popular views. Instead, it is sometimes devised rapidly by government in the face of a particular problem or crisis. The classic example is the case of British forest policy, which was largely non-existent until the crisis years of the First World War brought home the disadvantages of dependence on timber imports. Policies devised in this way are likely to have simple, single, well-defined objectives, and they are the direct product of government rather than the reflection of popular interest or concern. The urgency and immediacy of such a crisis may very effectively focus the attention of government on an otherwise neglected issue, and may lead to the general acceptance of the idea of a national policy.

Its origins will obviously determine the initial nature of a policy, but inertia may ensure that the original policy objectives and instruments persist while conditions and circumstances change. It has been suggested, for example, that the 'objectives of official forest management in post-Independence India have not [yet] been liberated from colonial legacies' (Shiva et al., 1985).

Subsequent crises – whether financial, military or political – may lead to radical revision of the original policy, but unless such crises arise any change is likely to be minor and incremental. Pressure from interest groups or other branches of government may result in adjustments, and new objectives may be added or the priorities of existing ones revised. In some instances new objectives are simply added to the existing ones without any clear indication of priorities, and without the addition of new instruments. As a result, the policies become increasingly complex, and even those charged with implementing them may lack clear direction of priorities. The principle of providing at least one policy instrument for each policy objective is probably ignored more often than it is honoured.

The origin and content of forest policies depend on a variety of factors including political will and the extent of the forest resource. In countries where the forest resource has largely disappeared, the stimulus of war or economic crisis may give rise to a policy geared to expanding the forest estate. In well-wooded countries, on the other hand, the gradual shrinking of the forest resource may lack the immediacy or urgency of such a crisis. When a policy is eventually devised, it is likely to be concerned initially with the protection of the resource, especially against threats such as fire. The combination of different degrees of resource endowment, different political systems and different levels of development mean that the search for common characteristics of forest policies, on the global scale, is at best likely to be only partly successful. Nevertheless, a number of common features can be identified.

Most forest policies refer to goals of timber production, as well as to environmental and social objectives. In many instances concern about the availability of timber led to the initial formulation or reformulation of forest policy, and in some cases to the setting-up of a state forestry service. During the seventeenth-century reign of Louis XIV, for example, it was reported that 'la forêt de France est en mauvais état' (ONF, 1966, p.8), despite attempts dating back to at least the fourteenth century to protect it by means of a forest code and ordinances. Fears about the availability of timber for naval purposes led to the famous ordinance of Colbert in 1669, and the laying of the foundation of modern French forest legislation. Another classic example is the case of the Britain, which embarked on a programme of forest expansion after the First World War: other countries have followed similar courses on the basis of fears that imports will become difficult to obtain in the future, and will become increasingly expensive as timber shortages develop. Increasing self-sufficiency, for reasons of physical or economic security, has been a primary objective in many national policies, and has in particular been the basis on which forest expansion programmes have been advocated.

Timber is one of the very few natural resource commodities to have increased in real price over prolonged periods of several decades, and thus arguments of increasing scarcity cannot be discounted. Furthermore, real wood shortages have already been encountered in many countries, especially in the more arid parts of the world. Nevertheless, the shortages predicted at various times in countries as diverse as the United States, Britain, Australia and New Zealand have not materialised. In the case of Britain, arguments of increasing scarcity, and hence rising prices, were used by the state forest service as recently as the 1970s in support of continued forest expansion (Forestry Commission, 1977). In the case of Australia, Carron (1980) notes that the 'scarcity' argument has been used for seventy years without the prediction coming to pass. Most 'scarcity' arguments have been directed at industrial wood: few (at least until recently) have been directed at fuelwood, where paradoxically real and acute shortages have been experienced in various parts of the world, including much of Britain by the seventeenth century and many parts of the tropics today. Perhaps the emphasis on industrial wood and the relative neglect of fuelwood simply reflects an 'industrial' bias in the forestry profession and in forestry policies.

Self-sufficiency or adequacy of timber reserves for emergency use are impermanent goals. In the case of Australia, for example, forest expansion during the 1960s and early 1970s was geared to self-sufficiency, but with a lowering of population estimates for the end of the century and beyond, demand estimates were revised downwards. The question then arose of whether planting rates should be reduced, or whether planting should be aimed at the export market (Hanson, 1980). It has been suggested that the level of uncertainty about future demand for timber has increased in recent years (Haynes and Adams, 1983; Adams and Haynes, 1985). If so, the translation of policy objectives into areal requirements may become increasingly difficult. In Britain, the advent of nuclear warfare meant that the original objective of building up a strategic reserve of timber for use during war was becoming irrelevant. This change did not, however, lead to a radical revision of the planting programme. Expansion continued, on the basis of economic strategy. In short, planting programmes can achieve a momentum that outlives the conditions in which they were established, and forest expansion may become a goal in its own right.

While increasing timber production through expansion of the forest area is a major theme in countries such as Britain, Ireland and New Zealand, it may also be an important issue in countries which are well endowed with forest resources. In some developed countries, private forest owners have little interest in maximising wood production. The needs of forest-products industries have meant that sub-maximal production from private forests has emerged as a particular issue to which policy is directed (for the example of Finland, see Vehkamaki, 1986). In many developing countries, stated or unstated policy has been focused on increasing timber production from natural forests in the hope that socio-economic development would be fostered (see p. 279).

Timber production is therefore usually a central or primary objective in national forestry policies. In addition, social objectives are frequently included, and these may be given special emphasis at certain times and in certain areas. Afforestation has often been viewed as a means of providing employment. A strong regional dimension is sometimes apparent, and forest expansion or development may be justified for social reasons even when the economic case for it is doubtful. It has been suggested that the forest service in New Zealand has suffered from being used as a social agency in providing employment (Willis and Kirby, 1987). Similar sentiments are widely held, if less directly expressed, elsewhere, and reflect something of the tension that arises when multiple objectives are pursued. The same authors refer to the repeated calls to the forest service in New Zealand to repair the environmental damage caused by burning and over-grazing. This is but one aspect of the environmental objectives that are incorporated in many national policies, especially since the 1970s (e.g. Schmithusen, 1986). Similarly, recreation has been increasingly acknowledged as a policy objective. As indicated in Chapter 6, various objectives were added incrementally to the management of state forests in New Zealand between the 1950s and the 1980s, including recreation, nature conservation and landscape conservation (Tilling, 1988). Similarly, recreation was added to the management objectives of state forests in the Netherlands in the 1960s, and nature conservation in the 1970s (Grandjean, 1987). In some countries the emergence of new issues such as the environment has resulted in new management agencies and changing relationships between agencies and divisions. Under such circumstances the integrity and coherence of policies becomes increasingly difficult to maintain.

The typical national forest policy has become more complex through time, and simultaneously has often become less precise and specific. Policy formulation has increasingly become a matter of compromise and of reconciling the views of different interest groups, rather than one of devising blueprints or guidelines for the management and use of the forest resource. Policy statements in the developed world frequently refer to multiple use, for example in the cases of the national forest strategy for Australia, as announced in 1986 (Bartlett, 1988) and in the United States. In the latter, the Multiple Use–Sustained Yield Act of 1960 was as much a compromise as a milestone (see Chapter 5; Cox et al., 1985): whilst it and subsequent legislation such as the National Forest Management Act of 1976 established multiple use as a general principle, many practical problems remained in translating this principle into practice. Multiple use was defined as the management of all the various resources of the national forests, in the combination that would best meet the needs of the American people. Such a definition seems unexceptionable, but it is also vague and lacking in specific criteria. The US Forest Service was left to interpret these definitional terms, and as a guide to decision-making or a standard for measuring performance the act had limited meaning. The bill leading to the act was attacked by the Sierra Club, a major and powerful environmental group. One of the fundamental points of criticism was that foresters were competent to identify resource problems and to propose possible solutions, but *not* to choose between uses (Steen, 1976). The bill contained a list of multiple uses, arranged in alphabetical order. Despite the fact that the order was held to be insignificant, some judicious manipulation is reported to have been undertaken: 'fish and wildlife' became 'wildlife and fish', for example, and 'forage' was translated into 'range' (Dana and Fairfax, 1980). Whatever the accuracy of the allegations and the significance of the reordering may have been, there is in this issue a reminder that the apparent policy as enshrined in law is but the tip of an iceberg: much lies below the surface.

Nevertheless, such legislation is of at least symbolic significance, indicating that the days of the 'industrial' forest, in which timber production was the sole or overwhelmingly dominant function, were over. The broadening of policies to incorporate environmental and recreational elements is perhaps epitomised by the Multiple Use–Sustained Yield Act in the United States, but many other countries demonstrate similar trends, whether or not they are manifested in major legislation.

When policies do evolve through time, they tend to become more complex and more vague: if they fail to evolve, they become increasingly irrelevant. Inertia may be a powerful factor even when evolution appears to occur: the typical pattern of incremental change may be basically too slow to respond to emerging forest issues (e.g. Tikkanen, 1986). Senior officials in forest services may have spent their formative years during periods of different or simpler policies, and unconsciously or otherwise may be strongly influenced by these earlier phases. Furthermore, the addition of new policy objectives (such as environmental and recreational goals), is not always matched by the provision of new instruments.

Therefore the effective policy may differ from the stated policy.

In some instances major differences can exist between policy as stated and as practised. Sometimes there is a simple inability or unwillingness to implement or enforce policy provisions. In Colombia, for example, a permit is required before forest is cleared and there may be a requirement for reforestation, but in practice few landowners observe these regulations and staff and resources are inadequate for enforcement (Green, 1984). Some plans or apparent policies have been dismissed by Westoby (1989) as 'window dressing'. His comments are directed especially towards certain developing countries where forest destruction continues despite the announcement of grandiose plans apparently directed at conserving the forest resource. In his view, such plans and policies are merely designed to mollify international conservationists. Elements of window dressing, however, are not confined to such situations, but extend to developed countries where environmental or recreational objectives are apparently incorporated into policy in order to satisfy interest groups. Whether their incorporation is always followed by changed practice is another matter.

Policy limitations

The gap between rhetoric and reality means that although national forest policies may be necessary for effective management of the forest resource, their existence is unlikely to be a sufficient condition for that management. In addition to the points just discussed, three other factors are significant.

First, the recent and continuing 'internationalisation' of the forest industry (Le Heron, 1988) may mean that national policies become increasingly inadequate in scale and scope, in the same way in which national governments may not always be a match for transnational corporations. Direct foreign involvement in some developing countries may be decreasing, but the international dimension in forestry in some developed countries is increasing. For example, in the United States, Canadian and Scandinavian forest-industry companies have been investing in forests, as have British financial institutions (e.g. Yoho, 1985). In response to such trends, some countries may feel a need to devise foreign forest policies, as well as domestic ones. For example, some importing countries such as France may be prompted to devise *foreign* forest policies as well as domestic ones, as supplies become scarcer and market conditions increasingly favour the seller. Such policies could include elements aimed at encouraging investment in joint ventures in tropical countries (Huguet, 1980). Whether such foreign policies can be effectively harmonised with national domestic policies in the host countries is debatable. A growing international or transnational dimension is also reflected by the attempts of the European Community to formulate a common policy. Such attempts encounter great difficulty, because the problems to which policy objectives need to be directed become more numerous as geographical scale increases. In Mediterranean Europe, for example, the problems are related more to fire and environmental protection, whereas production goals and the afforestation of 'surplus' land released from agriculture are relatively more important further north. On the still wider scale, it remains to be seen how successful international policies such as those enshrined in the Tropical Forestry Action Plan are in practice. None of the major international conventions deals directly with forest resources: of the 113 concluded between 1921 and 1983, fewer than ten are related to forest management, and then usually merely tangentially (Mayda, 1986). For example, one tree species (of mahogany) is included in the convention on International Trade in Endangered Species (CITES) concluded in Washington in 1973.

Second, national forest policies do not exist in isolation. Various other agricultural, economic and social policies are likely to be in operation at the same time. And if it has proved difficult to harmonise the various internal elements of forest policy, it is almost impossible to do so on the broader front. Adequate integration is often lacking at both the intrasectoral and inter-sectoral levels. In Canada, for example, the need to co-ordinate the host of government departments and agencies is seen as even greater than that of establishing a national policy (Wetton, 1978). In practice, non-forest policies may have a far greater effect on the use and management of the forest resource than have forest policies. In relation to forest problems in the developing world, Romm (1986) goes so far as to argue that '. . . the primary objectives of forest management policy must be outside the forest' (p.102). If indeed the main threats to the forest are from factors such as population growth and agricultural expansion, the validity of his argument is apparent. And the significance of non-forest policies for the forest resource are not confined to the developing world. Conflicts between sectors are numerous in the developed world also. In Britain, for example, policies of expansion of both agriculture and forestry were pursued after the Second World War. These policies were to a large extent worked out separately: *de facto*, however, agricultural expansion had priority, not least because it was administered by a larger and more powerful government department. Similarly, government positions on forestry and deforestation in developing countries in Africa and elsewhere are often confusing: deforestation may officially be decried, but at the same time land clearance for agriculture encouraged (e.g. Hosier, 1988). Numerous calls have been made for integrated land-use policies (e.g. Papanastasis, 1986), but these are likely to remain pipedreams. If agreed and meaningful policies cannot be devised for the forest sector, what hope is there for more general land-use policies?

If serious conflicts sometimes arise between forest and agricultural policies, much greater problems exist in the relationship between forest resource use and economic, fiscal and tenurial policies. Such policies may have a far greater impact on the extent and condition of the forest than forestry policies. This is as true of policies pursued at the supra-national and non-governmental levels as well as of those pursued by national governments. The classic example is Brazilian Amazonia, where fiscal incentives, tax holidays, and the nature of land tenure have contributed greatly to pasture-driven deforestation (e.g. Hecht, 1989): a scathing indictment of government development policies, sponsored by the World Bank, is presented by Mahar (1988). He proposes five immediate changes in policy: the discontinuation of fiscal incentives for livestock projects, a moratorium on disbursement of fiscal incentive funds for projects in the Carajas area, the modification of policies that recognise deforestation as a form of land improvement, and thus as a means of establishing tenurial rights. The character of land tenure, and hence of the pattern of forest ownership and of management objectives, is largely dependent, for better or worse, on government policy. Laws that assign property rights over public forests to private parties on condition that such lands are 'developed' or 'improved' favour expansion of agriculture at the expense of the forest (e.g. Gillis and Repetto, 1988). The significance of tenurial policies and enactments is not new: legislation on forest property and use rights in many European countries in the past facilitated the transition of the forest from the 'pre-industrial' to the 'industrial' stage in the same way as it has done so much more recently in much of the developing world. For example, an act of 1805 abolished all common rights in private forests in Denmark (Sabroe, 1954). Whether intentionally or otherwise, this prepared the way for a fundamental change in the pattern of forest use and management.

Similarly, the framing of tax regulations can wittingly or unwittingly have major effects on how the resource is managed. Tax 'holidays' to foreign corporations, in the hope that industrial development will be fostered, may mean that forest destruction is accelerated. Adjustments to tax regulations can have an almost overnight effect on afforestation rates in countries such as Britain, irrespective of whether they were intended to have any effect on forestry.

Third, planning, or the local implementation of policy, can pose major problems. By their very nature, national forest policies are formulated at the centre. To have effect, they have to flow 'outward' and 'downward'; to reach local inhabitants and forest owners. This problem is reviewed for the case of Japan by Shimotori (1986), but is by no means restricted to that country. In addition, there is the fundamental problem that policies are formulated nationally, but the implications vary regionally. Problems emerge especially in relation to planting targets. In the case of New Zealand, for example, these have been established without significant consultation with regional and local authorities (Moran, 1989). This is also true in other countries such as Britain, and highlights the tensions that exist between sectoral and land-use planning. Different degrees of support or enthusiasm for central government or sectoral policies exist at different levels. In New Zealand, for example, regional planning authorities have been more supportive of central government targets for afforestation than have the local planners (e.g. Abbiss, 1986). Local planning authorities have to cope with the local outworkings of these national policies, and often feel frustrated because of their limited or inappropriate powers and instruments. Furthermore, one of the traditional tools of land-use planning is zoning, but this practice of allocating zones of land to specific uses fits uncomfortably with the shift towards multiple use that is character-istic of the 'post-industrial forest'.

Table 9.2   Prescriptions for forest policies

- Forest policies need to be strengthened and implemented more rigorously
- Forest policies should give more emphasis to the needs and wishes of people
- There must be a close co-ordination between forest policy and other policies
- Forest policy must be treated as a coherent whole
- National policies should recognise the growing importance of forestry's international dimension
- Those responsible for forest policy should do what they can to protect forests against avoidable damage and destruction
- Forest administration and individual forest officers should become more outward looking, and become more concerned with people

---

Source: Compiled from Hummel (1984) (pp. xi–xii)

There are, therefore, several serious and basic limitations to forestry policy. Numerous prescriptions for more effective policies have been offered: one example is illustrated in Table 9.2. It is easy to identify defects and weaknesses in existing policies and to point to areas where improvement could and should be achieved. It is easy to urge, for example, that forest policy should be treated as a whole, and that forest policies need to be strengthened. It is much more difficult to convert the prescription into reality in the face of competing issues, changing political agendas and conflicting interests. It is doubtful whether a completely comprehensive and consistent forest policy can ever be formulated. To this extent, the fervent advocacy of national policies, as expressed by World Forestry Congresses and commentators such as Westoby (1985) is futile. To accept that all national forest policies are flawed and incomplete, however, is not to suggest that they are pointless and meaningless. Partial though they may be, they can still help to instil principles of management and to establish the broadest of guidelines for the use of the forest resource. In the final analysis, however, they can be but one of the preconditions for forest conservation.

10 REVIEW

Human use of forest resources resembles human use of the earth as a whole. It is characterised by destructive exploitation and damage both to the resource and to the wider environment. It is also characterised by friction and conflict over the control of the resource base and the type of use to which it should be put. Problems of forest resource use have been experienced in various parts of the world for thousands of years, and by the late twentieth century the condition and fate of major world forests have emerged as a major world issue. The most obvious conclusion to be drawn from a review of the global forest resource is that the lessons from the history of forest resources in one part of the world are not heeded in other parts.

The tropical forest is at present in the midst of a phase of use similar to that in the United States in the nineteenth century and parts of the Old World in earlier times. It is rapidly shrinking in the face of clearing for agriculture, lumbering and the gathering of fuelwood. As the forest area contracts, at least some of it changes in ecological character and often in usefulness as a resource. Resource shortages occur, especially of fuelwood, in the same way that they were suffered in parts of Europe, for example , in previous centuries. And environmental problems, such as soil erosion and increased flooding, are attributed to the pattern of forest resource use in the same way as they were in nineteenth-century North America.

Comparison of the tropical forest with that of temperate lands can lead to both optimism and pessimism. On the one hand, there is hope that a forest transition will occur in the tropics as it has done in higher latitudes: that the presently shrinking forest area will stabilise and begin to expand once more. There are grounds for hope that the transition will occur more abruptly and more rapidly in the tropics than it has done elsewhere, especially because of the growing and spreading concern about forest resource issues on the world scale. There is pessimism, however, because even if a rapid transition does occur, much of value will have been lost from the original resource, much human suffering will have been caused and much environmental damage done. Destructive exploitation is sometimes viewed as a step towards conservation and efficient resource use (Chapter 1): in the United States, for example, the destructive exploitation of the forests in the nineteenth century was certainly followed by the rise of a conservation movement and by a forest transition. In other countries such as Britain and Ireland, for example, as well as in parts of the

Mediterranean lands, destructive exploitation continued to a stage where the forest resource was almost completely exhausted, and a transition was long delayed and initially hesitant. Even if destructive exploitation were invariably followed by more conservative use, however, the tragedy of the damage and wastefulness remains: why has a resource such as the forest to be depleted before it can be conserved? Why can the clearing of the forest for agriculture not be carried out in a orderly, planned and controlled manner? Why can avoidable environmental effects not be avoided when the resource is utilised?

On the other hand, the scale of destruction should not be exaggerated. While much damage has been done, most of the pre-agricultural forest area still remains. It is true that some forest types and areas have been almost completely eliminated, but huge areas survive, and large areas survive almost intact. Much of the world forest has proved to be resilient in the face of human use, and much of it lies in areas so inaccessible that exploitation is unlikely to occur in the foreseeable future. Furthermore, while the current rate of deforestation is probably unprecedented in history, so also is the rate of reforestation and afforestation. The net trend is still one of contraction, but eventually it may give way to one of expansion, as afforestation continues in the developed world (perhaps at an accelerating rate, as land is transferred out of agriculture) and becomes more rapid and more widespread in the developing world.

The world forest resource is probably changing more rapidly at present than at any time in human history. It is changing in extent through direct human agency, and it may also change in extent and distribution as a result of climatic change arising from indirect human effects. There is some evidence that its health is being impaired in some parts of the world, again through indirect human agency. The perception of the forest resource is also altering. Throughout much of human history, it has been viewed as a source of a wide range of useful products including food, fodder and fibre. For what will perhaps prove to be a brief interlude, this 'pre-industrial' stage has been succeeded by an 'industrial' phase in many parts of the world. During this phase, the forest is seen solely or primarily as a source of wood for con-structional and industrial purposes. Around much of the world, however, there has been progress to a 'post-industrial' stage, in which the forest is perceived as much more than a source of timber. It is viewed also as having intrinsic value in terms of landscape and wildlife, as well as offering opportunity for recreation. It is increasingly seen as containing a wealth of actually or potentially valuable products and organisms. This trend applies alike to publicly and privately owned forests in much of the developed world. The distribution of the material or non-material benefits accruing from this 'post-industrial' forest resource is usually wider than that from the 'industrial' forest. Society (as opposed to individual owners) begins to value the resource, and it is probably no mere coincidence that the forest transition seems to take place as this change in perception or re-evaluation begins to occur. Perhaps the re-evaluation of the forest resource, like the forest transition, will happen more rapidly and more abruptly in the developing world than it did in Europe and North America in the past.

The fate of the world forest is also related to the other forest transition, from the 'hunting/gathering' form of use to that more closely resembling farming. This transition has been effected in many parts of the world, and an increasing area of forest plantation increasingly resembles farm crops such as wheat in terms of management. As the area of accessible and exploitable 'old growth' forest shrinks, the pressure to switch to 'farmed' forests, at least for timber supplies, will grow. While extensive areas of 'old growth' forests were available for use on the 'hunting/gathering' mode, there was little incentive to incur the higher costs arising from managed or man-made forests. As accessible and exploitable natural forests become fewer, however, the possible alternative of plantations (or other forms of intensive management) will be perceived ever more favourably. Perhaps this is one reason why forest resources have to be depleted before they are conserved.

Plantations are not a panacea to the problems of the world forest resource. They offer good prospects for timber supply, but are less attractive from the viewpoint of other goods and services such as wildlife conservation. They may suffer from serious problems of sustainability in terms of plant nutrients, pests and diseases. On the other hand, they can help to relieve the remaining natural forest from the role of timber production, and thus allow a fuller appreciation of other resource functions such as conservation and recreation. As plantations (and other intensively managed forest areas) expand, there may well be a relative shift towards lower latitudes as the main areas of timber production. These latitudes may have an advantage in terms of growth rates and ultimately of costs. Furthermore, much of the forest area in the developed world is in (or is approaching) the 'post-industrial' stage, where timber production is increasingly constrained by the preferences of forest owners and society alike for non-consumptive uses. While it is true that rapid afforestation may occur in parts of the developed world as land is transferred out of agriculture, there are signs that opposition towards extensive 'industrial' afforestation is growing in some developed countries. Perhaps these disparate factors will, in combination, be expressed in a tendency for the wood-production industry to move gradually towards lower latitudes. If so, the forest-area transition in tropical latitudes may be further hastened.

The publicity afforded to tropical forest issues in recent years has tended to give the impression that current forest problems are concentrated in the developing world, and has perhaps tended to divert attention from some of the problems of developed-world forestry. The fact that the forest area is stable or increasing in the developed world perhaps strengthens this effect. Nevertheless, serious problems remain in the use of boreal forest resource in particular. In both Canada and the Soviet Union, much of the boreal forest has been extensively modified and degraded as a result of human use, and it is very doubtful whether the forms of exploitation and management practised even in recent decades are in accordance with sustainable use. Perhaps the boreal forest issue will become more prominent in the years ahead, especially if rising temperatures lead to a mismatch between climate and vegetation and hence to apparent malaise in health and vigour or shrinkage in area.

The latent issue of the boreal forest is a reminder that forest problems are not confined to the tropics. It is also a salutary reminder that complacency on the part of the developed countries about their forest resources is unwarranted. It is readily understandable that developing countries should be resentful of what they see as interference from the 'North' over the stewardship of their tropical forest resources. Perhaps both local and global dimensions are required in the management of the global forest resource. If, as suggested in Chapter 3, incorporation into the world economy is one factor that can trigger destructive exploitation of the forest resource, then it follows that a global dimension is significant. Furthermore, some forest resource values, such as gene pools and possible sources of pharmaceuticals, are global rather than local. It is appropriate that the conservation of these resource values is supported, financially and in other ways, on a world-wide basis. Whether 'debt-for-nature' swaps and other recent initiatives offer promise that this can be done effectively and successfully remains to be seen (Chapter 8). It is apparent, however, that the creation of a global management framework for what amounts to a global resource, whilst respecting local use, values and control, is probably the biggest single challenge facing forest resource management at the end of the twentieth century. Problems of a technical nature still persist, not least in the sustained-yield management of the tropical rain forest. The basic problems, however, are economic, social and political. The example of the environmental effects of logging, as reviewed in Chapter 7, is a reminder that technical knowledge is available on how adverse effects of soil erosion and compaction, for example, can readily be mitigated through appropriate management, if the will is present. Perhaps this small example typifies the use of the forest resource as a whole. To regard the current problems of forest resource use as primarily technical in nature may conveniently deflect attention from fundamental human, social and political issues, but it is ultimately self-deluding. Technical knowledge for some forms of sustained-yield management (such as coppicing) was available in parts of the Ancient World. It did not safeguard the forest.

REFERENCES

Abbiss, J.E., 1986, Private forestry; planning conflicts, in Magee, A. and Chalmers, L. (eds.), *Proceedings of the 13th New Zealand Geographical Society Conference*, NZGS, Christchurch, pp. 118–121.

Abdullah, R., Kartawinata, K., and Sukardjo, S., 1981, Effects of mechanized logging in the lowland dipterocarp forest at Lempake, East Kalimantan, *Malaysian Forester*, **44**: 407–18.

Abo-Hassan, A.A., 1983, Forest resources in Saudi Arabia, *Journal of Forestry*, **81**: 239–41.

Adams, D.M. and Haynes, R.W., 1985, Changing perspectives on the outlook for timber in the United States, *Journal of Forestry*, **83**: 32–5.

Adas, M., 1983, Colonisation, commercial agriculture and the destruction of the deltaic rainforests of British Burma in the late nineteenth century, in Tucker, R.P. and Richards, J.F. (eds.), *Global deforestation and the nineteenth century world economy*, Duke University Press, Durham, pp. 95–110.

Adeyoju, S.K., 1976, Land use and tenure in the tropics, *Unasylva*, **28** (112–13); 26–41.

Agarwal, B., 1986, *Cold hearths and barren slopes*, Zed Press, London.

Aiken, S.R. and Leigh, C.H., 1985, On the declining fauna of peninsular Malaysia in the post-colonial period, *Ambio*, **14**: 15–22.

Aiken, S.R. and Leigh, C.H., 1987, Queensland's Daintree rain forest at risk, *Ambio*, **16**: 134–41.

Albion, R.G., 1926, *Forest and sea power: the timber problems of the Royal Navy 1652–1862*, Harvard University Press, Cambridge, Mass.

Aldwell, P.H.B., and Whyte, J., 1984, Impacts of forest-sector growth in Bruce County, Otago: a case study, *New Zealand Journal of Forestry*, **29**: 269–95.

Algar, W.H., 1981, The use of forests, in Day, M.F. (ed.), *Australia's forests: their role in our future*, Australian Academy of Science, Canberra, pp. 21–46.

Allan, N.J.R., 1986, Déforestation et agropastoralisme dans le Pakistan du Nord, *Revue de Géographie Alpine*, **74**: 405–20.

Allan, N.J.R., 1987, Impact of Afghan refugees on the vegetation resources of Pakistan's Hindukush–Himalaya, *Mountain Research and Development*, **7**: 200–4.

Allen, J.C. and Barnes, D.F., 1985, The causes of deforestation in developing countries, *Annals, Association of American Geographers*, **75**: 163–84.

Amaranthus, M.P., Rice, R.M., Barr, N.R. and Ziemer, R.R., 1985, Logging and forest roads related to increased debris slides in Southwestern Oregon, *Journal of Forestry*, **93**: 229–33.

Anderson, D., 1987, Managing the forest: the conservation history of Lembus, Kenya, 1904–63, in Anderson, D. and Grove, R. (eds.), *Conservation in Africa: people, policies and practice*, Cambridge University Press, Cambridge, pp. 249–68.

Anderson, H.W., Papadopol, C.S. and Zsuffa, L., 1983, Wood energy plantations in temperate climates, *Forest Ecology and Management*, **5**: 281–306.

Anderson, M.L. (ed.), 1967, *History of Scottish forestry* (2 vols.), Nelson, Edinburgh.

Anderson, P., 1989, The myth of sustainable logging: the case for a ban on tropical timber imports, *The Ecologist*, **19**: 166–8.

Andersson, F., 1986, Acidic deposition and its effects on the forests of Nordic Europe, *Water, Air and Soil Pollution*, **30**: 17–29.

Apin, T., 1987, The Sarawak timber blockade, *The Ecologist*, **17**: 186–9.

Arnalds, A., 1987, Ecosystem disturbance in Iceland, *Arctic and Alpine Research*, **19**: 508–13

Arnason, T., Hebda, R.J. and Johns, T., 1981, Use of plants for food and medicine by native peoples of eastern Canada, *Canadian Journal of Botany*, **59**: 2189–325

Arnold, J.E.M., 1983, Community forestry and meeting fuelwood needs, *Commonwealth Forestry Review*, **62**: 183–91.

Arnold, J.E.M., 1987a, Deforestation, in McLaren, D.J. and Skinner, B.J. (eds.) *Resources and world development*, John Wiley, Chichester, pp. 771–25.

Arnold, J.E.M., 1987b, Community forestry, *Ambio*, **16**: 122–8.

Arnold, J.E.H., and Jongma, J., 1977, Fuelwood and charcoal in developing countries, *Unasylva*, **29** (118): 2–9.

Arnold, R., 1976, The virgin forest harvest and the development of colonial New Zealand, *New Zealand Geographer*, **32**: 105–26.

Arovaara, H., Hari, P. and Kuusela, K., 1984, Possible effect of changes in atmospheric composition and acid rain on tree growth, *Communicationes Instituti Forestalis Fenniae*, **122**, 1–16.

Asabere, P.K., 1987, Attempts at sustained yield management in the tropical high forests of Ghana, in Mergen, F. and Vincent, J.R. (eds.) *Natural management of tropical moist forests*, Yale University, Newhaven, Conn. pp. 47–70.

Ashmore, M., Bell, N., and Rutter, J., 1985, The role of ozone in forest damage in West Germany, *Ambio*, **14**: 81–7.

Ashton, P.S., 1964, *Ecological studies in the mixed dipterocarp forests of Brunei State*, Clarendon Press, Oxford.

Astrom, S.-E., 1988, From tar to timber: studies in Northeast European forest exploitation and foreign trade 1660–1860, *Commentationes Humanarum Litteratum*, **85**, Societas Scientiarum Fennica, 229 pp.

Atkins, R.L., 1983, The role of joint ventures in world trade in wood, in Bethel, J.S. (ed.) *World trade in forest products*, University of Washington Press, Seattle, pp. 256–61.

Baharuddin, H.G., 1984, Peninsular Malaysia's timber industry in perspective, *Malaysian Forester*, **47**: 70–9.

Bailly, C., Barbier, C., Clément, J., Goudet, J.P. and Hamel, O., 1982, Les problèmes de la satisfaction des besoin en bois en Afrique tropicale sèche, *Bois et Forêts Tropiques*, **197**: 23–43.

Bajracharya, D., 1983a, Fuel, food or forest? Dilemmas in a Nepali village, *World Development*, **11**: 1057–74.

Bajracharya, D., 1983b, Deforestation in the food/fuel context: historical and political perspectives from Nepal, *Mountain Research and Development*, **3**: 227–40.

Bamford, P.W., 1956, *Forests and French sea power 1660–1789*, Toronto University Press, Toronto.

Bandyopadhyay, J. and Shiva, V., 1987, Chipko: rekindling India's forest culture, *The Ecologist*, **17**: 26–34.

Barney, G.O., 1980, *The Global 2000 report to the President of the U.S.*, Pergamon, New York.

Barr, B.M., 1984, The Soviet forest in the 1980s: changing geographical perspectives, in Demko, G.J. and Fuchs, R.J. (eds.) *Geographical studies on the Soviet Union*, Research paper 211, Department of Geography, University of Chicago, pp. 235–55.

Barr, B.M., 1988, Perspectives on deforestation in the USSR, in Richards, J.F., and Tucker, R.P. (eds.), *World deforestation in the twentieth century*, Duke University Press, Durham, pp. 230–261.

Barr, B.M. and Braden, K.E., 1988, *The disappearing Russian forest: a dilemma in Soviet resource management*, Rowman and Littlefield, Totowa, NJ.

Bartlett, A.G., 1988, National forest strategy for Australia, *Australian Forestry*, **51**: 209–21.

Baskerville, G.L., 1988, Redevelopment of a degrading forest system, *Ambio*, **17**: 314–22.

Battarbee, R.W., Appleby, P.G., O'Dell, K., and Flower, R.J., 1985, ^{210}Pb dating of Scottish lake sediments, afforestation and accelerated soil erosion, *Earth Surface Processes and Landforms*, **10**: 137–42.

Becker, M., 1989, The role of climate on present and past vitality of silver fir forests in the Vosges Mountains of northeastern France, *Canadian Journal of Forest Research*, **20**: 1110–17.

Bell, G.S., 1982, Forestry development corporations in Papua New Guinea, *Commonwealth Forestry Review*, **61**: 99–106.

Ben Salem, B. and van Nao, R., 1981, Fuelwood production in traditional farming systems, *Unasylva*, **33**: 13–8.

Bertrand, A., 1983, La déforestation en zone de forêt en Côte d'Ivoire, *Bois et Forêts des Tropiques*, **202**: 3–17.

Bethel, J.S. and Tseng, A.Y., 1986, Developing countries as markets for forest products, Schreuder, G.F. (ed.), *World trade in forest products*, University of Washington Press, Seattle, pp. 22–35.

Bingham, L.W., 1985, Rationale for intensive forestry management: a 1980s view, in Sedjo, R.A. (ed.) *Investments in forestry: resources, land use and public policy*, Westview, Boulder, pp. 21–31.

Binkley, C.S. and Dykstra, D.P., 1987, Timber supply, in Kallin, M., Dykstra, D.O. and Binkley, C.S. (eds.), *The global forest sector: an analytical perspective*, John Wiley, Chichester, pp. 508–33.

Binns, W.O., 1986, Forestry and fresh waters: problems and remedies, in Solbé, J.F.L.G. (ed,) *Effects of land use on fresh waters*, Water Research Centre and Ellis Horwood, Chichester, pp. 364–77.

Birch, T.W., 1986, Communicating with non-industrial private forestland owners, *Journal of Forestry*, **84**: 25–33.

Birch, T.W. and Dennis, D.F., 1980, The forest-land owners of Pennsylvania, *USDA Forest Service Research Bulletin* NE-66.

Birch, T.W., Lewis, D., and Kaiser, H.F., 1982, Private forest land owners in the United States, *US Forest Service Bulletin* WO-1.

Biswas, A.K., 1987, Environmental concerns in Pakistan, with special reference to water and forests, *Environmental Conservation*, **14**: 319–28.

Bjorklund, J. 1984, From the Gulf of Bothnia to the White Sea: direct Swedish investments in the sawmill industry of Tsarist Russia, in Steen, H.K. (ed.), *History of sustained-yield forestry: a symposium*, Forest History Society, Santa Cruz, pp. 145–54.

Blackie, J.R., and Newson, M.D., 1986, The effects of forestry on the quantity and quality of run off in upland Britain, in Solbé, J.F.L.G. (ed.) *Effects of land use on fresh waters*, Water Research Centre and Ellis Horwood, Chichester, pp. 398–412.

Blandon, P., 1983, *Soviet forest industries*, Westview Press, Boulder.

Blank, L.M., Roberts, T.M. and Skeffington, R.A., 1988, New perspective on forest decline, *Nature*, **336**: 27–30.

Blondal, S., 1987, Afforestation and reforestation in Iceland, *Arctic and Alpine Research*, **19**: 526–36.

Blondel, J., 1976, Reboisement et oiseaux dans le Mont Ventoux, *Annales des Sciences Forestières*, **33**: 221–45.

Blyth, M. and McCallum, A., 1987, Onsite costs of land degradation in agriculture and forestry, in Chisholm, A. and Dumsday, R. (eds.), *Land degradation: problems and policies*, Cambridge University Press, Cambridge.

Boado, E.L., 1988, Incentive policies and forest use in the Philippines, in Repetto, R., and Gillis, M. (eds.), 1988, *Public policies and the misuse of forest resources*, Cambridge University Press, Cambridge and New York, pp. 165–203.

Bonnicksen, T.M., 1982, The development of forest policy in the United States, in Young, R.A. (ed.) *Introduction to forest science*, John Wiley, New York, pp. 7–36.

Booth, T.H., 1984, Major forest plantations in Australia: their location, species composition and size, *Australian Forestry*, **47**: 184–93.

Borman, B.T., and Gordon, J.C., 1989, Can intensively managed forest eco-systems be self sufficient in nitrogen?, *Forest Ecology and Management*, **29**: 95–103.

Bosch, J.M., and Hewlett, J.D., 1982, A review of catchment experiments to determine the effect of vegetation changes on water yield and evapotranspira-tion, *Hydrology*, **55**: 3–23.

Bouchard, A., Dyrda, S., Bergeron, Y. and Meilleur, A., 1989, The use of notary deeds to estimate the changes in the composition of 19th century forests, in Haut-Saint-Laurent, Quebec, *Canadian Journal of Forest Research*, **20**: 1146–50.

Boutland, A. and Byron, N., 1987, Rethinking private forestry in Australia: 2 strategies to promote trees on farms, *Australian Forestry*, **50**: 245–52.

Bowonder, B., Prasad, S.S.R., and Unni, N.V.M., 1987a, Afforestation in India:

policy and strategy reforms, *Land Use Policy*, **4**: 133–46.

Bowonder, B., Prasad, S.S.R., and Unni, N.V.M., 1987b, Deforestation around urban centres in India, *Environmental Conservation*, **14**: 23–8.

Boxman, O., de Graaf, N.R., Hendrison, J., Jonkers, W.B.J., Poels, R.L.H., Schmidt, P. and Tjon Lim Sang, R., 1987, Forest land use in Surinam, in van Beusekom, C.F., van Goor, C.P., and Schmidt, P. (eds.) *Wise utilisation of tropical rain forest lands*, Amsterdam, UNESCO, pp. 119–29.

Boyd, R.G., Daniels, B.J., Fallon, R., and Hyde, W.F., 1988, Measuring the effectiveness of public forestry assistance programs, *Forest Ecology and Management*, **23**: 297–309.

Bradley, P.N., 1988, Methodology for woodfuel development planning in the Kenyan highlands, *Journal of Biogeography*, **15**: 157–64.

Brand, D.G., Kehoe, P. and Connors, M., 1986, Coniferous afforestation leads to soil acidification in Central Ontario, *Canadian Journal of Forest Research*, **16**: 1389–91.

Brandt, J., 1988, The transformation of rainfall energy by a tropical rain forest canopy in relation to soil erosion, *Journal of Biogeography*, **15**: 41–8.

Brandt, M., Bergstrom, S., and Gardelin, M., 1988, Modelling the effects of clearcutting on runoff—examples from central Sweden, *Ambio*, **17**: 307–13.

Brash, A.R., 1987, The history of avian extinction and forest conversion in Puerto Rico, *Biological Conservation*, **39**: 97–111.

Braudel, F., 1979, *Civilization and capitalism 15th–19th century: vol. 1. The structures of everyday life: the limits of the possible*, Collins, London.

Browder, J.O., 1988, Public policy and deforestation in the Brazilian Amazon, in Repetto, R. and Gillis, M. (eds.), *Public policies and the misuse of forest resources*, Cambridge University Press, Cambridge and New York, pp. 247–97.

Brünig, E.F., 1977, The tropical rainforest – a wasted asset or an essential biospheric resource?, *Ambio*, **6**: 187–91.

Brünig, E.F., 1984, Forest research and planning in South and Southeast Asia, *Applied Geography and Development*, **23**: 46–54.

Brünig, E.F., 1987a, The forest ecosystem: tropical and boreal, *Ambio*, 16: 68–79.

Brünig, E.F., 1987b, Die Entwaldung der Tropen und die Auswirkung auf das Klima, *Forst-wissenschaftliches Centralblatt*, **106**: 263–75.

Brünig, E.F., von Buch, M., Heuveldop, J., and Panzer, K.F., 1975, Stratification of the tropical moist forest for land use planning, *Plant Research and Development*, **2**: 21–44.

Buckley, G.P., 1987, The forests of the Jos Plateau, Nigeria: 1 The development of the forest estate, *Commonwealth Forestry Review*, **66**: 139–50.

Bull, P.C., 1981, The consequences for wildlife of expanding New Zealand's forest industry, *New Zealand Journal of Forestry*, **26**: 210–31.

Bunyard, P., 1989, Guardians of the forest: indigenist policies in the Colombian Amazon, *The Ecologist*, **19**: 255–58.

Burgess, P.F., 1971, Effects of logging on hill dipterocarp forests, *Malaysian Naturalist's Journal*, **24**: 231–7.

Buschbacher, R.J., 1987, Deforestation for sovereignty over remote frontiers, in Jordan, C.F. (ed.) *Amazonian rain forests: ecosystem disturbance and recovery*, Springer-Verlag, New York, pp. 46–57.

Buttond, G., 1986, Les politiques de réboisement des montagnes en France aux XIXe et XXe siècles: implications, techniques, économiques et sociales, Procéedings, Division 6, 18th IUFRO World Congress, pp. 227–37.

Byron, N., and Boutland, A., 1987, Rethinking private forestry in Australia: 1 Strategies to promote private timber production, *Australian Forestry*, **50**: 236–44.

Caird, J.B., 1980, The reshaped agricultural landscape, in Parry, M.L. and Slater, T.R. (eds.) *The making of the Scottish landscape*, Croom Helm, London, pp. 203–22.

Cameron, R.J., 1964, Destruction of the indigenous forests for Maori agriculture during the nineteenth century, *New Zealand Journal of Forestry*, **9**: 98–109.

Canadian Council of Forest Industries, 1987, A national forest sector strategy for Canada, *Forestry Chronicle*, **63**: 310–31.

Canadian Forestry Service, 1988, *Selected forestry statistics Canada 1987*, Information Report E-X-40, Economics Branch, CFS, Ottawa.

Cannel, M.G.R., 1982, *World forest biomass and primary production data*, Academic Press, London.

Cannel, M.G.R., Grace, J., and Booth, A., 1989, Possible impacts of climatic warming on trees and forests in the United Kingdom, *Forestry*, **62**: 337–64.

Carlson, A.M., 1986, A comparison of birds inhabiting pine plantations and indigenous forest patches in a tropical mountain area, *Biological Conservation*, **35**: 195–204.

Carroll, C.F., 1973, *The timber economy of Puritan New England*, Brown University Press, Providence.

Carron, L.T., 1979, Forestry in the Australian environment—the background, *Australian Forestry*, **42**: 63–73.

Carron, L.T., 1980, Self sufficiency in forest policy in Australia, *Australian Forestry*, **43**: 203–9.

Carron, L.T., 1983, National forest policy—myth, manifesto, mandate or mandala, *Australian Forestry*, **46**: 261–9.

Carson, W.W., 1983, Is New Zealand ready for steep country logging? *New Zealand Journal of Forestry*, **28**: 24–34.

Carter, F.W., 1985, Pollution problems in post-war Czechoslovakia, *Transactions, Institute of British Geographers*, NS **10**: 17–44.

Castro, A.P., 1988, Southern Mount Kenya and colonial forest conflicts, in Richards, J.F., and Tucker, R.P. (eds.) *World deforestation in the twentieth century*, Duke University Press, Durham, pp. 33–55.

Catinot, R., 1978, L'utilisation intégrale des forêts tropicales, est-elle possible? Référence à l'Afrique tropicale au sud du Sahara, *Bois et Forêts des Tropiques*, **181**: 3–14.

Caufield, C., 1987, Conservationists scorn plans to save tropical forests, *New Scientist*, 1566 (25 June 1987): 33.

C.E.C., 1987, *The state of the environment in the European Community 1986*, Office for Official Publications of the European Communities, Luxembourg.

Cherkasov, A.P., 1988, Classification of non-timber resources in the USSR, *Acta Botanica Fennica*, **136**: 3–5.

Chevone, B.I., and Linzon, S.N., 1988, Tree decline in North America, *Environ-*

mental Pollution, **50**: 87–99.

Christie, J.M. and Lines, R., 1979, A comparison of forest productivity in Britain and Europe in relation to climatic factors, *Forest Ecology and Management*, **2**: 75–102.

Ciriacy-Wantrup, S.V. and Bishop, R., 1975, 'Common property' as a concept in natural resources policy, *Natural Resources Journal*, **15**: 713–27.

Clark, T.D., 1984, *The greening of the South: the recovery of land and forest*, University of Kentucky Press, Lexington.

Clawson, M., 1976, The national forests, *Science*, **191**: 762–7.

Clawson, M., 1979, Forests in the long sweep of American history, *Science*, **204**: 1168–74.

Coats, R.N. and Miller, T.O., 1981, Cumulative silvicultural impacts on watershed: a hydrologic and regulatory dilemma, *Environmental Management*, **5**: 147–60.

Cohen, S.I., 1985, The afforestation of Israel, *Journal of Forestry*, **83**: 95–9.

Cole, D.W., 1986, Nutrient cycling in world forests, in Gersel, S.P. (ed.), *Forest site and productivity*, Martinus Nijhoff, Dordrecht, pp. 103–16.

Colinvaux, P.A., 1989, The past and future Amazon, *Scientific American*, **260**: 68–74.

Combes, F., 1982, Réflexions sur les problèmes d'érosion dans les Alpes de Haute-Provence, *Revue Forestière Française*, **34**: 61–76.

Conacher, A.J., 1977, Conservation and geography: the case of the Manjimup woodchip industry in Southwestern Australia, *Australian Geographical Studies*, **15**: 104–22.

Conacher, A., 1983, Environmental management implications of intensive forestry practices in an indigenous forest ecosystem: a case study from South-western Australia, in O'Riordan, T. and Turner, K.V. (eds.) *Progress in Resource Management and Environmental Planning*, Vol. 4, pp. 117–51.

Contreras, A., 1987, Transnational corporations in the forest-based sector of developing countries, *Unasylva*, **39**: 38–52.

Cornforth, J.S., 1970, Reafforestation and nutrient reserves in the humid tropics, *Journal of Applied Ecology*, **7**: 609, 15.

Correa de Lima, J.P. and Mercado, R.S., 1985, The Brazilian Amazon region: forestry industry opportunities and aspirations, *Commonwealth Forestry Review*, **64**: 151–6.

Cowling, E.B., 1989, Recent change in chemical climate and related effects on forests in North America and Europe, *Ambio*, **18**: 167–71.

Cox, T.R., 1983, Trade, development and environmental change: the utilisation of North America's Pacific Coast forests to 1914 and its consequences, in Tucker, R.P. and Richard, J.F. (eds), *Global deforestation and the nineteenth century world economy*, Duke University Press, Durham, pp. 14–29.

Cox, T.R., 1988, The North American–Japanese timber trade: a survey of its social, economic and environmental impact, in Richards, J.F. and Tucker R.P. (eds.) *World deforestation in the twentieth century*, Duke University Press, Durham, pp. 165–86.

Cox, T.R., Maxwell, R.S., Thomas, P.D. and Malone, J.J., 1985, *This well-wooded land: Americans and their forests from colonial times to the present*, University of Nebraska Press, Lincoln and London.

Crocker, M.D., 1984, Forest policy in post-Revolutionary Mexico 1917–1943, in Steen, H.K. (ed.), *History of sustained-yield forestry: a symposium*, Forest History Society, Santa Cruz, pp. 145–54.

Crocker, T.D. and Forster, B.A., 1986, Atmospheric deposition and forest decline, *Water, Air and Soil Pollution*, 31: 1007–17.

Cubbage, F.W. and Gunter, J.E., 1987, Conservation reserves, *Journal of Forestry*, 85: 21–7.

Cubbage, F.W. and Siegel, W.C., 1985, The law regulating private forest practices, *Journal of Forestry*, 83: 538–47.

Culhane, P.J. and Friesema, H.P., 1979, Land use planning for the public lands, *Natural Resources Journal*, 19: 43–74.

Cunningham, G.R., 1982, Private nonindustrial forests, in Young, R.A. (ed.) *Introduction to forest science*, John Wiley, New York, pp. 313–33.

Curtis, J.T., 1965, The modification of mid-latitude grasslands and forests by man, in Thomas, W.L. (ed.) *Man's role in changing the face of the earth*, Chicago University Press, Chicago, pp. 721–36.

da Fonseca, G.A.B, 1985, The vanishing Brazilian Atlantic forest, *Biological Conservation*, 34: 17–34.

Dana, S.T. and Fairfax, S.K., 1980, *Forest and range policy*, McGraw-Hill, New York.

Daniel, J.G. and Kulasingam, A., 1974, Problems arising from large-scale forest clearing for agricultural use — the Malaysian experience, *Malaysian Forester*, 37: 152–60.

Daniels, T.C., Lapping, M.B. and Keller, J.W., 1989, Rural planning in the United States: fragmentation, conflict and slow progress, in Cloke, P.J. (ed.) *Rural land-use planning in developed nations*, Unwin Hyman, London, pp. 152–77.

Darby, H.C., 1956, The clearing of woodland in Europe, in Thomas, W.L. (ed.) *Man's role in changing the face of the earth*, Chicago University Press, Chicago, pp. 183–216.

Dargavel, J., 1982, Employment and production: the declining forestry sector examined, *Australian Forestry*, 45: 255–61.

Davis, B.W., 1984, Non-wood values and state forestry policy: some socio-political dimensions, *Australian Forestry*, 47: 143–7.

Dean, W., 1983, Deforestation in Southwestern Brazil, in Tucker, R.P. and Richards, J.F. (eds.) *Global deforestation and the nineteenth century world economy*, Duke University Press, Durham, pp. 30–67.

DeBonis, J.N., 1986, Harvesting tropical forests in Ecuador, *Journal of Forestry*, 86: 43–6.

Delcourt, H.R. and Harris, W.F., 1980, Carbon budget of the Southeastern U.S. biota: analysis of historical change in trend from source to sink, *Science*, 210: 321–3.

Delgado-Calvo-Flores, R., Barcelo, G., and Parraga, J., 1985, Efectos de la deforestación sobre los suelos de la commarca de Antequera (Malaga) III Análisis y evaluacíon, *Anales de Edapología y Agrobiología*, 44: 1015–27.

de Montgofier, J., 1989, Heritage management and negotiated management in European forestry, in OECD *Renewable natural resources: economic incentives for improved management*, OECD, Paris, pp. 102–8.

Denevan, W.M., 1973, Development and the imminent demise of the Amazon rainforest, *Professional Geographer*, **25**: 130–5.

de Saussay, C., 1987, Land tenure systems and forest policy, *FAO Legislative Study No. 41*, 82 pp.

De Steigner, J.E. and Royer, J.P., 1986, Increasing forestry investments by means of public policy programs, *Silva Fennica*, **20**: 354–7.

Detwiler, R.P. and Hall, C.A.S., 1988, Tropical forests and the global carbon cycle, *Science*, **239**: 42–7.

Devaud, J., 1987, Agriculture and rural land: France, *European Environmental Yearbook*, London, DocTer, pp. 7–10.

Diamond, J., 1986, The design of a nature reserve system for Indonesian New Guinea, in Soulé, M.E. (ed.) *Conservation biology: the science of scarcity and diversity*, Sinauer, Sunderland, Mass., pp. 485–503.

Diamond, J.M., 1987, Human use of world resources, *Nature*, **328**: 479–80.

Dietrich, B.F.A., 1928, European forests and their utilisation, *Economic Geography* **4**: 141–58.

Digerness, T.H., 1979, Fuelwood crisis causing unfortunate land use—and the other way round, *Norsk Geografisk Tidskrift*, **33**: 23–32.

Dons, A., 1986, The effect of large-scale afforestation on Tarawera river flows, *Journal of Hydrology (NZ)*, **25**: 61–73.

Dosso, H., Guillaumet, J.L., and Hadley, M., 1981, The Tai forest: land use problems in a tropical forest, *Ambio*, **10**: 120–5.

Douglas, J.J., 1983, *A re-appraisal of forestry development in developing countries*, Martinus Nijhoff/Dr W. Junk, The Hague.

Douguedroit, A., 1981, Reafforestation in the French Southern Alps, *Mountain Research and Development*, **1**: 245–52.

Dourojeanni, M.J., 1985, Overexploited and underused animals in the Amazon Region, in Prance, G.T. and Lovejoy, T.E. (eds.) *Amazonia*, Pergamon, Oxford, pp. 419–33.

Douthwaite, R.J., 1987, Lowland forest resources and their conservation in southern Somalia, *Environmental Conservation*, **14**: 29–35.

Drent, P.J. and Woldendorp, J.W., 1989, Acid rain and eggshells, *Nature*, **339**: 431.

Dunbar, G.S., 1983, The forests of Cyprus under British stewardship, *Scottish Geographical Magazine*, **99**: 111–20.

Dunne, N., 1989, Ecuador in $9m debt-for-nature swap, *Financial Times*, 10 April 1989.

Dunster, J., 1987, Forestry conflicts in Canada, *Ambio*, **16**: 59–63.

Dunster, J.A., 1988, Land use planning in Canada: an overview of the forestry aspects, *Land Use Policy*, **6**: 83–93.

Durst, P.B., 1981, Problems facing reforestation in the Philippines, *Journal of Forestry*, **79**: 686–8.

Durst, P.B., 1986, Dendrothermal dreams threatened in the Philippines, *Journal of Forestry*, **84**: 45–8.

Dyck, W.J. and Beets, P.N., 1988, Managing for long-term site productivity, *New Zealand Journal of Forestry*, **32**: 23–6.

Dykstra, D.P., 1983, Forestry in Tanzania, *Journal of Forestry*, **83**: 742–6.

Earl, D.E., 1975, *Forest energy and economic development*, Clarendon Press, Oxford.

Eckerberg, K., 1985, Environmental considerations in Swedish forestry, *Environmental Management*, **9**: 19–25.

Eckerberg, K., 1986, Implementation of environmental protection in Swedish forestry: a policy perspective, *Forest Ecology and Management*, **17**: 61–72.

Eckholm, E., 1975, The deterioration of mountain environments, *Science*, **189**: 764–70.

Eckholm, E., Foley, G., Barnard, G. and Timberlake, L., 1984, *Fuelwood: the energy crisis that won't go away*, Earthscan, London and Washington.

Eckmüllner, O.S., 1986, Die Forstwirtschaft im Grünen Bericht und im Grühen Plan, *Centralblatt für das Gesamte Forstwesen*, **103**: 187–210.

Eckmüllner, O., and Madas, A., 1984, The production functions, in Hummel, F.C., (ed.) *Forest policy: a contribution to resource development*, Martinus Nijhoff/Dr W. Junk, The Hague, pp. 67–126.

Edwards, C.R., 1986, The human impact on the forest in Quitano Roo, Mexico, *Journal of Forest History*, **30**: 120–7.

Ellefson, P.V., Palm, S.L. and Lothner, D.C., 1982, From public lands to nonindustrial private forest: a Minnesota case study, *Journal of Forestry*, **80**: 219–22.

Ellenberg, H., 1986, The effects of environmental factors and use alternatives upon the species diversity and regeneration of tropical rainforests, *Applied Geography and Development*, **28**: 19–36.

Emanuel, W.R., Shugart, H.H., and Stevenson, M.P., 1985, Climatic change and the broad-scale distribution of terrestrial ecosystem complexes, *Climatic Change*, **7**: 29–43.

Environment Canada, 1989, Protecting natural resources means jobs, *Sustainable Development*, **10** (3): 4.

Erdelen, W., 1988, Forest ecosystems and nature conservation in Sri Lanka, *Biological Conservation*, **43**: 115–35.

Eronen, J., 1983, Routes of Soviet timber to world markets, *Geoforum*, **14**: 205–10.

Essman, H., 1985, Die Staatsforstverwaltung Japans bielet dem Bürger Mitbesitz am öffertlichen Wald an, Das Grünbesitzer-system, *Allgemeine Forstzeitschrift*, **20**: 504–7.

Estève, J., 1983, La destruction du couvert forestier consécutive à l'exploitation forestière de bois d'oeuvre en forêt dense tropicale humide Africaine ou Américaine, *Bois et Forêts des Tropiques*, **201**: 77–84.

Estève, J. and Lepitre, E., 1979, Conditions, téchniques et tendances d'exploitation en forêt tropicale Africaine, *Bois et forêts des tropiques*, **188**: 69–79.

Evans, J., 1982, *Plantation forestry in the tropics*, Clarendon Press, Oxford.

Evans, J., 1985, A time to plant – the complementary need to expand intensive forestry programmes in developed and developing countries, *Journal of World Forest Resource Management*, **1**: 151–61.

Evans, J., 1986, Plantation forestry in the tropics – trends and prospects, *International Tree Crops Journal*, **4**: 3–15.

Evans, J., 1987, Site and species selection – changing perspectives, *Forest Ecology and Management*, **21**: 299–310.

Ewins, P.J., and Bazely, D.R., 1989, Jungle law in Thailand's forests, *New Scientist*, **124**: (18 November 1989), 42–6.

Eyre, L.A., 1987, Jamaica: test case for tropical deforestation?, *Ambio*, **16**: 338–43.

Eyre, S.R., 1963, *Vegetation and soils: a world picture*, Edward Arnold, London.

Eyre, S.R., 1978, *The real wealth of nations*, Edward Arnold, London.

Fahnestock, G.R., Tarbes, J. and Yegres, L., 1987, The pines of Venezuela: can plantations supply domestic needs?, *Journal of Forestry*, **85**: 42–4.

Falk, B. and Mordnas, A., 1984, Multiple use in Swedish forest policy in Saastamoinen, O. et al, (eds.), Multiple use forestry in the Scandinavian countries, *Communicationes Instituti Forestalis Fenniae, 120*, pp. 19–22.

FAO (annual) *Production yearbook*, FAO, Rome.

FAO (annual) *Yearbook of forest products*, FAO, Rome.

FAO, 1946, *Forestry and forest products: world situation 1937–46*, FAO, Stockholm.

FAO, 1963, *World forest inventory*, FAO, Rome.

FAO, 1966, Wood: world trends and prospects, *Unasylva*, 20: 1–135.

FAO, 1982a, World forest products: demand and supply 1990–2000, *FAO Forestry Paper 29*.

FAO, 1982b, *Map of the fuelwood situation in the developing countries*, FAO, Rome.

FAO, 1985a, A world perspective: forestry beyond 2000, *Unasylva*, **37** (147): 7–16.

FAO, 1985b, Intensive multiple-use forest management in the Tropics: analysis of case studies from India, Africa, Latin America and the Caribbean, *FAO Forestry Paper 55*.

FAO, 1985c, *Tropical Forestry Action Plan*, FAO, Rome.

FAO, 1986a, Forest products: world outlook projections 1985–2000, *FAO Forestry Paper 73*.

FAO, 1986b, Are eucalypts ecologically harmful?, *Unasylva*, **38** (152): 19–22.

FAO, 1986c, Tropical Forestry Action Plan, *Unasylva*, **38** (152): 37–64.

FAO, 1986d, Forest industries in socio-economic development, *Unasylva*, **38** (153), 2–9.

Farnsworth, M.C., 1983, The social impact of forest development in Northland, *New Zealand Journal of Forestry*, **28**: 246–54.

Fearnside, P.M., 1983, Land-use trends in the Brazilian Amazon Region as factors in accelerating deforestation, *Environmental Conservation*, **10**: 141–8.

Fearnside, P.M., 1986, Spatial concentration of deforestation in the Brazilian Amazon, *Ambio*, **15**: 74–81.

Fearnside, P.M., 1989a, Deforestation in Brazilian Amazonia: the rates and causes of forest destruction, *The Ecologist*, **19**: 214–8.

Fearnside, P.M., 1989b, The charcoal of Carajas: a threat to the forests of Brazil's Eastern Amazon Region, *Ambio*, **17**: 141–3.

Fearnside, P.M., 1989c, Forest management in Amazonia: the need for new criteria in evaluation development options, *Forest Ecology and Management*, **27**: 61–79.

Fearnside, P.M. and Salati, E., 1985, Explosive deforestation in Rondônia, Brazil,

Environmental Conservation, **12**: 355–6.

Feeny, D., 1988, Agricultural expansion and forest depletion in Thailand 1900–1975, in Richards, J.F. and Tucker, R.P., (eds.) *World deforestation in the twentieth century*, Duke University Press, Durham, pp. 112–43.

Fenton, R., 1985, New Zealand's exports of logs and sawntimber to Japan, *New Zealand Journal of Forestry*, **29**: 225–48.

Fenton, R.T., 1986, The Japanese market as viewed from Oceania, in Schreuder, G.F. (ed.) *World trade in forest products*, University of Washington Press, Seattle, pp. 113–24.

Fergus, M., 1983, Firewood or hydropower: a case study of rural energy markets in Tanzania, *Geographical Journal*, **142**: 29–38.

Filius, A.M., 1986, Forestry strategy and land-use policy in areas with high population pressure, *Forest Ecology and Management*, **15**: 181–93.

Flenley, J.R., 1988, Palynological evidence for land use changes in South-East Asia, *Journal of Biogeography*, **15**: 185–97.

Florence, R.G., 1983, A perspective of the eucalypt forests: their characteristics and role in wood production, *New Zealand Journal of Forestry*, **28**: 372–3.

Florence, R.G., 1986, Cultural problems of eucalypts as exotics, *Commonwealth Forestry Review*, **65**: 141–63.

Foley, G., 1985, Wood fuel and conventional fuel demands in developing countries, *Ambio*, **14**: 253–8.

Foley, G., 1987, Exaggerating the Sahelian woodfuel problem, *Ambio*, **16**: 367–71.

Fontaine, R.G., 1986, Management of humid tropical forests, *Unasylva*, **38** (154), 16–21.

Forestier, K., 1989, The degreening of China, *New Scientist*, **123** (1671) (18 July 1989), 52–4.

Forestry Commission, 1977, *The wood production outlook in Britain*, Forestry Commission, Edinburgh.

Fox, J.E.D., 1976, Constraints on the natural regeneration of tropical moist forest, *Forest Ecology and Management*, **1**: 37–65.

Fox, M.F., 1988, Canada's agricultural and forest lands: issues and policy, *Canadian Public Policy*, **14**: 266–81.

Fraser, G.A., 1985, *The potential impact of the long range transport of air pollutants on the Canadian forests*, Canadian Forestry Service, Ottawa.

Freedman, B., Duinker, P.N. and Morash, R., 1986, Biomass and nutrients in Nova Scotian forests, and implications of intensive harvesting for future site productivity, *Forest Ecology and Management*, **15**: 103–27.

French, R.A., 1983, Russians and the forest, in Bater, J.H. and French, R.A. (eds.) *Studies in Russian Historical Geography*, Academic Press, London, Vol. 1, pp. 24–42.

Friend, G.R., 1980, Wildlife conservation and softwood forestry in Australia: some considerations, *Australian Forestry*, **43**: 217–24.

Friend, G.R., 1982, Mammal populations in exotic pine plantations and indigenous eucalypt forests in Gippsland, Victoria, *Australian Forestry*, **45**: 3–18.

Froelich, H.A., 1979, Soil compaction from logging equipment: effects on growth of young Ponderosa pine, *Journal of Soil and Water Conservation*, **34**: 276–8.

Gallagher, G.J. and Gillespie, J., 1984, The economics of peatland afforestation, *Proceedings of 7th International Peat Congress*, Dublin, Vol. III, 271–85.

Gamlin, L., 1988, Sweden's factory forests, *New Scientist*, **117** (28 January 1988), 41–78.

Gammie, J.I., 1981, World timber to the year 2000, *Special Report No. 98*, Economist Intelligent Unit, London.

Gane, M., 1983, Forest policy-making, *Commonwealth Forestry Review*, **62**: 85–92.

Garfunkel, H.L. and Brubaker, L.B., 1980, Modern climate-tree growth relationships and climatic reconstruction in sub-Arctic Canada, *Nature*, **286**: 872–4.

Gaunitz, S., 1984, Resource exploitation on the North Swedish timber frontier in the 19th and beginning of the 20th centuries, in Steen, H.K. (ed.) *History of sustained-yield forestry: a symposium*, Forest History Society, Santa Cruz, pp. 134–44.

Gedney, D.R., 1983, Diverse owners of nonindustrial private timberland in Western Oregon, *Journal of Forestry*, **83**: 727–9.

Gentry, A.H. and Lopez-Parodi, J., 1980, Deforestation and increased flooding in the upper Amazon, *Science*, **210**: 1354–6.

Gentry, A.H. and Vasquez, R., 1988, Where have all the ceibas gone? A case history of mismanagement of a tropical forest resource, *Forest Ecology and Management*, 23: 73–6.

Giaimo, M.S., 1988, Deforestation in Brazil: domestic political imperative – global ecological disaster, *Environmental Law*, **18**: 537–70.

Gillis, M., 1988a, West Africa: resource management policies and the tropical forest, in Repetto, R. and Gillis, M. (eds.) *Public policies and the misuse of forest resources*, Cambridge University Press, Cambridge and New York, pp. 299–35.

Gillis, M., 1988b, Malaysia: public policies and the tropical forest, in Repetto, R. and Gillis, M. (eds.) *Public policies and the misuse of forest resources*, Cambridge University Press, Cambridge and New York, pp. 115–64.

Gillis, M., 1988c, Indonesia: public policies, resource management and the tropical forest, in Repetto, R. and Gillis, M. (eds.) *Public policies and the misuse of forest resources*, Cambridge University Press, Cambridge and New York, pp. 43–113.

Gillis, R.P. and Roach, T.R., 1986, *Lost initiatives: Canada's forest industries, forest policy and forest conservation*, Greenwood Press, New York.

Gilmour, D.A., 1971, The effects of logging on streamflow and sedimentation in a north Queensland rainforest catchment. *Commonwealth Forestry Review*, 50: 38–48.

Glück, P., 1987, Social values in forestry, *Ambio*, **16** 158–60.

Golley, F.B. (ed.), 1983, *Tropical rainforest ecosystems: structure and function*, Elsevier, Amsterdam.

Gondard, P., 1988, Land use in the Andean region of Ecuador, *Land Use Policy*, **5**: 341–8.

Goodman, G.T., 1987, Biomass energy in developing countries: problems and challenges, *Ambio*, **16**: 111–19.

Goreau, T.J. and de Mello, W.Z., 1988, Tropical deforestation: some effects on atmospheric chemistry, *Ambio*, **17**: 275–81.

Gornitz, V., 1985, A survey of anthropogenic vegetation changes in West Africa during the last century – climatic implications, *Climatic Change*, **8**: 285–325.

Gottfried, G.J., 1982, Forests and forestry in Israel, *Journal of Forestry*, **80**: 516–20.

Goucher, C.L., 1988, The impact of German colonial rule on the forests of Togo, in Richards, J.F. and Tucker, R.P., (eds.) *World deforestation in the twentieth century*, Duke University Press, Durham, pp. 56–69.

Goudie, A., 1981, *The human impact*, Basil Blackwell, Oxford.

Grainger, A., 1982, *Desertification*, Earthscan, London.

Grainger, A., 1984a, Quantifying changes in forest cover in the humid tropics: overcoming current limitations, *Journal of World Forest Resource Management*, **1**: 3–63.

Grainger, A., 1984b, Increasing the effectiveness of afforestation projects in the tropics involving non-governmental organizations, *International Tree Crops Journal*, **3**, 33–47.

Grainger, A., 1986, Deforestation and progress in afforestation in Africa, *International Tree Crops Journal*, **4**: 33–48.

Grainger, A., 1988, Future supplies of high-grade tropical hardwoods from intensive plantations, *Journal of World Forest Resource Management*, **3**: 15–29.

Grandjean, A.J., 1987, Forêts domaniales et politique forestière néerlandaise depuis 1945 Evolution et resultats, *Revue Forestière Française*, **39**: 219–30.

Graumlich, L.J., Brubaker, L.B. and Grier, C.C., 1989, Long-term trends in forest net primary productivity: Cascade Mountains, Washington, *Ecology*, **70**: 405–10.

Gray, J.W., 1983, Forest revenue systems in developing countries, *FAO Forestry Paper 43*.

Graynoth, D., 1979, Effects of logging on stream environments and faunas in Nelson, *N.Z. Marine and Freshwater Research*, **13**: 70–109.

Greacen, E.L. and Sands, R., 1980, Compaction of forest soils: a review, *Australian Journal of Soil Research*, **18**: 163–89.

Green, G.C., 1984, Priorities of land use: a South American examples, *Commonwealth Forestry Review*, **63**: 185–92.

Green, G.C. and Barborak, J., 1987, Conservation for development: success stories from Central America, *Commonwealth Forestry Review*, **66**: 91–102.

Greene, J.C. and Blatner, K.A., 1986, Identifying woodland owner characteristics associated with timber management, *Forest Science*, **32**: 135–46.

Greig, P.J., 1984, Environmental constraints in the forestry and wood manufacturing sectors, *Australian Forestry*, **47**: 69–75.

Gritzner, J.A., 1988, The West Africa Sahel: human agency and environmental changes, *Research Paper 226*, Department of Geography, University of Chicago.

Grouev, I., 1984, Forest management in Bulgaria, *Unasylva*, **36** (145): 40–6.

Guess, G.M., 1981, Technical and financial policy options for development forestry, *Natural Resources Journal*, **21**: 37–55.

Guillard, J., 1983, Les forêts et leur gestion, *Revue Forestière Française*, numéro spéciale, 30–8.

Guppy, N., 1983, Proposals for an organisation of timber exporting countries (O.T.E.C.), *Malaysian Forester*, **47**: 1–19.

Guppy, N., 1984, Tropical deforestation: a global view, *Foreign Affairs*, **62**: 928–65.

Gustafsson, L., 1987, Plant conservation aspects of energy forestry – a new type of land use in Sweden, *Forest Ecology and Management*, **21**: 141–61.

Hachenberg, F., 1985, Kommunalwald, *Forst- und Holzwirt*, **40**: 178–84, 186–90, 192–3.

Haden-Guest, S., Wright, J.K. and Teclaff, E.M., 1956, *A world geography of forest resources*, American Geographical Society, New York.

Haeruman Js, 1988, Conservation in Indonesia, *Ambio*, **17**: 218–22.

Hagner, S., 1983, *Pinus contorta*: Sweden's third conifer, *Forest Ecology and Management*, **6**: 185–99.

Hagner, S.O.A., 1986, From mining to industrial forestry: some Canadian forest problems in an international perspective, *Forestry Chronicle*, **62**: 101–3.

Hahtola, K., 1973, The rationale of decision-making by forest owners, *Acta Forestalia Fennica*, **130**: 1–112.

Halkett, J.C., 1983, The conservation of natural forest in New Zealand, *New Zealand Journal of Forestry*, **28**: 263–74.

Hall, J.B., 1983, Positive management for strict natural reserves: reviewing effectiveness, *Forest Ecology and Management*, **7**: 57–66.

Hamilton, A.C., 1984, *Deforestation in Uganda*, Oxford University Press, Nairobi.

Hamilton, L.S., 1987, What are the impacts of Himalayan deforestation on the Ganges–Brahmaputra lowlands and delta? Assumptions and facts, *Mountain Research and Development*, **7**: 256–63.

Hamilton, L.S., 1988, Forestry and watershed management, in Ives, J.D. and Pitt, D.C. (eds.), *Deforestation: social dynamics in watershed and mountain ecosystems*, Routledge, London and New York, pp. 99–131.

Hamilton, L.S. and Pearce, A.J., 1988, Soil and water impacts of deforestation, in Ives, J.D. and Pitt, D.C. (eds.), *Deforestation: social dynamics in watershed and mountain ecosystems*, Routledge, London and New York, pp. 75–98.

Hamilton, L.S. with King, P.N., 1983, *Tropical forested watersheds: hydrologic and soils response to major uses or conversion*, Westview Press, Boulder.

Hamzah, Mohd-Basri, Kamis, A. and Rusli, Mohd, 1983, Issues in Malaysian forestry, *Malaysian Forester*, **46**: 409–24.

Hanson, A.G., 1980, Should Australia plan to export forest products? *Australian Forestry*, **43**: 70–4.

Hardin, G., 1968, The tragedy of the commons, *Science*, **163**: 1243–8.

Harou, P.A., 1981, Forest ownership in the European Community, *Journal of Forestry*, **79**: 298–308.

Harriman, R., 1978, Nutrient leaching from fertilised forest watershed in Scotland, *Journal of Applied Ecology*, **15**: 933–42.

Harriman, R. and Morrison, B.R.S., 1981, Forestry, fisheries and acid rain in Scotland, *Scottish Forestry*, **35**: 89–95.

Harrington, J.B., 1987, Climatic change: a review of causes, *Canadian Journal of Forest Research*, **17**: 1313–39.

Hase, H. and Foelster, H., 1983, Impact of plantation forestry with teak (*Tectona grandis*) on the nutrient status of young alluvial soils in West Venezuela, *Forest Ecology and Management*, **6**: 33–57.

Haynes, R.W. and Adams, D.M., 1983, Changing perceptions of the US forest sector: implications for the RPA timber assessment, *American Journal of Agricultural Economics*, **65**: 1002–9.

Head, C.G., 1975, An introduction to forest exploitation in nineteenth century Ontario, in Wood, J.D. (ed.) *Perspectives on landscape settlement in nineteenth century Ontario*, McClelland and Steward, Toronto, pp. 78–112.

Hebbert, M., 1989, Rural land-use planning in Japan, in Cloke, P.J. (ed.) *Rural land-use planning in developed nations*, Unwin Hyman, London, pp. 30–51.

Hecht, S.B., 1989, The sacred cow in the green hell: livestock and forest conversion in the Brazilian Amazon, *The Ecologist*, **19**: 229–34.

Hecht, S., and Cockburn, A., 1989, Defenders of the Amazon, *New Statesman and Society*, **2** (23 June 1989): 16–21.

Hendee, J.C., 1984, Public opinion and what foresters should do about it, *Journal of Forestry*, **82**: 340–4.

Hendershot, W.H. and Jones, A.R.C., 1989, Maple decline in Quebec: a discussion of possible causes and the use of fertilisers to limit damage, *Forestry Chronicle*, **65**: 280–7.

Henderson-Sellers, A. and Gornitz, V., 1984, Possible climatic impacts of land cover transformation, with particular emphasis on tropical deforestation, *Climatic Change*, **6**: 231–57.

Henly, R.K. and Ellefson, P.V., 1986, Cost and effectiveness of legal mandates for the practice of forestry on private land: experiences with state forest practice laws in the United States, *Silva Fennica*, **85**: 31–5.

Hickman, C.A., 1987, Preserving rural lands: legislative strategies to curb excessive conversions, *Journal of Forestry*, **85**: 31–5.

Hickman, C.A. and Gehlhausen, R.J., 1981, Landowner interest in forestry assistance programs in East Texas, *Journal of Forestry*, **79**: 211–3.

Hildyard, N., 1989, Amazonia: the future in the balance, *The Ecologist*, **19**: 207–10.

Hillis, W.E., 1988, A review of forest products utilisation in Australia, *Commonwealth Forestry Review*, **67**: 71–80.

Hilton, R.G.B. and Johns, R.J., 1984, The future of forestry in Papua New Guinea, *Commonwealth Forestry Review*, **63**: 103–6.

Hingston, F.J., Dimmock, G.M., and Turton, A.G., 1981, Nutrient distribution in a jarrah (*Eucalyptus marginata*) ecosystem in south-western Western Australia, *Forest Ecology and Management*, **3**: 183–207.

Hinrichsen, D., 1986, Multiple pollutants and forest decline, *Ambio*, **15**: 258–65.

Hinrichsen, D., 1987, The forest decline enigma, *BioScience*, **37**: 542–6.

Hirsch, P., 1986a, Deforestation and development in Thailand, *Singapore Journal of Tropical Geography*, **8**: 129–38.

Hirsch, P., 1986b, Problems of forest settlement in Western Thailand, *Australian Geographical Studies*, **26**: 295–308.

Hodgson, G. and Dixon, J.A., 1989, Logging versus fisheries: the effects of soil erosion on marine resources, *The Ecologist*, **19**: 139–43.

Hoffman, J.S., 1984, Carbon dioxide and future forests, *Journal of Forestry*, **82**: 164–7.

Holowacz, J., 1985, Forests in the USSR, *Forestry Chronicle*, **61**: 366–73.

Honer, T.G., 1986, Assessing change in Canada's forest resource 1977–1981, *Forestry Chronicle*, **62**: 423–8.

Horn, P.J., 1986, Environmental constraints on the availability and production of wood for industry in New Zealand, *Appita*, **39**: 184–6.

Hornbeck, J.W. and Smith, R.B., 1985, Documentation of red spruce growth decline, *Canadian Journal of Forest Research*, **15**: 1199–201.

Hornbeck, J.W., Martin, C.W., Pierce, R.S., Bormann, F.H., Likens, G.E. and

Eaton, J.S., 1986, Clearcutting northern hardwoods: effects on hydrologic and nutrient ion budgets, *Forest Science*, **32**: 667–86.

Hornung, M., 1985, Acidification of soils by trees and forests, *Soil Use and Management*, **1**: 24–8.

Horrick, J.R., Zerbe, J.I., and Whitmore, J.L., 1984, Jari's success, *Journal of Forestry*, **82**: 663–7.

Hosier, R.H., 1988, The economics of deforestation in eastern Africa, *Economic Geography*, **64**: 121–36.

Hosteland, J., 1989, The role of the environment in forest resource management, in OECD, *Renewable natural resources: economic incentives for improved management*, OECD, Paris, pp. 95–101.

Houghton, R.A., Boone, R.D., Melillo, J.M., Palm, C.A., Woodwell, G.M., Myers, N., Moore III, B., and Skole, D.L., 1985, Net flux of carbon dioxide from tropical forests in 1980, *Nature*, **316**: 617–20.

Houghton, R.A. and Woodwell, G.M., 1989, Global climatic change, *Scientific American*, **260**, 18–27.

House of Lords, 1979, Scientific aspects of forestry (Report of Select Committee on Science and Technology), *House of Lords Paper 381*, HMSO, London.

Howard, T.E. and Lacy, S.E., 1986, Forestry limited partnerships, *Journal of Forestry*, **84** 39–43.

Hsiung, W., 1983, Forestry progress in China, *Commonwealth Forestry Review*, **62**: 191–3.

Hughes, F., 1987, Conflicting uses for forest resources in the Lower Tana River basin of Kenya, in Anderson, D. and Grove, R. (eds.) *Conservation in Africa: people, policies and practice*, Cambridge University Press, Cambridge, pp. 211–28.

Hughes, J.D. and Thirgood, J.V., 1982, Deforestation in Ancient Greece and Rome: a cause of collapse?, *The Ecologist*, **12**: 196–208.

Hughes, J.D. with Thirgood, J.V., 1982, Deforestation, erosion and forest management in ancient Greece and Rome, *Journal of Forest History*, **26**: 60–75.

Huguet, L., 1980, Une politique forestière éstrangère pour la France, *Bois et Forêts des Tropiques*, **195**: 3–19.

Huguet, L., 1982, Que penser de la 'disparition' des forêts tropicales? *Bois et Forêts des Tropiques*, **195**: 7–22.

Huguet, L., 1983, The future of the world's tropical forests, *Commonwealth Forestry Review*, **62**: 195–200.

Hummel, F.C. (ed.) 1984, *Forest policy: a contribution to resource development*, Martinus Nijhoff/Dr W. Junk, The Hague.

Hummel, F.C., 1988, Biomass forestry: implications for land use policy in Europe, *Land Use Policy*, **5**: 375–384.

Hurst, P., 1987, Forest destruction in South-east Asia, *The Ecologist*, **17**: 170–4.

Husch, B., 1982, Forestry in Chile, *Journal of Forestry*, **80**: 735–7.

Husch, B., 1987, Guidelines in forest policy formulation, *FAO Forestry Paper 81*.

Hyde, W.F. and Krutilla, J.V., 1979, The question of development or restricted use of Alaska's interior forests, *Annals of Regional Science*, **13**: 1–10.

Idso, S.B., 1985, The search for global CO_2 etc 'Greenhouse effects', *Environmental Conservation*, **12**: 29–35.

Imamura, K., 1982, Human resources in Japanese forestry, *Unasylva*, **34** (135): 13–9.

IUCN (International Union for the Conservation of Nature), 1985, *The United Nations list of national parks and protected areas*, IUCN, Gland.

Ives, J.D., 1988, Development in the face of uncertainty, in Ives, J.D. and Pitt, D.C. (eds.) *Deforestation: social dynamics in watershed and mountain ecosystems*, Routledge, London, pp. 54–74.

Ives, J.D., 1989, Deforestation in the Himalayas: the cause of increased flooding in Bangladesh and northern India?, *Land Use Policy*, **6**: 187–93.

Jabil, D.M., 1983, Problems and prospects in tropical rainforest management for sustained yield, *Malaysian Forester*, **46**: 398–408.

Jacobs, M., 1988, *The tropical rain forest: a first encounter*, Springer Verlag, Berlin and Heidelberg.

Jadot, B. and Sernsiaux, E., 1987, Forestry: Belgium, *European Environmental Yearbook*, DocTer, London, p.250.

Jäger, D., 1985, Gefährdung von Existenzen im Bereich von Forst und Holz durch das Waldsterben, *Holz-Zentralblatt*, **111**: 1549–50, 1573–4, 1581–2.

Jakucs, P., 1988, Ecological approach to forest decay in Hungary, *Ambio*, **17**: 267–74.

Jammick, M.S. and Beckett, D.R., 1988, A logit analysis of private woodlot owners' harvesting decisions in New Brunswick, *Canadian Journal of Forest Research*, **18**: 330–6.

Jarvelainen, A.-P., 1986, Effects of forestry extension on the use of allowable cut in non-industrial private forests, *Silva Fennica*, **20**: 312–8.

Jennings, K.S., 1980, The need for regulation of private forestry investment in Australia, *Australian Forestry*, **43**: 264–9.

Jensen, K.M., 1986, Marginale landbrugsarealer, *Geografisk Tidsskrift*, **86**: 69–73.

Johann, E., 1984, The change of conception of sustained yields within the forestry of Austria during the last 200 years, in Steen, H.K. (ed.) *History of sustained-yield forestry*, Forest History Society, Santa Cruz, pp. 183–91.

Johns, A.D., 1985, Selective logging and wildlife conservation in tropical rainforest: problems and recommendations, *Biological Conservation*, **31**: 355–75.

Johns, A.D., 1988, Effects of selective timber extraction on rainforest structure and composition and some consequences for frugivores and folivores, *Biotropica*, **20**: 31–7.

Johns, A.D., 1989, Economic development and wildlife conservation in Brazilian Amazonia, *Ambio*, **17**: 302–6.

Johnson, B., 1985, Chimera or opportunity? An environmental appraisal of the recently concluded International Tropical Timber Agreement, *Ambio*, **14**: 42–4.

Johnson, J.A. and Price, C., 1987, Afforestation, employment and depopulation in the Snowdonia National Park, *Journal of Rural Studies*, **3**: 195–205.

Johnson, M.G. and Beschta, R.L., 1980, Logging, infiltration capacity and surface erodibility in Western Oregon, *Journal of Forestry*, **78**: 334–7.

Johnson, N.E., 1976, Biological opportunities and risks associated with fast-growing plantations in the tropics, *Journal of Forestry,* **74**: 206–11.

Johnston, A., Mace, J. and Laffan, M., 1981, The saw, the soil and the sounds, *Soil and Water*, **17**: 4–8.

Johnston, T., 1952, *Memories*, Collins, London.

Jones, G., 1979, *Vegetation productivity*, Longman, London.

Jordan, C.F., 1983, Productivity of tropical rainforest ecosystems and the implications for their use as future wood and energy sources, in Golley, F.B. (ed.) *Tropical rainforest ecosystems: structure and function*, Elsevier, Amsterdam, pp. 117–37.

Jordan, C.F., 1986, Local effects of tropical deforestation, in Soulé, M.E. (ed.), *Conservation biology: the science of scarcity and diversity*, Sinauer, Sunderland, Mass., pp. 410–26.

Jordon, C.F. (ed.), 1987, *Amazonian rain forest. Ecosystem disturbance and recovery. Case studies of. ecosystem dynamics under a spectrum of land-use intensities*, Springer-Verlag, New York.

Joyce, C., 1988, The tree that caused a riot, *New Scientist*, **117** (1600): 54–8.

Kardell, L., 1985, Recreation forests – a new silvicultural concept?, *Ambio*, **14**: 139–47.

Kardell, L., Steen, E., and Fabiao, A., 1986, Eucalyptus in Portugal – a threat or a promise?, *Ambio*, **15**: 6–13.

Kartawinata, K., Adisoemarto, S., Riswan, S., and Vayda, A.P., 1981, The impact of man on a tropical forest in Indonesia, *Ambio*, **10**: 115–9.

Kauppi, P., 1987, Forests and the changing composition of the atmosphere, in Kallio, M., Dykstra, D.P. and Binkley, C.S. (eds.) *The global forest sector*, John Wiley, Chichester, pp. 32–56.

Kauppi, P., and Posch, M., 1985, Sensitivity of boreal forests to possible climatic warming, *Climatic Chance*, **7**: 45–54.

Keeves, A., 1966, Some evidence of loss of productivity with successive rotations of *Pinus radiata* in the south-east of South Australia, *Australian Forestry*, **30**: 51–63.

Kelly, K., 1974, The changing attitude of farmers to forest in nineteenth century Ontario, *Ontario Geography*, **8**: 64–77.

Kelta, J.D., 1987, Wood or charcoal – which is better? *Unasylva*, **39** (157/8): 61–6.

Kemf, E., 1988, The re-greening of Vietnam, *New Scientist*, **118** (1616) (23 June 1988): 52–7.

Kennedy, J.J., 1981, A view of New Zealand forestry in 'mid-life' transition, *New Zealand Journal of Forestry*, **26**: 43–54.

Kennedy, J.J., 1985, Conceiving forest management as providing for current and future social value, *Forest Ecology and Management*, **13**: 121–32.

Keogh, R.M., 1986, A preliminary model to determine forest cover history of Central America, *Forest Ecology and Management*, **15**: 95–102.

Keresztesi, B., 1984, The development of Hungarian forestry 1950–1980, *Unasylva*, **36** (145), 34–40.

Kiljunen, K., 1986, Growth of Third World forest industry: possible impact on Finland, *Silva Fennica*, **20**: 159–79.

Kimmins, J.P., 1977, Evaluation of the consequences for future tree productivity of the loss of nutrients in whole-tree harvesting, *Forest Ecology and Management*, **1**: 169–83.

King, K.F.S., 1975, It's time to make paper in the tropics, *Unasylva*, **109**: 2–5.

Kingsley, N.P. and Birch, T.W., 1980, The forestland owners of Maryland, *USDA Forest Service Research Bulletin NE-63*.

Kio, P.R.O., 1979, Management strategies in the natural tropical high forest, *Forest Ecology and Management*, **2**: 207–31.

Kio, P.R.O. and Ekwebelam, S.A., 1987, Plantations versus natural forests for meeting Nigerian wood needs, in Mergen, F., and Vincent, J.R., (eds.) *Natural management of tropical moist forests*, Yale University, Newhaven, Conn., pp. 149–76.

Kirkland, A., 1988, The rise and fall of multiple-use forest management in New Zealand, *New Zealand Forestry*, **33**: 9–12.

Ki-Zerbo, J., 1981, Women and the energy crisis in the Sahel, *Unasylva*, **33** (133): 5–10.

Klein, R.M., and Perkins, T.D., 1987, Cascades of causes and effects of forest decline, *Ambio*, **16**: 86–93.

Knight, H.A., 1987, The pine decline, *Journal of Forestry*, **85**: 25–8.

Knudsen, F.D., 1987, Forestry: Denmark, *European Environmental Yearbook*, DocTer, London, pp. 251–2.

Koch, N.E., 1984, Multiple-use forestry – Danish statistics, in Saastamoinen, O. et al. (ed.) Multiple use forestry in the Scandinavian countries, *Communicationes Instituti Forestalis Fenniae* 120, pp. 33–38.

Konrad, G.D., and Harou, P.A.W., 1985, An economic evaluation of the Massachusetts forestry yield tax program, *Forestry Chronicle*, **62**: 358–62.

Kornai, G., 1987, Historical analysis of international trade in forest products, in Kallin, M., Dykstra, D.P. and Binkley, C.S., (eds.) *The global forest sector*, John Wiley, Chichester, pp. 432–56.

Krag, R., Higginbotham, K. and Rothwell, R., 1986, Logging and soil disturbance in south-east British Columbia, *Canadian Journal of Forest Research*, **16**: 1345–54.

Kreutzwiser, R.D. and Crichton, L.M., 1987, An evaluation of the United States experience in controlling forest practices on private lands, *Forestry Chronicle*, **63**: 43–7.

Kroth, W., 1985, Zur Bewertung de Waldschäden, *Forst-wissenschaftliches Centalblatt*, **104**: 255–63.

Kumar, R., 1986, *The forest resources of Malaysia: their economics and development*, Oxford University Press, Singapore.

Kumar, P. 1987, The practice of forestry on Albert's Indian Reserves, *Environmental Conservation*, **14**: 260–2.

Kurtz, W.B. and Lewis, B.J., 1981, Decision-making framework for nonindustrial private forest owners: an application in the Missouri Ozarks, *Journal of Forestry*, **79**: 285–8.

Kuusela, K., 1987, Forest products – world situation, *Ambio*, **16**: 80–5.

Laarman, J.G., 1987, Household demand for fuelwood, in Kallio, M., Dykstra, D.P. and Binkley, C.S. (eds.) *The global forest sector: an analytical perspective*, John Wiley, Chichester, pp. 355–68.

Laarman, J.G., 1988, Export of tropical hardwoods in the twentieth century, in Richard, J.F. and Tucker, R.P. (eds.) *World deforestation in the twentieth century*, Duke University Press, Durham, pp. 148–63.

Laarman, J.G. and Wohlgenant, M.K., 1984, Fuelwood consumption: a cross-country comparison, *Forest Science*, **30**: 383–92.

Laffan, M.D., 1979, Slope stability in the Charleston–Punakaiki region, South Island, New Zealand, *New Zealand Journal of Science*, **22**: 193–201.

Lal, R., 1986, Conversion of tropical rainforests: agronomic potential and ecological consequences, *Advances in Agronomy*, **39**: 173–264.

La Marche, V.C., Greybill, D.A., Fritts, H.C. and Rose, M.R., 1984, Increasing atmospheric carbon dioxide: tree ring evidence for growth enhancement in natural vegetation, *Science*, **225**: 1019–21.

Lang, W., 1986, Knowing the forest, *Naturopa*, **52**: 8–9.

Lanly, J.P., 1982, Tropical forest resources, *FAO Forestry Paper 30*.

Lanly, J.P., 1985, Defining and measuring shifting cultivation, *Unasylva*, **37** (147), 17–21.

Lanly, J.P. and Clement, J., 1979, Present and future natural forest and plantation areas in the tropics, *Unasylva* **31** (123): 12–20.

Le Heron, R.B., 1986, Changing private-state relations during an era of exotic afforestation 1960–1985, in Magee, A. and Chalmers, L. (eds.) *Proceedings of the 13th New Zealand Geographical Society Conference*, NZGS, Christchurch, pp. 112–17.

Le Heron, R.B., 1988, The internationalisation of New Zealand's forestry companies and the social reappraisal of New Zealand's exotic forest resource, *Environment and Planning* A, **20**: 489–515.

Le Heron, R.B. and Roche, M.M., 1985, Expanding exotic forestry and the extension of competing use for rural land in New Zealand, *Journal of Rural Studies*, **1**: 211–29.

Leslie, A.J., 1980, Logging concessions, Unasylva, **32** (129): 2–7.

Leslie, A.J., 1987, The economic feasibility of natural management of tropical forests, in Mergen, F. and Vincent, J.R. (eds.) *Natural management of tropical moist forests*, Yale University, Newhaven, Conn., pp. 178–88.

Lieth, H., 1975, Primary production of the major vegetation units of the world, in Lieth, H. and Whittaker, R.H. (eds.) *Primary productivity of the biosphere*, Springer Verlag, New York, pp. 202–15.

Lieth, H., 1976, Biological productivity of tropical lands, *Unasylva*, **28** (114), 24–31.

Li J., Kong, F., He, N. and Ross, L., 1988, Price and policy: the keys to revamping China's forestry resources, in Repetto, R. and Gillis, M. (eds.) *Public policies and the misuse of forest resources*, Cambridge University Press, Cambridge and New York, pp. 205–45.

Likens, G.E., Bormann, F.H., Pierce, R.S. and Reiness, W.A., 1978, Recovery of a deforested ecosystem, *Science*, **199**: 327–35.

Linares, O., 1976, Garden hunting in the American tropics, *Human Ecology*, **4**: 331–49.

Little, P.D. and Brokensha, D.W., 1987, Local institutions, tenure and resource management in East Africa, in Anderson, D. and Grove, R. (eds.) *Conservation in Africa*, Cambridge University Press,, Cambridge, pp. 193–209.

Livingstone, D.N., 1980, Nature and man in America: Nathaniel Southgate Shaler and the conversation of natural resources. *Transactions, Institute of British*

Geographers, **NS 5**: 369–82.

Lofgren, K.G., 1986, Effects of permanent and non-permanent forest policy means on timber supply, *Silva Fennica*, **20**: 308–11.

Logan, W.E.M., 1967, FAO world symposium on man-made forests and their industrial importance: 1 Policy, *Unasylva*, **21** (86–7): 8–23.

Lohmann, L., 1989, Forestry in Thailand: the logging ban and its consequences, *The Ecologist*, **19**: 76–7.

Lönnstadt, L., 1984, Stability of forestry and stability of regions: contradictory goals? The Swedish case, *Canadian Journal of Forest Research*, **14**: 707–11.

Lortie, M., 1983, Private nonindustrial forest ownership and public programs in Eastern Canada, *Journal of Forestry*, **81**: 382–4, 405.

Lothner, D.C., 1986, State, county and municipal forests, *Journal of Forestry*, **84**: 31–2.

Lowe, R.G., 1977, Experience with the tropical shelterwood system of regeneration in natural forest in Nigeria, *Forest Ecology and Management*, **1**: 193–212.

Lowe, R.G., 1984, Forestry and forest conservation in Nigeria, *Commonwealth Forestry Review*, **63**: 129–36.

Lower, A.R.M., 1973, *Great Britain's woodyard: British America and the timber trade*, McGill-Queens University Press, Montreal and London.

Lowenthal, D. (ed.) 1965, *Man and nature, or physical geography as modified by human action, by George Perkins Marsh*, Harvard University Press, Cambridge, Mass.

Lugo, A.E. and Brown, S., 1980, Tropical forest ecosystems: sources or sinks of atmospheric carbon?, *Unasylva*, **32** (129): 8–13.

Lugo, A., Schmidt, R. and Brown, S., 1981, Tropical forests in the Caribbean, *Ambio*, **10**: 318–24.

Lundgren, B., 1985, Global deforestation, its causes and effects, *Agroforestry Systems*, **3**: 91–5.

Lundmark, T., 1986, Private forests and public recreation in Germany, *Journal of Forestry*, **84**: 44–6.

Lutzenberger, J.A., 1987, Who is destroying the Amazon rainforest?, *The Ecologist*, **17**: 155–60.

Lyons, G.J. and Vasievich, J.M., 1986, Economic analysis of short-rotation forests for energy in Ireland, in Kallio, M., Anderson, A.E., Seppala, R. and Morgan, A., (eds.) *Systems analysis in forestry and forest industries*, Elsevier, North Holland, Amsterdam, pp. 311–23.

MacConnell, W.P., and Archey, W.E., 1986, Short-term landowners and timber management, *Journal of Forestry*, **84** (10): 25, 45.

MacDonald, G.T., 1989, Rural land-use planning in Australia, in Cloke, P.J. (ed.) *Rural land-use planning in developed nations*, Unwin Hyman, London, pp. 207–37.

MacKenzie, D., 1988, Uphill battle to save Filipino trees, *New Scientist*, **118** (1619): 42–4.

MacKinnon, J., MacKinnon, K., Child, G. and Thorsell, J., 1986, *Managing protected areas in the tropics*, IUCN, Gland.

McCashion, J.D., and Rice, R.M., 1981, Erosion on logging roads in northwestern California: how much is avoidable?, *Journal of Forestry*, **81**: 23–6.

McComb, W.H., 1975, Mismanagement by the small landowner – fact or fiction?, *Journal of Forestry*, **73**: 224–5.

McDonald, S.E. and Krugman, S.L., 1986, Worldwide planting of southern pines, *Journal of Forestry*, **84**: 21–4.

McKay, D., 1979, The Canadian logging frontier, *Journal of Forest History*, **23** 4–17.

McNeil, D.L., 1981, Tropical forest industries: a transnational corporation view, *Commonwealth Forestry Review*, **60**: 105–12.

McNeill, J.R., 1988, Deforestation in the Araucaria zone of southern Brazil 1900–1983, in Richards, J.F., and Tucker, R.P. (eds.) *Global deforestation in the twentieth century*, Duke University Press, Durham, pp. 15–32.

McTaggart, W.D., 1983, Forestry policy in Bali, Indonesia, *Singapore Journal of Tropical Geography*, **4**: 147–61.

Madeira, M.A.V., 1989, Changes in soil properties under Eucalyptus plantations in Portugal, in Pereira, J.A. and Landsberg, J.J. (eds.), *Biomass production by fast-growing trees*, Kulwer, Dordrecht, pp. 81–99.

Mahar, D.J., 1988, Government policies and deforestation in Brazil's Amazon Region, *Environment Department Working Paper 7*, World Bank, Washington.

Maitre, H.F., 1986, Growth and yield of natural stands in the tropical rain forests of Africa, *Bois et Forêts des Tropiques*, **213**: 13–20.

Malingreau, J.-P., and Tucker, C.J., 1988, Large-scale deforestation in the Southeastern Amazon Basin of Brazil, *Ambio*, **17**: 49–55.

Mather, A.S., 1987, The structure of forest ownership in Scotland, Journal of *Rural Studies*, **3**: 175–82.

Mather, A.S. and Murray, N.C., 1986, Disposal of Forestry Commission land in Scotland, *Area*, **18**: 109–116.

Mathur, H.M., Rambabu, P.J. and Singh, B., 1976, Effect of clearfelling and reforestation on run off and peak rates in small watersheds, *Indian Forester*, **102**: 219–26.

Matsui, M., 1980, Japan's forest resources, *Unasylva*, **32** (128): 19–20.

Matthews, E., 1983, Global vegetation and land use: new high-resolution data bases for climatic studies, *Journal of Climatic and Applied Meteorology*, **22**: 474–87.

Mayda, J., 1986, Malaysia's 'new' plantations, *New Zealand Forestry*, **33**: 12–14.

Mead, D.J., 1989, Malaysia's 'new' plantations, *New Zealand Forestry*, **33**: 12–14.

Meeks, G. Jr 1982, State incentives for nonindustrial private forestry, *Journal of Forestry*, **80**: 18–22.

Megahan, W.F. and Kidd, W.J., 1972, Effects of logging and logging roads on erosion and sediment deposition from steep terrain, *Journal of Forestry*, **70**: 136–41.

Megahan, W.F. and King, P.N., 1985, Identification of critical areas on forest lands for control of nonpoint sources of pollution, *Environmental Management*, **9**: 7–18.

Meiggs, R., 1982, *Trees and timber in the ancient Mediterranean world*, Clarendon Press, Oxford.

Melillo, J.M., Palm, C.A., Houghton, R.A., Woodwell, G.M. and Myers, N., 1985, A comparison of two recent estimates of disturbance in tropical forests, *Environmental Conservation*, **12**: 37–40.

Mergen, F. and Vincent, J.R. (eds.), 1987, *Natural management of tropical moist forests*, Yale University, New.haven, Conn.

Metz, A.-M., 1986, Influence of forest owners as an interest group in achieving forest policy goals in Finland, *Silva Fennica*, **20**: 286–92.

Meulenhoff, M. 1986, Indonesia as a lumber exporter, in Schreuder, G.F. (ed.) *World trade in forest products*, University of Washington Press, Seattle, pp. 197–206.

Meyer, R.D., Klemperer, W.D. and Siegel, W.C., 1986, Cutting contracts and timberland leasing, *Journal of Forestry*, **84**: 35–7.

Miles, J. and Young, W.F., 1980, The effects on heathland and moorland soils in Scotland and northern England following colonisation by birch (*Betula* spp.) *Bulletin d'Ecologie*, **11**: 233–42.

Miles, D.W.R., Swanson, F.J. and Youngberg, C.T., 1984, Effects of landslide erosion on subsequent Douglas fir growth and stocking levels in the western Cascades, Oregon, *Soil Science Society of America Journal*, **48**: 667–71.

Miller, E.L., 1984, Sediment yield and storm flow response to clear-cut harvest and site preparation in the Ouachita Mountains, *Water Resources Research*, **20**: 471–5.

Miller, T.B., 1981, Growth and yield of logged-over mixed Dipterocarp forest in East Kalimantan, *Malaysian Forester*, **44**: 419–24.

Miller, H.G., 1989, Internal and external cycling of nutrients in forest stands, in Pereira, J.S. and Landsberg, J.J. (eds.) *Biomass production by fast-growing trees*, Kluwer, Dordrecht, pp. 73–80.

Miller, D. and Rose, R., 1985, Changes in the urban land base and the consequences for the future of forestry, in Sedjo, R.A. (ed.) *Investments in forestry: resources, land use and public policy*, Westview, Boulder, pp. 73–119.

Mnzava, E.M., 1981, Village industries vs. savanna forests, *Unasylva*, **33** (131): 24–9.

Modinos, M. and Tsekouras, G., 1987, Forestry: Greece, *European Environmental Yearbook*, DocTer, London, p. 262.

Moncrief, L.W., 1970, The cultural basis for our environment crisis, *Science*, **170**: 508–12.

Montalembert, M.R. and Clement, J., 1983, Fuelwood supplies in the developing countries, *FAO Forestry Paper 42*.

Moran, W., 1989, Sectoral and statutory planning for rural New Zealand, in Cloke, P.J. (ed.) *Rural land-use planning in developed nations*, Unwin Hyman, London, pp. 238–63.

Moss, D., 1978, Even-aged plantations as a habitat for birds, in Ford, E.D., Malcom, D.C. and Atterson, J. (eds.) *The ecology of even-aged forest plantations*, Edinburgh, IUFRO, pp. 423–27.

Mueller-Dombois, D., 1987, Natural dieback in forests, *BioScience*, **37**: 575–81.

Mumeka, A., 1986, The effect of deforestation and subsistence agriculture on runoff of the Kafue River headwaters, Zambia, *Hydrological Sciences Journal*, **31**: 543–54.

Murphey, R. 1983, Deforestation in modern China, in Tucker, R.P. and Richards, J.F. (eds.) *Global deforestation and the nineteenth century world economy*, Duke University Press, Durham pp. 111–28.

Murphy, G., 1982, Soil damage associated with production thinning, *New Zealand Journal of Forestry science*, **12**: 281–92.

Muthiah, S. (ed.), 1987, *A social and economic atlas of India*, Oxford University

Press, Delhi.

Myers, 1979, *The sinking ark: a new look at the problem of disappearing species*, Pergamon, Oxford.

Myers, N., 1980a, *Conversion of tropical moist forests*, National Academy of Science, Washington.

Myers, N., 1980b, The problems of disappearing species: what can be done? *Ambio* 9: 229–35.

Myers, N., 1981, The hamburger connection: how Central America's forests became North America's hamburgers, *Ambio*, 10: 3–8.

Myers, N., 1983a, Conversion rates in tropical moist forests, in Golley, F.B. (ed.) *Tropical rain forest ecosystems: structure and function*, Elsevier, Amsterdam, pp. 289–300.

Myers, N., 1983b, The tropical forest issue, *Progress in Resource Management and Environmental Planning*, 4: 1–28.

Myers, N., 1983c, Tropical moist forests: over-exploited and under-utilized?, *Forest Ecology and Management*, 6: 59–79.

Myers, N., 1983d, Reduction of biological diversity and species loss, *Ambio*, 12: 72–4.

Myers, N., 1984, Genetic resources in jeopardy, *Ambio*, 13: 171–4.

Myers, N., 1986a, Forestland farming in Western Amazonia: stable and sustainable, *Forest Ecology and Management*, 15: 81–93.

Myers, N., 1986b, Tree-crop based agroecosystems in Java, *Forest Ecology and Management*, 17: 1–11.

Myers, N., 1986c, Tropical deforestation and a mega-extinction spasm, in Soulé, M.E. (ed.) *Conservation biology: the science of scarcity and diversity*, Sinauer, Sunderland, Mass., pp. 394–409.

Myers, N., 1988, Tropical forests: much more than stocks of wood, *Journal of Tropical Ecology*, 4: 209–21.

Myers, N., 1989, Tropical deforestation and climatic changes, *Environmental Conservation*, 15: 293–8.

National Research Council, 1982, *Ecological aspects of development in the humid tropics*, NRC, Washington.

Nautiyal, J.C. and Rawat, J.K., 1985, Role of forest tenure in the investment behaviour of integrated Canadian forestry firms, *Canadian Journal of Forest Research* 16: 456–63.

Nedelin, G., and Gulev., V., 1987, (Special purpose parks and the natural environment) *Gorko Stopanstro Gorkska Promislenost*, 43: 17–18 (*Forestry Abstracts* 49/ 2802).

Nef, J.U., 1977, An early energy crisis and its consequences, *Scientific American*, 237: 140–8.

Neumann, R.P. and Machlis, G.E., 1989, Land use and threats to parks in the Neotropics, *Environmental Conservation*, 16: 13–18.

Netsch, W., 1985, Möliche Auswirkungen der Waldschäden auf bäuerliche Forstbetriebe, *Forst-wissenschaftliches Centralblatt*, 104: 263–71.

Newell, R.E., Reichle, H.G. and Seiler, W., 1989, Carbon monoxide and the burning earth, *Scientific American*, 261: 58–65.

Ngugi, N., 1988, Cultural aspects of fuelwood shortages in the Kenyan highlands,

Journal of Biogeography, **15**: 165–70.

Nilsson, S.G., 1979, Effect of forest management on the breeding bird community in Southern Sweden, *Biological Conservation*, **16**: 135–44.

Nilsson, S.I., Miller, H.G. and Miller, J.D., 1982, Forest growth as a possible cause of soil and water acidification: an examination of the concepts, *Oikos*, **39**: 40–9.

Nomura, I., 1986, Demand and supply outlook of forest products in Japan, in Schreuder, G.F. (ed.) *World trade in forest products*, University of Washington Press, Seattle.

Nor, S.M., 1983, Forestry in Malaysia, *Journal of Forestry*, **81**: 164–6, 187.

Nordin, C.F. and Meade, R.H., 1982, Deforestation and increased flooding on the Amazon, *Science*, **215**: 427.

Normandin, D., 1987, La gestion des patrimonies forestiers privés structures et activités. Essai de typologie sur 46 départments français, *Revue Forestière Française*, **39**: 393–408.

Noronha, R., 1981, Why is it so difficult to grow fuelwood?, *Unasylva*, **33** (131): 4–12.

Nortcliff, S. and Dias, A.C.D.C.P., 1988, The change in soil physical conditions resulting from forest clearance in the humid tropics, *Journal of Biogeography*, **15**: 61–6.

Nwoboshi, L.C., 1987, Regeneration success of natural management, enrichment planting and plantations of native species in West Africa, in Mergen, F., and Vincent, J.R. (eds) *Natural management of tropical moist forests*, Yale University, Newhaven, Conn., pp. 71–92.

Nykvist, N. and Rosen, K., 1985, Effects of clear-felling and slash removal on the acidity of northern coniferous soils, *Forest Ecology and Management*, **11**: 157–69.

Nylund, L., Nylund, M., Kellomaki, S., and Haapenen, A., 1980, Radial growth of Scots pine and soil conditions at some camping sites in southern Finland, *Silva Fennica*, **14**: 1–13.

OECD, 1987, *OECD environmental data compendium 1987*, OECD, Paris.

OECD, 1988, *Environmental policies in Finland*, OECD, Paris.

OECD, 1989a, *OECD environmental data compendium 1989*, OECD, Paris.

OECD, 1989b, *Renewable natural resources: economic incentives for improved management*, OECD, Paris.

Oedekoven, K., 1981, Small private forests in the Federal Republic of Germany, *Journal of Forestry*, **79**: 161–2.

Ofcansky, T.P., 1984, Kenya forestry under British colonial administration 1895–1963, *Journal of Forest History*, **28**: 136–43.

Ohba, K., 1983, Risk evaluation and tree improvement as components of intensive forest management in Japan, *Forest Ecology and Management*, **6**: 245–62.

Ohler, F.M.J., 1985, The fuelwood production of wooded savanna fallows in the Sudan zone of Mali, *Agroforestry Systems*, **3**: 15–23.

O'Keefe, P., and Kristoferson, L., 1984, The uncertain energy path – energy and Third World development, *Ambio*, **13**: 15–23.

Oldfield, S., 1989, The tropical chainsaw massacre, *New Scientist*, **123** (1683) (23 September 1989), 54–7.

Olechowski, A., 1987, Barriers to trade in wood and wood products, in Kallio, M., Dykstra, D.P. and Binkley, C.S. (eds.), *The global forest sector: an analytical perspective*, John Wiley, Chichester, pp. 371–90.

O'Loughlin, C.L. and Owens, I.F., 1987, Our dynamic environment, in Holland, P.G. and Johnston, W.B. (eds.) *Southern approaches: geography in New Zealand*, NZGS, Christchurch, pp. 59–90.

Olson, S.H., 1971, *The depletion myth: a history of railroad use of timber*, Harvard University Press, Cambridge, Mass.

ONF (Office National des Forêts), 1966, *Office National des Forêts*, ONF, Paris.

Osaka, M.M., 1983, Forest preservation in Tokugawa Japan, in Tucker, R.P. and Richards, J.F. (eds.) *Global deforestation and the nineteenth century world economy*, Duke University Press, Durham, pp. 129–45.

Osara, N.A., 1984, World forestry: some trends and prospects, *Acta Forestalia Fennica*, **190**: 91–107.

Osemeobo, G.J., 1988, The human causes of forest depletion in Nigeria, *Environmental Conservation*, **15**: 17–28.

Ovington, J.D. (ed.), 1983, *Temperate broad-leaved evergreen forests*, Elsevier, Amsterdam.

Palca, J., 1987, High-finance approach to protecting tropical forests, *Nature*, 328: 373.

Paille, G.G. and Deffrasnes, R., 1988, Le nouveau régime forestier du Québec, *Forestry Chronicle*, **64**: 3–8.

Palm, C.A., Houghton, R.A., Melillo, J.M. and Skole, D.L., 1986, Atmospheric carbon dioxide from deforestation in South-east Asia, *Biotropica*, **18**: 177–88.

Palmer, J.R., 1986, Jari: leçons pour les responsables de mise en valeur des terres sous les tropiques, *Bois et Forêts des Tropiques*, **212**: 3–15.

Palo, M., 1987, Deforestation perspectives for the Tropics: a provisional theory with pilot applications, in Kallio, M., Dykstra, D.P. and Binkley, C.S. (eds.) *The global forest sector: an analytical perspective*, John Wiley, Chichester, pp. 57–89.

Palo, M. and Mery, G., 1986, Deforestation perspectives in the tropics with a global view: a pilot quantitative human population growth approach, *18th IUFRO Congress Report*, Ljubljana, 552–85.

Papanastasis, V.P., 1986, Policy analysis and integrated land use, *Silva Fennica*, **20**: 274–9.

Pardé, J., 1980, Forest biomass, *Forestry Abstracts*, **41**: 343–62.

Pardo, R.D., 1985, The social dimension of forest utilization agreements, *Unasylva*, **37**: 36–43.

Parker, P.K., 1987, Australian rain-forest sub-divisions and conservation strategies, *Environmental Conservation*, **14**: 37–43.

Parsons, H.L., 1977, Marx and Engels on ecology, Greenwood Press, Westport.

Pastor, J. and Post, W.M., 1988, Response of northern forests to CO_2-induced climatic change, *Nature*, **334**: 55–7.

Paterson, S.S., 1956, *The forest area of the world and its potential productivity*, Royal University of Gothenburg.

Patric, J.H., 1976, Soil erosion in the eastern forest, *Journal of Forestry*, **74**: 671–7.

Patric, J.H., 1980, Some environmental effects of cable logging in Appalachian forests, *USDA Forest Service General Technical Report NE 55*.

Patric, J.H., Evans, J.O. and Helvey, J.D., 1984, Summary of sediment yield data from forested land in the United States, *Journal of Forestry*, **82**: 101–3.

Pavlovskii, E.S., 1986, (Protective forestry in the USSR), Agropromizdat, Moscow, *Forestry Abstracts* 50/ 2141.

Payette, S., Fillion, L., Gauthier, L. and Boutin, Y., 1985, Secular climatic change in old-growth tree-line vegetation in northern Quebec, *Nature*, **315**: 135–8.

Peck, T., 1984, The world perspective, in Hummel, F.C. (ed.) *Forest policy: a contribution to resource development*, Martinus Nijhoff/Dr W. Junk, The Hague, pp. 21–66.

Pearse, P.H., Land, A.J. and Todd, K.L., 1986, The backlog of unstocked forest land in British Columbia and the impact of reforestation programs, *Forestry Chronicle*, **62**: 514–21.

Pellek, R., 1983, Depletion of the Mauritanian forest, *Journal of Forestry*, **81**: 320–1.

Perry, D.A. and Maghembe, J., 1989, Ecosystem concepts and current trends in forest management: time for reappraisal, *Forest Ecology and Management*, **26**: 123–40.

Persson, R., 1974, World forest resources: review of the world's forest resources in the early 1970s, *Research Note 17*, Royal College of Forestry, Stockholm.

Persson, J., 1986, Trees, plans and a rural community in the southern Sudan, *Unasylva*, **38** (152): 32–43.

Peters, C., Gentry, A. and Mendelsohn, O., 1989, Valuation of an Amazonian rainforest, *Nature*, **339**: 655–6.

Piearce, G.D., 1986, How to save the Zambezi teak forests, *Unasylva*, **38** (152): 29–36.

Pimentel, D., Dazhong, W., Eigenbrode, S., Lang, H., Emerson, D. and Karasik, M., 1986, Deforestation: interdependency of fuelwood and agriculture, *Oikos*, **46**: 404–12.

Pitelka, L.F. and Raynal, D.J., 1989, Forest decline and acid deposition, *Ecology*, **70**: 2–10.

Pittock, A.B., 1987, Forests beyond 2000 – effects of atmospheric change, *Australian Forestry*, **50**: 205–15.

Plamoudou, A.P., 1982, Augmentation de la concentration des sédiments en suspension suite à l'exploitation forestière et durée de l'effet, *Canadian Journal of Forest Research*, **12**: 883–92.

Pollard, D.F.W., 1985, A forestry perspective on the carbon dioxide issue, *Forestry Chronicle,* **61**: 312–8.

Posey, D.A., 1985, Indigenous management of tropical forest ecosystems: the case of the Kayapo Indians of the Brazilian Amazon, *Agroforestry Systems*, **3**: 139–58.

Postel, S. and Heise, L., 1988, Reforesting the earth, *Worldwatch Paper 83*, Washington.

Potter, G.L., Elkaesser, H.W., McCracken, M.C., and Luthere, F.M., 1975, Possible climatic impact of tropical deforestation, *Nature*, **258**: 697–8.

Poulsen, G., 1982, The non-wood products of African forests, *Unasylva*, **34** (137); 15–21.

Prance, G.T., 1986, The Amazon: paradise lost? in Kaufman, L. and Mallory, K. (eds.) *The last extinction*, MIT Press, Cambridge, Mass., pp. 62–106.

Prats Llaurado, J. and Speidel, G., 1981, Public forestry administration in Latin America, *FAO Forestry Paper 25*.

Priasukmana, S., 1986, The trade and investment opportunities of the forestry sector in East Kalimantan, in Schreuder, G.F. (ed.) *World trade in forest products*, University of Washington Press, Seattle, pp. 207–23.

Price, M.F., 1988, Legislation and policy for forests of the Swiss Alps, *Land Use Policy*, 5: 314–28.

Prieur, M., 1987, Forestry: France, *European Environmental Yearbook*, DocTer, London, pp. 252–8.

Pringle, S.L., 1977, The future availability of wood pulp: a world picture, *Unasylva*, 29 (115): 18–25.

Pringle, S.L., 1979, The outlook for tropical wood imports, *Unasylva*, 31 (125): 10–8.

Prins, K., 1987, European timber: 2000 and beyond, *Unasylva*, 39 (156): 51–60.

Pullan, R.A., 1988, Conservation and the development of national parks in the humid tropics of Africa, *Journal of Biogeography*, 15: 171–83.

Pyatt, D.G. and Craven, M.M., 1978, Soil changes under even-aged plantations, in Ford, E.D., Malcolm, D.C. and Atterson, J. (eds.) *The ecology of even-aged forest plantations*, IVFRO, Edinburgh, pp. 369–86.

Raison, R.J. and Crane, W.J.B., 1986, Nutritional costs of shortened rotations in plantation forestry, in Gessel, S.P. (ed.) *Forest and site productivity*, Martinus Nijhoff, Dordrecht, pp. 117–25.

Rakestraw, L., 1955, *A history of forest conservation in the Pacific Northwest*, Arno Press, New York.

Ramade, F., 1984, *Ecology of natural resources*, John Wiley, Chichester.

Ramm, C.W., Potter, K.L., and Rudolph, V.J., 1987, Toward a national forest system in the Dominican Republic, *Journal of Forestry*, 85: 47–9.

Rankin, J.M., 1985, Forestry in the Brazilian Amazon, in Prance, G.T. and Lovejoy, T.E. (eds.) *Amazonia*, Pergamon, Oxford, pp. 369–92.

Ratcliffe, D.A. and Oswald, P.H., 1986, (eds.) *Birds, bogs and forestry: the peatlands of Caithness and Sutherland*, Nature Conservancy Council, Peterborough.

Rauf, Abd. S., 1983, Employment in the primary wood-based industries of Peninsular Malaysia, *Malaysian Forester*, 46: 20–5.

Raumolin, J., 1984, The formation of the sustained yield forestry system in Finland, in Steen, H.K. (ed.) *The history of sustained-yield forestry: a symposium*, Forest History Society, Santa Cruz, pp. 155–69.

Reclus, E., 1871, *The earth*, Chapman and Hall, London.

Redpath, D.K., Lacate, D.S. and Moore, K.E., 1986, Land-use changes on prime forest land in the Prince George, B.C., Region 1965–1981, *Forestry Chronicle*, 62: 236–9.

Reed, F.L.C., 1983, Forest renewal in Canada, *Commonwealth Forestry Review*, 62: 169–77.

Rees, J.A., 1985, *Natural resources: allocation, economics and policy*, Methuen, London.

Rehfuess, K.E., 1985, On the causes of decline of Norway spruce (*Picea abies Karst*) in Central Europe, *Soil Use and Management*, **1**: 30–1.

Reid, L.M. and Dunne, T., 1984, Sediment production from forest road surfaces, *Water Resources Research*, **20**: 1753–61.

Repetto, R., 1988, *The forest for the trees? Government policies and the misuse of forest resources*, World Resources Institute, Washington.

Repetto, R. and Gillis, M. (eds.), 1988, *Public policy and the misuse of forest resources*, Cambridge University Press, Cambridge and New York.

Rich, B.M., 1989, The greening of the development banks: rhetoric and reality, *The Ecologist*, **19**: 44–52.

Richards, J.F., 1986, World environmental history and economic development, in Clark, W.C. and Munn, R.E. (eds.) *Sustainable development of the biosphere*, Cambridge University Press, Cambridge, pp. 53–71.

Richards, J.F., Haynes, E.S. and Hagen, J.R., 1985, Changes in land and human productivity in Northern India 1870–1970, *Agricultural History*, **59**: 523–48.

Richards, J.F. and McAlpin, M.B., 1983, Cotton cultivating and land clearing in the Bombay Deccan and Karnatak 1818–1920, in Tucker, R.P. and Richards, J.F. (eds.) *Global deforestation and the nineteenth century world economy*, Duke University Press, Durham. pp. 68–94.

Richards, J.F., and Tucker, R.P. (eds.), 1988, *World deforestation in the twentieth century* Duke University Press, Durham and London.

Richards, P., 1952, *The tropical rain forest*, Cambridge University Press, Cambridge.

Riethmuller, P. and Fenelon, J., 1988, *Japanese agricultural policies: a time of change*, Australian Government Publishing Service, Canberra.

Riley, S.J., 1984, Effect of clearing and roading operations on the permeability of forest soils, Karnah catchment, New South Wales, Australia, *Forest Ecology and Management*, **9**: 283–93.

Risbrudt, C.D., Kaiser, H.F. and Ellefson, P.V., 1983, Cost effectiveness of the 1979 Forestry Incentives Program, *Journal of Forestry*, **81**: 298–301.

Robbins, W.G., 1985, *American forestry: a history of national, state and private co-operation*, University of Nebraska Press, Lincoln.

Roberts, R.G. and Church, M., 1986, The sediment budget in a severely disturbed watershed, Queen Charlotte Ranges, B.C., *Canadian Journal of Forest Research*, **15**: 1092–106.

Robinson, M. and Blyth, K., 1982, The effect of forestry drainage operations on upland and sediment yields: a case study, *Earth Surface Processes and Landforms*, **7**: 85–90.

Rochadi, A., Kartawinata, K., and Sukardjo, S., 1981, Effects of mechanized logging in the lowland dipterocarp forest at Lempake, East Kalimantan, *Malaysian Forester*, **44**: 407–18.

Roche, L., 1979, Forestry and the conservation of plants and animals in the tropics, *Forest Ecology and Management*, **2**: 103–22.

Roche, M.M., 1984, Reactions to scarcity: the management of forest resources in nineteenth century Canterbury, New Zealand, *Journal of Forest History*, **28**: 82–91.

Roche, M.M., 1986, Company afforestation: patterns and processes during the 'first planting boom', in Magee, A. and Chalmers, L. (eds.), *Proceedings of the*

13th New Zealand Geographical Society Conference, NZGS, Christchurch, pp. 107–11.

Roche, M.M., 1987, 'New Zealand timber for the New Zealanders', Regulatory controls and the dislocation of the Pacific timber trade in the 1920s and 1930s, in Le Heron, R., Roche, M. and Shepherd, M. (eds.), *Proceedings of the 14th New Zealand Geography Conference and 56th ANZAAS Congress Geographical science*, NZGS, Palmerston North, pp. 195–203.

Rollet, B., 1980, Jari: succès ou échec, *Bois et Forêts des Tropiques*, **192**: 3–34.

Romm, J., 1986, Forest policy and development policy, *Journal of World Forest Resource Management*, **2**: 85–103.

Romm, J., Tuazon, R., and Washburn, C., 1987, Relating forestry investment to the characteristics of nonindustrial private forestland owners in northern California, *Forest Science*, **33**: 197–209.

Romm, J. and Washburn, C., with Tuazon, R. and Bendix, J., 1987, Public subsidy and private forestry investment: analyzing the selectivity and leverage of a common policy form, *Land Economics*, **62**: 157–67.

Rosen, K., 1984, Effect of clear felling on run off in two small watersheds in central Sweden, *Forest Ecology and Management*, **9**: 267–81.

Ross, M.S., 1985, The development and current status of land clearing for transmigration in Indonesia, *Journal of World Forest Resource Management*, **2**: 119–36.

Rotaru, C., 1985, Les phénomènes de tassement du sol forestier dus à l'exploitation mécanisée du bois, *Revue Forestière Française*, **37**: 359–70.

Roth, D.M., 1983, Philippine forests and forestry 1565–1920, in Tucker, R.P. and Richards, J.F. (eds.) *Global deforestation and the nineteenth century world economy*, Duke University Press, Durham, pp. 30–49.

Rotty, R.M., 1986, Estimates of CO_2 from woodfuel based on forest harvest data, *Climatic Changes*, **9**: 311–25.

Routley, R. and Routley, V., 1974, *The fight for the forests: the takeover of Australian forests for pines, woodchips and intensive forestry*, Australian National University, Canberra.

Royer, J.P. and Kaiser, H.F., 1983, Reforestation decisions on harvested southern timberlands, *Journal of Forestry*, **81**: 657–9.

Royer, J.P., and Moulton, R.J., 1987, Reforestation incentives, *Journal of Forestry*, **85**: 45–7.

Rubner, H., 1984, Sustained-yield forestry in Europe and its crisis during the era of the Nazi dictatorship, in Steen, H.K. (ed.) *History of sustained-yield forestry: a symposium*, Forest History Society, Santa Cruz, pp. 170–5.

Russell, B.P., 1985, Why invest in private woodlands or continue with them?, *Quarterly Journal of Forestry*, **79**: 169–74.

Ryti, N., 1986, Trends and likely structural changes in the forest industry worldwide, in Kallio, M., Anderson, A.E., Seppala, R. and Morgan, A. (eds.) *Systems analysis in forestry and forest industries*, Elsevier – North Holland, Amsterdam, pp. 27–39.

Saastamoinen, O., 1982, Economics of multiple-use forestry in the Saariselka forest and fell area, *Communicationes Instituti Forestalis Fenniae No. 104*, 102 pp.

Sabroe, A.S., 1954, *Forestry in Denmark*, Danish Forestry Society, Copenhagen.

Sader, S.A. and Joyce, A.T., 1988, Deforestation rates and trends in Costa Rica, 1940 to 1983, *Biotropica*, **20**: 11–9.

Salatti, E. and Vose, P.B., 1983, Depletion of tropical rain forests, *Ambio*, **12**: 67–71.

Salatti, E. and Vose, P.B., 1984, Amazon Basin: a system in equilibrium, *Science*, **225**: 129–38.

Sankovich, M.M., 1984, (Production and utilisation of minor forest products), Lesovedenie: Lesnoe Khoryaistro, 19: 119–22, *Forestry Abstracts 49/ 1347*.

Sassaman, R.W. and Miller, R.W., 1986, Native American forestry, *Journal of Forestry*, **84**: 26–32.

Savill, P.S. and Evans, J., 1986, *Plantation silviculture in temperate regions*, Clarendon, Oxford.

Sauer, C.O., 1938, Theme of plant and animal destruction in economic history, in Leighly, J. (ed.) (1963) *Land and life*, University of California Press, Berkeley and Los Angeles, pp. 45–54.

Schmidt, R., 1987, Tropical rain forest management, *Unasylva*, **39** (156): 2–17.

Schmithusen, F., 1976, Forest utilization contracts on public land in the tropics, *Unasylva*, **28** (112–3): 52–73.

Schmithusen, F., 1979, Logging and legislation, *Unasylva*, **31** (124): 2–10.

Schmithusen, F., 1986, The changing role of legislation related to forest conservation and forest resources development, *Silva Fennica*, **20**: 270–3.

Schöpfer, W. and Hradetzky, J., 1984, Der Indizienbeweis: Luftverschuntzung massgebliche Ursache de Walderkrankung, *Forst-wissenschaftliches Central-blatt*, **103**: 231–48.

Schrepfer, S.R., 1983, *The fight to save the redwoods: a history of environmental reform 1917–1978*, University of Wisconsin Press, Madison.

Schreuder, G.F. and Vlosky, R.P., 1986, Indonesia as an exporter and importer of forest products, in Schreuder, G.F. (ed.) *World trade in forest products*, University of Washington Press, Seattle, pp. 172–84.

Schutz, C.J., 1986, Monitoring the long-term effects of management practices on site productivity in South African forestry, in Gessel, S.P. (ed.) *Forest site and productivity*, Martinus Nijhoff, Dordrecht, pp. 137–44.

Schwartz, T., 1989, The Brazilian forest people's movement, *The Ecologist*, **19**: 245–7.

Seddon, G., 1984, Logging in the Gogol Valley, Papua New Guinea, *Ambio*, **13**: 351–4.

Sedjo, R.A., 1980, Forest plantations in Brazil and their possible effects on world pulp markets, *Journal of Forestry*, **78**: 702–5.

Sedjo, R.A., 1984, An economic assessment of industrial forest plantations, *Forest Ecology and Management*, **9**: 245–57.

Sedjo, R.A. (ed.) 1985, *Investments in forestry: resources, land use and public policy*, Westview, Boulder.

Sedjo, R.A., 1986, Forest plantations of the Tropics and Southern Hemisphere and their implications for the economics of temperate climate forestry, in Kallio, M., Andersson, A.E., Seppala, R. and Morgan, A. (eds.) *Systems analysis in forestry and forest industries*, Elsevier – North Holland, Amsterdam, pp. 55–72.

Sedjo, R.A., 1987, Forest resources of the world: forests in transition, in Kallio, M., Dykstra, D.P., and Binkley, C.S. (eds.) *The global forest sector: an analytical perspective*, John Wiley, Chichester, pp. 7–31.

Sedjo, R.A., 1989, Forests: a tool to moderate global warming, *Environment*, **31** (1): 14–20.

Sedjo, R.A. and Clawson, M., 1983, Tropical deforestation: how serious?, *Journal of Forestry*, **81**: 792–4.

Sedjo, R.A. and Clawson, M., 1984, Global forests, in Simon, J.L. and Kahn, H. (eds.) *The resourceful earth: a response to Global 2000*, Basil Blackwell, Oxford, pp. 128–170.

Seiler, W. and Crutzen, P.J., 1980, Estimates of carbon flux between biosphere and atmosphere from biomass burning, *Climatic Change*, **1**: 207–47.

Shands, W.E. and Hoffman, J.S. (eds.), 1987, *The greenhouse effect, climatic change and U.S. forests*, Conservation Foundation, Washington.

Sheffield, R.M. and Cost, N.D., 1987, Behind the decline: why are natural pine stands in the Southeast growing slower?, *Journal of Forestry*, **85**: 29–33.

Shelton, N., 1985, Logging versus the natural habitat in the survival of tropical forests, *Ambio*, **14**, 39–41.

Shimokawa, E., 1977, Japan's dependence upon wood chips for pulp, *Unasylva*, **29**: 26–7.

Shimotori, S., 1984, Trends and problems in national forest management in Hokkaido since World War II, in Steen, K.H. (ed.) *History of sustained-yield forestry*, Forest History Society, Santa Cruz, pp. 281–8.

Shimotori, S., 1986, Private and municipal forests and the forestry planning system in Japan: trends and problems after World War II, *Silva Fennica*, **20**: 385–93.

Shiva, V., 1987, Forestry myths and the World Bank, *The Ecologist*, **17**: 142–9.

Shiva, V. and Bandyopadhyay, J., 1988, The Chipko movement, in Ives, J.D. and Pitt, D.C. (eds.), *Deforestation: social dynamics in watershed and mountain ecosystems*, Routledge, London and New York, pp. 224–41.

Shiva, V., Bandyopadhyay, J. and Jayal, N.D., 1985, Afforestation in India: problems and strategies, *Ambio*, **14**: 329–33.

Shugart, H.H., Antonovsky, M.Y., Jarvis, P.G. and Sandford, A.P., 1986, CO_2, climatic change and forest ecosystems, in Bolin, B., Doos, B.R., Jager, J. and Warrick, R.A. (eds.), *The greenhouse effect, climatic change and ecosystems*, John Wiley, Chichester, pp. 475–521.

Shuttleworth, W.J., 1988, Evaporation from Amazonian rainforest, *Proceedings of the Royal Society of London B Biological Sciences*, **233**: 321–46.

Shyamsunder, S. and Parameswarappa, S., 1987, Forestry in India: a forester's view, *Ambio*, **16**: 332–7.

Siebert, S.F., 1987, Land-use intensification in tropical uplands: effects on vegetation, soil fertility and erosion, *Forest Ecology and Management*, **21**, 37–56.

Simberloff, D., 1986, Are we on the verge of a mass extinction in tropical rain forests? in Elliot, D.K. (ed.), *Dynamics of extinction*, John Wiley, New York, pp. 165–82.

Simmons, I.G., 1989, *Changing the face of the earth*, Basil Blackwell, Oxford.

Simon, J.L., 1986, Disappearing species, deforestation and data, *New Scientist*, **110**: 60–3.

Simon, J.L. and Wildavsky, A., 1984, On species loss, the absence of data and risk to humanity, in Simon, J.L. and Kahn, H. (eds.), *The resourceful earth: a response to Global 2000*, Basil Blackwell, Oxford, pp. 171–83.

Simons, P., 1989, Nobody loves a canal with no water, *New Scientist*, **124** (7 October 1989): 48–52.

Sinduredjo, K., 1986, Indonesia as a plywood exporter, in Schreuder, G.F. (ed.), *World trade in forest products*, University of Washington Press, Seattle, pp. 191–6.

Sioli, H., 1985a, The effects of deforestation in Amazonia, in Hemming, J. (ed.), *Change in the Amazon Basin, Vol. 1: man's impact on forests and rivers*, Manchester University Press, pp. 58–65.

Sioli, H., 1985b, The effects of deforestation in Amazonia, *Geographical Journal*, **151**: 197–203.

Skog, K.E., and Watterson, I.A., 1984, Residential fuelwood use in the United States, *Journal of Forestry*, **82**: 742–7.

Smiet, F., 1987, Tropical watershed forestry under attack, *Ambio*, **16**: 156–8.

Smil, V., 1983, Deforestation in China, *Ambio*, **12**: 226–31.

Smith, W.H., 1985, Forest quality and air quality, *Journal of Forestry*, **83**: 82–94.

Smith, B. and Wilson, P., 1984, The public's evaluation of land-use options in two New Zealand regions, *New Zealand Journal of Forestry*, **29**: 249–68.

Solbrig, O.T., 1984, Forests and woodlands (Southern Andes), *Mountain Research and Development*, **4**: 163–73.

Sommer, A., 1976, Attempt at an assessment of the world's tropical moist forests, *Unasylva*, **28**: 5–24.

South, P.M., 1981, World view and Australian perspective, in Day, M.F. (ed.), *Australia's forests: their role in our future*, Australian Academy of Science, Canberra, pp. 4–20.

Spears, J.S., 1979, Can the wet tropical forest survive?, *Commonwealth Forestry Review*, **58**: 165–80.

Spears, J.S., 1983, Tropical reforestation: an achievable goal?, *Commonwealth Forestry Review*, **62**: 201–17.

Speth, W.W., 1977, Carl Ortwin Sauer on destructive exploitation, *Biological Conservation*, **11**: 273–7.

Spray, C.J., Crick, H.Q.P. and Hart, A.D.M., 1987, Effects of aerial applications of fenitrothion on bird populations of a Scottish pine plantation, *Journal of Applied Ecology*, **24**: 29–47.

Spurr, S.H. and Vaux, H.J., 1976, Timber, biological and economic potential, *Science*, **191**: 752–6.

Statistics Canada, 1986, *Human activity and the environment: a statistical compendium*, Statistics Canada, Ottawa.

Steen, H.K., 1976, *The U.S. Forest Service: a history*, University of Washington Press, Seattle.

Steinlin, H.J., 1982, Monitoring the world's tropical forests, *Unasylva*, **34** (137): 2–9.

Steinlin, H. and Pretsch, J., 1984, Der tropische Feuchtwald in der internationalen Forstpolitik, *Holz-Zentralblatt*, **110**: 2053–7, Forestry Abstracts 46/563.

Sternberg, H.O., 1987, Aggravation of floods in the Amazon River as a consequence of deforestation? *Geografiska Annaler*, **69A**: 201–9.

Straka, T.J., Wisdom, H.W. and Moak, J.E., 1984, Size of forest holding and investment behaviour of nonindustrial private owners, *Journal of Forestry*, **82**: 495–6.

Streyffert, T., 1968, *World pulpwood*, Almqvist and Wiksell, Stockholm.

Stridsberg, E., 1984, Multiple-use forestry in former days, in Saastamoinen, O., Hultman, S.G., Kock, N.E. and Mattson, L. (eds.), Multiple use forestry in the Scandinavian countries, *Communicationes Instituti Forestalis Fenniae*, **120**, pp. 14–8.

Struhsaker, T.T., 1987, Forestry and conservation in Uganda, *Biological Conservation*, **39**: 209–34.

Struhsaker, T.T., Kasenene, J.M., Gaither, J.G., Larsen, N., Mussango, S. and Bancroft, R., 1989, Tree mortality in the Kibale forest, Uganda: a case study of dieback in a tropical rainforest adjacent to exotic conifer plantations, *Forest Ecology and Management*, **29**: 165–86.

Styrman, M., and Wibe, S., 1986, Wood reserves and availability as determinants of the supply of timber, *Canadian Journal of Forest Research*, **16**: 256–9.

Suffling, R. and Michalenko, G., 1980, The Reed affair: a Canadian logging and pollution controversy, *Biological Conservation*, **17**: 5–24.

Suran, J.C., 1985, Indonesia's plywood industry, *Bois et Forêts des Tropiques*, **210**: 141–50.

Sutton, W.R.J., 1975, Forest resources of the USSR: their exploitation and potential, *Commonwealth Forestry Review*, **54**: 110–38.

Swank, W.T. and Douglass, J.E., 1974, Streamflow greatly reduced by converting deciduous hardwood to pine, *Science*, **185**: 857–9.

Swanston, D.N. and Dyrness, C.T., 1973, Stability of steepland, *Journal of Forestry*, **71**, 264–9.

Takeuchi, K., 1983, Market prospects for tropical hardwoods from South-east Asia, in Bethel, J.S. (ed.), *World trade in forest products*, University of Washington Press, Seattle, pp. 432–46.

Tamm, C.O., 1989, Comparative and experimental approaches to the study of acid deposition effects on soils as substrate for forest growth, *Ambio*, **18**: 184–91.

Tamm, C.O. and Hallbacken, L., 1988, Changes in soil acidity in two forest areas with different acid deposition: 1920s to 1980s, *Ambio*, **17**: 56–61.

Tang, H.T., 1980, Factors affecting regeneration methods for tropical high forests in South-east Asia, *Malaysian Forester*, **43**: 469–80.

Tang, H.T., 1987, Problems and strategies for regenerating Dipterocarp forests in Malaysia, in Mergen, F. and Vincent, J.R. (eds.), *Natural management of tropical moist forests*, Yale University, Newhaven, Conn., pp. 23–45.

Teeguarden, d.E., 1985, Effects of public policy on forestry investments, in Sedjo, R.A. (ed.), *Investments in forestry: resources, land use and public policy*, Westview Press, Boulder, pp. 215–40.

Thang, H.C., 1987, Forest management systems for tropical high forest, with special reference to Peninsular Malaysia, *Forest Ecology and Management*, **21**: 3–20.

Thirgood, J.V., 1981, *Man and the Mediterranean forest*, Academic Press, London.

Thirgood, J.V., 1986a, The Barbary forests and forest lands, environmental destruction and the vicissitudes of history, *Journal of World Forest Resource management*, **2**: 137–84.

Thirgood, J.V., 1986b, The struggle for sustension on the island of Cyprus, *Journal of World Forest Resource Management*, **2**: 21–41.

Thirgood, J.V., 1987, *Cyprus: a chronicle of its forests, land and people*, University of British Columbia Press, Vancouver.

Thompson, R.P. and Jones, J.G., 1981, Classifying nonindustrial private forestland by tract size, *Journal of Forestry*, **79**: 288–91.

Thompson, M. and Warburton, M., 1988, Uncertainty on a Himalayan scale, in Ives, J.O. and Pitt, D.C. (eds.), *Deforestation: social dynamics in watersheds and mountain ecosystems*. Routledge, London and New York, pp. 1–53.

Thomson, J.T., 1988, Deforestation and desertification in twentieth century arid Sahelian Africa, in Richards, J.F. and Tucker, R.P. (eds.), *World deforestation in the twentieth century*, Duke University Press, Durham, pp. 70–90.

Tibbits, W.N., 1986, Eucalypt plantations in Tasmania, *Australian Forestry*, **49**: 219–25.

Tikkanen, I., 1986, Search for innovative forest policies and programs: the future and role of policy and program analysis, *Silva Fennica*, **20**: 265–9.

Tilastokeskus (annual) *Suomen Tilastollinen Vuosikirja*, Tilastokeskus, Helsinki.

Tilling, A.J., 1988, Multiple use indigenous forestry on west coast of South Island, *New Zealand Forestry*, **32**: 13–8.

Tillman, D.A., 1978, *Wood as an energy resource*, Academic Press, New York.

Totman, C., 1982, Forestry in early modern Japan 1650–1850: a preliminary survey, *Agricultural History*, **56**: 415–26.

Totman, C., 1984, From exploitation to plantation forestry in early modern Japan, in Steen, H.K. (ed.), *History of sustained yield forestry: a symposium*, Forest History Society, Santa Cruz, pp. 270–80.

Totman, C., 1986, Plantation forestry in early modern Japan: economic aspects of its emergence, *Agricultural History*, **60**: 23–51.

Trimble, S.W. and Weirich, F.H., 1987, Reforestation reduces streamflow in the south-eastern United States, *Journal of Soil and Water Conservation*, **42**: 274–6.

Trotmann, I.G. and Thomson, A.P., 1988, 65 years of state forest recreation, *New Zealand Forestry*, **33**: 9–12.

Tsay, T.B., 1987, Forestry in Japan, *Forestry Chronicle*, **63**: 97–102.

Tseplyaev, V.P., 1965, *The forests of the USSR*, IPST, Jerusalem.

Tucker, R.P., 1983, The British colonial system and the forests of the western Himalayas, 1815–1914, in Tucker, R.P. and Richard, J.F. (eds.), *Global deforestation in the nineteenth century*, Duke University Press, Durham, pp. 146–66.

Tucker, R.P., 1984a, The historical context of social forestry in the Kumaon Himalayas, *Journal of Developing Areas*, **16**: 341–55.

Tucker, R.P., 1984b, The forests of the western Himalayas: the legacy of British colonial administration, *Journal of Forest History*, **26**: 112–23.

Tucker, R.P., 1986, Major sources of deforestation in the Tropics since 1800, *Proceedings, Division 6, 18th IUFRO World Congress Voluntary Papers*, pp. 300–11.

Tucker, R.P., 1987, Dimensions of deforestation in the Himalayas: the historical setting, *Mountain Research and Development*, **7**: 328–33.

Tucker, R.P., 1988, The British Empire and India's forest resources: the timberlands of Assam and Kumaon 1914–1950, in Richards, J.F. and Tucker, R.P. (eds.), *Global deforestation in the twentieth century*, Duke University Press, Durham, pp. 91–111.

Tucker, R.P. and Richards, J.F. (eds.), 1983, *Global deforestation and the nineteenth century world economy*, Duke University Press, Durham.

Tyler, C., 1989, Towards a warmer world, *Geographical Magazine*, **61**: 40–3.

Udvârdy, M.F.D., 1975, *A classification of the biogeographical provinces of the world*, IUCN, Gland.

Uhl, C. and Buschbacher, R., 1985, A disturbing synergism between cattle ranch burning practices and selective tree harvesting in the Eastern Amazon, *Biotropica*, **17**: 265–8.

Uhl, C., Buschbacher, R. and Serrao, E.A.S., 1988, Abandoned pastures of Eastern Amazonia, I: Pattern of plant succession, *Journal of Ecology*, **76**: 663–81.

Uhl, C., Nepstad, D., Buschbacher, R., Clark, K., Kauffman, B., and Subler, S., 1989, Disturbance and regeneration in Amazonia: lessons for sustainable land use. *The Ecologist*, **19**: 235–40.

Uhlrich, B., 1986, Die Rolle der Bodenversanerung beim Waldsterben: Langfristige Konsequenzem und forstliche Möglichkeiten, *Forst-Wissenschaftliches Centralblatt*, **105**: 421–35.

UN Conference on Desertification, 1977, *Desertification: its causes and consequences*, Pergamon, Oxford.

UNECE and FAO, 1985, *The forest resources of the ECE Region*, ECE/FAO, Geneva.

USDA, 1981, An assessment of the forest and rangeland situation in the United States, *Forest Service Report 22*.

USDA, 1982, As analysis of the timber situation in the United States, *Forest Service Report 23*.

US Department of Commerce, Bureau of the Census (annual) *Statistical Abstract of the United States*, Washington.

van den Berg, L.M., 1989, Rural land-use planning in the Netherlands: integration or segregation of functions? in Cloke, P.J. (ed.), *Rural land-use planning in developed nations*, Unwin Hyman, London, pp. 47–75.

van Hise, C.R., 1910, *Conservation of natural resources in the United States*, Macmillan, New York.

van Hook, R.I., Johnson, D.W., West, D.C. and Mann, L.K., 1982, Environmental effects of harvesting forests for energy, *Forest Ecology and Management*, **4**: 79–84.

Vannière, B., 1977, Influence de l'environnement économique sur l'aménagement forestier en afrique tropicale, *Bois et Forêts Tropiques*, **175**: 3–14.

Veblen, T.T., 1978, Forest preservation in the Western Highlands of Guatemala, *Geographical Review*, **68**: 417–34.

Veblen, T.T., 1984, Degradation of native forest resources in Southern Chile, in Steen, H.K. (ed.), *History of sustained yield forestry: a symposiums*, Forest History Society, Santa Cruz, pp. 344–52.

Vehkamaki, S., 1986, The economic basis of forest policy, *Acta Forestalia Fennica*, **194**: 1–60.

Veijalainen, H., 1976, Effect of forestry on the yields of wild berries and edible fungi, in Tamm, C.O. (ed.), *Man and the boreal forest*, Ecological Bulletin, Stockholm, 21: 63–5.

Victor, M.A.M., Kronka, F.J.N., Timoni, J.L. and Yamazoe, G., 1986, Land classification for industrial afforestation in the state of São Paolo, Brazil, in Gessel, S.P. (ed.), *Forest site and productivity*, Martinus Nijhoff, Dordrecht, pp. 69–91.

Vincent, J.R., Chamberlain, J.L. and Warren, S.T., 1987, Summary in Mergen, F. and Vincent, J.R., *Natural management of tropical moist forests*, Yale University, Newhaven, Conn., pp. 200–7.

von Maydell, H.J., 1985, The contribution of agroforestry to world forestry development, *Agroforestry Systems*, 3: 83–90.

Wadsworth, F.H., 1983, Production of usable wood from tropical forests, in Golley, F.B. (ed.), *Tropical rain forest ecosystems: structure and function*, Elsevier, Amsterdam, pp. 279–88.

Wadsworth, F.H., 1987, Applicability of Asian and African sylvicultural systems to naturally regenerated forests in the Neotropics, in Mergen, F. and Vincent, J.R. (eds.), *Natural management of tropical moist forest*, Yale University, Newhaven, Conn., pp. 93–111.

Walker, R.T., 1987, Land use transition and deforestation in developing countries, *Geographical Analysis*, 19: 18–30.

Walker, L.C. and Hoesada, J.A., 1986, Indonesia: forestry by degree, *Journal of Forestry*, 84: 38–43.

Wallace, T.D. and Newman, D.H., 1986, Measurement of ownership effects on forest productivity in North Carolina from 1974 to 1984, *Canadian Journal of Forest Research*, 16: 733–8.

Walsh, J., 1987, Bolivia swops debt for conservation, *Science*, 237: 598–7.

Walter, H., 1985, *Vegetation of the earth*, Springer–Verlag, New York.

Wardle, P., and Palmieri, M., 1981, What does fuelwood really cost?. *Unasylva*, 33 (131): 20–23.

Weetman, G.F., 1986, The state of Canadian forest management, *Forestry Chronicle*, 62: 348–54.

Wegener, H.-J., 1987, Forestry: Germany, in *European Environmental Yearbook*, DocTer, London, pp. 259–61.

Wert, S. and Thomas, B.R., 1981, Effects of skid roads on diameter, height and volume growth in Douglas fir, *Soil Science Society of America Journal*, 45: 629–32.

Westoby, J.C., 1962, The role of forest industries in the attack on economic underdevelopment, *Unasylva*, 16: 168–201.

Westoby, J.C., 1985, Foresters and politics, *Commonwealth Forestry Review*, 64: 105–16.

Westoby, J., 1987, *The purpose of forests: follies of development*, Basil Blackwell, Oxford.

Westoby, J., 1989, *Introduction to world forestry*, Basil Blackwell, Oxford.

Wetton, F., 1978, Evolution of forest policies in Canada, *Journal of Forestry*, 76: 563–6.

Whitaker, J.R., 1940, World view of destruction and conservation of natural resources, *Annals, Association of American Geographers*, 30: 143–62.

Whitby, M. and Ollerenshaw, J. (eds.), 1988, *Land use and the European environment*, Belhaven Press, London.

White, S., 1978, Cedar and mahogany logging in eastern Peru, *Geographical*

Review, **68**: 394–416.

White, D.E., 1987, New Zealand forestry, *Journal of Forestry*, **85**: 41–3.

Whitmore, T.C., 1984, *Tropical rain forests of the Far East*, Clarendon, Oxford.

Whitmore, J.L., 1987, Plantation forestry in the tropics of Latin America, *Unasylva*, **39** (156): 36–41.

Whitmore, J.L. and Burwell, B., 1986, Industry and agroforestry, *Unasylva*, **38** (153): 28–34.

Whitney, G.G., 1987, An ecological history of the Great Lakes forest of Michigan, *Journal of Ecology*, **75**: 667–84.

Whitney, G.G. and Somerlot, W.J., 1985, A case study of woodland continuity and change in the American Midwest, *Biological Conservation*, **31**: 265–87.

Wigston, D.L., 1984, Historical aspects of forestry problems in Papua New Guinea, in Steen, H.K. (ed.), *History of sustained yield forestry: a symposium*, Forest History Society, Santa Cruz, pp. 306–12.

Williams, M., 1982, Clearing the United States forests: pivotal years 1810–1860, *Journal of Historical Geography*, **8**: 12–28.

Williams, M., 1983, Ohio: microcosm of agricultural clearing in the Midwest, in Tucker, R.P. and Richard, J.F., *Global deforestation and the nineteenth century world economy*, Duke University Press, Durham, pp. 3–13.

Williams, M., 1989a, *Americans and their forest: an historical geography*, Cambridge University Press, Cambridge and New York.

Williams, M., 1989b, Deforestation: past and present, *Progress in Human Geography*, **13**: 176–208.

Willis, K.G. and Benson, J.F., 1989, Recreational values of forests, *Forestry*, **62**: 93–110.

Willis, R.P. and Kirby, J.M., 1987, Using the lowlands and hill country, in Holland, P.G. and Johnston, W.B. (eds.), *Southern approaches: geography in New Zealand*, NZGS, Christchurch, pp. 219–37.

Wilson, E.O., 1989, Threats to biodiversity, *Scientific American*, **261**: 60–9.

Wilson, W.L. and Johns, A.D., 1982, Diversity and abundance of selected animal species in undisturbed forest, selectively logged forest and plantations in East Kalimantan, *Biological Conservation*, **24**: 205–18.

Wingate-Hill, R., and Jakobsen, B.F., 1982, Increased mechanisation and soil damage in forests – a review, *New Zealand Journal of Forestry Science*, **12**: 380–93.

Winterbottom, R., and Hazlewood, P.T., 1987, Agroforestry and sustainable development: making the connection, *Ambio*, **16**: 100–10.

Woodruffe, B.J., 1989, Rural land-use planning in West Germany, in Cloke, P.J. (ed.), *Rural land-use planning in developed nations*, Unwin Hyman, London, pp. 104–29.

Woodwell, G.M., Hobbie, J.E., Houghton, R.A., Melillo, J.M., Moore, B., Peterson, B.J. and Shaver, G.R., 1983, Global deforestation: contribution to atmospheric carbon dioxide, *Science*, **222**: 1081–6.

World Bank, 1978, *Forestry: sector policy paper*, World Bank, Washington.

Worrell, A.C., and Ireland, L.C., 1975, Alternative means for motivating investment in private forestry, *Journal of Forestry*, **73**: 206–9.

WRI (World Resources Institute), 1985, *Tropical forests: a call for action*, WRI, Washington.

WRI, 1986, *World resources 1986*, Basic Books, New York.
WRI, 1989, *World resources 1988–89*, Basic Books, New York.
Wunder, W., 1983, Die Forstpolitik Schwedens unter veränderten gesamt-politischer Konzeption, *Allegemeine Forstzeitschrift*, **43**: 1171–2.
Wyatt-Smith, J., 1987, Problems and prospects for natural management of tropical moist forests, in Mergen, F. and Vincent, J.R. (eds.), *Natural management of tropical moist forests*, Yale University, Newhaven, Conn., pp. 5–22.
Wynn, G., 1979, Pioneers, politicians and the conservation of forests in early New Zealand, *Journal of Historical Geography*, **5**: 171–88.
Wynn, G., 1981, *Timber colony: a historical geography of early nineteenth century New Brunswick*, University of Toronto Press, Toronto.

Yoho, J.G., 1985, Continuing investments in forestry: private investment strategies, in Sedjo, R.A. (ed.), *Investments in forestry: resources, land use and public policy*, Westview, Boulder, pp. 151–66.
Young, W., 1984, Development of sustained yield forest management in British Columbia, in Steen, H.K. (ed.), *History of sustained yield forestry: a symposium*, Forest History Society, Santa Cruz, pp. 220–5.
Young, R.A. and Reichenbach, M.R., 1987, Factors influencing the timber harvest intention of nonindustrial private forest owners, *Forest Science*, **33**: 381–93.
Young, S.S. and Wang, Z.-J., 1989, Comparison of secondary and primary forests in the Ailao Shan Region of Yunnan, China, *Forest Ecology and Management*, **28**: 281–300.
Yuan, H., 1986, Forestry and forest product development in the PRC: a Chinese perspective in Schreuder, G.F. (ed.), *World trade in forest products*, University of Washington Press, Seattle.

Zedaker, S.M., Hyink, D.M. and Smith, D.W., 1987, Growth decline in red spruce, *Journal of Forestry*, **85**: 34–6.
Zhu, X., James, L.M., and Hanover, J.W., 1987, Timber supply and demand in China, *Journal of Forestry*, **85**: 41–3.
Ziemer, R.R., 1981, Roots and the stability of forest slopes, in *Erosion and sediment transport in Pacific Rim steeplands*, International Association of Hydrological Sciences Publication 132, Christchurch.
Zimmerman, E.W., 1951, *World resources and industries*, New York.
Zinn, G.W., and Miller, G.W., 1984, Increment contracts: Southern experience and potential use in the Appalachians, *Journal of Forestry*, **82**: 747–9.
Zivnuska, J., 1961, The multiple problems of multiple use, *Journal of Forestry*, **50**: 555–60.
Zobel, B.J., van Wyk, G. and Stahl, P., 1987, *Growing exotic forests*, John Wiley, New York.
Zon, R., 1920, Forests and human progress, *Geographical Review*, **10**: 139–66.
Zon, R. and Sparhawk, W.W., 1923, *Forest resources of the world*, McGraw-Hill, New York.

INDEX